Freedom from Nicotine
The Journey Home

by John R. Polito

ISBN-13: 978-1478333029

Medical Advice Disclaimer - This book (FFN-TJH) is designed to support, not replace, the relationship that exists between a reader and his/her physician. Do not rely upon any information in this book to replace individual consultations with your doctor or other health care provider.

Published: 12/31/08   4th Revision: 09/04/13

Dedication

FFN-TJH is dedicated to all still captive to nicotine's influence. May mastery of the "Law of Addiction" make freedom a keeper.

Acknowledgments

FFN-TJH would not exist if not for the insights of Joel Spitzer, the support of Patricia P. Arnold and the encouragement and inspiration of Harriet McBryde Johnson, deceased.

Table of Contents

Introduction

Your Greatest Awakening Ever

You may be like me, not a big book reader. But if wanting to end nicotine use, Freedom from Nicotine - The Journey Home (FFN-TJH) is worthy of your time. If allowed, it will aid in turning fear to excitement, dread to delight, anxiety to calm, bondage to freedom, and destruction to healing.

As hard as this may be to believe, ending nicotine use need not be horrible or even bad. In fact, someday soon you'll look back upon this temporary journey of re-adjustment as possibly the most amazing chapter of your life, your greatest personal awakening ever.

You see, nicotine addiction is about living a lie. Life here on Easy Street is calm, rich and wonderful, not more stressful, boring and empty. With knowledge as your ally, you're about to discover that you've journeyed far from that peaceful pre-addiction mind that was once home.

How many times have we heard the phrase "knowledge is power"? But when it comes to breaking nicotine's grip, until now, you've likely failed to devote the time needed to educate your intelligence. Instead, most of us turned to worthless products, pills or procedures; to quick fix magic cures promising fast, easy or effortless success.

You are about to become far smarter than your addiction is strong. And as you journey home, somewhere along the way it will hit you, that knowledge and insight truly is a recovery method. Think about how hard it would be to notice and savor the healing and benefits that recovery gradually unfolds before us, if consumed and gripped by anxiety and fear. Understanding and the confidence it breeds destroy needless fears, fears that ignorance was capable of festering into anxiety or even panic.

And during prior attempts (if any), our fears were many: fear of failure, fear that life as an ex-user would be horrible, that we were leaving something valuable behind, that we'd be unable to cope with stress, that the next challenge would be too big to handle, or even fear of success, that we really had used nicotine for the last time ever.

Who is John?

The anguish of attempting to break free in ignorance and darkness can easily overwhelm freedom's dreams. How do I know? Because I squandered three decades of desire to stop using by not knowing how.

My name is John, John R. Polito, and I'm a former 3 pack-a-day smoker. Failure after failure, after one final failed anxiety-riddled attempt in early 1999, I surrendered. I totally gave up on giving up. It was then that I first admitted to myself who I really was. I was a "real" drug addict, no different

from the alcoholic or heroin addict. And I accepted my fate. The pace of my failing health was accelerating, and I would die an addict's death. My most liberating admissions ever, I no longer needed the many excuses I'd invented to explain that next cigarette.
They all boiled down to just one. It was simple. "My name is John and I'm a REAL drug addict." Having achieved acceptance, strangely, I was no longer afraid. For some still unknown reason, on May 13, 1999, I typed the words "quit smoking" into an Internet search engine. A couple of clicks later, I found myself reading messages inside a stop smoking group.

There, watching the caring support between strangers, people who'd never met, I was overwhelmed. So, I typed my own little message. I told them that what they were doing in supporting each other was beautiful, but that it was too late for me, that I'd given-up trying. The rest is history. A flood of caring replies reached through the screen, tried pulling me in, and left me in tears. Two days later, on May 15, 1999, I smoked my last cigarette ever.

Totally consumed by long overdue success, on my two month anniversary, July 15, 1999, I created a website. I named it WhyQuit.com. Originally, it simply sought to preserve and share the tragic story of a 34 year-old Marlboro smoker. It was a story that hit home. It left me feeling lucky, that I'd somehow, maybe, dodged a bullet.

His name was Bryan. He was a 20-year smoker who had started at age thirteen. The news article included a sobbering photo of a totally emaciated young man lying dead in his bed. According to the story, the death bed photo was taken just two months after Bryan was diagnosed with lung cancer. In the photo, his grieving widow is sitting in a chair beside him, hugging the couple's two year-old son, Bryan Jr.

Over the years, WhyQuit's content grew into a mega-recovery site that today attracts 2.2 million unique annual visitors (different IP addresses). I've since presented roughly 100 live recovery programs, and written hundreds of cessation articles, including a handful that have appeared in peer-reviewed medical journals. Today, I continue to serve as director of two online support groups, Freedom and Turkeyville, which together have nearly 9,000 members.

Which brings us to this book, FFN-TJH. First released on December 31, 2008, it's unique in taking direct aim at our addiction's root cause, nicotine. It also documents the abrupt nicotine cessation ("cold turkey") science-base. It's a body of knowledge that pharmaceutical industry financial influence has done its very best to suppress, hide and destroy.

I wish I could claim credit for most of what you are about to read. I can't. The insights that follow were not discovered during my own thirty-years of chemical captivity. Nor do they flow from my own failed history, reflecting roughly a dozen serious attempts.

This book, FFN-TJH, is not the result of the invention of some new method or product, or of ideas or concepts born inside this mind. Instead, it simply shares the keys to the method that each year generates more successful ex-smokers than all others combined.

Nearly every lesson shared was mined from the discoveries and accomplishments of others. It's the reason for more than 400 footnotes. But as you'll soon discover, most of the key discoveries shared were made by an amazing man with almost super-human observational skills, a man with the ability to discern fact from fiction.

Who is Joel?

Frankly, FFN-TJH would not exist without the insights and teachings of Joel Spitzer of Chicago. Since 2000, I've studied and shared Joel's clinical observations. They are insights he began harvesting as early as 1972, first as a volunteer smoking prevention speaker for the American Cancer Society, and then as a smoking cessation counselor and paid staff member beginning in 1977.

I challenge you to locate any other person who has devoted their entire work-life, nearly 40 years, full-time, to helping smokers break free. More than 350 six-session stop smoking clinics, 690 single-session seminars, and an additional dozen years working online with smokers, Joel truly is the Henry Aaron or Babe Ruth of smoking cessation.

On January 20, 2000, out of the blue, a man I'd never met e-mailed me offering to share the more than 80 stop smoking articles he'd written.

A young Joel Spitzer holding wrapped slices from the lungs of a smoker and non-smoker.

Joel's articles quickly became the primary lessons shared at Freedom, what was then an anything-goes, free online peer-support group that Joel could clearly see was floundering horribly.[1]

Joel had written his collection of articles as follow-up reinforcement and relapse prevention letters, which were sent to graduates of his two-week clinics. During those clinics he'd taught new ex-smokers to take recovery just one challenge and day at a time. Now, for the first time, he used the closing of each article to remind them how to stay free, by simply sticking with their original commitment to "Never Take Another Puff!"

As I read through the 80 or so articles, I was hammered by ringing truths on a wide range of cessation issues. Joel raised scores of concerns that I'd never once considered. How could I have overlooked all these factors?

I was left stunned and humbled by how little I actually knew about either smoking or stopping. Who was I to think that I was somehow qualified to create and co-manage an online stop smoking support group? This guy was the real deal!

---

1 Freedom from Tobacco - Quit Smoking Now was founded on September 8, 1999 as a free peer support forum at MSN Groups. On February 21, 2009 MSN shut down all MSN Groups. In anticipation of the closing we moved Freedom to Yuku's free forums where we officially opened "Freedom from Nicotine" at www.ffn.yuku.com on January 18, 2009.

Nicotine's relationship to eating, stress, alcohol, vitamin C, anger, its influence upon heart rate,
depression, and sleep, how did I miss all this? Where
had I been? Why hadn't I seen smoking nicotine as
true chemical dependency decades earlier, or realized
that replacement nicotine actually undercuts success, or
grasped the importance of extinguishing use cues while
avoiding crutch creation?

Before Joel arrived, Freedom's co-founder, Joanne
Diehl, and I had grown horribly frustrated. Members
were relapsing to smoking left and right. Failure was
everywhere. It was as if our support group was
somehow fostering defeat.

Joel on Fox News on May 12, 2004
challenging pharma industry assertions
that nicotine gum is not addictive.

Each new announcement of a member's failure and return to smoking brought lots of virtual
member hugs, and encouragement for them to once again jump into the pool. It was as if the
group's affection and attention was an invitation for others to relapse too, so that they could return
and enjoy their own relapse party.

More than once Joanne had wanted to pull the plug and shut Freedom down. But now, here was a
guy whose entire life had prepared him to deliver on the forum's name, Freedom from Tobacco.

Without hesitation, we begged Joel to take charge of what was then little more than an anything-
goes motivational pep-rally. Although he declined, he did agree to join us and assist as a co-
manager and to serve as WhyQuit's director of education.

I named his large collection of reinforcement letters "Joel's
Library" and placed the library enter-stage at WhyQuit.
More than a decade later, that's where they remain, freely
available to all.

Joel's Library is today home to more than 100 articles and
nearly 200 free video counseling lessons. Joel's life's work
continues to be the heart and soul of our online work.[2]

Today, the often-repeated title of Joel's popular free e-
book, "Never Take Another Puff," has become relapse
prevention insurance for countless thousands.

Joel presenting one of his more than
190 free video counseling lessons.

Roy, who was six weeks into recovery, said it well. "The 'Never Take Another Puff' mantra is one
of the most powerful phrases I've ever heard in my life. It can move mountains. It was my only
shining light in a mass of darkness and guided me back to a normal nicotine-free life. It is effective
because it is so simple and innocent. It has the power of innocence."

A simple four word restatement of the Law of Addiction, you'll find that I've broadened it a bit in

2   Spitzer, J, Joel's Library, www.WhyQuit.com/joel

FFN-TJH to "never take another puff, vape, dip or chew."

I've searched long and hard for any work comparable to Joel's. Except for individual lessons here and there by particular counselors and authors, and Allen Carr's excellent assault upon smoking rationalizations, I've been unable to locate any collection of work that comes close.

What I did find were individual studies by scores of dedicated researchers, studies that aid us in better understanding the amazing effects upon humans of this chemical called nicotine.

Since the summer of 2000, I've also been on a quest for answers as to how government health officals were duped into feeding replacement nicotine to those addicted to it. And I have shared what I've learned at WhyQuit.

I've learned that those selling approved cessation products need for you to fear your natural instinct to abruptly end use of nicotine. In that most go cold turkey, if a pharmaceutical company wishes to increase its product's market share, it has no choice but to lie to you about how most real-world ex-users succeed, including "your" real odds of success.

Take your own poll of all the former nicotine users you know who have been free from all nicotine and all stop smoking products for at least a year. How did they do it? You'll discover a giant turkey in the room, that someone has been lying to you.

A July 31, 2013 Gallup Poll found that only 8 percent of U.S. ex-smokers owe their success to replacement nicotine (NRT), Zyban, Chantix or Champix, that 92 percent succeeded without it.

A careful reading of the poll suggests that the vast majority of ex-smokers (roughly 75 percent) credit their success to tactics normally associated with and defined as cold turkey (the abrupt cessation of nicotine without use of cessation products or procedures).[3]

Included within the 8 percent attributed to approved products, the Gallup Poll found that only 1 in 100 ex-smokers credited nicotine gum for their success. That's after 40 years and billions spent marketing Nicorette nicotine gum, while zero was spent encouraging cold turkey attempts.

Search as you might, you will never see any pharmaceutical industry commercial or website telling smokers that, depending on the nation in which you live, cold turkey continues to be the method responsible for generating 70-90% of long-term successful ex-smokers.[4]

These ex-users owe their success to ending use of all nicotine, not to devices that replace it, designer drugs that imitate it, vaccines that partially block its entry into the brain, or to magic herbs, vitamins, hypnosis, needles, lasers that imitate needles, to motion sickness shots that make you too sick to smoke, or (as we'll discuss later) to Billy Bob's Lima Bean Butter.

---

3   Gallup Poll, Most U.S. Smokers Want to Quit, Have Tried Multiple Times, July 31, 2013,
    http://www.gallup.com/poll/163763/smokers-quit-tried-multiple-times.aspx
4   Doran CM et al, Smoking status of Australian general practice patients and their attempts to quit, Addictive Behaviors, May
    2006, Volume 31(5), Pages 758-766; Fiore MC et al, Methods used to quit smoking in the United States: do cessation
    programs help? Journal of the American Medical Association, May 1990, Volume 263(20), Pages 2760-2765.

A Journey to Unconscious Competence

FFN-TJH teaches the world's most productive and effective method. In doing so, it attempts to remove the mystery and as much anxiety as possible from recovery, so as to afford you the ability to notice and savor the richness of coming home.

Smart turkey is about to put you back into the driver's seat of your mind. It's my hope that you'll learn to relax and embrace your healing. Already, hundreds of millions of worldwide cold turkey success stories, it's my hope that FFN-TJH contributes to swelling their numbers even greater.

Although free PDF versions of FFN-TJH are available at WhyQuit, it's my hope that the paperback and Kindle versions available online through Amazon.com allow our work to reach beyond the Internet, to enter libraries and schools, and become loving gifts to entrenched users.

So here it is in a nutshell. As health care futurist Joe Flower puts it, you're about to find yourself "in the mush," the same mush I was wading though when Joel entered my life on January 20, 2000.

According to Flower, there are four phases to change induced learning: (1) unconscious incompetence [not knowing that I knew almost nothing about my addiction], (2) conscious incompetence [Joel making me aware of how little I knew], (3) conscious competence [mastering Joel's teachings], and (4) unconscious competence [having those lessons become as second nature as walking].

As Flower suggests, once competence is achieved it becomes difficult to recall how we could ever have been anything else.[5]

If FFN-TJH aids you in achieving conscious competence, please don't allow it to collect dust on some book or cyber shelf. Consider sharing it with a friend or loved one still trapped in active dependency. Frankly, there is no more loving gift we can give that the insights need to reclaim our priorities, health and life.

If just starting out, congratulations on your decision to reclaim your mind! You are about to live the time-tested adage that "knowledge is power. Just that first brave step in saying "no" to that next fix, yes you can!

Breathe deep, hug hard, live long

John R. Polito
Nicotine Cessation Educator

---

5   Flower J, In the mush, Physician Executive, Jan-Feb 1999, Volume 25(1), Pages 64-66.

Chapter 1

Nicotine Addiction 101

That First Subtle "Aaah"

Remember how your body reacted to that first-ever inhaled puff, dip or chew of tobacco? Although some took to smoking like ants to sugar, what most recall is how utterly horrible it tasted.

You may have felt dizzy, nauseous or if like me, your face cycled through six shades of green. My mouth was filled with a terrible taste, my throat on fire, and my lungs in full rebellion as scores of powerful toxins assaulted, inflamed and numbed all tissues touched.

Prior to that moment, you may have heard that tobacco can be addictive. But after such an unpleasant introduction, you were convinced that it couldn't possibly happen to you.

How could it? If like most, you didn't like what just happened. How could you possibly get hooked?

As strange as this may sound, like or dislike have little to do with chemical dependency.

Beneath our body's rebellion to that toxic chemical onslaught, nicotine had activated our brain dopamine pathways, the mind's survival instincts teacher and motivator. The primary purpose of that brain circuitry is to make activating events extremely difficult to forget or ignore.

How do brain dopamine pathways teach and motivate action? Knowing will aid in understanding both how we became hooked and why breaking free appears vastly more daunting than it is.

Remember how you felt as a child when first praised by your parents or teachers for keeping

your coloring between the lines or for spelling your name correctly? Remember the "aaah" satisfaction sensation? Remember that same feeling after making and bonding with a new friend? "Aaah!"

We had just sampled the mind's motivational reward for accomplishment and peer bonding. An earned burst of dopamine was followed by an "aaah" wanting satisfaction sensation. It caught our attention, alerted us to what was important, and created a memory of the event that would help establish future priorities.

Bursts of dopamine were also felt when we anticipated accomplishment, peer bonding or other species survival activities. We were now being motivated and working to satisfy dopamine pathway wanting, the "aaah" relief sensation felt when anticipating or experiencing desire's satisfaction.

Our sense of wanting being satisfied is generated by the release of dopamine within multiple brain regions, primarily in our mid brain, inside cell structures known as the ventral tegmental area (VTA) and the nucleus accumbens.[6]

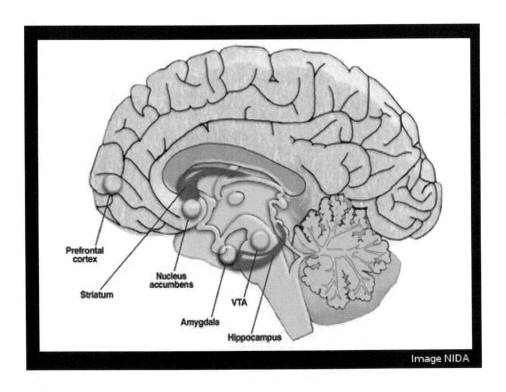

Two different yet overlapping dopamine pathways are responsible for wanting and its satisfaction. Our "tonic," background or baseline dopamine level determines our level of wanting, if any. Our "phasic" level or bursts of dopamine generate the "aaah" sensations sensed as wanting is satisfied.

Generally, as our tonic or background dopamine level begins to decline we begin to experience wanting. As phasic burst releases occur, our tonic level is gradually replenished by burst overflow

---

6   Rowell PP, Volk KA, <u>Nicotinic activation of mesolimbic neurons assessed by rubidium efflux in rat accumbens and ventral</u> <u>tegmentum</u>, Neurosignals, 2004 May-June; Volume 13(3), Pages 114-121.

into our tonic pathway, and wanting subsides.[7] The word "tonic" means to restore normal tone.

Brain dopamine pathways were not engineered to act as wanting satisfaction brain candy. Satisfaction is earned. Both a carrot (phasic) and a stick (tonic), they are a preprogrammed and hard-wired survival tool that teaches and reinforces our basic survival instincts.

Dopamine pathways are present and strikingly similar in the brains of all animals. They originate in the deep inner primitive, compulsive region of the brain known as the limbic mind, and extend forward into the conscious, rational, thinking portion of the brain.

Pretend for a moment that you're extremely thirsty. Really thirsty! Can you sense "wanting" beginning to build? Now, imagine drinking a nice, cool glass of refreshing water. Did you notice the "wanting" subside, at least a little?

Compliance with wanting generates a noticeable "aaah" relief sensation. The greater our wanting, the more intense our "aaah."

Our dopamine pathways are the source of survival instinct anticipation, motivation and reinforcement. Hard-wired instincts include eating food, drinking liquids, accomplishment, companionship, group acceptance, reproduction and child rearing.[8]

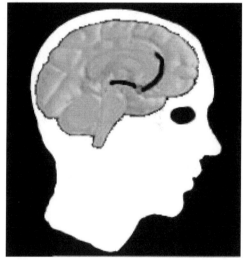

Our brain dopamine pathways cause our compliance with wanting to be recorded in high definition memory, in our forehead just above our eyes (our prefrontal cortex). It's what researchers call "salient" or "pay attention" memories.[9]

Although still poorly understood, the intensity of dopamine pathway wanting appears to stem from a combination of at least three factors. Those factors include a diminishing tonic dopamine level, the collective tease and influence of old wanting satisfaction memories, and self-induced anxiety if satisfaction is delayed.

The tease of thousands of old wanting satisfaction memories can be triggered by a physical bodily need, by subconscious habit conditioning, or by conscious concentration, fixation and desire.

Once their collective influence is triggered, as though bombarded by a thousand points of light, we have no choice but to recall exactly what needs to be done in order to satisfy wanting.

7   Grieder TE et al, <u>Phasic D1 and Tonic D2 dopamine receptor signaling double dissociate the motivational effects of acute nicotine and chronic nicotine withdrawal</u>, Proceedings of the National Academy of Science U S A. 2012 Feb 21;109(8); pages 3101-3106. Epub 2012 Jan 20.

8   Stefano GB, et al, <u>Nicotine, alcohol and cocaine coupling to reward processes via endogenous morphine signaling: the dopamine-morphine hypothesis</u>, Medical Science Monitor, June 2007, Volume 13(6), Pages RA91-102.

9   Kathleen McGowan, <u>Addiction: Pay Attention</u>, Psychology Today Magazine, Nov/Dec 2004, an article reviewing the drug addiction research of Nora Volkow, Director of the National Institute of Drug Abuse; also see Jay TM, Dopamine: a potential substrate for synaptic plasticity and memory mechanisms, Progress in Neurobiology, April 2003, Volume 69(6), Pages 375-390.

If you felt any wanting or relief with our pretend water-drinking example, it was due to old thirst and replenishment memories, not a biological need.

Yes, our "pay attention" pathways are a built-in, circular, self-reinforcing survival training school.

Wanting is triggered by our tonic dopamine level declining in response to a need, conditioning or desire. Old wanting satisfaction memories fuel wanting by constantly reminding us of exactly what needs to be done to make it end. Anticipating satisfaction may generate additional anxieties which further inflame wanting.

Obedience releases a sudden phasic burst of dopamine. Wanting ends once our need, conditioning or desire is satisfied and our tonic dopamine level returns to normal. The release also creates a vivid new high definition memory of how wanting was satisfied.

So, how does all of this relate to nicotine addiction?

Chemical Slavery's Onset

What would happen if, by chance, an external chemical so closely resembled the properties of the neuro-chemical responsible for activating brain dopamine pathways (acetylcholine) that once inside the brain it was capable of generating a stolen and unearned dopamine "aaah" wanting relief sensation?

Unfortunately, entirely by chance, nicotine is such a chemical.

Nicotine's polarities and chemical structure are so similar to acetylcholine, the brain's natural chemical messenger responsible for initiating normal dopamine pathway stimulation, that it bonds to acetylcholine receptors.

In those of us whose genetics or development made us susceptible to nicotine addiction, our dopamine pathways began to document and record nicotine use as though a pre-programmed species survival event.

Clearly, no inner "wanting" or desire existed when we first used nicotine. But if susceptible to dependency, it probably didn't take using too many times before repeated activation caused physical changes within our dopamine pathways.

Those changes would combine with constantly falling blood serum nicotine levels to cause our tonic dopamine level to decline. This would trigger subtle background wanting, wanting that would motivate us to use again and again and again.

Each new supply of nicotine would be followed by a phasic dopamine release. The lower our tonic dopamine level, the more noticeable our "aaah" wanting relief sensation, the more vivid our newest use reinforcement memory.

Soon, an increasing number of high definition nicotine use memories would themselves begin suggesting that we use early and often, so as to avoid sensing the onset of wanting.

As though bars to a prison cell, our thinking, planning and day became surrounded by hundreds and then thousands of durable use memories, each forcing us to vividly recall how wanting gets satisfied.

We had developed a physical need that we couldn't then possibly understand. We found ourselves inventing reasons to explain and justify our continued use. Those reasons (false use rationalizations) would act as additional bars in our prison cell.

Collectively, our wanting satisfaction memories quickly became more durable and vivid than any negative memory of any toxic unpleasantness felt during our first few uses of tobacco. In fact, it wasn't long before a growing number of high definition use memories buried all remaining memory of what life was like without nicotine.

Try recalling the calm, quiet and relaxed mind you enjoyed before getting hooked. Try hard to remember going entire days and weeks without once wanting to use nicotine. You can't do it, can you! Don't feel alone. None of us can. It's a drug addiction hallmark.

Prisoners of hijacked pay-attention circuitry, wanting's satisfaction became our #1 priority.[10]   We quickly forgot that it was ever possible to function without nicotine.

Our priorities teacher had been taken hostage. If we resisted and delayed using, we were disciplined with anxieties for failure to apply the lessons taught.

The brain's control room for coordinating and routing dopamine pathway functions appears to be the right insula. It's an oval, prune-sized brain structure above our ear.

The insula receives a wide range of input from our senses, emotions, dopamine pathways, and from the prefrontal cortex, home to previously recorded "pay attention" memories.

A 2007 study found that smokers who sustained brain damage

---

10 McGowan, K, <u>Addiction: Pay Attention</u>, Psychology Today Magazine, Nov/Dec 2004, Article ID: 3571; also see, Rosack, J, <u>Volkow May Have Uncovered Answer to Addiction Riddle</u>, Psychiatric News June 4, 2004, Volume 39 Number 11, Page 32.

to the right insula actually lost the urge to smoke,[11] suggesting that it also routes or coordinates use urges, craves and anxieties.

Thank goodness it doesn't take traumatic brain injury or a stroke to make us stop craving nicotine. Thank goodness that recovery isn't nearly as difficult as our brain wanting disorder suggests.

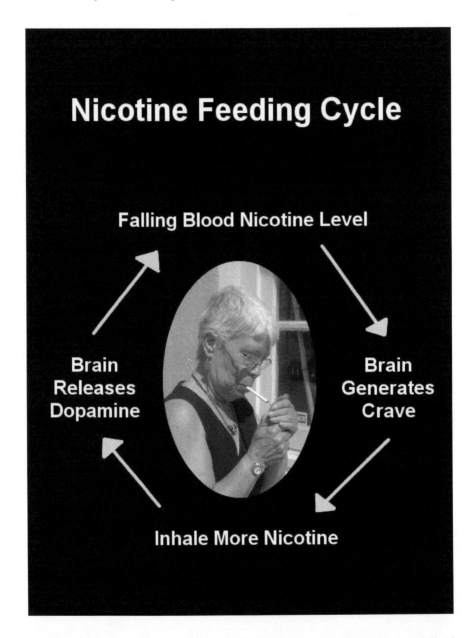

Whether heroin, cocaine, methamphetamines, alcoholism or nicotine, drug addiction is about the brain's dopamine pathways being taken hostage by an external chemical.

We nicotine smokers didn't suck tissue destroying tars that included ammonia, formaldehyde, arsenic, butane, hydrogen cyanide, lead, mercury, vinyl chloride, methane or vast quantities of carbon monoxide into our bodies because we wanted to watch each puff destroy a bit more of our capacity to receive and circulate life-giving oxygen. We did so to replenish constantly falling

---

11 Naqvi, NH, et al, <u>Damage to Insula Disrupts Addiction to Cigarette Smoking</u>, Science, January 2007, Vol. 315 (5811), Pages 531-534.

nicotine reserves.

Nicotine is a small molecule. This allows it to cross through our protective blood-brain filter. Once through, it docks with acetylcholine receptors and stimulates dopamine flow.

Smoked nicotine contains at least one other as yet unidentified chemical that somehow diminishes dopamine cleanup enzymes MAO A and MAO B. Diminished MAO means delay in normal dopamine cleanup following a phasic release. It means that smoked nicotine's wanting relief sensation is allowed to linger longer than normal.

Think about how short-lived the "aaah" sensation is following a single potato chip or a sip of water when thirsty. Longer wanting relief is thought to make smoked nicotine possibly the most perfectly designed form of addiction.

It may also help explain why oral tobacco users generally have higher blood nicotine concentrations than smokers. Smokeless tobacco does not inhibit MAO or normal dopamine clean-up. It may be that users of all non-smoked forms of nicotine require higher levels of nicotine in order to keep their wanting at bay.

Whether smoked or oral, an endless cycle of wanting and its brief absence following use left us totally yet falsely convinced that nicotine was essential to survival.

Our nicotine feeding cycle left many of us believing that use defined who we were, that nicotine gave us our edge, helped us cope, and that life without it would be horrible or even meaningless.

Punished with wanting that was satisfied by use, we quickly grew to believe that we could not function comfortably without it.

Why can't we starve ourselves to death? Not only is wanting for food satisfied with dopamine "aaah" relief sensations when we anticipate eating or actually do so, we are punished with anxieties and cravings when we wait too long between meals.

As for nicotine levels, like food, what goes up must come down. As our body slowly metabolized and rid itself of nicotine, we gradually experienced increasing mood deterioration and escalating distress, punctuated by anxiety, anger and depression.

In fact, it's work living life as a nicotine addict. We endured greater extremes in daily mood swings than non-users, greater problematic anger,[12] and the greater our dependency the more unstable our moods.[13]

Our hijacked priorities teacher was fooled and started teaching a false lesson, that bringing a new supply of nicotine into the bloodstream was every bit as important as eating.

Extensive dopamine circuitry overlap,[14] nicotine cravings became as real as food cravings. Nicotine "aaah" wanting relief sensations became as important as food "aaah"s. Nearly indistinguishable, we experienced the same anxiety beatings, and similar dopamine wanting relief sensations upon surrender.

But there is one massive difference between dependency upon food and dependency upon nicotine. Without food we starve, without nicotine we thrive!

Unfortunately, our hostage dopamine circuitry is incapable of distinguishing fact from fiction. By design, it has buried and suppressed the beauty of never wanting or needing that existed prior to nicotine's arrival.

Would coming home to your calm and quiet yet forgotten mind be a good thing or bad? If good, what sense does it make to fear it?

The problem is that attempts to end nicotine use are often met with a rising tide of anxieties. Soon, our thousands of old nicotine use "aaah" relief memories begin looking like life jackets.

While we only needed to remain nicotine-free and stay afloat for a maximum of three days in order to navigate the roughest seas and move beyond peak withdrawal, hungry for calm, most of us took the hook and bit on our "aaah" memory bait.

We obeyed the false lessons generated by our chemically hijacked teacher. In doing so, we abandoned the only path home in exchange for a few minutes of relief.

When trying to stop using, it isn't unusual to find our mind's addiction chatter insanely trying to convince us that things will be fine if we just have a little more nicotine now, that we can stop using while using more.

I hate to think about how many times I told myself during a prior attempt that using just once more was my reward for having briefly succeeded in going without.

Obviously, this quick fix isn't a solution at all. It shows a total lack of understanding as to the

---

12 Cougle JR, Delineating a Relationship Between Problematic Anger and Cigarette Smoking: A Population-Based Study, Nicotine and Tobacco Research, May 13, 2012

13 Parrott AC, Cigarette-derived nicotine is not a medicine, The World Journal of Biological Psychiatry, April 2003, Volume 4(2), Pages 49-55.

14 Blum K, et al, Reward circuitry dopaminergic activation regulates food and drug craving behavior, Current Pharmaceutical Design, 2011; Volume 17(12), Pages 1158-1167; also Kelley AE, et al, Neural systems recruited by drug- and food-related cues: studies of gene activation in corticolimbic regions, Physiology & Behavior. 2005 September, Volume 15;86(1-2):11-14.

purpose and function of brain dopamine pathways, to make circuitry activating activities nearly impossible, in the short term, to forget or ignore.

But bondage is more than a rising tide of anxieties being fostered by a diminishing tonic dopamine level, in response to constantly declining blood-serum nicotine reserves. And it's more than thousands of old use memories screaming the wrong way out.

Tolerance

As if nicotine taking our dopamine pathways captive wasn't enough, imagine the brain physically needing and requiring more nicotine over time.

Definitions of tolerance include:

- Decreased responsiveness to a stimulus, especially over a period of continued exposure
- Diminution in the response to a drug after prolonged use, or
- Physiological resistance to a poison.[15]

The brain attempts to fight back against its toxic intruder. As if somehow knowing that too much unearned dopamine is flowing, it attempts to diminish nicotine's influence by more widely disbursing it. It does so by growing or activating millions of extra nicotinic-type acetylcholine receptors in as many as eleven different brain regions.[16]

Although you'll generally see the average nicotine intake per cigarette stated as being about 1mg (milligram), in truth it varies significantly. For example, average intake is 30% greater in African Americans at 1.41 milligrams of nicotine per cigarette, as compared to 1.09 milligrams in Caucasians.

Although often stated that the average user's body depletes and eliminates (metabolizes) nicotine at the rate of roughly one-half every two hours, there's variation there too. For example, nicotine's elimination half-life is 129 minutes in Caucasians and 134 minutes in African

Photo MarionVA.gov

---

15 tolerance. (n.d.). The American Heritage Stedman's Medical Dictionary. Retrieved September 14, 2008, from Dictionary.com website: http://dictionary.reference.com/browse/tolerance

16 Mugnaini M et al, Upregulation of [3H]methyllycaconitine binding sites following continuous infusion of nicotine, without changes of alpha7 or alpha6 subunit mRNA: an autoradiography and in situ hybridization study in rat brain, The European Journal of Neuroscience, November 2002, Volume 16, Pages 1633-1646.

Americans.[17]

Tolerance ever so gradually pulls us deeper and deeper into dependency's forest. While nicotine's elimination half-life remains fixed, over time we gradually find ourselves sucking a wee bit harder, holding the smoke a bit longer, or using more nicotine in order to avoid wanting or achieve relief from it.

Two a day, three, four, four smoked hard, our brain gradually grew additional nicotinic-type acetylcholine receptors. Over the years, we gradually required a bit more nicotine to maintain our sense of nicotine-normal.

My "aaah" relief sensations were no more powerful smoking five cigarettes a day at age fifteen than when smoking sixty per day at age forty. I needed that much more in order to keep pace with wanting.

I know, you're probably thinking, you've been at the same nicotine intake level for some time now and it's likely vastly less than the three packs-a-day I was smoking. While we don't yet fully understand wide variations in levels of nicotine use, we know that genetics probably explains most differences.[18]

There is also the fact that some of our mothers, like mine, smoked during pregnancy. I was born with a brain already wired for nicotine. I came into this world as nicotine's slave and likely spent my first few days in withdrawal.[19]

For me, those first few cigarettes at age 15 were not about initial addiction. They were about relapse to a condition my brain had known since formation and creation of my very first acetylcholine receptor. That first receptor almost immediately became occupied by nicotine that was smoked by mom.

It was an event that occurred three to four weeks following conception.[20] The problem is that receptors are being activated before formation of the brain cell to which the receptor will eventually be attached.

As Duke University Professor Slotkin puts it, "nicotine alters the developmental trajectory of acetylcholine systems in the immature brain, with vulnerability extending from fetal stages

Me feeding my need at 19. I was already making failed attempts.

---

17 Perez-Stable EJ et al, Nicotine metabolism and intake in black and white smokers, Journal of the American Medical Association, July 1998, Volume 280(2), Pages 152-156.

18 Berrettini W, et al, Alpha-5/alpha-3 nicotinic receptor subunit alleles increase risk for heavy smoking, Molecular Psychiatry, April 2008, Volume 13(4), Pages 368-373.

19 Law KL, et al, Smoking during pregnancy and newborn neurobehavior, Pediatrics, June 2003, Volume 111(6 Pt 1): Pages 1318-1323.

20 Slotkin TA, If nicotine is a developmental neurotoxicant in animal studies, dare we recommend nicotine replacement therapy in pregnant women and adolescents? Neurotoxicology and Teratology, January 2008, Volume 30, Issue 1, Pages 1-19.

through adolescence."[21]

In addition to genetics and prenatal nicotine exposure, the younger we were when we started using, the more profound the altered development trajectory experienced by our still developing brain.

Research suggests that nicotine inflicted damage to dopamine and serotonin pathways is significantly greater in males than females, but that this female advantage disappears if the female brain is exposed to both prenatal and adolescent nicotine.[22]

The dependent mind is capable of using a low level of nicotine tolerance as justification for continued chemical servitude.

It's easy for those who use less often to rationalize that they are somehow superior or better able to control their addiction than heavy users. In reality, they're hooked solid too. Their slavery is just as permanent and just as real.

The smoker smoking five times a day may also face health risks as great or greater than heavier smokers. This too may be due to genetic factors, to differing toxin and cancer causing chemical levels found in different brands of tobacco, or to how intensely each cigarette was smoked.

It may also be due in part to environmental factors that subject us to other chemical agents such as radon, or to employment or hobby chemical exposures, or due to the quality of the water we drink and the air we breathe.

Over the years I've met many smokers, myself included, who experienced a significant increase in the number of cigarettes smoked and higher nicotine tolerance following relapse after a failed attempt.

Hawaii.gov

Why? We don't know. Smoking more cigarettes harder, it was almost like binge eating after dieting, as if my brain was trying to make up for missed nicotine feedings. But seeing increases in the level of smoking following relapse is becoming less common.

Like a hurricane requiring warm water to strengthen, the fuel for a nicotine tolerance increase is additional time and opportunities to use.

The smoke-free indoor-air movement is gradually sweeping the globe. Smoking is also increasingly being prohibited in and around parks, playgrounds, beaches, hospitals, schools and college campuses, and in the presence of children.

21 Slotkin TA, et al, Adolescent nicotine treatment changes the response of acetylcholine systems to subsequent nicotine administration in adulthood, Brain Research Bulletin, May 15, 2008, Volume 76 (1-2), Pages 152-165.

22 Jacobsen LK, et al, Gender-specific effects of prenatal and adolescent exposure to tobacco smoke on auditory and visual attention, Neuropsychopharmacology, December 2007, Volume 32(12); Pages 2453-2464.

Smokers face fewer replenishment opportunities as non-smokers become increasing less tolerant of smoking in their presence, homes or vehicles. I suspect that the smoker's nicotine tolerance level will increasingly be associated with trying to obtain more nicotine by smoking fewer cigarettes harder.

But the opposite is often seen in smokers transferring their dependency to oral tobacco or NRT products, where around-the-clock use becomes possible.

"I started out with about 6 pieces a day and now chew about 15 pieces of 2mg per day. Probably more nicotine than when I smoked," asserts a 48 year-old, three-year female gum user.

"There is one in my mouth 24 hours a day, 7 days a week ... yes for real," claims a 32 year-old, three-year male gum user who chews 40-50 pieces a day and thinks he may "chew more than anyone in the world."[23]

Regardless of method of delivery or level of nicotine tolerance, the millions of extra acetylcholine receptors grown by the addicted brain desensitized it to its own natural sense of neuro-chemical normal.

We became wired to function with a precise amount of nicotine in our bloodstream. Not too much, not too little, we worked to maintain and remain within our zone of nicotine-normal. Any attempt to stop using brought potential for a brief emotional train wreck, as we found ourselves not only desensitized to nicotine but briefly to life as well.

"Dependent human smokers have decreased dopamine activity during withdrawal" and withdrawal is accompanied by "a decrease in tonic dopamine activity."[24]

But the brain makes substantial progress in reversing tolerance-induced de-sensitivities within 72 hours of ending all nicotine use. It's primarily a matter of patience, as withdrawal anxieties peak within three days, putting the worst behind us.

Within three weeks the brain will restore the number of receptor to levels seen in non-smokers. Although feeling physically normal again, nicotine's tolerance wiring paths have been permanently burned and etched into our brains.

Although we can arrest our chemical dependency we cannot cure, eliminate or destroy it. We each remain wired for relapse for life.

While this may sound like a curse, it can become our greatest peace of mind. Once confident of victory, this time we know exactly what it takes to both stay free and fail.

But arrival here on Easy Street involves more than simply arresting a chemical need and level of

23 Polito JR, Long-Term Nicorette Gum Users Losing Hair and Teeth, WhyQuit.com, December 1, 2008.

24 Grieder TE et al, Phasic D1 and Tonic D2 dopamine receptor signaling double dissociate the motivational effects of acute nicotine and chronic nicotine withdrawal, Proceedings of the National Academy of Science U S A. 2012 Feb 21;109(8); pages 3101-3106. Epub 2012 Jan 20.

tolerance.

Use Conditioning

The term "addiction" is is generally viewed as being broader than "dependency." Among other factors, it includes the consequences of years of nicotine feedings that involved replenishment patterns and habits that did not go unnoticed by our subconscious mind.

Use habits were fathered by endless compliance with our brain's chemical dependence upon nicotine. Although covered in detail in Chapter 11 (Subconscious Recovery), a basic understanding of nicotine addiction must include mention of use conditioning.

Our subconscious mind became conditioned to associate various activities, locations, times, people, events and emotions with using nicotine. It learned to expect arrival of a new supply when specific situations or circumstances occurred.

Insula routed urges, craves and anxieties alerted us when conditioned use cues were encountered. Normally the bell ringing use cue and urge was so subtle that it went unnoticed. Almost as if on autopilot, we'd reach for nicotine to satisfy it nonetheless.

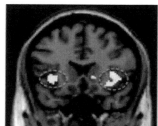

Left Insula   Right Insula

You've likely heard of Pavlov, who actually used the ringing of a bell to induce classical conditioning in dogs. He conditioned them to expect food upon hearing a bell. The dogs would actually begin salivating when he rang the bell, even as he started to delay food's arrival longer and longer.

Your unique patterns of nicotine use have conditioned your subconscious too. Encountering a nicotine feeding cue can trigger a response ranging from a barely notice urge to a full blown anxiety episode, depending upon your tonic dopamine level.

Teased by thousands of old wanting satisfaction memories, if allowed, the anxiety episode can become emotionally inflamed.

Self-induced anxieties and fears can build, eventually triggering the body's fight or flight panic response. It happens when stress associated with a need, conditioning or desire escalates to the point of registering within the deep inner primitive mind as a threatening event.

During panic, normal cessation time distortion is made worse, as time seemingly stands still. It can make a less than three minute crave episode feel like three hours, and entirely unmanageable.

Contrary to what is then felt, those three minutes are extremely short lived in comparison to active dependency's never ending cycle of want, urge, use and satisfy.

Nicotine addiction is about living false priorities, needless conditioning, dishonest use justifications, and denial of all of the above. It's about use of a tiny molecule called nicotine becoming the most frequent lesson taught by a hijacked survival instincts teacher.

Think about it. While we might forget to take our vitamin or medicine, procrastinate regarding work, skip meals, interrupt quality time with family or friends, how often would we fail to respond to the bell for that next mandatory nicotine feeding?

What is Nicotine?

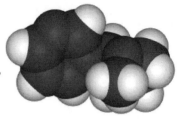

I was surprised to learn that all nicotine comes from the tobacco plant, including nicotine in nicotine replacement products such as the patch, gum and lozenge.

Although creation of synthetic nicotine is possible, imagine the regulatory hoops that the industry would need to jump through in order to be allowed to market synthetic nicotine for human consumption.

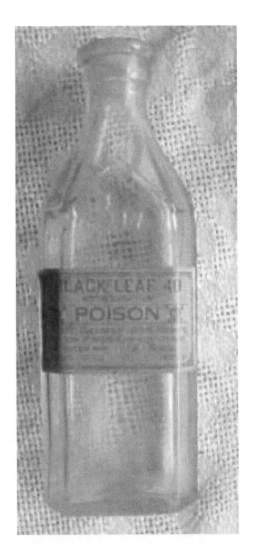

Instead, the pharmaceutical industry competes with the tobacco industry in purchasing tobacco from tobacco farmers and extracting nicotine from it.

Nicotine is a colorless, odorless, liquid organic-based alkaloid in the same family as cocaine, morphine, quinine and strychnine. It slowly yellows when exposed to air, is bitter tasting and gives off a slight fishy odor when warmed.[25]

When holding dry tobacco in your hand, the weight of nicotine within it will vary depending upon the type of tobacco. While nicotine's weight averages about 3% in cigarettes[26] and moist snuff, it

comprises 1.6% of a tobacco plug's weight and about 1% of the weight of chewing tobacco.[27]

One of the most toxic of all poisons,[28] nicotine is a fetal teratogen that damages the developing brain.[29] A natural insecticide formed in the roots of the tobacco plant, it helps protect the plant's roots, stalk and leaves from being eaten by insects and animals.

Nicotine was originally sold as an alkaloid insecticide in America under the brand name Black Leaf 40, a mixture that

---

25 Cornell University, Nicotine (Black Leaf 40) Chemical Profile, April 1985.

26 Blakely T et al, New Zealand Public Health Report on Nicotine, May 27, 1997.

27 Tilashalski, K et al, Assessing the Nicotine Content of Smokeless Tobacco Products, Journal of the American Dental Association, May 1994, Volume 125, Pages 590-594.

28 de Landoni, JH, Nicotine, IPCS INCHEM, March 1991.

29 Roy TS, et al, Nicotine evokes cell death in embryonic rat brain during neurulation, The Journal of Pharmacology and

was 40% nicotine sulfate.[30] Use of similar nicotine products continues to be touted in organic gardening as a means for killing insects.

Neonicotinoids are synthetic forms of the natural insecticide nicotine, and possibly the most widely used insecticides worldwide.

Sold under brand names such as Imidacloprid and Thiamethoxam (TMX), neonicotinoids attach to the insect's acetylcholine receptors. The insect then exhibits leg tremors, rapid wing motion and disoriented movement followed by paralysis and death.

There is growing concern that widespread use of neonicotinoids may be responsible for killing bees and colony collapse disorder.[31]

How deadly is nicotine? It's nearly twice as deadly as black widow spider venom (.5 mg/kg versus .9mg/kg) and at least three times deadlier than diamondback rattlesnake venom (.5 mg/kg versus 1.9mg/kg).

LD50 is an abbreviation for the lethal dose of a toxic chemical. It represents the amount of the chemical needed to kill 50% of humans weighing 160 pounds. Nicotine's minimum adult LD50 is 30mg (milligrams) and if ingested in liquid form death can occur within 5 minutes.[32]

Drop for drop, that makes nicotine as deadly as strychnine, which also has a minimum adult LD50 of 30mg,[33] and more deadly than arsenic (50mg)[34] or cyanide (50mg).[35]

Nicotine kills by eventually paralyzing breathing muscles. Prior to death, symptoms include salivation, nausea, vomiting, abdominal pain, diarrhea, dizziness, weakness and confusion progressing to convulsions, hypertension and coma.[36]

Although the average American cigarette contains 8 to 9 milligrams of nicotine,[37] some is burned, some escapes through cigarette ventilation and the filter traps some. The lungs absorb nearly 90% of inhaled nicotine.[38]

It results in the average smoker introducing 1.17 to 1.37 milligrams of nicotine into their bloodstream with each cigarette smoked.[39] Average intake can vary significantly from smoker to

Experimental Therapeutics, December 1998, Volume 287(3), Pages 1136-1144.

30 Cornell University, nicotine (Black Leaf 40) Chemical Profile, Pesticide Management Education Program (PMEP), April 1985.

31 Whitehorn PR, et al, Neonicotinoid pesticide reduces bumble bee colony growth and queen production, Science, April 20, 2012, Volume 336(6079), pages 351-352.

32 Cornell University, Nicotine (Black Leaf 40) Chemical Profile, April 1985.

33 Borges, A et al, Strychnine (PIM 507), March 1989, IPSC INCHEM.

34 Benedetti, JL, Arsenic (PIM G042), July 1996, IPSC INCHEM.

35 van Heijst, ANP, Cyanides (PIM G003), February 1988, IPSC INCHEM.

36 de Landoni, JH, Nicotine (PIM 373), March 1991, IPCS INCHEM.

37 Benowitz NL, et al, Establishing a nicotine threshold for addiction. The implications for tobacco regulation, New England Journal of Medicine, July 14, 1994, Volume 331(2), Pages 123-125.

38 Philip Morris, Memorandum, Media Presentation - Draft Outline, April 7, 1998, Bates Number: 2064334296.

39 Jarvis MJ, et al, Nicotine yield from machine-smoked cigarettes and nicotine intakes in smokers: evidence from a representative population survey, Journal of the National Cancer Institute, January 17, 2001, Volume 93(2), Pages 134-138.

smoker, ranging from 0.3 to 3.2 mg of nicotine per cigarette.[40]

Picture the largest rat you have ever seen. It would weigh about a pound. The 1mg of nicotine that entered your bloodstream from your last nicotine fix would be sufficient to kill that rat.

A smoker smoking 30 cigarettes per day is, over an entire day, bringing enough nicotine into their body to have killed a 160-pound human, if the entire 30 milligrams had arrived all at once. Two to three drops of nicotine in the palm of the hand of someone weighing 160 pounds or less and he or she is dead.

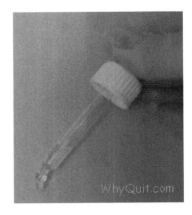

Those pushing a growing array of nicotine products often falsely assert that they are as safe as caffeine. Far from it. Nicotine is at least 166 times more toxic than caffeine. Caffeine's lethal dose is 10 grams or 10,000 milligrams, compared to 30 milligrams for nicotine.

Picture a substance more toxic than rattlesnake or black widow venom being fed to your brain day after day after day. Is it any wonder that a 2004 study using brain MRI imaging found that "smokers had smaller gray matter volumes and lower gray matter densities than nonsmokers?"[41]

Contrary to findings from studies examining the short-term (acute) effects of nicotine,[42] studies of the long-term (chronic) effects of smoking nicotine report decline and impairment of attention, concentration, and the accuracy of working and verbal memory.[43]

Visualize nicotine's neuro-toxic effects upon the human brain slowly destroying it,[44] while damaging what remains.[45] Possibly the most frightening of all the risks posed by our addiction is its ability to destroy all memory of why we need to stop.

As for those selling a growing array of nicotine products, their marketing ploys and the research backing their sales pitch will always micro-focus upon the effects of just a few of the more than 200 neuro-chemicals that nicotine controls (usually the stimulants), while ignoring the big picture.

Their goal is to make money by selling us nicotine, not to free us from requiring it. Their marketing will never value the loss of personal freedom to a never-ending need to feed, nor discuss in a fair and honest manner the harms inflicted by nicotine upon those addicted to it.

40 Benowitz NL, et al, <u>Establishing a nicotine threshold for addiction. The implications for tobacco regulation</u>, New England Journal of Medicine, July 14, 1994, Volume 331(2), Pages 123-125.

41 Brody, AL et al, <u>Differences between smokers and nonsmokers in regional gray matter volumes and densities</u>, Biological Psychiatry, January 1, 2004, Volume 55(1), Pages 77-84.

42 Jubelt LE, et al, <u>Effects of transdermal nicotine on episodic memory in non-smokers with and without schizophrenia</u>, Psychopharmacology, July 2008, Volume 199(1), Pages 89-98.

43 Jacobsen LK, et al, <u>Effects of smoking and smoking abstinence on cognition in adolescent tobacco smokers</u>, Biological Psychiatry, January 1, 2005, Volume 57(1), Pages 56-66; also see, Counotte DS,et al, <u>Long-Lasting Cognitive Deficits Resulting from Adolescent Nicotine Exposure in Rats</u>, Neuropsychopharmacology, June 25, 2008.

44 Gallinat J, et al, <u>Abnormal hippocampal neurochemistry in smokers: evidence from proton magnetic resonance spectroscopy at 3 T</u>, Journal of Clinical Psychopharmacology, February 2007, Volume 27(1), Pages 80-84.

45 Gallinat, J, et al, <u>Smoking and structural brain deficits: a volumetric MR investigation</u>, European Journal of Neuroscience, September 2006, Vol. 24, pp. 1744-1750.

Do you know of any alcoholic rehabilitation program that recommends switching from whiskey to pure alcohol, and then trying to slowly wean yourself off over a period of 90 days?

Who benefits from such a treatment method when it takes just 3 days to rid the body of all nicotine and move beyond peak withdrawal?

As Addictive as Heroin?

On May 17, 1988, the U.S. Surgeon General warned that nicotine is as addictive as heroin and cocaine.[46]

Canada's cigarette pack addition warning label reads, "WARNING - CIGARETTES ARE HIGHLY ADDICTIVE - Studies have shown that tobacco can be harder to quit than heroin or cocaine."
But how on earth can nicotine possibly be as addictive as heroin? It's a legal product, sold in the presence of children, near candies, sodas, pastries and chips at the neighborhood convenience store, drug store, supermarket and gas station.

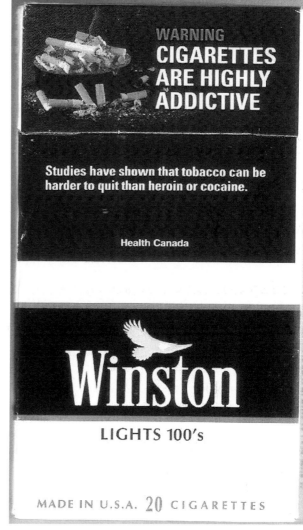

Heroin addicts describe their dopamine pathway wanting satisfaction sensation as being followed by a warm and relaxing numbness. Racing energy, excitement and hyperfocus engulf the methamphetamine or speed addict's wanting satisfaction. Satisfaction of the alcoholic's wanting is followed by the gradual depression of their central nervous system. And euphoria (intense pleasure) is the primary sensation felt when the cocaine addict satisfies wanting.

The common link between drugs of addiction is their ability to stimulate and captivate brain dopamine pathways.

Should the fact that nicotine's dopamine pathway stimulation is accompanied by alert central nervous system stimulation blind us as to what's happened, and who we've become?

Nicotine is legal, openly marketed, taxed and everywhere. Its acceptance and availability openly invites denial of a super critical recovery truth, that we had become "real" drug addicts in every sense.

Definitions of nicotine dependency vary greatly. One of the most widely accepted is the American Psychiatric Association's as published in the Diagnostic and Statistical Manual of Mental

---

46 The Health Consequences of Smoking: Nicotine Addiction: A Report of the Surgeon General, May 17, 1988.

Disorders, 4th edition (DSM IV).[47] Under DSM IV, a person is dependent upon nicotine if at least 3 of the following 7 criteria are met:

1. Difficulty controlling nicotine use or unable to stop using it.
2. Using nicotine more often than intended.
3. Spending significant time using nicotine (note: a pack-a-day smoker spending 5 minutes per cigarette devotes 1.5 hours per day, 10.5 hours per week or 13.6 forty-hour work weeks per year to smoking nicotine).
4. Avoiding activities because they might interfere with nicotine use or cutting activities short so as to enable replenishment.
5. Nicotine use despite knowledge of the harms tobacco is inflicting upon your body.
6. Withdrawal when attempting to end nicotine use.
7. Tolerance - over the years gradually needing more nicotine in order to achieve the same desired effect.

A 2008 study found that 98% of chronic smokers have difficulty controlling use.[48] Although often criticized, the problem with DSM nicotine dependency standards is not its seven factors. It's getting those hooked upon nicotine to be honest and accurate in describing its impact upon their life.

It isn't unusual for the enslaved and rationalizing mind to see leaving those we love in order to go smoke nicotine as punctuating life, not interrupting it. And the captive mind can invent a host of excuses for avoidance of activities lasting longer than a couple of hours. It can explain how the ashtray sitting before them became filled and their cigarette pack empty without realizing it was happening.

In February 2008, I finished presenting 63 nicotine cessation seminars in 28 South Carolina prisons that had recently banned all tobacco. Imagine paying $8 for a hand-rolled cigarette. Imagine it being filled with tobacco from roadside cigarette butts, tobacco now wrapped in paper torn from a prison Bible.

47 American Psychiatric Association, Diagnostic and Statistical Manual of Mental Disorders, 4th edition, Washington, D.C. 1994.
48 Hendricks, P. et al, Evaluating the validities of different DSM-IV-based conceptual constructs of tobacco dependence, Addiction, July 2008, Volume 103, Pages 1215-1223.

Eight dollars per cigarette was pretty much the norm in medium and maximum-security prisons. The price dropped to about $2 in less secure pre-release facilities. Imagine not having $8. I heard horrific stories about the lengths to which inmates would go for a fix.

Two inmates housed in a smoke-free prison near Johnson City, Tennessee ended a six-hour standoff in February 2007 when they traded their hostage, a correctional officer, for cigarettes. According to a prison official, "They got them some cigarettes, they smoked them and went back to their cell and locked themselves back in."

I stood before thousands of inmates whose chemical addictions to illegal drugs landed them behind bars. During each program I couldn't help but comment on the irony that those caught using illegal drugs ended up in prison, while we nicotine addicts openly and legally purchase our drug at neighborhood stores.

According to the CDC, during 2011 tobacco killed 11 times more Americans than all illegal drugs combined (443,690 versus 40,239).

As discussed in the intro, Joel Spitzer may well be the world's most insightful nicotine cessation educator. My mentor since January 2000, he tells the story of how during a 2001 two-week stop smoking clinic, a participant related that he was briefly tempted to smoke after finding a single cigarette and lighter setting atop a urinal in a men's public bathroom.

What made it so tempting was that the cigarette was his brand. He thought to himself how easy it would have been to smoke it. Joel then asked the man, "When was the last time you ever saw anything else atop a urinal in a men's room that you felt tempted to put in your mouth?" At that, the man smiled and said, "Point well taken."

Over the years, ex-users have shared stories of leaving hospital rooms where their loved one lay dying of lung cancer so they could smoke, of smoking while pregnant, of accidentally lighting their car, clothing, hair or dog on fire, of smoking while battling pneumonia, and of sneaking from their hospital room into the staircase to light-up while dragging along the stand holding their intravenous medication bag.

Another story shared by Joel relates how one clinic participant had long kept secret how his still smoldering cigarette butt on the floor had lit the bride's wedding dress on fire.

We each have our own dependency secrets. As a submarine sailor, I went to sea on a 72-day underwater deployment in 1976 thinking that stopping would be a breeze if I didn't bring any cigarettes or money along. I was horribly, horribly wrong. I spent two solid months begging, bumming and digging through ashtray after ashtray in search of long butts.

Even worse was losing both of my dogs to cancer. One of them, Billy, died at age five of lymphoma. It wasn't until after breaking free that I read studies suggesting that smoke from my cigarettes may have contributed to their deaths.[49] If so, all this recovered addict can do now is to

---

49 Roza MR, et al, <u>The dog as a passive smoker: effects of exposure to environmental cigarette smoke on domestic dogs</u>, Nicotine and Tobacco Research, November 2007, Volume 9(11), Pages 1171-1176; also see, Bertone ER, <u>Environmental</u>

keep them alive in his heart while begging forgiveness.

Again, the primary difference between the illegal drug addict and us is that our chemical is legal and our dopamine wanting relief sensation accompanied by alertness.

Yes, there are social smokers called "chippers." And yes, their genetics may allow them to use yet always retain the ability to simply turn and walk away.[50] But, I'm clearly not one of them. And odds are, neither are you, as you wouldn't be reading a book about how to arrest your dependency.

I often think about the alcoholic's plight, in having to watch 90% of drinkers do something the 10% who are alcoholics cannot themselves do, control their alcohol intake. We've got it much easier.

The dependency figures for nicotine are almost the exact opposite of alcohol's. Roughly 90% of daily adult smokers are chemically dependent under DSM-III[51] standards, while 87% of students smoking at least 1 cigarette daily are already dependent under DSM-IV standards.[52]

Addiction Not News to Tobacco Industry

Nearly 50 million pages of once secret tobacco industry documents are today freely available and fully searchable online.[53] Collectively, they paint a disturbing picture of an industry fully aware that its business is drug addiction.

The industry cannot ignore that, historically, roughly 27% of new smokers have been age 13 or younger, 60% age 15 or under, 80% age 17 or younger, and 92% under the age of 19.[54]

Contrary to "corporate responsibility" image campaigns, with nearly five million annual tobacco related deaths worldwide,[55] the industry knows that it must either face financial ruin or somehow entice each new generation of youth to experiment and get hooked.

---

tobacco smoke and risk of malignant lymphoma in pet cats, American Journal of Epidemiology, 2003, Volume156 (3), Pages 268-273; also Brazell RS et al, Plasma nicotine and cotinine in tobacco smoke exposed beagle dogs, Toxicology and Applied Pharmacology, 1984, Volume 73, Pages 152-158, also Bertone-Johnson ER et al, Environmental tobacco smoke and canine urinary cotinine level, Environmental Research, March 2008, Volume 106(3), Pages 361-364.

50 Kendler KS, et al, A population-based twin study in women of smoking initiation and nicotine dependence, Psychological Medicine, March 1999, Volume 29(2), Pages 299-308.

51 Hughes, JR, et al, Prevalence of tobacco dependence and withdrawal, American Journal of Psychiatry, February 1987, Volume 144(2), Pages 205-208.

52 Kandel D, et al, On the Measurement of Nicotine Dependence in Adolescence: Comparisons of the mFTQ and a DSM-IV Based Scale, Journal of Pediatric Psychology, June 2005, Volume 30(4), Pages 319-332.

53 Legacy Tobacco Documents Library, University of California, San Francisco, http://legacy.library.ucsf.edu/; also see TobaccoDocuments.org at http://tobaccodocuments.org

54 Polito, JR, WhyQuit's Smoking Initiation Survey, June 3, 2005, www.WhyQuit.com

As a Lorillard executive wrote in 1978, "The base of our business is the high-school student."[56]

Philip Morris USA (PM) is America's largest tobacco company, holding a 49% share of the U.S. retail cigarette market in 2011.[57] Based in Richmond, Virginia and founded in 1854, PM brands include Alpine, Basic, Benson & Hedges, Bristol, Cambridge, Chesterfield, Commander, Dave's, English Ovals, L&M, Lark, Merit, Parliament, Players, Saratoga and Virginia Slims.

Today, Philip Morris' website openly proclaims, "PM USA agrees with the overwhelming medical and scientific consensus that cigarette smoking is addictive" and "smokeless tobacco products are addictive."[58]

Remember that fateful "what the heck" moment when you surrendered and gave tobacco that first serious try? What you probably don't recall are the thousands of invitations to surrender and experiment that tobacco industry marketing had by then burned into your subconscious.

As shown by the following quotes from once secret Philip Morris corporate documents, it was fully aware that it was in the drug addiction business while hammering your brain with those invitations:

- 1972 - "The cigarette should not be construed as a product but a package. The product is nicotine. Think of a puff of smoke as the vehicle for nicotine. The cigarette is but one of many package layers."

  "There is the carton, which contains the pack, which contains the cigarette, which contains the smoke. The smoke is the final package. The smokers must strip off all these package layers to get to that which he seeks."[59]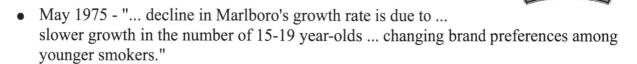

- May 1975 - "... decline in Marlboro's growth rate is due to ... slower growth in the number of 15-19 year-olds ... changing brand preferences among younger smokers."

  "Most of these studies have been restricted to people age 18 and over, but my own data, which includes younger teenagers, shows even higher Marlboro market penetration among 15-17 year-olds."

  "The teenage years are also important because those are the years during which most smokers begin to smoke, the years in which initial brand selections are made, and the period in the life-cycle in which conformity to peer-group norms is greatest.[60]

55 World Health Organization. WHO report on the global tobacco epidemic, 2008, Geneva, Switzerland: World Health Organization; 2008.

56 Lorillard, Memo, August 30, 1978, Bates Number: 94671153; http://legacy.library.ucsf.edu/tid/nlt13c00.

57 Philip Morris USA, Market Information, July 2012, http://www.philipmorrisusa.com

58 Philip Morris USA, Products, June 2008, http://www.philipmorrisusa.com

59 Philip Morris Research Center, William L. Dunn, Jr., Confidential: Motives and Incentives in Cigarette Smoking, 1972, Bates Number: 2024273959; http://legacy.library.ucsf.edu/tid/txy74e00.

60 Philip Morris U.S.A. memo: The Decline in the Rate of Growth of Marlboro Red, May 21, 1975, Bates Number: 2077864755; http://legacy.library.ucsf.edu/tid/srs84a00.

- November 1977 - "I was amazed at the trend that the [Council for Tobacco Research] work is taking. For openers, Dr. Donald H. Ford, a new staff member, makes the following quotes: 'Opiates and nicotine may be similar in action' ... 'There is a relationship between nicotine and the opiates.' ... It is my strong feeling that with the progress that has been claimed, we are in the process of digging our own grave."[61]

Based in Winston-Salem, North Carolina, R.J. Reynolds' Tobacco Company (RJR) has been around since 1874. Before RJR's 2004 merger with Brown and Williamson, its cigarette brands included Camel, Doral, Eclipse, Monarch, More, Now, Salem, Vantage and Winston.

While RJR cigarette store marketing claims that smokers smoke its brands for a host of reasons (flavor, pleasure, adventure, price, to be true, make new friends, have fun, great menthol or to look more adult), its once secret documents tell a different story.

A nine page 1972 confidential memo by a senior RJR executive is entitled "The Nature of the Tobacco Business and the Crucial Role of Nicotine Therein."[62] The next 11 paragraphs share direct quotes from this now famous and extremely informative memo:

"In a sense, the tobacco industry may be thought of as being a specialized, highly ritualized and stylized segment of the pharmaceutical industry. Tobacco products, uniquely, contain and deliver nicotine, a potent drug with a variety of physiological effects."

"Thus a tobacco product is, in essence, a vehicle for delivery of nicotine, designed to deliver the nicotine in a generally acceptable and attractive form. Our Industry is then based upon design, manufacture and sale of attractive dosage forms of nicotine ..."

"If nicotine is the sine qua non of tobacco products and tobacco products are recognized as being attractive dosage forms of nicotine, then it is logical to design our products -- and where possible, our advertising -- around nicotine delivery ..."

"He does not start smoking to obtain undefined physiological gratifications or reliefs, and certainly he does not start to smoke to satisfy a non-existent craving for nicotine. Rather, he appears to start to smoke for purely psychological reasons -- to emulate a valued image, to conform, to experiment, to defy, to be daring, to have something to do with his hands, and the like."

"Only after experiencing smoking for some period of time do the physiological "satisfactions" and habituation become apparent and needed. Indeed, the first smoking experiences are often unpleasant until a tolerance for nicotine has been developed."

---

61 Philip Morris U.S.A. Inter-Office Correspondence, Seligman to Osdene, November 29, 1977, Bates Number: 207799380; http://legacy.library.ucsf.edu/tid/ggy75c00.

62 RJR Confidential Research Planning Memorandum, The Nature of the Tobacco Business and the Crucial Role of Nicotine Therein, Claude E. Teague, Jr., RJR Assistant Director of Research, April 14, 1972, Bates Number: 501877121, http://legacy.library.ucsf.edu/tid/sjw29d00.

"This leaves us, then, in the position of attempting to design and promote the same product to two different types of markets with two different sets of motivations, needs and expectations."

"If, as proposed above, nicotine is the sine qua non of smoking, and if we meekly accept the allegations of our critics and move toward reduction or elimination of nicotine from our products, then we shall eventually liquidate our business."

"If we intend to remain in business and our business is the manufacture and sale of dosage forms of nicotine, then at some point we must make a stand." "If our business is fundamentally that of supplying nicotine in useful dosage form, why is it really necessary that allegedly harmful 'tar' accompany that nicotine?"

"There should be some simpler, "cleaner", more efficient and direct way to provide the desired nicotine dosage than the present system involving combustion of tobacco or even chewing of tobacco ..."

"It should be possible to obtain pure nicotine by synthesis or from high-nicotine tobacco. It should then be possible, using modifications of techniques developed by the pharmaceutical and other industries, to deliver that nicotine to the user in efficient, effective, attractive dosage form, accompanied by no 'tar', gas phase, or other allegedly harmful substances."

"The dosage form could incorporate various flavorants, enhancers, and like desirable additives, and would be designed to deliver the minimum effective amount of nicotine at the desired release-rate to supply the 'satisfaction' desired by the user."

As shown, more than 40 years ago, RJR's 1972 memo accurately predicted both the arrival of nicotine replacement products (NRT) and the combustion-free electronic or e-cigarette.

The lines between the tobacco and pharmaceutical industry nicotine are now blurring horribly. A 2003 nicotine gum study found that 37% of gum users were hooked on the cure, each being chronic long-term gum users of at least 6 months.[63] It's a trend that will continue.

Brown & Williamson (B&W) was a cigarette company that merged with RJR in 2004. B&W brands - now owned by RJR - include Barclay, Belair, Capri, Carlton, GPC, Kool, Laredo, Lucky Strike, Misty, North State, Pall Mall, Private Stock, Raleigh, Tareyton and Viceroy. Here are a few quotes from once secret B&W corporate documents:

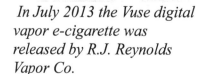

In July 2013 the Vuse digital vapor e-cigarette was released by R.J. Reynolds Vapor Co.

- July 18, 1977: "How to market an addictive product in an ethical

---

63 Shiffman S, Hughes JR, et al, <u>Persistent use of nicotine replacement therapy: an analysis of actual purchase patterns in a population based sample</u>, Tobacco Control, November 2003, Volume 12, Pages 310-316.

manner?"[64]

● June 24, 1978: "Very few consumers are aware of the effects of nicotine, i.e., its addictive nature and that nicotine is a poison."[65]

● March 25, 1983: "Nicotine is the addicting agent in cigarettes. It, therefore, seems reasonable that when people switch brands, if they have a certain smoking pattern (i.e. number of sticks/day), they will switch to a brand at the same nicotine level."[66]

Founded in 1760, Lorillard Tobacco Company is the oldest U.S. tobacco company. Its brands include Kent, Maverick, Max, Newport, Old Gold, Satin, Triumph and True. The following telling quotes are from once secret Lorillard documents:

● April 13, 1977: "Tobacco scientists know that physiological satisfaction is almost totally related to nicotine intake."[67]

● November 3, 1977: "I don't know of any smoker who at some point hasn't wished he didn't smoke. If we could offer an acceptable alternative for providing nicotine, I am 100 percent sure we would have a gigantic brand."[68]

● February 13, 1980: "Goal - Determine the minimum level of nicotine that will allow continued smoking. We hypothesize satisfaction cannot be compensated for by psychological satisfaction. At this point smokers will quit, or return to higher tar & nicotine brands."[69]

Last but not least is British American Tobacco (BAT), which dates to 1902 and sells more than 300 brands worldwide. BAT's international brands include Dunhill, Kent, Lucky Strike, Pall Mall, Vogue, Rothmans, Peter Stuyvesant, Benson & Hedges, Winfield, John Player, State Express 555, Kool and Viceroy. It does not own all these brands but is licensed by other companies to distribute them. Here are a few BAT admissions.

November 1961: Smoking "differs in important features from addiction to other alkaloid drugs, but

64 Brown & Williamson Advertising Conference Report: Synectics Problem Laboratory, July 18, 1977, Bates Number: 770101768; http://legacy.library.ucsf.edu/tid/mri63f00/pdf.

65 Brown & Williamson, Memorandum: Future Consumer Reaction to Nicotine, June 24, 1978, Bates Number: 665043966; http://legacy.library.ucsf.edu/tid/zfi21f00.

66 Brown & Williamson, Internal Correspondence, Project Recommendations, March 25, 1983, Bates Number: 670508492; http://legacy.library.ucsf.edu/tid/uly04f00.

67 Lorillard, Present Status of the Nicotine Enrichment Project, April 13, 1977, Bates Number: 83251103; http://legacy.library.ucsf.edu/tid/bgm09c00

68 Lorillard, Letter, November 3, 1977, Bates Number: 03365541; http://legacy.library.ucsf.edu/tid/cze91e00

69 Lorillard, Memorandum Secret, RT Information Task Force, February 13, 1980, Bates Number: 94672618; http://legacy.library.ucsf.edu/tid/ust13c00

yet there are sufficient similarities to justify stating that smokers are nicotine addicts."[70]

1967: "There has been significant progress in understanding why people smoke and the opinion is hardening in medical circles that the pharmacological effects of nicotine play an important part... It may be useful, therefore, to look at the tobacco industry as if a large part its business is the administration of nicotine (in the clinical sense)."[71]

August 1979: "We are searching explicitly for a socially acceptable addictive product. The essential constituent is most likely to be nicotine or a direct substitute for it."[72]

April 1980: "In a world of increased government intervention, B.A.T should learn to look at itself as a drug company rather than as a tobacco company."[73]

In light of the above tiny sampling of tobacco industry admissions, should there be any doubt in our minds as to who was slave and who was master, who profited and who lost?

Freedom Starts with Admitting Addiction

It was not easy looking in the mirror and at last seeing a true drug addict looking back. I felt like I was surrendering, that after all those failed attempts I'd lost. I felt like a total and complete failure. But as horrible as that moment felt, doing so was the most liberating event in my life.

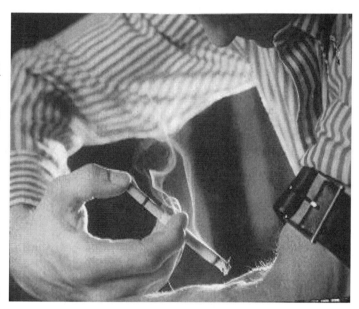

It was then and there that I no longer needed the long list of lies I'd invented to try to explain my captivity, my need for that next fix.

Yes, there were countless times during my 3 decades of bondage where I'd told myself that I was hooked. But not until early 1999, after one last failed attempt, did it hit me. Like alcoholism, my addiction was for real. It was then that I awoke to realize that I was no different from the meth or heroin addict

---

70 Honorable Gladys Kessler, <u>Final Opinion</u>, U.S. District Court, U.S. vs. Phillip Morris USA, Page 416, August 17, 2006.
71 British American Tobacco Memo, 1967, as stated in Federal Court of Australia, New South Wales, N-1089 of 1999, <u>Statement of Claim</u>, Page 370.
72 British American Tobacco, Memo, <u>Key Areas - Product Innovation Over Next 10 Years for Long Term Development</u>, August 28, 1979, Bates Number: 321469581; http://bat.library.ucsf.edu/tid/fyz34a99
73 British American Tobacco, <u>Brainstorming II</u>, April 11, 1980, Bates Number: 109884190; http://bat.library.ucsf.edu/tid/oli85a99

Dr. M.A.H. Russell, a psychiatrist and addiction researcher at London's Institute of Psychiatry had me pegged in 1974:

> "There is little doubt that if it were not for nicotine in tobacco smoke, people would be little more inclined to smoke than they are to blow bubbles or to light sparklers."

> "Cigarette-smoking is probably the most addictive and dependence-producing form of object-specific self-administered gratification known to man."[74]

Over the years, millions of nicotine addicts have tried proving Dr. Russell wrong. In January 2003, a Miami based company, the Vector Group Ltd., began marketing a nicotine-free cigarette called Quest in seven northeastern U.S. states.

A novelty item, thousands of smokers rushed out to purchase their first pack of nicotine-free smokes. But locating any smoker who returned to purchase a second pack proved nearly impossible.

We would no more smoke nicotine-free cigarettes than we'd smoke dried leaves from the backyard. Hello! My name is John and I'm a comfortably recovered nicotine addict.

It is not normal for humans to light things they place between their lips on fire and then intentionally suck the fire's smoke deep into their lungs. Nor is it normal to chew or suck a highly toxic non-edible plant, hour after hour, day after day, year after year.

We rationalized irrational behavior because of the neuro-chemical relief from wanting it generated. What we didn't realize that each use reinforced future wanting by creation of yet another high definition use memory.

Cuddling up to the warm, cozy rationalization that, at worst, all we have is some "nasty little habit" serves the tobacco industry well. While habits can be manipulated, modified, toyed with and controlled, nicotine addiction is an all or nothing proposition.

The nicotine industry knows that so long as its adult free-choice marketing continues to brainwash nicotine addicts into believing that they're in full control, that they are likely to continue to hand the industry their money until the day they die.

Regardless of the delivery device or method used to introduce nicotine into the bloodstream, fully accepting that our addiction is as real and permanent as alcoholism greatly simplifies the rules of recovery. In fact, there's really only one.

Chapter 2 reviews the only rule that we each need follow in order to spend the balance of life on the free side of dependency's bars. It's called the "Law of Addiction."

---

74 Russell, MA, The Smoking Habit and Its Classification, The Practitioner, June 1974 Volume 212 (1272), Pages 791-800.

Chapter 2

The Law of Addiction

"Administration of a drug to an addict will cause re-establishment of chemical dependence upon the addictive substance."

The Law Defined

According to the World Health Organization, "In the 20th century, the tobacco epidemic killed 100 million people worldwide. During the 21st century, it could kill one billion."[75]

Year after year, at least 70% of surveyed smokers say they want to stop,[76] and each year 40% make an attempt of at least one day.[77]

There is no lack of desire or effort. What's lacking is know-how. Key to breaking and staying free is understanding the "Law of Addiction."

Whether users know it by name or simply understand the basic premise, failure to self-discover or to be taught this law is a horrible reason to die. The "Law of Addiction" is not man-made law. It's as fundamental as the law of gravity and refusal to abide by it will result in injury or death.

The Law is rather simple. It states, "Administration of a drug to an addict will cause re-establishment of chemical dependence upon the addictive substance."

Mastering it requires acceptance of three fundamental principles:

    (1) That dependency upon using nicotine is a true chemical addiction, captivating the same brain dopamine wanting relief pathways as alcoholism, cocaine or heroin addiction;

    (2) That once established we cannot cure or kill an addiction but only arrest it; and

75   World Health Organization, <u>WHO Report on the Global Tobacco Epidemic, 2008</u>, The MPOWER Package, Fresh and Alive, Forward by WHO Director General, 2008.

76   U.S. Centers for Disease Control, <u>Cigarette Smoking Among Adults - United States, 2000</u>, Weekly MMWR, July 26, 2002, Volume 51(29), Pages 642-645.

77   U.S. Centers for Disease Control, <u>Cigarette Smoking Among Adults - United States, 2007</u>, Weekly MMWR, November 14, 2008, Volume 57(45), Pages 1221-1226.

(3) That once arrested, regardless of how long we have remained nicotine-free, that just one hit of nicotine creates an extremely high probability of full relapse.

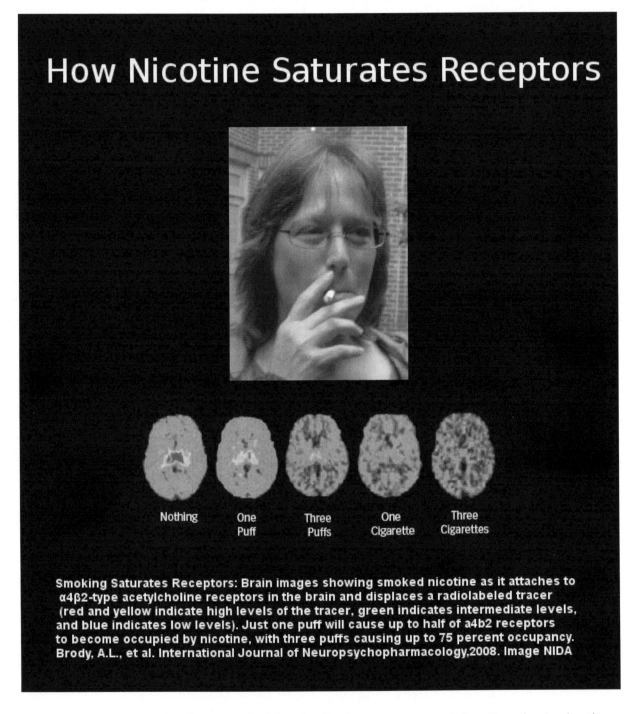

How Nicotine Saturates Receptors

Nothing   One Puff   Three Puffs   One Cigarette   Three Cigarettes

Smoking Saturates Receptors: Brain images showing smoked nicotine as it attaches to α4β2-type acetylcholine receptors in the brain and displaces a radiolabeled tracer (red and yellow indicate high levels of the tracer, green indicates intermediate levels, and blue indicates low levels). Just one puff will cause up to half of a4b2 receptors to become occupied by nicotine, with three puffs causing up to 75 percent occupancy. Brody, A.L., et al. International Journal of Neuropsychopharmacology,2008. Image NIDA

We need not guess as to what happens inside a brain that attempts to "cheat" and use nicotine during recovery. The evidence seen on brain PET scans is undeniable. Just one puff of nicotine and up to 50 percent of the brain's nicotinic-type acetylcholine receptors become occupied by nicotine.[78]

---

78 Brody AL et al, Cigarette smoking saturates brain alpha 4 beta 2 nicotinic acetylcholine receptors, Archives of General Psychiatry, August 2006, Volume 63(8), Pages 907-915.

During relapse, while the smoker's conscious mind may find itself struggling with tobacco toxin tissue burning sensations and carbon monoxide induced dizziness, well-engineered dopamine pay-attention pathways are recording the event and will make the resulting dopamine "aaah" wanting relief sensation nearly impossible, in the short-term, to forget.

In fact, most actually walk away from their relapse experience thinking that they have gotten away with cheating and using just once. But it won't be long before their awakened dependency is again wanting and begging for more.

Recovery isn't about battling an entire pack, pouch, tin or box. It's about that first bolus of nicotine striking the brain, a hit that will end our journey, cost us liberty, and land us back behind bars.

Unfortunately, conventional recovery wisdom invites relapse with statements such as "Don't let a little slip put you back to smoking." As Joel says, it's like telling the alcoholic, "Don't let a sip put you back to drinking" or the heroin addict, "Don't let shooting-up put you back to using."

Experts are fond of stating that "on average, it takes between 3-5 serious recovery attempts before breaking free of tobacco dependence," and that "every time you make an effort you're smarter and you can use that information to increase the likelihood that your subsequent attempt is successful."

What these so called experts fail to reveal is the precise lesson eventually learned. Why? And why can't that lesson be taught and mastered before a user's first attempt ever?

They don't teach it because most don't understand it themselves. Instead they excuse failure before it occurs, as if trying to protect the particular smoking cessation product they are pushing from being blamed for defeat.

The lesson eventually gleaned from the school of hard-recovery-knocks is that "if I take so much as one puff, dip or chew I will relapse." Just one, just once and defeat is all but assured.

"The idea that you can't stop the first time is absolutely wrong," says Joel.[79] "The only reason it takes most people multiple attempts is that they don't understand their addiction to nicotine. How could they, no one really teaches it."

"People have to learn by screwing up one attempt after another until it finally dawns on them that each time they lost it, it happened by taking a puff. If you understand this concept from the get-go, you don't have to go through chronic [stopping and starting]."

The Law Reflected in Studies

Yes, once all nicotine use ends, a single subsequent use is extremely accurate in predicting full and complete relapse.

The 1990 Brandon lapse/relapse study followed 129 smokers who successfully completed a two-

---

79 Spitzer J, Is this your first time quitting? http://www.ffn.yuku.com/topic/11623 - December 29, 2001.

week stop smoking program for two additional years.[80]   Lapse was defined as any tobacco use regardless of how much.

Among those who lapsed, the mean number of days between the end of the smoking cessation program and lapse was two months (58 days), with nearly all lapsing within the first three months.

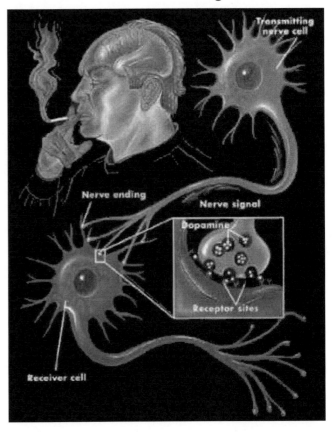

While 14% took only one or two puffs, 42% smoked the entire cigarette, while the average smoked about two-thirds.   A second cigarette was smoked by 93.5% who had lapsed. Nearly half (47%) smoked that second cigarette within 24 hours, with one in five smoking it within an hour (21%).

The Brandon study found that 60% who lapsed "asked for" the cigarette (bummed it), 23% purchased it, 9% found it, 6% stole it, and 2% were offered it. Also of note, 47% who lapsed drank alcohol before doing so.

Overall, the study found that 88% who "tasted" a cigarette relapsed. In discussing the finding Brandon wrote:

> "The high rate of return to regular smoking (88%) once a cigarette is tasted suggests that the distinction between an initial lapse and full relapse may be unnecessary." "In our study, high initial confidence levels may have reduced subjects' motivation to acquire skills and engage productively in treatment."

The Brandon study's finding was echoed by the 1990 Boreland study, which followed callers to an Australian telephone stop smoking line. There, among 339 participants who lapsed (123 who didn't make it an entire day and 172 who stopped for at least 24 hours) 295 or 87% experienced relapse within 90 days.[81]

The 1992 Garvey study followed 235 adult smokers for one full year after attempting to quit. It found that, "Those who smoked any cigarettes at all in the post-cessation period (i.e. lapsed) had a 95% probability of resuming their regular pattern of smoking subsequently."[82]

Although the challenges of recovery have ended for hundreds of millions of now comfortable ex-

---

80 Brandon, TH et al, Postcessation cigarette use: the process of relapse, Addictive Behaviors, 1990; 15(2), pages 105-114.
81 Borland R., Slip-ups and relapse in attempts to quit smoking, Addictive Behaviors, 1990, Volume 15(3), Pages 235-45.
82 Garvey AJ et al, Predictors of smoking relapse among self-quitters: a report from the Normative Aging Study, Addictive Behaviors, 1992, Volume 17(4), Pages 367-377.

users, each lives with nicotine dependency's imprint permanently burned into their brain. Even after 10, 20 or 30 years of freedom we remain wired for relapse.

We're not stronger than nicotine but then we don't need to be. It is only a chemical. Like the salt or pepper in our shakers, it has an I.Q. of zero. Like the sugar in our sugar bowl, it cannot plot, plan, think or conspire. And it is not some big or little monster that dwells inside us.

Our blood serum becomes nicotine-free and withdrawal peaks in intensity within three days of ending all use. But just one powerful jolt of nicotine and the deck gets stacked against us. The odds of us having the stamina to withstand and endure nicotine's influence upon the brain without relapsing are horrible.

Brandon, Boreland and Garvey teach us that while relapse isn't 100% guaranteed, that the odds are so high, that to not treat lapse as relapse is a recipe for defeat, disease and death.

Our greatest weapon has always been our infinitely superior intelligence. As taught by Garvey, the most important recovery lesson our intelligence can master is that being 99% successful at not using nicotine produces up to 95% odds of defeat.

As Joel Spitzer's lessons have burned deeply into my brain, there's just one controlling principle determining the outcome for all. It's that total adherence to a personal commitment to not violate the law of addiction provides a 100% guarantee of success. Although obedience may not always be easy, the law is clear, concise and simple - no nicotine today, not one puff, dip or chew!

Missed Relapse Lesson

In 1984 Joel wrote an article with the heartless sounding title, "The Lucky Ones Get Hooked."[83] Frankly, it's anything but callous.

It makes the important point that those who experience full relapse within a few days of taking a puff, dip or chew are fortunate in that the experience offers potential to self-teach them the most critical recovery lesson of all, "The Law of Addiction."

In the Brandon study, while nearly half who lapsed experienced full relapse within one day, the study's mean average from lapse to relapse was nine days.

---

83 Spitzer, J, Joel's Library, <u>The Lucky Ones Get Hooked</u>, 1984, http://whyquit.com/joel

Those who quickly experience full relapse increase the likelihood of learning, right away, the critical lesson of the power of using nicotine just once.

But the more time and distance between that first use and full dependency resumption, the greater likelihood there is of learning the wrong lesson, a lesson that for far too many smokers proves deadly.

"The ex-smoker who takes a drag and doesn't get hooked gets a false sense of confidence," writes Joel. "He thinks he can take one any time he wants and not get hooked. Usually, within a short period of time sneaking a drag here and there, he will become hooked."

"One day he too may try to stop and actually succeed. He may stop for a week, month, or even years. But always in the back of his mind he feels, 'I know I can have one if I really want to. After all, I did it last time and didn't get hooked right away.'"

"One day, at a party or under stress or just out of boredom he will try one again. Maybe this time he will get hooked, maybe not. But you can be sure that there will be a next time. Eventually he will become hooked again."

Living a series of perpetual relapses, trying to break free again and again and again, each time enduring withdrawal and recovery is no way to live. "Taking the first drag is a no-win situation," cautions Joel.

Over the years, hundreds of millions of ex-users have discovered the power of one puff, dip or chew totally on their own. But over the years, with arrival of each new magic cure, self-discovery of the Law of Addiction has become increasingly difficult.

If old enough, think back to 1980, before arrival of nicotine replacement therapy (NRT) and nicotine gum. Remember the traveling smoking cessation hypnotist coming to town? There really wasn't much else.

The only real alternatives to cold turkey were gradual weaning or tapering schemes, with extremely dismal results (roughly half as effective as cold turkey/abrupt cessation).[84]

---

84 Cheong Y, Yong HH and Borland R, <u>Does how you quit affect success? A comparison between abrupt and gradual methods</u>

The likelihood of any particular attempt being cold turkey was substantial. Thus, the odds of self-discovering the Law of Addiction were good. Absent was the negative influence of pharmaceutical company marketing, marketing designed to intentionally shatter confidence in our natural recovery instincts.

Cold turkey had cornered the recovery market. When NRT arrived the industry saw no alternative but to attack it. Three decades of industry brainwashing has falsely painted cold turkey as nearly impossible with few succeeding.

Cold turkey is free yet poor. It has no bank account, economic muscle or political clout. The industry's attacks, false representations and gradual takeover of government cessation policy went largely unnoticed and unchallenged.[85]

Today, pharmaceutical industry financial influence has played a major role in authoring official national cessation policy in nearly every developed nation on earth.[86]

Unopposed, by June 2000 the industry's muscle had grown so powerful here in the U.S. that cessation policy was rewritten so as to make use of pharmaceutical industry cessation products mandatory unless the user's medical condition prohibited it.[87]

Instead of teaching the Law of Addiction and the power of nicotine to foster relapse, the pharmaceutical industry teaches that nicotine is "medicine" and its use is "therapy."

It has never made a commercial announcing to smokers that it redefined "stopping smoking" from its traditional meaning of ending both smoking and nicotine use, to just a single method of nicotine delivery, smoking it.

The industry has yet to reveal that its more than 200 "medication" studies were not about drug addicts arresting their chemical dependency upon nicotine. Those studies did not test body fluids to see if any participant actually became nicotine-free. Instead, they tested the breath of participants for expired carbon monoxide, to see if participants had stopped smoking it.

One of the best-kept industry secrets is the percentage of former smokers who continued to remain dependent upon replacement nicotine at study's end or who turned to oral tobacco.

That's why it's so important that each of us teach the Law of Addiction to users within our sphere of influence. Why? Because jumping from product to product while fearing your natural recovery instincts, it's getting hard to self-discover the Law, and that's a horrible reason to die.

---

using data from the International Tobacco Control Policy Evaluation Study, Nicotine & Tobacco Research, August 2007, Volume 9(8), Pages 801-810; also see West R, Fidler J, Smoking and Smoking Cessation in England 2010, August 13, 2011, www.smokinginengland.info, STS 23.

85 Polito, JR, Flawed research equates placebo to cold turkey, WhyQuit.com, March 12, 2007.

86 Helliker, K, Nicotine Fix - Behind Antismoking Policy, Influence of Drug Industry, Wall Street Journal - February 8, 2007, Page A1; also see, Polito JR, U.S. quit smoking policy integrity drowns in pharmaceutical influence, WhyQuit.com, May 13, 2008.

87 Polito, JR, Does updated tobacco treatment "Guideline" reflect sham science? WhyQuit.com, May 5, 2008.

Just one rule - "No Nicotine Today!"

While there are scores of stop smoking books and quick-fix magic cures promising near painless and sure-fire success, there is but one principle that affords a 100% guarantee to all adhering to it ... "no nicotine today."

While the Brandon, Boreland and Garvey studies afford the junkie mind a tiny sliver of junkie thinking wiggle-room in believing that the "Law of Addiction" can be cheated, it's impossible to fail by living the "Law" as an absolute.

Why test the ability of our dopamine pathways to make pathway-activating events extremely difficult to forget or ignore? Why challenge our brain's design? Why toy with disastrous odds?

One hit will be too many, while a thousand never enough. We cannot fail so long as all nicotine remains on the outside. Just one rule to staying free, none today!

Chapter 3

Quitting "You"

The real "you" never, ever needed nicotine. You were fine on your own. The real "you" didn't need the sense of wanting satisfaction that arrived with each new supply, or the anxieties associated with needing more.

The real us typically functioned more towards the center, without nicotine's feeding cycle mood swings.

So what if you never, ever needed to inhale or juice nicotine again? What if your mind was once again allowed to be itself, filled with a rich sense of calm while stimulating its dopamine pathways the natural way, via great flavors, big hugs, cool water, a sense of accomplishment, friendship, nurturing, love and intimacy?

What if days, weeks or even months passed comfortably, without once thinking about wanting to use nicotine? Would that be a good thing or bad?

Recovery Instead of Quitting

Quitting is a word that tugs at emotion. By definition it associates itself with departing, leaving, forsaking and abandonment.

But the real abandonment took place on the day nicotine dependent pathways suppressed all remaining memory of the beauty of life without nicotine, when no longer able to recall how fantastic we functioned without it.

FFN-TJH isn't about quitting. It's about recovering a person long ago forgotten, the real and wonderful "you!"

The word "quitting" tends to paint nicotine cessation in gray and black, in the doom and gloom of bad and horrible. It breeds anticipatory fears, inner demons, needless anxieties, external enemies and visions of suffering. It fosters a natural sense of self-deprivation, of leaving something valuable behind.

Now, contrast quitting with recovery. Recovery doesn't run or hide from our addiction. Instead, it boldly embraces who we became, and every aspect of this temporary journey of re-adjustment.

When knowledge based, we're looking for recovery symptoms, emotions, conditioning and junkie thinking, and view each encounter as an opportunity to reclaim another piece of a nicotine-free life.

Nicotine dependency recovery presents an opportunity to experience what may be our richest period of repair and self-discovery ever. Tissues are allowed to heal. Senses awaken and brain's neuro-chemicals again flow in response to life not nicotine.

It's a period where each challenge overcome awards us another piece of our puzzle, a puzzle that once complete reflects a life reclaimed.

It is not necessary that we delete the word "quit" from our thinking, vocabulary or this book (at least not entirely). But it might be helpful to reflect upon when the real "quitting" took place, when freedom ended and that next fix became life's primary objective.

Although probably impossible to believe right now, you won't be leaving anything of value behind. Nothing! Everything done while under nicotine's influence can be done as well as or better as "us."

Buried Alive by Nicotine "Aaah"s

Again, try to remember. What was it like being you? What was it like to function every morning without nicotine, to finish a meal, travel, talk on the phone, have a disagreement, start a project or take a break without putting nicotine into your body?

What was it like before nicotine took control? What was it like residing inside a mind that did not want for nicotine?

Possibly the most fascinating aspect of drug addiction is just how quickly all remaining memory of life without the drug gets buried by high-definition wanting-relief memories.

As explored in Chapter 4, how can we claim to like or love something when we have almost no remaining memory of what life without it was like? What basis exists for honest comparison?

Why be afraid of returning to a calm and quiet place where you no longer crave a chemical that today, every day, you cannot seem to get off your mind, a chemical that is a mandatory part of each day's plan?

Why fear arriving here on Easy Street with nearly a billion comfortably recovered nicotine addicts? Is freedom of thought and action a good thing or bad? If good, why fear it?

How wonderful would it be to again reside inside a quiet mind where our addiction's chatter gradually becomes infrequent and then rare?

Slave to our world of nicotine-normal, we were each provided a new identity. Captive brain dopamine pathways did their designed job and did it well. They left us convinced that our next nicotine fix was central to survival, as important as water or food.

I recently read disturbing comments posted by more than one hundred long-term nicotine gum addicts. One, a 36 year-old woman, wrote, "I have to say, I traded one problem for another. I chew 4 mg 24/7 and can go through 170 pieces in less than 6 days. I have been chewing Nicorette now for 12 years. If I run out for a short time my mood becomes irrational. It is costing me more money than I have. I have chosen Nicorette over food many times."[88]

We can only hope that such honesty leads her to ask and answer the bigger question, "why?" Hopefully someday soon she'll feel what it's like to comfortably engage her entire day without once wanting for nicotine.

Contrary to the false survival training lesson constantly being pounded into her brain by her hijacked priorities teacher, she'd be leaving nothing of value behind. Even the love in her heart, she'd get to bring it with her.

An Infected Life

Whether a closet user who hides their addiction, a low tolerance level addict whose twice daily use has them denying it, or a heavy and open addict like I was, our dependency infected far more of life than we care or cared to admit. Once we permit ourselves to begin looking closely, it becomes hard to find any aspect of life that wasn't, to some degree, touched by our addiction.

Our endless feeding cycle was a perpetual interruption. Aside from the time devoted to use, there was non-stop use planning, the need to re-supply, clean-up and returning to the activity use had previously interrupted, or to a new one.

---

88 AskAPatient.com , Nicorette User Database, January 25, 2008 comments by a 36 year-old female user. Also see Polito JR, Long-term Nicorette gum users losing hair and teeth, WhyQuit.com, December 1, 2008.

As smokers, how many times daily did we suck 1 milligram of nicotine into our lungs? As snuff users, how many times did a 2.5 gram pinch stay in your mouth until generating 3.6 milligrams of pure nicotine juice? If a chewer, how many times daily was 7.9 grams of loose tobacco jawed until letting go of 4.5 milligrams?[89]

And then we'd wait for nicotine's two-hour elimination half-life and a falling tonic dopamine level to command us to use again. Or we could accelerate elimination by encountering stress, drinking alcohol or consuming vitamin C.[90]

Nicotine's presence altered our body's natural sensitivities. It destroyed our ability to relax, hijacked our priorities and consumed precious time. Smoking it diminished lung function while gradually destroying our body's ability to receive and transport oxygen.

Whether smoked, chewed or sucked, tobacco diminished the accuracy of our smell and taste, while making us home to smoke's more than 4,000 chemicals or oral tobacco's more than 2,550.[91] If a smoker, we introduced up to 81 cancer causing chemicals[92] and up to 28 carcinogens if an oral tobacco user.[93]

Like a mouse on an exercise wheel, there can be no end to this endless cycle of madness unless we get off, unless nicotine's arrival ends.

Forgotten Relaxation

Photo SierraWild.gov

Two million years of evolution prepared us to fight or flee the now extinct saber tooth tiger. Our

89 Benowitz NL, Systemic Absorption and Effects of Nicotine from Smokeless Tobacco, Advances in Dental Research, September 1997, Volume 11(3), Pages 336-341.

90 Spitzer, J, Never Take Another Puff, WhyQuit.com, 2003.

91 U.S. Surgeon General, Reducing the Health Consequences of Smoking: 25 Years of Progress: A Report of the Surgeon General: 1989, Page 79.

92 Smith CJ et al, IARC carcinogens reported in cigarette mainstream smoke and their calculated log P values, Food and Chemical Toxicology, June 2003, Volume 41(6), Pages 807-817.

93 IARC Monographs on the Evaluation of Carcinogenic Risks to Humans, Smokeless Tobacco and Some Tobacco-specific N-Nitrosamines, 2007, Volume 89.

body's response to sensing danger or sudden stress is activation of the "fight or flight" pathways of the sympathetic nervous system. Nicotine also activates these pathways.[94]

Nicotine's arrival in the brain causes the release of noradrenaline (nor-epinephrine), which in turn causes more than 100 neuro-chemicals to prepare the body to run for its life or fight.

Is it normal to spend the balance of life under the influence of an adrenaline releasing central nervous system stimulant?

Before climbing into bed to sleep, is it normal to consume a chemical that will make our heart pound up to 17.5 beats per minute faster,[95] that elevates blood pressure, restricts extremity blood flow causing the temperature of our fingers to drop up to seven degrees,[96] that accelerates breathing, dilates our pupils, perks our senses, shuts down digestion, and that triggers the release of glucose and fats from our body's energy stores?

As active addicts, most of us claimed that nicotine helped us relax. But activating our fight or flight response shows just how neuro-chemically confused we became regarding nicotine's impact upon us. Try to imagine what it is like to go hours or an entire day without having adrenaline being pumped into your bloodstream.

What would it feel like to stop endlessly beating yourself as if whipping a tired horse, to stop responding to non-existent saber tooth tigers, to again know and bask in full, deep and complete relaxation for extended periods of time?

Forgotten Calm During Crisis

Have you ever noticed what you reach for during crisis? That's right - as just reviewed - a nervous system stimulant that activates the body's fight or flight response. While stressful situations often by themselves activate our fight or flight response, why guarantee that it happens? When confronted with stress, why intentionally make your heart pound faster, elevate your blood pressure and induce additional anxiety?

Even more disturbing, intentionally adding your body's fight or flight response to every stressful

94 Haass M, et al, Nicotine and sympathetic neurotransmission, Cardiovascular Drugs and Therapy, January 1997, Volume 10(6), Pages 657-665.

95 Parrott AC et al, Nicotine chewing gum (2 mg, 4 mg) and cigarette smoking: comparative effects upon vigilance and heart rate, Psychopharmacology (Berlin). 1989, Volume 97(2), Pages 257-261 (2 mg gum average increase of 5 beats per minute [bpm], 4 mg gum 10 bpm, smoking nicotine 17.5 bpm); also see, Houlihan ME, et al, A double blind study of the effects of smoking on heart rate: is there tachyphylaxis? Psychopharmacology (Berlin), May 1999 Volume 144(1), Pages 38-44 (max increase of 15 bpm); also see, Najem B, et al, Acute cardiovascular and sympathetic effects of nicotine replacement therapy, Hypertension, June 2006, Volume 47(6), Pages 1162-1167 (average increase of 7 bpm).

96 Lorillard Tobacco Company, Killian Research Laboratories, Inc., 1949-1955, http://tobaccodocuments.org/lor/95309579-9589.html

situation was nothing compared to the reason why we reached for nicotine during crisis, because stress caused the onset of early withdrawal.

We'll review in detail how stressful situations threw us into withdrawal in the next chapter (Use Rationalizations) under the heading "Use helps me concentrate."

Here, simply ask yourself this. What would encounters with stress be like if fewer of them activated your fight or flight response, and none threw you into withdrawal?

Imagine being far calmer during crisis. What would it be like to again be you?

Forgotten Breathing & Endurance

Smokers not only suffer from nicotine addiction but the ravaging effects of thousands of inhaled chemicals upon their lungs and respiratory system.

What was it like to run like the wind, to engage in an extended period of brisk physical activity without becoming seriously winded?

What was it like to climb flight after flight of stairs, to play full-court basketball, or to chase a child or the family pet without ending up gasping for air?

Every now and then I meet a current smoker who proudly boasts that they enjoy running. What they don't seem to appreciate is the tremendous strain they subject their heart and body to when doing so. It's a matter of the availability of sufficient oxygen to keep vigorously working muscles well fueled and alive.

Carbon monoxide is a colorless, odorless toxic gas produced when any carbon-based material is burned, including tobacco. When smoking, the amount of carbon monoxide entering the bloodstream varies greatly (up to 25mg per cigarette) depending upon such factors as how intensely the smoker smokes, whether or not they cover the filter ventilation holes with their lips, and the particular brand smoked.

Without oxygen the body's cells suffocate and die. The primary function of our lungs is to allow the entry of life-giving oxygen from the atmosphere into our bloodstream, and to then transfer carbon dioxide from our bloodstream back out into the atmosphere.

This exchange of gases takes place within an estimated 480 million thinly walled air sacs called alveoli.[97]   But sucking large quantities of carbon monoxide into our lungs changes the playing field.

Hemoglobin is the portion of each red blood cell that transports a new supply of oxygen from the alveoli (air sacs) in our lungs to more than 50 trillion living cells throughout the body. One hemoglobin molecule can transport up to 4 oxygen molecules.

The problem is, when smoking, if both an oxygen molecule and a carbon monoxide molecule arrive at an air sac at the same time, the carbon monoxide molecule always wins and the oxygen molecule is always left behind.

The chemical attraction between carbon monoxide and hemoglobin is 200-250 times greater than with oxygen.[98] What's worse, once attached to hemoglobin, carbon monoxide's long chemical bloodstream half-life of 2 to 6.5 hours[99] destroys the ability of red blood cells to engage in transporting oxygen.

Think about that last puff. One-half of the carbon monoxide it contained will still be circulating inside your bloodstream roughly four hours later. Is it any wonder that our heart and body rebelled when we attempted vigorous exercise, even hours after smoking?

We don't just deprive our heart and muscles of oxygen. We daily paint our lungs with the 4,000 chemicals that the tobacco industry collectively refers to as tar. It's too little oxygen and too much gunk.

We like to think that most of what we suck into our lungs is exhaled but it just isn't so. Ninety-seven percent of NNN (possibly the most potent lung cancer causing chemical of all) is not exhaled but remains inside.

It's the same absorption rate as nicotine. Ninety-seven percent of inhaled nicotine isn't exhaled.[100] Imagine traveling through life with lungs so marinated and caked in toxic tars that it significantly diminishes lung function.

What would it be like to allow nearly destroyed bronchial tube sweeper brooms, our cilia, to re-grow and begin the process of sweeping gunk from air passages? Imagine allowing all still functioning air sacs time to clean and heal.

What would it be like to experience a significant increase in overall lung function? Imagine gifting yourself the ability to build cardiovascular endurance again, to have nearly all of your hemoglobin transporting life-giving oxygen.

---

97 Ochs M et al, The number of alveoli in the human lung, American Journal of Respiratory and Critical Care Medicine, January 1, 2004, Volume 169(1), Pages 120-124.
98 Meredith T et al, Carbon monoxide poisoning, British Medical Journal, January 1988, Volume 296, Pages 77-79.
99 World Health Organization. Environmental Health Criteria 213 - Carbon Monoxide (Second Edition) , WHO, Geneva, 1999; ISBN 92 4 157213 2 (NLM classification: QV 662). ISSN 0250-863X.
100 Feng S, A new method for estimating the retention of selected smoke constituents in the respiratory tract of smokers during cigarette smoking, Inhalation Toxicology, February 2007, Volume 19(2), Pages 169-179.

Forgotten Sensitivities

Where is the real neuro-chemical you? Is it normal to administer a stimulant that makes the heart pound 17 beats per minute faster when trying to relax?

Is it normal to use an external chemical to induce a dopamine "aaah" wanting relief sensation upon hearing that a friend has been hurt or a loved one has died?

Our dependency robs us of our emotional self-identity and sensitivities. The millions of extra acetylcholine receptors it grew inside our brain not only created a barrier to feeling nicotine's full effects but an insensitivity to life itself.

It isn't that the basic person and personality underlying nicotine dependency is significantly different. It's that their addiction has disrupted their sensitivities, and has the wrong chemicals flowing at the wrong times.

Aside from dopamine, nicotine has command and control of serotonin, our stress busting neurotransmitter, with ties to mood, impulse control, anger and depression.[101]

Included among the estimated 200 neuro-chemicals that nicotine controls, mediates or regulates are acetylcholine, arginine vasopressin,[102] GABA,[103] glucose,[104] glutamate,[105] neuropeptide S,[106] anti-apoptotic XIAP,[107] epinephrine and nor-epinephrine.

What is it like to navigate nicotine dependency recovery, arrive home and for the first time in a long time allow life, not nicotine, to decide which neuro-chemicals your awareness will sense?

Forgotten Senses

Some nicotine users claim to smoke, chew, dip or vape for the flavor or aroma. If you haven't heard others say it, you've certainly seen tobacco industry marketing suggest it. Truth is, powerful tobacco toxins rob users of the ability to accurately smell and taste.

I used to barely get through the bank door to make the daily deposit when one cashier, without looking up, would say, "Hi John!"

---

101 Rausch JL et al, Effect of nicotine on human blood platelet serotonin uptake and effluxm, Progress in Neuropsychopharmacology & Biological Psychiatry, 1989, Volume 13(6), Pages 907-916.

102 Yu G, et al, Nicotine self-administration differentially regulates hypothalamic corticotropin-releasing factor and arginine vasopressin mRNAs and facilitates stress-induced neuronal activation, Journal of Neuroscience, March 12, 2008, Volume 28(11), Pages 2773-2782.

103 Zhu PJ, et al, Nicotinic receptors mediate increased GABA release in brain through a tetrodotoxin-insensitive mechanism during prolonged exposure to nicotine, Neuroscience, 2002, Volume 115(1), Pages 137-144.

104 Morgan TM, et al, Acute effects of nicotine on serum glucose insulin growth hormone and cortisol in healthy smokers, Metabolism, May 2004, Volume 53(5), Pages 578-582.

105 Liechti ME, Role of the glutamatergic system in nicotine dependence, CNS Drugs, 2008, Volume 22(9), Pages 705-724.

106 Lage R, et al, Nicotine treatment regulates neuropeptide S system expression in the rat brain, Neurotoxicology, November 2007, Volume 28(6), Pages 1129-1135.

107 Zhang J, et al, Nicotine Induces Resistance to Chemotherapy by Modulating Mitochondrial Signaling in Lung Cancer, American Journal of Respiratory Cell and Molecular Biology, August 1,2008.

One day I made the mistake of asking how she knew it was me. "When the door closes behind you," she said, "a rush of air that smells like smoke announces your arrival." It hurt. I didn't know whether to change banks or brands.

Sensory nerve endings in the mouth and nasal passages begin healing within three days of ending tobacco use. Will everything smell and taste better? No. As Joel puts it, you smell and taste everything more accurately, but that does not necessarily mean better.

As Joel notes, that first spring will bring the aroma of flowers that will likely be far more intense than you perceived while smoking. But

Photo by National Cancer Institute

wait until you drive by a garbage dump or sewage treatment plant.

The same is true of taste. With an accurate sense of taste, there may be flavors you thought you liked that no longer appeal to you, or foods you were convinced were horrible that suddenly become wonderful.

What is it like to smell coffee brewing more than a hundred feet away? Imagine being able to identify every smoker you meet by the thousands of chemicals that coat their hair, skin and clothing.

Flour isn't just white and rain just wet. They both offer subtle yet distinct aroma experiences.

Think about having missed out on the natural smell of those you love, the scent of a new baby, the aromas that tease as we walk past a bakery, or feeling compelled to stop and smell every flower, as if planted just for you.

What is it like to live with healed senses? "Come to where the flavor is." Come home to you!

Forgotten Mealtime

I almost never ate breakfast and usually skipped lunch. However, that's not entirely accurate. You see, nicotine was my spoon.

With each puff, nicotine activated my body's flight or flight response, which would almost instantly dump stored fats and sugars (glucose) from my liver into my bloodstream.

I'd normally eat just one large meal at the end of each day. A portion of that meal was stored and the next day I'd use nicotine to release it.

The consequences of torturing our body this way were many, including a 44% increase in the risk of developing type II diabetes (29% for light smokers and 61% for heavy smokers of more than 20 cigarettes per day).[108]

I had long ago forgotten how to properly fuel my body. Smoking 60 cigarettes per day, about one every 15 minutes, I had few hunger cravings and little experience satisfying them.

I repeatedly tried to navigate early recovery without awareness that nicotine had become my spoon. Not only did I endure nicotine cravings, I added hunger cravings. I endured a number of hypoglycemic-type symptoms including mind fog and an inability to concentrate.

An utter mess, I tried to eat my way out of food craves. It made recovery vastly more challenging than it needed to be. The result was always the same: needless cravings, anxieties, extra pounds, relapse and failure.

But back to our theme, what was it like to feed yourself, to fuel your body on a regular basis, to sit with friends and eat like a normal person?

What would it be like to no longer make excuses to leave meals early in order to replenish missing nicotine, to stay and comfortably savor the after dinner conversation for as long as possible?

Extra Workweeks

A 12 cigarette per day smoker who spends an average of 5 minutes per cigarette devotes one hour per day to smoking. That's 365 smoking hours per year. Broken down into 40-hour workweeks, that's 9 full workweeks per year spent servicing their addiction.

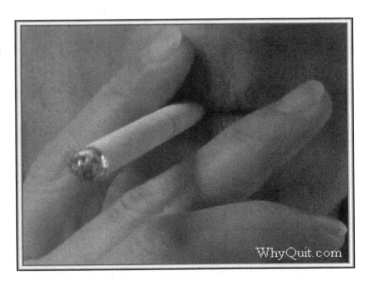

Even while spitting, oral tobacco users easily blend in and hide where bellowing smoke cannot. Usually they require fewer nicotine fixes, each delivering substantially more nicotine than inhaled from a cigarette. But honest calculation of the total time each day spent servicing the oral user's addiction is likely to show as much or more than for smokers.

Time spent locating a spit container, your tin, can, pouch, bag or box, tapping the lid, packing the can or opening the package, sniffing or otherwise packing or loading up, working the dip, wad, pouch, orb, strip, gum or lozenge, sucking or chewing while waiting for nicotine to slowly penetrate mouth tissues and enter the bloodstream as anxieties gradually build, spitting or swallowing juices, parking periods, and disposing of spit, used tobacco or gum, it all adds up.

Imagine giving yourself a two-month vacation from work each year. What would it be like to

---

108 Willi C et al, Active smoking and the risk of type 2 diabetes: a systematic review and meta-analysis, Journal of the American Medical Association, December 2007, Volume 12;298(22), Pages 2654-2664.

reclaim such a massive chunk of life? What would it be like for your days to be entirely yours?

What if your mouth, hands and time were again yours without precondition? Where would you go, what would you do, and what would you become if not chained to mandatory feedings?

Forgotten Priorities, Forsaken Life

It is entirely normal for drug addicts to truly and deeply believe that drug use enhances life, that it punctuates rather than interrupts it. Rarely did we stop and reflect upon the realities of captivity and full price of bondage.

Nicotine's two-hour elimination half-life in human blood serum is a feeding clock without feeling or conscience. It cannot respect life, time or priorities. When nicotine reserves and tonic dopamine begin falling, it will not matter if the moment being interrupted is the most wonderful of our entire day, year or life.

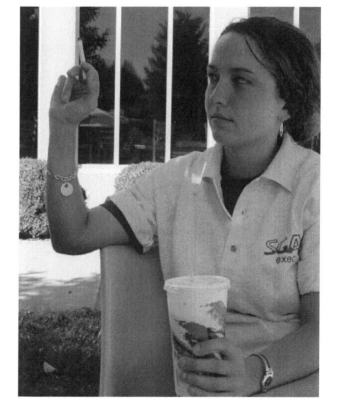

The mind's survival instincts motivator is captive to nicotine. The lesson this circuitry's design now compels it to vividly and firmly implant within our brain is that nicotine use is core to survival, as important as food. In fact, nicotine use becomes more frequent and trumps eating instincts. Part of our body's fight or flight response is to shut down digestion, so as to divert more blood to large muscles.

Any activity lasting longer than the time we could comfortably go between nicotine feedings became a sacrificial lamb. Where might we have gone, what might we have done and whom might we have met? What learning was missed?

Chemical dependency onset did more than simply modify our core survival instincts. It became elevated above family, friends, food, work, accomplishment, romance, love and concentration.

You'd think we would have immediately questioned such a massive shift in priorities. How could we not notice the amount of time devoted to nicotine and its impact upon our senses, sensitivities, relaxation, crisis management, meals and moods?

We didn't notice because nicotine had our focus diverted elsewhere. All we could think about was that next fix, satisfying that next urge, and feeling nicotine-normal again.

Once brave enough to venture beyond nicotine's influence, hidden truths become obvious. "Real choice" gets introduced into the equation. We become the jailer, and our dependency the inmate.

Once home, the full flavor of life can be savored and celebrated. What's there to lose by coming home for a visit? And there's just one rule to arriving ... none today.

Chapter 4

Use Rationalizations

W hat if you truly believed that there was absolutely nothing good about spending the balance of life as nicotine's slave? Nothing!

Imagine being totally unafraid to let go entirely of your chemical relationship to nicotine. Willing to let go, imagine recovery involving far fewer fear driven anxieties than during any prior attempt. Instead of fighting recovery, imagine welcoming and embracing it.

This chapter will aid in recognizing, analyzing and destroying common use justifications, if that is your desire. And I hope it is. Imagine how much easier letting go would be if totally convinced that absolutely nothing of value was being left behind.

Inventing Use Rationalizations

How many times did we tell ourselves that we needed to use nicotine because we were happy or sad, to stimulate or relax us, to accompany a thrill or because we were bored, to help us concentrate or to take our mind off things, or because we were around other smokers or alone and lonely?

To "rationalize" is to attempt to explain or justify our actions or beliefs, often with little or no regard for truth. We invented a reason as to why this was the perfect time to use for nearly every situation imaginable.

Rationalizations are defense mechanisms for making threatening conduct non-threatening. They are a means by which we attempt to justify or make tolerable feelings, behaviors and motives that would otherwise be intolerable.[109]

Rationalizations are often personal and compelling. While a young smoker, I looked upon my chain-smoking mother with her emphysema-riddled lungs and non-stop cough and rationalized to myself, "I'm still young, far younger than she is." "I haven't hurt myself yet, so it's still safe for me

---

109 Online Medical Dictionary, <u>Rationalization</u>, Department of Medical Oncology, University of Newcastle upon Tyne, July 2, 2008.

to smoke, at least for now."

Little did I then appreciate that I was already just as addicted as mom. I also couldn't foresee how emphysema would so weaken her that it would diminish her cancer treatment options, and that she'd die just two years after her own mother's death.

It's normal to think that plenty of time remains to get serious about breaking free. It's logical to think that we'll get serious at the first sign of a serious tobacco related health concern. Unfortunately, when truth slaps such rationalizations hard, we simply invent new ones.

What percentage of the roughly half of U.S. adult smokers who'll lose an average of 13 to 14 years of life will ride the "there's still time" rationalization until it collides with "it's too late now" hopelessness? How many will journey from "I'll stop soon" to "you have to die of something"?

Will seriousness arrive once the doctor diagnoses you with your first smoking related disease, once told that you have chronic bronchitis, circulatory disease, adult onset diabetes or emphysema? If an oral user, will that first precancerous leukoplakia or that first root canal be enough?

The problem is, while fear can and often does motivate action, it has little sustaining power. We can only remain afraid for so long before growing numb to it.

A 2002 study found that only 22% of lung cancer patients who attempted to stop smoking by enrolling in the Mayo Clinic Nicotine Dependence Center were smoke-free six months after the program.[110]

Imagine the birth of hundreds of additional use rationalizations between "I'm still young" and "It's too late." Imagine each being invented by a mind that knows amazingly little about nicotine dependency or recovery from it.

Imagine being the user who always justified today's nicotine purchase (always only a single day's supply) by promising yourself that tomorrow you'd stop. Alternatively, imagine being the user who always purchased a multiple days' supply, inviting the rationalization that now isn't the right time to stop because your remaining supply would go to waste.

Tobacco industry marketing is designed to support the addict's need for alternative use explanations.

Pleasure, taste, a 2 for 1 sale, improved menthol, a coupon, your store's new "come to where the flavor

110 Sanderson CL, et al, Tobacco use outcomes among patients with lung cancer treated for nicotine dependence, Journal of Clinical Psychology, August 2002, Vol. 20, Issue 16, Pages 3461-3469.

is" sign, a fantastic price on cartons, U.S. tobacco companies spend at least $14 billion annually to keep us convinced that we use their products for every reason imaginable, except the truth.

We use them because we must. We do so because tonic dopamine declines and anxieties rise when we don't. Stated another way, the tobacco industry spends billions each year to keep you brainwashed and believing that there's value in using, to make you fear letting go.

Even the names of most brands, a name repeated each time we purchased more, burned into our brain a sense that we'd lose something if we stopped. Think about the emotional sense of loss in breaking strong self-identity ties to such brand names as:

Alpine, Apple Jack, Basic, Beech Nut, Belair, Belmont, Best Value, Big Mountain, Black Owl, Blu, Bond, Bucks, Buglar, Cambridge, Camel, Cannon Ball, Capital, Captain Black, Champion, Chesterfield, Class A, Copenhagen, Cleopatra, Cloud 9, Cougar, Dark Horse, Derby, Eagle, Eclipse, Envy, Focus, Gold Coast, Gold River, Golden Gate, Grand Prix, Green Smoke, Grizzly, Half & Half, Husky, Jade, Kayak, Kent, King Edward, Kiss, Kodiak, Kool, Knights, L & M, Lady, Lark, Liberty, Lucky Strike, Main Street, Marlboro, Marshal, Maverick, Merit, Mild

Seven, Misty, Monarch, Montecristo, More, Mustang, Natural American Spirit, Newport, Njoy, Now, Palace, Paladin, Parliament, Passion, Passport, Peachy, Players, Pride, Prince, Prince Albert's, Pure Natural, Pyramid, Quality, Rave, Red Man, Red River, Rich, Riviera, Romeo y Julieta, Rooster, Rosebud, Rosetta, Samson, Satin, Savannah, Signature, Silver Creek, Sir Walter Raleigh, Sky Dancer, Sonic, South Beach Smoke, Southern Harvest, Sport, Springwater, Style, Sundance, Swisher Sweets, Tempo, Top, Tourney, Triumph, True, USA Gold, Vantage, Velvet, Viceroy, Virginia Slims, Vogue, Wave, White Cloud, Wild Geese, Wildfire, Wildhorse, Wind, Windsail, Winston, Workhorse, Yours and Zig Zag.

Clearly, the industry fully understands chemical dependency upon nicotine and intentionally plays upon the wanting within in keeping users hooked.

Our lack of dependency understanding made us rather inventive when trying to explain our continuing need to feed. Let's look at a few common use rationalizations that were bred and fueled by our lack of understanding.

As we review common use rationalizations, notice that there are three basic types: (1) alternative use explanations that aid in denying dependency; (2) rationalizations that minimize the costs and harms of use; and (3) recovery avoidance or relapse justifications.

"Just One" or "Just Once"

Let's start with the most costly and destructive tease of all, that we can cheat the Law of Addiction (Chapter 2).

Why torment your yourself with a lie? Why pretend that brain imaging studies were all wrong, that one hit of nicotine won't cause up to half of your brain dopamine pathway receptors to become occupied by nicotine, that your brain won't soon be wanting or even begging for more?

"Just one" or "just once" denies who we are, real drug addicts.

Whether free for 10 hours, 10 days, 10 months or 10 years, just one hit of nicotine and permanently compromised brain dopamine pathways will again re-assign using nicotine again, the same priority as eating food.

And that re-established use priority shall remain until you once again successfully navigate recovery, if ever.

Let go of thoughts of "just one" or "just once." Laugh at them. You're far too intelligent to see the dopamine pathway wanting, urges and craves that you felt for nicotine as being any different than the dopamine pathway wanting, urges and craves felt by the alcoholic, heroin or meth addict for their drug.

While focus and fixation upon the thought of "just one" or "just once" is the most common cessation torture inflicted upon the unschooled mind, that's not us anymore. We now understand exactly what happens if we use again. We know that for us, one will always equal all, that lapse will always equal relapse, and one puff, vape, dip, pinch or chew will always be too many, while thousands are never enough.

And be honest about it. As Joel says, don't say that we don't want one when we do. Rather, acknowledge the desire, but then ask yourself, do I want all the others that go with it? When the thought of "just one" or "just once" enters your mind, try to picture all of them, the thousands upon thousands that would follow.

"Use relieves stress and anxiety"

The falsehood that nicotine use relieves stress is almost as destructive as the tease of "just one" or "just once." For example, a June 2013 study found that roughly 1 million U.S. ex-smokers relapsed to smoking following the World Trade Center terrorist attacks on September 11, 2001.[111]

Library of Congress

Nearly all of those 1 million ex-smokers deeply believed that smoking relieves stress. It is normal and natural to believe that smoking is a stress-buster, that it calms us during crisis. How could we not believe it? We felt it happen hundreds or maybe even thousands of times. Or, did we?

Stress relief is the most deeply believed yet easily debunked use rationalizations of all. And this false belief certainly isn't news to the nicotine addiction industry.

According to a once secret 1983 Brown & Williamson research memo, "People smoke to maintain nicotine levels" and "stress robs the body of nicotine, implying a smoker smokes more in times of stress due to withdrawal, not to relax."[112]

The physiological effects of stress cause urine to turn more acidic. Urine acidification accelerates elimination of nicotine from the bloodstream, forcing early replenishment.[113] Additionally, nicotine itself is an alkaloid and extremely sensitive to acids.

GlaxoSmithKline's Nicorette website warns nicotine gum chewers that, "Eating or drinking even mildly acidic foods and beverages directly before using or during use of Nicorette inhibits nicotine absorption into your bloodstream."[114]

Whether inhaled or juiced, nicotine does not relieve anxiety but only its own absence. Hundreds or even thousands of times, the time needed for replenishment combined with arrival of a new supply of nicotine to relieve intense wanting felt by a nicotine addict in the throws of early withdrawal. It left us totally yet falsely convinced that nicotine was an emotional solution to crisis.

A never-smoker and a smoker both experience flat tires while driving in a freezing rain. They stop, get out and look at the flat. The never-smoker sighs and then immediately reaches for a jack to change the tire. And the smoker reaches for a ....? That's right, a cigarette. But why?

---

111 Caba, J, 9/11 <u>Attacks Made 1 Million Former Smokers Pick Up Cigarettes Again</u>, MedicalDaily.com, Jun 21, 2013.

112 Brown & Williamson Tobacco Corporation, <u>Internal Correspondence</u>, March 25, 1983, Bates Number: 670508492; http://legacy.library.ucsf.edu/tid/uly04f00

113 Benowitz NL, Jacob P 3rd, <u>Nicotine renal excretion rate influences nicotine intake during cigarette smoking</u>. Journal of Pharmacology and Experimental Theraputics, July 1985, Volume 234(1), Pages 153-155.

114 GlaxoSmithKline, Nicorette: Frequently Asked Questions, Nicorette.com/faqs.aspx, May 23, 2012.

Stress, anger, worry and fear cause our urine to turn more acidic. Stress generated acids accelerate elimination of the alkaloid nicotine from the bloodstream. The more stressful the situation, the faster nicotine is eliminated. The further from your last nicotine replenishment when stress occurs, the greater the decline in tonic dopamine, and the sooner and more intense stress induced wanting is felt.

The stressed nicotine addict is forced to reach for a central nervous system stimulant in order to battle the sudden onset of early nicotine withdrawal, before turning their attention to the underlying stressful event (the flat tire).

Whether urine acidification is caused by sudden emotional turmoil, alcohol use or acidic foods or juices, the more acidic our urine, the greater the rate of nicotine depletion.[115] Although it sounds totally backwards, the literature suggests that the rate of elimination has to do with how the kidneys function.

In one study, an increase in urine acidity from a pH of 5.6 to a pH of 4.5 (making it 11 times more acidic) caused a 206% increase in the rate nicotine was eliminated from the bloodstream by the kidneys.[116]

Urine acidification during crisis occurs in stressed never-smokers and ex-smokers too. The difference is that there is no nicotine in their bloodstreams, no accelerated nicotine elimination, and no battle against the onset of withdrawal.

Life as a nicotine addict is hard. It's more stressful, not less. We compounded stressful situations by adding withdrawal to them. And once done servicing our addiction the tire was still flat.

Never once in our life did nicotine resolve the underlying crisis. If the tire was flat, it was still flat. If some other event made us frightened or angry, escape into servicing our addiction totally ignored the event.

And if the flat tire or other stressful situation is tackled and resolved without using, the nicotine addict is still not going to feel good or satisfied. Why? Because addressing the initial cause of stress does not ease withdrawal. Only re-administration of nicotine, or navigating withdrawal and the up to 72 hours needed to eliminate nicotine from the body and move beyond peak withdrawal, can bring relief.

Unlike total nicotine elimination, replenishment's relief is temporary. While it calms for the

---

115 Schachter, S et al, Studies of the interaction of psychological and pharmacological determinants of smoking: II. <u>Effects of urinary pH on cigarette smoking</u>, Journal of Experimental Psychology: General, March 1977, Volume 106(1), Pages 13-19.

116 Benowitz NL et al, <u>Nicotine renal excretion rate influences nicotine intake during cigarette smoking</u>, Journal of Pharmacology and Experimental Therapy, July 1985, Volume 234(1), Pages 153-155.

moment, the user will again soon be forced to confront the chemical clock governing their life (nicotine's two-hour chemical half-life), or witness accelerated depletion brought on by encountering stress, consuming alcohol or by drinking or eating acidic foods.

Joel makes one final yet important point here. Nicotine's false calming effect quickly becomes a rationalization crutch reached for during stressful situations. The crutch and nicotine's impact upon the user's life is "more far-reaching than just making initial stress effects more severe."

According to Joel, "it affects how the person may deal with conflict and sadness in a way that may not be obvious, but is nonetheless serious. In a way, it affects the ability to communicate and maybe even in some ways, to grow from the experience."[117]

Joel shares an example. "Let's say you don't like the way a significant other in your life squeezes toothpaste. If you point out how it's a problem to you in a calm rational manner, maybe the person will change and do it in a way that is not disturbing to you. By communicating your feelings you make a minor annoyance basically disappear."

"But now let's say you're a smoker who sees the tube of toothpaste, gets a little upset, and is about to say something, again, to address the problem. But wait. Because you are a little annoyed, you lose nicotine, go into withdrawal, and before you are able to deal with the problem, you have to go smoke."

"You smoke, alleviate the withdrawal and, in fact, you feel better. At the same time, you put a little time between you and the toothpaste situation and on further evaluation, you decide it's not that big of a deal, and you forget it."

"Sounds like and feels like you resolved the stress. But in fact, you didn't. You suppressed the feeling. It is still there, not resolved, not communicated. Next time it happens again, you again get mad. You go into withdrawal. You have to smoke. You repeat the cycle, again not communicating and not resolving the conflict," explains Joel. "Over and over again, maybe for years this pattern is repeated."

"One day you stop smoking. You may in fact be off for weeks, maybe months. All of a sudden, one day the exact problem presents itself again, that annoying toothpaste. You don't have that automatic withdrawal kicking in and pulling you away from the situation. You see it, nothing else affecting you and you blow up. If the person is within earshot, you may explode."

"When you look back, in retrospect, you feel you have blown up inappropriately, that your reaction was greatly exaggerated for the situation. You faced it hundreds of times before and nothing like this ever happened. You begin to question what happened to you, to turn you into such a horrible or explosive person."

"Understand what happened," writes Joel. "You are not blowing up at what just happened, you are blowing up for what has been bothering you for years. And now, because of the build up of

---

117 Spitzer, J, New Reactions to Anger as an Ex-smoker, an article in Joel's free PDF book Never Take Another Puff, http://whyquit.com/joel

frustration, you are blowing up much more severely than you ever would have if you had addressed it early on. It is like pulling a cork out of a shaken carbonated bottle: the more shaken, the worse the explosion."

Sooner or later, even if we fail to break free from nicotine, that unresolved stress will most probably result in either a blowup or onset of one or more anxiety related diseases.

Don't for a second think that hiding from life by escaping into a stimulated wanting relief sensation is an answer or solution. It's our problem.

As we climb back into our mind's driver's seat we need to listen to our feelings and emotions. We may discover that we need to learn to address the root causes of once suppressed anxiety or anger in positive and healthy ways.

The only lasting solution to anxieties brought on by rapidly falling nicotine reserves - anxieties that interfere with healthy conflict resolution - is to bring active dependency to an end. And as you do, dump the destructive falsehood that a stimulant relieves stress.

"Nicotine is my friend"

Imagine the illness inside a mind that looks upon nicotine as a "friend." It was always there, never let us down, calmed us during crisis (or so we thought), never argued, a loyal and trusted companion more dependable than a dog. Pretending that our addiction is human comes easily, at least until honesty arrives.

Like table salt, nicotine cannot talk. Not a word. Unlike a dog, it never, ever demonstrates affection or is happy to see us. Nicotine's most dependable attribute is its ability to keep us dependent upon it, to ever so briefly silence wanting.

"My Cigarette, My Friend" is likely the most famous "friend" rationalization buster ever.[118] Written by Joel, in it he asks, "How do you feel about a friend who has to go everywhere with you? Not only does he tag along all the time, but since he is so offensive and vulgar, you become unwelcome when with him. He has a peculiar odor that sticks to you wherever you go. Others think both of you stink."

As Joel notes, nicotine addiction is about surrendering control. It's about putting life on pause come replenishment time. It compels smokers to find an acceptable place to feed, even during bad

118 Spitzer, J., "My Cigarette, My Friend," WhyQuit.com, Joel's Library, 1990.

weather. It's about being forced to go buy more, spending thousands upon thousands during our years as users.

As a nicotine smoker it deprives us of engaging in prolonged vigorous activities. "Your friend won't let you," writes Joel. "He doesn't believe in physical activity. In his opinion, you are too old to have that kind of fun. So he kind of sits on your chest and makes it difficult for you to breathe. Now you don't want to go off and play with other people when you can't breathe, do you?"

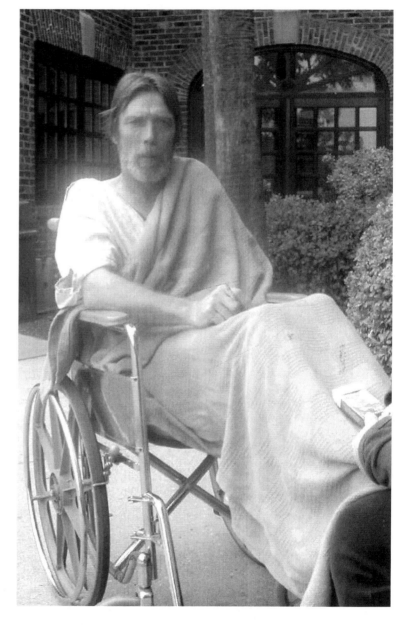

Our "friend," notes Joel, "does not believe in being healthy. He is really repulsed by the thought of you living a long and productive life. So every chance he gets he makes you sick. He helps you catch colds and flu." "He carries thousands of poisons with him, which he constantly blows in your face. When you inhale some of them, they wipe out cilia in your lungs which would have helped you prevent these diseases."

"But colds and flu are just his form of child's play. He especially likes diseases that slowly cripple you - like emphysema. He considers this disease great. Once he gets you to have this, you will give up all your other friends, family, career goals, activities - everything. You will just sit home and caress him, telling him what a great friend he is while you desperately gasp for air."

"But eventually your friend tires of you," Joel reminds us. "He decides he no longer wishes to have your company. Instead of letting you go your separate ways, he decides to kill you. He has a wonderful arsenal of weapons behind him. In fact, he has been plotting your death since the day you met him. He picked all the top killers in society and did everything in his power to ensure you would get one of them. He overworked your heart and lungs. He clogged up the arteries to your heart, brain, and every other part of your body. In case you were too strong to succumb to this, he constantly exposed you to cancer causing agents. He knew he would get you sooner or later."

Our cigarette, e-cig, cigar, pipe, chew, dip, snus, gum or lozenge was simply the means by which nicotine entered our bloodstream. It is no more a friend than is a stainless steel spoon.   "Friend," asks Joel? Cigarettes are "expensive, addictive, socially unacceptable and deadly."

Expense, time demands, and increasing social unacceptability are common to all forms of nicotine delivery. While each poses different levels and types of risks, the form of delivery does not alter the super-toxin nicotine's risks, including its ability to keep us its slave.

It's increasingly common to see those hooked on nicotine replacement products or e-cigarettes treat their form of delivery as though their savior or hero. Clearly, the risks posed by nicotine alone are vastly less than smoking's. However, nicotine's continued use, in any form, is NOT safe.

If you have Internet access, go to www.PubMed.gov. PubMed is the U.S. government's medical study search engine. Search the word "nicotine." My search on August 29, 2008, produced 10,205 journal articles having nicotine in the title.

In the footnote below I cite titles to a few of the nicotine medical journal articles published during August 2008, when this chapter was written.[119] As you can see, it isn't necessary for anyone to resort to scare tactics or exaggeration regarding nicotine's effects upon the body. The truth is frightening enough.

While personifying any chemical artificially inflates emotional bonds and attachments to it, it's still just a chemical. While nicotine cannot think or feel, just one puff will activate up to half of our brain's dopamine pathway receptors.

One sure fire way to end the need to invent chemical friends is to make sure all nicotine stays on the outside.

"I like it" "I love it"

Think hard. What, if anything, do you love about smoking, vaping or about using oral tobacco or NRT?

If a smoker, what's so wonderful that we were willing to destroy this body, creating a 50/50 chance of departing earth 5,000 days early? If an oral tobacco user, how much love does it take to permanently expose your mouth to unadulterated tobacco's 2,550 chemicals?
As dependent users we lived a constant struggle to maintain a narrow range of nicotine in our

---

119 Vaglenova J, Long-lasting teratogenic effects of nicotine on cognition: Gender specificity and role of AMPA receptor function, The Neurobiology of Learning and Memory, August 12, 2008 [Epub ahead of print]; also see, Somm E, et al, Prenatal Nicotine Exposure Alters Early Pancreatic Islet and Adipose Tissue Development with Consequences on the Control of Body Weight and Glucose Metabolism Later in Life, Endocrinology, August 7, 2008 [Epub ahead of print]; also see Huang YY, et al, Chronic nicotine exposure induces a long-lasting and pathway-specific facilitation of LTP in the amygdala, Learning & Memory, August 6, 2008, Volume 6;15(8), Pages 603-610; also see, Zhang J, et al, Nicotine Induces Resistance to Chemotherapy by Modulating Mitochondrial Signaling in Lung Cancer, American Journal of Respiratory Cell & Molecular Biology, August 1, 2008 [Epub ahead of print]; also see, Baykan A, et al, The protective effect of melatonin on nicotine-induced myocardial injury in newborn rats whose mothers received nicotine, Anadolu Kardiyol Dergisi, August 2008, Volume 8(4), Pages 243-248; also see, Marchei E, et al, Ultrasensitive detection of nicotine and cotinine in teeth by high-performance liquid chromatography/tandem mass spectrometry, Rapid Communications in Mass Spectrometry, August 2008, Volume 22(16), Pages 2609-2612.

bloodstream, so as to remain in our nicotine-normal zone of comfort. Each time our blood serum nicotine level fell below our minimum limit, our tonic dopamine level declined and we starting sensing the onset of urges and wanting.

We grew tense, anxious, irritable and depressed, and the only path to immediate relief was more nicotine. Once replenished, we were left totally convinced that we "enjoyed smoking," "liked chewing," "relished vaping," or "loved our snus."

On the other end, we also had to be cautious not to use too much nicotine and exceed our upper limit of tolerance, or risk suffering varying degrees of nicotine poisoning. Early symptoms can include feeling sick, nauseous and dizzy.

As Joel notes, being a successful user is like being an accomplished tightrope walker, constantly maintaining a balance between these two painful extremes of too much or too little.[120]

According to Philip Michels, PhD, a USC School of Medicine professor and cessation facilitator, it is normal for us to look to our own behavior in order to obtain clues about our attitudes and beliefs. We tend to draw conclusions about what we must like, by watching what we see ourselves doing. Such self-analysis goes like this:

Logical Yet False Reasoning

- **I don't do things I don't like to do.**
- **I smoke lots and lots of cigarettes.**
- **Thus, I must really love smoking.**

Ignorance is bliss. Now let's look at how informed analysis might flow:

Logical & True Reasoning

- **I don't do things I don't like to do.**
- **I smoke lots and lots of cigarettes.**
- **Each puff destroys more of my body.**
- **I'm actually slowly killing myself.**
- **I've learned nicotine is highly addictive.**
- **I've tried breaking free but failed.**
- **Thus, I'm probably a "real" drug addict.**

The most compelling argument supporting like or love revolves around the undeniable dopamine

---

120 Spitzer, J, "I smoke because I like smoking," an article in Joel's free PDF book Never Take Another Puff,
http://whyquit.com/joel

"aaah" wanting relief sensation that arrives following replenishment. However, even here the rationalization relies heavily upon selective memory.

When valuing replenishment, is it fair to ignore the urges and anxieties that preceded our "aaah" relief sensation? If we had waited longer prior to using, wouldn't every wanting relief sensation have had a corresponding anxiety and depression riddled low preceding it? Tanking up early and often allowed us to avoid the downside.

Still, most nicotine addicts know that "WHERE ARE MY CIGARETTES?" feeling, and the emotions that accompany the "I need a nicotine fix ... AND NOW" feeling!!!

At Joel's clinics he identifies the two pack-a-day smokers who insist that they smoke because of the "good cigarettes" or because they "like" smoking.

"First I ask them to tell me which cigarettes stand out in their mind as being really great cigarettes on any given day. Usually they will offer up the first one or two they have when they wake up, the ones after meals and maybe one or two others that they have on certain breaks."

Joel watches as they try to think of other good ones but none seem to come to mind.[121]

"I simply point out that we have a mathematical problem occurring here. They have come up with five to seven good cigarettes yet they are smoking forty or more cigarettes a day. Where are those other cigarettes?"

As Joel points out, a few were smoked and tasted nasty while others were marginal but as soon as they were snuffed out they can't even be recalled. "So here we have a few good cigarettes, a few lousy cigarettes and a whole bunch of what now seem to be insignificant cigarettes."

As Joel notes, while there may be some good ones, they have to be accompanied by all of the mediocre and miserable ones, and when it comes down to it, "all of them, even the good ones, are killing them."

Regarding the few identified as "good cigarettes," Joel poses a follow-up question. "How much do you like smoking? Do you like smoking more than you like something like, oh, I don't know. ... something like maybe ... breathing?"

If we say we "like smoking" are we also saying we like the morning phlegm in our lungs and the need for water for a "horribly dry throat"? What about the nasty taste it leaves in our mouth and how it makes foods taste bland? If a pack-a-day smoker, do we like devoting an hour and a half each day to feeding our addiction?

What about often feeling hurried, the dirty brown film on the inside of the car windshield, rush hour anxieties depleting nicotine reserves quicker, being unable to smoke while at work, attempting to run and being left with a throbbing heart that wants to explode, or standing in line to buy more

---

121 Spitzer, J, "I smoke because I like smoking" February 21, 2001, http://www.ffn.yuku.com/topic/17137

nicotine, are we saying we like those things too?[122]

How can we claim to like or love something when we have no legitimate basis for comparison?

If no longer able to remember and explain what it felt like to reside inside our mind before nicotine took control, if we cannot recall the calm and quiet mind we once called home, then what basis exists for asserting that we love using nicotine more than we miss the pre-nicotine us?

How can we talk about love if we cannot remember who we were before climbing aboard an endless roller-coaster ride of nicotine-dopamine-adrenaline highs and lows?

As real drug addicts in every sense, with blind obedience to the wanting within, "what's love got to do with it"?

"I'm just a little bit addicted"

Nicotine dependency diagnostic standards are reflected by official looking acronyms such as DSM-IV, FTND, MNWS, M-NRQ and HONC. These standards claim to measure the onset, existence or depth of nicotine dependency. But being a little bit addicted is like being a little bit pregnant.

It's normal to want to rationalize that we don't have a problem, or if we do that it's just some "nasty little habit,"or if not and we really are addicted that we're just a little bit addicted. It's

normal to compare our situation with that of other drug or nicotine addicts and rationalize that it isn't nearly as bad.[123]

The easiest such minimization is to compare how frequently we use nicotine, our level of tolerance. But let's not kid ourselves. Whether our brain demands a single nicotine fix daily or twenty, having lost the autonomy to simply turn and walk away, why pretend superiority once a full-fledged addict?

Pretending superiority is a dependency minimization rationalization that helps keep millions trapped behind bars.

"I do it for flavor and taste"

Flavor? Taste? How many tastebuds are inside human lungs, the place we suck and briefly hold all smoke? Answer: zero, none!

Imagine blaming continuing use on what we describe as tobacco's wonderful smells and tastes. This rationalization ignores the hundreds of smell and flavor additives used by the tobacco industry to engineer a vast spectrum of sensory sensations.

122 Spitzer, J, "Boy, do I miss smoking!" March 9, 2001. http://www.ffn.yuku.com/topic/20665
123 Craig, Kathleen, Not Much of a Smoker, Originally posted at MSN's Freedom from Tobacco's on February 29, 2004, and today shared on Yuku's Freedom from Nicotine forum on the site's Rationalizations message board.

It also ignores the fact that hundreds of other plants, products and people smell good too but never once did we find it necessary to light any of them on fire and suck their smoke deep into our lungs in order to complete the experience. But if soaked in nicotine, stand back. We'll likely try chewing or lighting them ablaze too.

A 1972 memo from Brown & Williamson consultants entitled "Youth Cigarette - New Concepts" recommends the company create a "sweet flavor cigarette."s "It's a well-known fact that teenagers like sweet products. Honey might be considered." It also recommends apple-flavored cigarettes. "Apples connote goodness and freshness and we see many possibilities for our youth-oriented cigarette with this flavor."[124]

Since 1972, almost 700 industry tobacco flavor additives have been identified including:

> Alfalfa extract, allspice extract, anise, angelica root extract, apple fructose, apricot extract, balsam oil, banana fructose, bark oil, basil oil, bay leaf, beet juice, black current buds, blackberry fructose, beeswax, bergamot oil, brandy, caffeine, cajeput oil, camphor oil, cananga oil, carob bean extract, caramel, caraway oil, carrot seed oil, cassia cocoa, cedarwood oil, celery seed extract, chocolate, chicory extract, cinnamon leaf oil and extract, citric acid, clary sage oil, clove oil, coffee extract, cognac oil, coriander oil, corn oil, corn syrup, corn silk, costus root oil, cubeb oil, cypress oil, dandelion root extract, date fructose, davana oil, dill seed oil, fennel sweet oil, fenugreek, fig juice, ginger oil, geranium rose oil, gentian root extract, grape fructose, honey, hops oil, jasmine, lactic acid, juniper berry oil, leucine, lavandin oil, kola nut extract, lemon oil, lavender oil, licorice, lemongrass oil, lime oil, linaloe wood oil, lovage oil, longosa oil, locust bean gum, linden flowers, menthol, mandarin oil, maple syrup, milk solids, wild mint oil, garden mint oil, mullein flowers, nutmeg, oak moss, oak bark extract, olibanum oil, olive oil, orange leaf, orange blossoms, orange peel oil, orris root, palmarosa oil, peach extract, pear extract, plum extract, peruvian oil, patchouli oil, parsley seed oil, peach kernel oil, pectin, pepper oil, peppermint oil, plumb juice, pimenta leaf oil, pine needle oil, pineapple extract, pipsissewa leaf extract, prune extract, quebracho bark, raisin extract, raspberry extract, rose water, rose oil, rosemary oil, rum, saccharin, saffron, sage oil, sandalwood oil, sclareolide, sherry, smoke flavor, sodium, spearmint oil, spike lavender oil, snakeroot oil, starch, star anise oil, strawberry extract, styrax gum, sucrose syrup, tamarind extract, solanone, tangerine oil, sugar alcohols, sugars, tarragon oil, thyme oil, rye extract, thymol, toasting flavors, tobacco extracts, tolu balsam gum, tagetes oil, tuberose oil, turpentine oil, urea, vinegar, valine, wild cherry bark, xanthan gum, valerian root, vanilla beans and extract, vanillin, vetiver oil, violet leaf oil, walnut extractables, wheat extract, wine, whiskey, yeast and ylang ylang oil.

Tobacco's smells and flavors are highly engineered. The few brands that do not use additives use flue curing for sweetness, genetic engineering, blending and/or faster nicotine delivery (more free-base nicotine) in order to make tobacco's natural harshness more acceptable to the senses.

If you like one or more additives in your brand such as licorice or chocolate, then purchase licorice or chocolate and savor their flavors. I doubt you'll feel a need to light them on fire.

---

124 Marketing Innovations Inc., <u>Project: Youth Cigarette - New Concepts</u>, September 1972, Brown & Williamson Document, Bates Number: 170042014

Again, there are zero tastebuds inside our lungs. Advertising that suggests that flavor or taste is the reason smokers suck nicotine laden smoke deep into their lungs is an insult to the smoker's intelligence.

Likewise, it's pathetic for oral tobacco product marketing to suggest that taste is the reason users cannot stop putting taste bud damaging and sensitivity destroying tobacco toxins into their mouth.

"My coffee won't taste the same"

There's some truth here but probably not for the reason you're thinking. Toxins in tobacco smoke seriously impair our ability to accurately smell both coffee and cigarettes.

It also increases the risk of taste impairment (an inability to detect very small amounts of one or more of the four basic tastes: sweet, salty, sour and bitter) by 71% in smokers smoking 20 or more cigarettes per day. [125]

As Joel teaches, smells and flavors may not be better after ending tobacco use but will certainly be more accurate. Once our senses heal, many find that coffee's smell and taste actually improves.

Your morning coffee experience can be far richer than when smoking. Imagine smelling the aroma of brewing coffee when the pot is more than 50 feet away.

"It helps me concentrate"

Although nicotine is undeniably a stimulant that activates fight or flight pathways and excites certain brain regions, it's also a super toxin that constricts blood vessels and promotes artery hardening. While a stimulant, so are three minutes of physical activity.

If smoked, large quantities of carbon monoxide and other toxins combine with nicotine to slowly destroy brain gray and white matter. And don't forget that concentration can be eliminated entirely by a nicotine-induced stroke, early dementia or a tobacco-induced death.

And where's the honesty is saying that being constantly interrupted by an endless cycle of wanting and urges,

---

125 Vennemann MM, et al, <u>The association between smoking and smell and taste impairment in the general population</u>, Journal of Neurology, July 28, 2008.

while pausing to refuel, aids concentration? As an excited Turkeyville newbie posted this morning, "I just finished programming for 4 hours straight with full concentration and forgot totally about nicotine. I don't remember the last time I did this."

Not only did wanting and urges break concentration while using, skipping breakfast or lunch during withdrawal impairs concentration by causing blood sugar to plummet. Experiencing this low blood sugar induced sense of mind fog reinforced the false belief that use aids concentration.

Avoid low blood sugar concentration impairment by sipping on natural fruit juice the first three days. Cranberry juice is excellent. Also, try not to skip meals for the first few weeks. It isn't necessary to eat more food but to learn to spread our normal calorie intake out more evenly over the day, so as to keep blood sugars as stable as possible.

Yes, where's the self-honesty in calling constantly interrupted concentration concentration? Protect your ability to concentrate. Fresh air and activity are vastly healthier stimulants.

"I do it to relieve boredom"

It's easy to relate nicotine use to boredom. However, as actively feeding addicts we needed to replenish constantly falling nicotine reserves whether bored to death, having the time of our life, and at all points in-between.

Nicotine use is more noticeable, and thus more memorable when bored. If doing nothing, it's hard not to notice when feeding time arrives. Yet, if busy, thinking or excited, we often didn't notice our refueling.

Although nicotine's half-life is roughly 2 hours, a falling tonic dopamine level

Photo by National Cancer Institute

would get our attention long before serious depletion anxieties arrived. We learned to tank up early and often, whether bored or not.

Have you ever noticed the minor anxieties that occur when bored? It's why we talk of "relieving" boredom.

Boredom is thought to be a means by which the mind motivates action. It causes us to seek accomplishment and the dopamine "aaah" that comes with anticipating completion or completing each task.

What's sad is a mind that views successful nicotine replenishment as itself an important accomplishment.

Maybe that's why we make such a powerful association between not using nicotine and boredom. Instead of earning the phasic burst of dopamine that boredom's anxieties attempt to motivate, we'd steal it, over and over and over again.

Recovery presents a substantial increase in opportunities to experience boredom and to blame it on recovery. If we normally used nicotine 12 times per day, and each replenishment averaged 5 minutes, we now have an extra hour each day to either fill with some new activity or to sense boredom's anxieties.

But don't kid yourself. We didn't smoke, chew, dip or vape due to boredom. Never-users get horribly bored too but the thought of nicotine replenishment never once crosses their mind.

Nicotine depletion anxieties attempt to motivate replenishment. Boredom anxieties attempt to motivate activity. Unfortunately, the nicotine addict's act of replenishment satisfied both.

Boredom can be a productive emotion. Recovery will clearly add additional free time to each day. Hopefully, you'll learn to spend it in healthy, productive and satisfying ways.

"I do it for pleasure"

"I smoke for pleasure." Pleasure? It's the Newport sales cry and it's highly effective.

Pleasure is defined as a state of gratification, a source of delight, satisfaction or joy. Wanting is defined as feeling a need, strong desire, suffering from the lack of something, or requiring it.

Calling the satisfaction of wanting pleasure is akin to saying that it feels good to stop pounding your thumb with a hammer. Still, it's high quality bait, one of the most powerful use rationalizations of all, and the industry loves it.

The tobacco industry knows how easy it is to confuse

wanting with pleasure. Look around. Industry pleasure marketing is everywhere, subliminal and constantly assaulting the subconscious mind.

Intentionally substituting joy for need, if pleasure marketing wasn't highly effective we wouldn't see so much of it.

Have you ever seen an advertisement showing a smoker badly in need of a smoke? And you won't. When photos or pictures are used with pleasure marketing they show smokers laughing, carefree and having the time of their life.

Our pleasure rationalization sinks its teeth into nicotine's dopamine induced "aaah" while totally ignoring the wanting, urge and anxiety that preceded it.

We are true drug addicts. This isn't about pleasure but about the mind's survival instincts teacher teaching another false lesson after having again been activated by nicotine.

Pleasure? Try to imagine anything more intellectually dishonest than suggesting that smokers smoke for pleasure. Try to imagine anything more criminal than to hang signs along public streets that falsely teach children that smoking is about pleasure.

"It's my choice and I choose to use"

"Quitters never win and I'm no quitter." "It's my choice and I choose to continue using!" Truth is, we lost "choice" the day nicotine took control.

But that doesn't stop the tobacco industry from spending billions building mighty neighborhood store marketing facades that each scream the message "smoking is an adult free-choice activity."

Think about the message and collective tease of hundreds of colorful and neatly arranged boxes, packs and tins behind the

Nicotine withdrawal in the mouse

I just can't quit

Withdrawal signs

Increased shaking
Increased grooming
Increased scratching

National Institute on Drug Abuse

checkout counter. Each time we stepped-up to buy a new supply, our senses were flooded with the subconscious message that using is all about choice, lots and lots of choices.

Apparently, few tobacco executives are buying the "choice" lie. A former Winston Man, David Goerlitz, asked R.J. Reynolds executives, "Don't any of you smoke?" One executive answered, "Are you kidding? We reserve that right for the poor, the young, the black and the stupid."[126]

Once hooked, our only real alternative is the up to 72 hours needed to purge nicotine from our system and move beyond peak withdrawal. Choice? The only choice made while still using is to

126 New York Times, In America, Tobacco Dollars, by Bob Hebert, November 28, 1993.

avoid withdrawal.

It isn't that we like using nicotine but that we don't like what happens when we don't.

Then there are those who claim to smoke knowing full well that it's killing them. They suggest that they don't care what happens, that they don't want to get old, that we have to die of something, so why not smoking?

This self-destruction "choice" rationalization can be used to hide fears born of a history of failed attempts. It's often rooted in a false belief that we are somehow different from those who succeed, that we will never be able to stop.

But try to find any user who isn't shocked upon arrival of lung cancer, emphysema, a heart attack or stroke. As Joel writes, "no one ever called me enthusiastically proclaiming, 'It worked, it's killing me!' On the contrary, they were normally upset, scared and depressed."[127]

Choice? The only way to restore free choice is to come out from under our dependency's control. But even then, just one puff, dip or chew and our freedom and autonomy will again be lost, as our brain is soon wanting and begging for more.

"It's just a nasty little habit"

"Nasty little habit?" We are true drug addicts in every sense. That's right, look in the mirror and you'll see an honest to goodness drug addict looking back.

One of the most harmful rationalizations of all is pretending that all we have is nasty "habit." It confuses children and encourages experimentation.

Children and teens believe that it takes time and repetition to develop a habit. But research shows that "experimenting" with smoking nicotine just once may be sufficient to begin fostering the loss of autonomy to stop using it. it.[128]

Adoption of the "habit" rationalization is also disabling to those already enslaved. Imagine pretending that someday, we'll awaken and at last discover how to mold, modify, manipulate and control our nicotine use, so as to allow us to use, or not use, as often as we please.

Imagine pretending that someday, we'll discover how to "have our cake and eat it too."

The phrase "nasty little habit" is simply more junkie thinking. Such soft fuzzy words minimize the hard cold reality of being chemically married to and dependent upon nicotine.

It's much easier to tell ourselves that all we have is some "nasty little habit." The warmth of the phrase is akin to the cute and cuddly word "slip," the addict's tool for sugarcoating relapse.

---

127 Spitzer, J, "I Smoke Because I'm Self-Destructive," an article in Joel's free PDF book Never Take Another Puff, http://whyquit.com/joel

128 DiFranza JR, Hooked from the first cigarette, Scientific American, May 2008, Volume 298(5), Pages 82-87.

Failing to use turn signals while driving is a "habit" and so is using too many cuss words, cracking our knuckles or losing our temper too often. But we will not experience physical withdrawal if we start using turn signals, stop cussing or cracking our knuckles, or learn to keep our temper in check.

Chemical dependence does foster habits. It does so by forcing us to select patterns for the regular delivery of nicotine. Our dependency fathered our drug feeding habits, not the other way around. Calling chemical dependence a habit is like calling a young child a parent.

Yes, it was almost always nearing time for another fix. And yes, we developed habits, but not just for the sake of having habits. There were only two choices - use again or prepare for withdrawal.

I wish it were just a "nasty little habit," I truly do. There would be no need for FFN-TJH and fewer deaths.

Truth is, my name is John and I'm a recovered nicotine addict. Effortlessly and comfortably, I live just one puff away from three packs a day. If I want to stay free, and to stay me, all I have to do is to ... never take another puff, dip or chew!

"I'll lose my friends"

Imagine convincing ourselves that if we arrest our chemical dependency that our friends won't want to be around us, or that we won't be able to be around them. Yes, it takes a bit of practice getting comfortable around users. But extinguishing all use conditioning is a necessary part of healing.

According to Philip Morris research, over 85% of smokers strongly agree with the statement, "I wish I had never started smoking."[129]

Secretly, most of our friends who use feel the same. They wish they knew how to stop. Imagine them soon having a friend who is both knowledgeable and skilled regarding nicotine dependency recovery.

Through use conditioning and association, most of us became convinced that nicotine use was central to our life, including friendships with other users.

While recovery means that we'll no longer use while with friends who do, no relationship whose foundation is deeper than shared drug use need be adversely affected by nicotine's absence.

Successful recovery need not deprive us of a single friend or loved one. On the contrary, tobacco use has likely cost us relationships. Fewer and fewer non-users are willing to tolerate being around the smells, smoke and stink. And oral tobacco use can be a major turn-off.

---

129 Philip Morris, The Cigarette Consumer, March 20, 1984, Bates Number: 2077864835;
      http://legacy.library.ucsf.edu/tid/wos84a00

Aside from no longer using nicotine, our current lives do not need to change at all unless we want them to change. Mine did. I no longer sought situations that allowed me to feel comfortable smoking.

Fellow nicotine addicts don't normally try to make each other feel guilty for being hooked and using. In fact, there can be a very real sense of dependency camaraderie. We also serve as a form of "use" insurance for each other on those occasions when our supply runs out.

Obviously, I no longer frequented community ashtrays. In fact, for the

first time in my adult life I found myself totally comfortable sitting beside non-users and ex-users for extended periods of time.

Gradually, yet increasingly, my circle of friends and acquaintances grew to include far more non-users and ex-users. It was as if my addiction had been picking friends for me.

"I'm still healthy"

Millions and millions ride the "I'm still healthy" rationalization until it collides with a massive heart attack, stroke, or until diagnosed with incurable cancer.

Each nicotine use activates the body's fight or flight response. That response releases extra fuel. You can't hear or see it but stored energy is released into the bloodstream, including cholesterol, the bad kind, LDL.

This energy was supposed to be burned and used fleeing or fighting to save our life. Instead, we sit or stand around doing little or nothing. Instead, released LDL cholesterol begins forming fatty deposits along artery walls.

On the outside, your body mass or size may have looked normal or even thin. Yet, on the inside an artery started acting as a gathering spot and roadblock for cholesterol, dead cells, waste and other fats. Use after use, the plaques build, gather and grow. They become hardened by nicotine through a process known as angiogenesis. Eventually, the artery becomes totally blocked. All tissues serviced with oxygen via the artery suffocate and die. Whether the result is a heart or stroke, there may have been little warning that disaster was about to strike.

And we never once used tobacco without introducing more cancer causing chemicals into our body. There's no feeling, sensation or warning before a house falls on you and that first cancerous cell begins to divide and multiply.

"I feel fantastic." "I'm as healthy as a horse!" "I do aerobics." "I eat healthy." "I walk and run." "I'm athletic."

What does any of that have to do with preventing the scores of cancer causing chemicals that you daily introduced into your body from eventually causing cancer? Wishful thinking?

Let's turn our attention to three common recovery rationalizations: (1) that we can't stop; (2) that if we try, internal forces will plot against us; and (3) that using "just once" won't hurt.

"I can't stop"

I've made no secret over the years about which Joel Spitzer article is my favorite.[130] It's about a woman who enrolled in one of Joel's two-week clinics.

Prior to the start of the first session, she came up to Joel and told him, "I don't want to be called on during this clinic. I am stopping smoking but I don't want to talk about it. Please don't call on me."

Joel said, "Sure. I won't make you talk, but if you feel you would like to interject at anytime, please don't hesitate to."

She grew angry. "Maybe I am not making myself clear, I don't want to talk! If you make me talk I will get up and walk out of this room. If you look at me with an inquisitive look on your face, I am leaving!

130 Spitzer, J, I Can't Quit or I Won't Quit, WhyQuit.com, Joel's Library, 1986.

Am I making myself clear?"

Surprised by the force of her reaction, Joel said he'd honor her request. Although he still hoped she'd change her mind and share her experiences with the group, Joel was no longer expecting it.

With approximately 20 participants, it was a good group except for two women in back who "gabbed constantly." Others were forced to turn around and ask them to be quiet. The women would stop for a few seconds and then were right back at it.

Sometimes, when other people were sharing sad, personal experiences, they'd be laughing at some humorous story they'd shared with each other, oblivious to surrounding happenings, recalls Joel.

On the third day of the clinic it happened. The two women in the back were talking away as usual when a younger participant asked if she could speak to the group first, because she had to leave early. The two in the back continued their private conversation as if she wasn't there.

The young woman said, "I can't stay, I had a horrible tragedy in my family today, my brother was killed in an accident. I wasn't even supposed to come tonight. I am supposed to be helping my family making funeral arrangements. But I knew I had to stop by if I was going to continue to not smoke."

She'd remained nicotine-free for two days and not smoking was obviously important. Joel recalls that the group "felt terrible, but were so proud of her. It made what happened in their days seem so trivial. All except the two ladies in the back of the room. They actually heard none of what was happening," recalls Joel.

"When the young woman was telling how close she and her brother were, the two gossips actually broke out laughing. They weren't laughing at the story. They were laughing at something totally different not even aware of what was being discussed in the room."

The young woman excused herself to return to her family, said she'd keep in touch and thanked the group for their support.

A few minutes later Joel was relating a story to the group when all of a sudden the woman who had requested anonymity interrupted him. "Excuse me Joel," she said loudly.

"I wasn't going to say anything this whole program. The first day I told Joel not to call on me. I told him I would walk out if I had to talk. I told him I would leave if he tried to make me talk. I didn't want to burden anyone else with my problems. But today I feel I cannot keep quiet any longer. I must tell my story." The room went quiet.

"I have terminal lung cancer. I am going to die within two months. I am here to stop smoking. I want to make it clear that I am not kidding myself into thinking that if I stop I will save my life. It is too late for me. I am going to die and there is not a damn thing I can do about it. But I am going to stop smoking."

"You may wonder why I am stopping if I am going to die anyway. Well, I have my reasons. When my children were small, they always pestered me about my smoking. I told them over and over to leave me alone, that I wanted to stop but couldn't. I said it so often they stopped begging."

"But now my children are in their twenties and thirties, and two of them smoke. When I found out about my cancer, I begged them to stop. They replied to me, with pained expressions on their faces, that they want to stop but they can't."

"I know where they learned that, and I am mad at myself for it. So I am stopping to show them I was wrong. It wasn't that I couldn't stop smoking, it was that I wouldn't!"

"I am off two days now, and I know I will not have another cigarette. I don't know if this will make anybody stop, but I had to prove to my children and to myself that I could stop smoking. And if I could stop, they could stop, anybody could stop."

"I enrolled in the clinic to pick up any tips that would make stopping a little easier and because I was real curious about how people who really were taught the dangers of smoking would react. If I knew then what I know now - well, anyway, I have sat and listened to all of you closely."

"I feel for each and every one of you and I pray you all make it. Even though I haven't said a word to anyone, I feel close to all of you. Your sharing has helped me. As I said, I wasn't going to talk. But today I have to. Let me tell you why."

She turned to the two women in the back who had listened to her every word. "The only reason I am speaking up now is because you two BITCHES are driving me crazy. You are partying in the back while everyone else is sharing with each other, trying to help save each other's lives."

She told them about the young woman whose brother was killed and how they laughed, totally unaware of her loss.

"Will you both do me a favor, just get the hell out of here! Go out and smoke, drop dead for all we care, you are learning and contributing nothing here." Joel recalls they sat stunned. He had to calm the group as things had become "quite charged."

Needless to say, recalls Joel, "that was the last of the gabbing from the back of the room for the entire two-week clinic."

All present that night were successful in remaining nicotine-free. The two women who had earlier talked only to each other were applauded by all during graduation, even by the woman with lung cancer.

"All was forgiven," recalls Joel. The woman who'd lost her brother was also present, nicotine-free and proud. And the lady with lung cancer proudly accepted her diploma and introduced one of her children. He had stopped smoking for over a week at that time. Actually, when the lady with cancer was sharing her story with us, she had not told her family yet that she had even stopped smoking."

Six weeks later his mother was dead.

When Joel telephoned to see how she was doing her son answered. He thanked Joel for helping her stop at the end, and told him how proud she was and how proud he was of her. "She never went back to smoking, and I will not either," he said.

She'd taught her children a falsehood and as her final lesson she corrected it. It wasn't that she couldn't stop but that she wouldn't.

I too was once totally convinced that I couldn't. But it was a lie, a lie born inside a hostage mind, a mind convinced that that next fix was more important than life itself.

"I'm fighting monsters and demons"

Once we decide to make an attempt, imagine turning our imaginary "friend" into an imaginary "foe." Imagine inventing destiny controlling monsters and demons that make successful recovery all but impossible.

The most famous smoking rationalization book is "The Easy Way to Stop Smoking" by the late Allen Carr of England.[131]

We lost Allen to lung cancer on November 29, 2006 at age 72. Like me, Allen was a former thirty-year smoker. Ending his five pack-a-day dependency clearly contributed to buying him another 26 years of life.

Allen's book focuses almost exclusively on a single aspect of recovery, using honesty to demolish and destroy smoking rationalizations. Yet, more than 40 times he teaches readers that successful recovery involves killing "monsters" that reside within.

I wrote a smoking rationalization article in early 2000 that I entitled "Nicodemon's Lies." Clearly the the title suggests demon involvement. It wasn't long before Joel set me straight.

I first read Allen's book in May 2006 and found myself chuckling at all the references to monsters. Imagine two ex-smokers, an ocean apart, inventing and blaming continuing captivity on demons and monsters.

While Allen's work has helped millions to critically analyze their smoking justifications, there are no monsters and there is no Nicodemon. There never was.

Nicotine is simply a chemical. Like table salt, it cannot think, plan, plot or conspire and is not some monster or demon that dwells within. The fact that nicotine has an I.Q. of zero is reason for celebration.

131 Carr, A, The Easy Way to Stop Smoking, 1985, 2004 Edition, Sterling Publishing Company, Inc.

Although nicotine activates brain dopamine pathways, causes up-regulation of receptors and creates durable memories of how wanting gets satisfied, recovery is not some strength or willpower contest.

In fact, we will never be stronger than nicotine. We don't need to be. Our greatest weapon has always been our infinitely superior intelligence, but only if put to work.

As Joel puts it, although nicotine is the addictive chemical, it is "no more evil than arsenic or carbon monoxide or hydrogen cyanide - all chemicals found in tobacco smoke."[132] It is the mind's design that generates crave episodes, not some evil force.

According to Joel, terms such as Nicodemon or monster "make nicotine seem to have more power than it actually does. The personification given to it can make an individual feel that nicotine has the potential of tricking him or her into smoking. An inanimate object such as a chemical has no such power." "People do not overcome the grip of chemical addictions by being stronger than the drug but rather by being smarter than the drug."

"Lets not give nicotine more credit than it is due," writes Joel. "Lets not make it some cute and cuddly or evil and plotting entity. It is a chemical that alters brain chemistry. It is no different than heroin, cocaine or alcohol."

"These drugs don't have cute names given to them and giving cute names to nicotine can start to make it seem different than these other substances -- more trivial or less serious in a way. Nicotine is not more trivial than other drugs of addiction and in fact kills more people than all other drugs of addiction combined."

Monsters and demons are inventions of the uneducated mind. We needed them to help explain a want and yearning we couldn't understand.

Nicotine is just a chemical. So long as it does not enter our bloodstream, there will be no need to invent explanations for its continued presence. Adherence to just one guiding principle will prevent the need to invent demons ... no nicotine today.

---

132 Spitzer, J, <u>Once and for all, there is no Nicodemon</u>, June 9, 2004, http://www.ffn.yuku.com/topic/12829

Chapter 5

Packing for the Journey Home

When to Start Home - Now or Later?

Short answer? Now!

Regrettably, both smoking cessation product and tobacco industry websites continue to proclaim that a "key" to success is to not stop using today or tomorrow but to pick some future date such as our birthday, New Years or your nation's national stop smoking day, and then plan around it.

While such advice makes it far more likely that you'll purchase and toy with replacement nicotine, it's deadly. Why? Because delay deprives smokers of significantly greater odds of success. A 2006 study found that about half of all smokers attempt to stop smoking without any planning whatsoever. That's right, no planning and no packing at all.

The study's authors were shocked to learn that unplanned attempts were 2.6 times more successful in lasting at least six months than attempts planned in advance.[133] Results from a 2009 study were nearly identical, also generating increased odds of 2.6.[134]

According to Joel Spitzer, the real experts on this question are millions of long-term successful ex-users, and this isn't news to them. "Rarely do those with the longest initials for credentials do real research on how people stop smoking," he says.

"Conventional wisdom in smoking cessation circles says that people should make plans and preparations for some unspecified future time," writes Joel.

"Most people think that when others stop smoking that they must have put a lot of time into preparations and planning, setting a date and following stringent protocols until the magic day arrives. When it comes down to it, this kind of action plan is rarely seen in real-world [cessation]."[135]

In an email to me Joel wrote, "My gut feelings here, I think the difference between planned and unplanned is that a person who is planning to stop isn't really committed." "If he were committed to it he would just do it - not plan it."

Waiting on some future day to arrive invites silly and exaggerated fears and anxieties about ending use, to gradually erode confidence and destroy core motivations. Imagine being emotionally

---

133 West R, et al, <u>"Catastrophic" pathways to smoking cessation: findings from national survey</u>, British Medical Journal, February 2006, Volume 332(7539), Pages 458-460.

134 Ferguson SG, et al, <u>Unplanned quit attempts--results from a U.S. sample of smokers and ex-smokers</u>, Nicotine & Tobacco Research, July 2009, Volume 11(7), Pages 827-832.

135 Spitzer, J, <u>Setting Quit Dates</u>, 2006, WhyQuit.com/joel

drained and physically whipped before ever getting started.

According to Joel, most successful ex-users fall into one of three groups:

(1) Those who awoke one day and were suddenly sick and tired of smoking, who threw their cigarettes over their shoulder and never looked back;

(2) Those given an ultimatum by their doctor - "stop smoking or drop dead" and

(3) Those who became sick with a cold, the flu or some other illness, went a few days without smoking and then decided to try to keep it going.

"All of these stories share one thing in common - the technique that people use. They simply stop smoking one day. The reasons varied but the technique used was basically the same."

"If you examine each of the three scenarios you will see that none of them lend themselves to long-term planning. They are spur of the moment decisions elicited by some external circumstance."

I visited the Philip Morris USA website during the initial draft of FFN-TJH. Philip Morris is the company that then held a 50% share of the U.S. cigarette market. Its "Quit Assist" pages told those hooked on nicotine to:

"Plan and prepare - that's the first key to quit-smoking success."

"Choose a specific quit date - perhaps your birthday or anniversary, or your child's birthday - and mark it on your calendar. If you give yourself at least a month to prepare, you're more likely to succeed than if you decide New Year's Eve to quit the next day. Pick a week when your stress level is likely to be low." **Philip Morris USA**[136]

Delay recovery for at least a month? Until your next birthday? Wait for life to become nearly stress free? Wrong!

Joel wrote an article attacking such insanity back in 1984.[137] It opens with the following rather lengthy list of cessation delay rationalizations that fit snuggly with Philip Morris' advice to continue using.

"I will stop when my doctor tells me I have to." "I can't stop now, it's tax season." "Maybe I will stop on vacation." "School is starting and I'm too nervous to stop." "I will stop in the summer when I can exercise more." "When conditions improve at work I'll stop." "Stop now, during midterms, you must be nuts!" "Maybe after my daughter's wedding." "My father is in the hospital. I can't stop now." "If I stop now it will spoil the whole trip." "The doctor says I need surgery. I'm too nervous to try now." "After I lose 15 pounds." "I'm making too many other changes right now." "I've smoked for years and feel fine, why should I stop smoking now?" "I'm in the process of moving, and it's a real headache." "It's too soon after my new promotion, when things settle

136 Philip Morris USA, Quit Assist, Get Ready, web site visited July 31, 2008.
137 Spitzer, J, "I will quit when ..." Joel's Library, 1985, note that article references to the word "quit" have been here been replaced with the word "stop" in hopes of diminishing any sense of having left something behind. www.WhyQuit.com/joel

down." "When we have a verifiable bilateral disarmament agreement, I'll consider stopping." "It is too late. I'm as good as dead now."

"The best time to stop is NOW. No matter when now is. In fact, many of the times specifically stated as bad times to stop may be the best."

"I actually prefer that people stop when experiencing some degree of emotional stress. In most cases, the more stress the better. This may sound harsh, but in the long run it will vastly improve the chances of long term success in abstaining from cigarettes," suggests Joel.

He knows that if successful during a period of significant stress, that stress would never again be the mind's excuse for relapse.

Joel is careful to distinguish real-world cessation from the Internet phenomenon where some spend substantial time at WhyQuit.com reading, planning and watching many of his more than 190 free video stop smoking lessons before taking the plunge.

While Internet use is tremendous in industrialized nations, only about 1 in 3 humans were Internet users in 2012 (32.7%).[138]

I suspect that the percentage of the world's nicotine addicts turning to the Internet to master their dependency, who have ever heard of the Law of Addiction, Joel Spitzer or WhyQuit.com, is vastly less than 1 percent.

Even with Internet access, while knowledge is power, time devoted to studying incorrect or false lessons can prove deadly. Regrettably, the primary lessons shared at the majority of websites are about toying with replacement nicotine and deadly. We wish it wasn't so but it is.

When to get started? Unless delay is associated with quality learning that is diminishing needless fears and anxieties, the sooner the better. But even then, you can pack and learn as you go.

Ask yourself, when will there ever be a more perfect time to take back control of your mind than when wanting flowing from hijacked dopamine pathways is again commanding you to use?

FFN-TJH's lessons are presented in an order roughly paralleling recovery's sequencing and priorities. So, don't worry about finishing it before departure.

Pack for Recovery

Ready for day #1 packing? For starters, are you packing for quitting or recovery? Instead of leaving wiggle room for mind games such as "quitters never win, winners never quit," why not start by adopting a positive vision of what's about to happen?

Synonyms for the word "quit" include: abandon, break-off, chuck, desert, forsake, give-up, leave,

---

138 Internet World Stats, Internet Usage Statistics - The Internet Big Picture, www.internetworldstats.com - 07/17/12.

push-out, relinquish, resign, surrender and terminate.

Abandoning us? Giving up? Forsaking, terminating or quitting ourselves? As reviewed in Chapter 3, the real "quitting" took place on the day that nicotine took control of our mind, not the day we decide to take it back.

Why not pack a healthy mental image of what happens during this temporary journey of re-adjustment? The taking back of control, "recovering" the real us!

Although it'll feel a bit awkward at first, try replacing the phrase "I'm quitting" with "I'm recovering."

You'll be pleasantly surprised at the calming effect upon needless anxiety generating fears by thinking in terms of taking back, returning and getting, instead of abandoning, forsaking and quitting.

Document Your Core Motivations

What is the inner source that allows us to end once mandatory nicotine feedings? Strength, willpower or desire?

It's natural to think that it's some combination. However, none of us are stronger than nicotine's influence upon brain dopamine pathways, as clearly evidenced by our inability to live the active addict's greatest desire, to control the uncontrollable.

Yes, we can temporarily muster mountains of willpower. But can willpower make any of us endure a challenge that we lack the desire to complete?

Photo by National Cancer Institute

Once nicotine gets inside, all the strength and willpower on earth cannot stop it from traveling to the brain and activating acetylcholine receptors.

We cannot beat our dependency into submission. Nor can we handle one hit of nicotine without stimulating brain circuitry designed to make activating events nearly impossible to forget, pathways engineered to generate wanting for more.

If incapable of using strength to control our addiction and we cannot "will" it into hibernation or submission, what remains?

As simple as it may sound, dreams and desire have always been the fuel of human accomplishment. Born of the honest recognition of nicotine's negative impact upon our life, desire is the fuel for change.

But it takes keeping those motivations vibrant and on center-stage, so that they can both consciously and unconsciously stimulate, motivate and fuel our journey home.

Those successful in navigating recovery found creative ways to protect and safeguard their dreams and desires. They somehow kept them robust, invigorated and available at a moment's notice.

Our core motivations aid in fostering the patience needed to transition an up to 3 minute subconsciously triggered crave episode. They provide resistance to the nicotine addict's romantic use fixations. Desire's energy stands up to junkie thinking that at times may linger inside the recovering mind.

This temporary period of re-adjustment is about fulfilling recovery's dreams and desires. We enhance our chances by protecting desire's juices. Those juices are accurate and vivid memories of the daily nightmare of living life as nicotine's slave.

Success is about well-protected and remembered recovery motivations. It's about uniting the realities of use with an understanding of the Law of Addiction (Chapter 2).

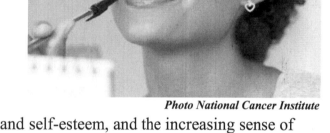

What will you do during the heat of battle (if there is any - as cakewalk recoveries can and do occur) to remind yourself of the importance of victory? Which desires will control?

Will you be able to vividly recall the full price of life as nicotine's slave? What will aid you in

Photo National Cancer Institute

recalling dependency's prison cell, your lost pride and self-esteem, and the increasing sense of feeling like a social outcast?

What will help you remember standing at the counter and handing over your money to purchase a chemical that you knew would force you to return to buy more? During moments of challenge, how do we bring honesty and the desire flowing from it, to the forefront of our mind?

Dreams and desire embrace recovery as freedom's stepping-stone. Consider allowing honest dependency memories to keep desire excited and stimulated. Let honesty transport you home. Allow it to gift you the inner quiet and calm that arrives once addiction's daily chatter goes silent.

When packing, bring along the thousands of negative nicotine use memories that motivated you to begin reading FFN-TJH. Doing so will provide all the wind your dream's wings will need.

One way to do so is to sit down and write yourself a caring (or even loving) letter in which you list your reasons for wanting to be free. Then, carry it with you, pull it out during challenge and use as a front-line defense.

I admit, it sounds rather silly for a fully-grown man or woman to write a letter to themselves, carry it, and then reach for it when threatened. But when your greatest moment of challenge is upon you and an anxiety-riddled mind is seriously considering throwing it all away, it won't seem so silly then.

You'll reach for a powerful resource -- "you" -- to remind yourself why victory here and now is oh so important.

Fear and panic may at times suggest that you flee toward your dependency's grasp; that you leave recovery behind. Failure to document and recall dependency's bad and ugly makes saying "no" to it more challenging.

Why allow your core recovery motivations and the dreams they fuel to be absent, erode or die?

The human mind suppresses negative memories. While daily chemical dependency kept dependency's memories vivid and alive, it's amazing how quickly they begin to erode once nicotine use ends. As impossible as this may be to believe, it won't be long before you'll find it extremely difficult to picture yourself having ever used nicotine.

Why allow time, challenge and memory suppression to destroy freedom's dreams? Pack sufficient fuel to transport you home. Consider spending a few minutes now to document life as an addict. While your list will never grow shorter, consider adding to it the benefits noticed during recovery.

Take a glance now at the Appendix at the end of FFN-TJH. It's a simple journal form that you can copy, complete and carry with you. Or, make your own!

Pack Durable Motives

Do this for "you," not others - It's wonderful that we'd be willing to attempt recovery because some other person wants us to. But navigating battle after battle for someone who isn't in there fighting with us, and who isn't there afterward expressing thanks for our sacrifice, naturally fosters a sense of self-deprivation that can quickly eat away and destroy motivation.

- "My husband can't stand it when I smoke. I'm stopping for him."
- "My dentist is constantly nagging me about my dip causing gum disease. I'll stop before my next appointment."
- "I'm hooked on nicotine gum and my two teenagers are telling everyone that dad is a drug addict. I can't take it. I'll stop if they stop."
- "I'm pregnant and stopped for the baby."
- "Our pediatrician claims that my smoking is causing our daughter's illnesses. I'm stopping for her."
- "My doctor says that she won't do surgery if I'm still smoking. She leaves me no choice."
- "My neighbor said my cat smells like cigarettes. My cat deserves better."

While each is making an attempt, they are doing so for the wrong reasons. "While they may have gotten through the initial withdrawal process, if they don't change their primary motivation for abstaining, they will inevitably relapse," wrote Joel in 1984.[139]

Ending nicotine use for someone else pins our success to him or her. Should they do something wrong or disappoint us we have at our disposal the ultimate revenge, relapse.

"I deprived myself of my cigarettes for you and look how you pay me back! I'll show you, I'll smoke a cigarette!"

As Joel notes from this example, "He will show them nothing. He is the one who will return to smoking and suffer the consequences. He will either smoke until it kills him or have to stop again. Neither alternative will be pleasant."

We can't stop for our doctor, religious leader, parents, spouse, children, grandchildren, best friend, employer, insurance company, support group, pet, some guy who wrote a nicotine cessation book, or for the developing life inside a woman's womb.

While all with whom we share our lives will clearly inherit the fruits of our recovery, it must first and foremost be our gift to us.

Journey for better health, not fear of failing health - While fear of bad or even failing health can be a powerful motivator in causing us to contemplate recovery, the human body is a healing machine. If allowed, it mends and repairs.

What if the primary force driving our recovery is an escalating fear flowing from noticeable dependency related harms? What will happen to those fears if nearly all noticeable harms quickly improve after stopping? What will happen to our determination and resolve?

If an oral nicotine user, imagine a white spot on your gum that quickly disappears.[140] If a smoker, picture dramatic improvement in your sense of smell and a noticeable change in taste. Imagine a chronic cough or wheeze that vanishes in a couple of weeks.

Healing is normally an extremely positive thing. But if recovery is driven almost exclusively by fear of failing health, it can feel like our motivational rug is being pulled out from under us as our primary concerns evaporate before our eyes.

Imagine healing breeding such thoughts as, "I guess smoking hadn't hurt my body as much as I'd thought. I guess it's safe to go back to smoking."

Obviously, we don't correct years of mounting damage to lungs and blood vessels within a few months. Long-term cancer and circulatory disease risks take years to reverse.

But to a mind that commenced recovery primarily due to worries about declining health, disappearance of a chronic cough or a noticeable improvement in breathing may fuel junkie

---

139 Spitzer, J, Joel's Library, Quitting for Others, 1984, http://whyquit.com/joel
140 Polito JR, Long-Term Nicorette Gum Users Losing Hair and Teeth, WhyQuit.com, December 1, 2008.

thinking about the impact of smoking upon the body.

The flip side of fear of declining or poor health is hope for improved health. While it may seem like word games, when packing durable and sustaining motives the distinction could prove critical.

Instead of using fear of failing health as a motivator, imagine recasting those fears into a dream of seeing how healthy your body can once again become.

What if instead of each new health improvement realization eating away at our primary motivation, we looked upon it as a reward that left us wanting to celebrate? Imagine the disappearance of each concern stirring our imagination about the limits of possible improvement?

Again, initially, fear can be an extremely positive force. It may have been what motivated you to start reading FFN-TJH. But fear suffers from a lack of sustainability. We can only remain afraid for so long. We can only look at so many photographs of diseased lungs or mouth cancers before growing numb to them.

As to noticeable tobacco related health concerns, why not use their potential for healing and some degree of noticeable improvement as a means of refueling core dreams and desires?

These bodies are built for healing. If given the opportunity, all tissues not yet destroyed will mend and repair. Why not put your body's ability to heal to work for you?

Do it for total savings, not daily cost - The final motivation we may want to consider shifting and recasting is cost.

The cost of satisfying the brain's demand for nicotine continues to rise as governments increasingly turn to tobacco tax increases as motivation to induce cessation, or so they say.

Fewer smokers mean that the tobacco industry must charge remaining smokers more money in order to satisfy profit-seeking shareholders. Still, if the cost of today's supply of nicotine is our primary recovery motivation, what's the actual price of relapse?

How much does it cost to bum or be offered a cigarette, cigar, pinch, wad or piece? What's the cost of a single pack, tin, pouch or box? A few dollars?

But if we focus upon total savings instead of the cost of our daily or weekly supply, our core motivation is allowed to grow instead of serve as a source of increasing temptation.

I just glanced and according to my computer's desktop recovery calculator, at $3.00 per pack of cigarettes (an addict's paradise, South Carolina continues to have almost the cheapest nicotine in America), during my 13 years of healing I've saved $52,462.01 (U.S.) by skipping 285,749 once mandatory nicotine feedings. But in reality, my savings have been far greater.

When calculating savings don't forget the price of fuel if travel was necessary to re-supply. And what about the value of our time? And don't forget tobacco use related doctor and dentist visits.

When smoking 3 packs a day, I lived with chronic bronchitis and respiratory illness, including being diagnosed with early emphysema. I had pneumonia two years in a row and six root canals in the two years prior to my final attempt.

Amazingly, the madness of paying the tobacco industry to destroy this body ended after arresting my dependency. I can't begin to guess at my medical savings but clearly they've been substantial, including being alive here today to type these words.

Dream about the big picture and total savings, not just what you'd spend for tomorrow's or next week's supply.

Pack Patience: One Day and Challenge at a Time

Derived from the French word "pati," which means to suffer or endure, patience is the "quality of being patient in suffering."[141] Ironically, nicotine users suffer from the fact that stimulation of dopamine pathways by use of an external chemical fosters impulsiveness,[142] the opposite of patience.

Yes, the speed with which we were each able to satisfy wanting via a new supply of nicotine conditioned us to develop varying degrees of impatience. As you embark upon this temporary journey of re-adjustment, practice developing patience as an aid to navigating both recovery and challenge.

One day at a time: today versus forever - How will you measure victory? "One day at a time" allows us to declare total victory within 24 hours, while focusing on tomorrow's concerns once tomorrow arrives. It encourages abandonment of all victory standards that fail to permit celebration today.

"One day at a time," "baby steps," and "one hour" or "one challenge at a time" (when first starting out) are patience focus techniques that break large tasks down

Photo National Cancer Institute

---

141 Patience. (n.d.). Online Etymology Dictionary. Retrieved July 27, 2008, from Dictionary.com website.
142 van Gaalen MM, et al, <u>Critical involvement of dopaminergic neurotransmission in impulsive decision making</u>, Biological Psychiatry, July 2006, Volume 1;60(1), Pages 66-73.

into entirely manageable events.

As Joel notes "this concept is taught by almost all programs which are devoted to dealing with substance abuse or emotional conflict of any kind. The reason that it is so often quoted is that it is universally applicable to almost any traumatic situation."[143]

Think about the needless anxiety and delayed satisfaction of those who insist that victory can only occur if they stop using for the rest of their lives. Forget about tomorrow. Truth is, any worry or concern about tomorrow is wasted emotion unless we succeed today.

Photo National Cancer Institute

Many fail at breaking free because they convince themselves that the mountain is simply too big to climb. Still, it doesn't stop them from trying. Every few years they take a few steps up it, stop, and decide that it's still too big.

"Big bite" anxieties occur when we perceive that the task before us is bigger than our ability to navigate or endure it. "One day at a time" is a patience development skill that once mastered causes "big bite" anxieties to evaporate.

When cliff climbing, it's wise to focus on gaining a solid hold upon the rock beneath our hands, not looking up ahead at the remaining mountain to be climbed. It's wise to focus on where we'll next place our foot, not repeatedly looking down at the ground far below. Why intentionally foster needless anxieties?

How many times have we said, "This time I'm stopping forever!" "Forever" is an awfully big psychological bite that can make any task appear larger than life, or all but impossible.

For example, picture yourself sitting down at the dinner table and having to eat 67 pounds of beef. Imagine the anxieties associated with thinking we need to eat a large portion of a cow. It sort of destroys the image of a

143 Spitzer, J, Take it One Day at a Time, WhyQuit.com, Joel's Library, 1985.

nice juicy steak, doesn't it? Yet the average American consumes 67 pounds of beef annually.[144]

I start each seminar with the same two questions. "I need an honest show of hands. How many of you deeply and honestly believe that you'll never, ever smoke another cigarette for the rest of your life?" Rarely will a hand go up.

I then ask everyone to look around and to never forget what he or she is seeing. I want them to realize that they're not alone. Next I ask, "How many of you deeply and honestly believe that you can go one hour without smoking nicotine?" Without exception, every hand goes up.

Why adopt a recovery philosophy that we are convinced cannot and will not succeed, when we already have a building block in which we deeply believe? Just one hour or challenge at a time, allow the hours to build into a day.

How does a person recover from a broken bone or nicotine addiction? By allowing time to heal, just "one day at a time."

If we insist on seeing and measuring victory only in terms of "stopping forever," then on which day do we allow ourselves to celebrate? Why wait until dead to celebrate? Who is coming to that party? Instead, consider adopting a recovery philosophy that celebrates every day that we remain free and healing.

And try not to see this recovery as being in competition with prior attempts. Although I've remained 100 percent nicotine-free since May 15, 1999, if we both remain 100 percent free today, your day's worth of freedom will have been no longer, shorter or less real than mine. We'll also remain equals in being just one hit of nicotine away from relapse. And when our head hits our pillow tonight we'll both have achieved full and complete victory today.

One challenge at a time: a task focus skill - Patience allows us navigate anxieties when confronted by challenge. Our goal is simple, to navigate challenge until challenge subsides, until our addiction's daily chatter goes silent.

We cannot build a beautiful wall with only one brick, receive a new baby after only one month of pregnancy, obtain a college degree after only one class, or cook a delicious holiday dinner in a few short minutes? Imagine getting half the meal cooked and then fleeing the kitchen, or building half a wall and then walking away.

Going the distance in life, completing each challenge and accomplishing our goal is normal and expected. Swimming half way across the river and then stopping is not.

144 Davis CG et al, Factors Affecting U.S. Beef Consumption, USDA, October 2005, Outlook Report No. LDPM13502.

So how do we navigate the up to 72 hours needed to move beyond peak withdrawal? Just one hour and challenge (if any) at a time. Managing impatience can be as simple as turning lemons to lemonade, while making each task smaller and savoring victory sooner.

Whether confronting a physical withdrawal symptom, struggling with a recovery emotion, encountering an un-extinguished subconscious crave trigger, or fixating on conscious thoughts about using, the objective is the same, to summon the patience needed to experience victory here and now. But how?

The first huge step is mustering the courage to initially say "no" to normal wanting within. Allow your rational thinking mind (your prefrontal cortex) to realize and discover that it has the ability to say "no" to the primitive impulsive mind (the limbic or lizard brain).

We smokers became conditioned to expect to sense satisfaction of nicotine urges and craves within 8-10 seconds of inhaling a puff of smoke. Is it any wonder that it may take a few victories before growing confident and skilled at saying "no" to use impulses?

Try to embrace recovery don't fight it. For example, crave episodes are good not bad. There is a prize at the end of each, breaking and silencing another use cue and return of another aspect of a nicotine-free life. When we take recovery just one challenge at a time, it isn't long before so many aspects of life are reclaimed that we have no choice but to accept the simple truth that everything done while nicotine's slave can be done as well or better without it.

Photo by National Cancer Institute

As Joel notes, we're forced to realize that our thoughts of what life would be like as an ex-user were all wrong, that there is life afterwards and that "it is a cleaner, calmer, fuller and most importantly, a healthier life."

Challenge may involve an internal debate and the need to call upon the patience needed to allow time for honesty and reason to prevail. Chapter 11 is loaded with coping techniques for handling subconscious crave episodes. And Chapter 12 shares tips associated with navigating periods of conscious thought fixation.

Once off and running it's important to keep in mind that recovery is a journey not an event. Online at Freedom and Turkeyville, our support groups, we often see those in early recovery growing impatient.

"Why am I still craving?" "When will comfort come?" Some endure a substantial degree of self-inflicted anxiety by intense focus upon the question of how long it will take for challenge to end. I like to think of it in terms of the time needed to heal a broken bone, but with greater variation from person to person, as every recovery is different.

In regard to psychological recovery, some let go and put their relationship with nicotine behind them far sooner than others. Some insist on clinging to varying use rationalizations for months. Some even longer.

But the ultimate result is the same for all. Patience transports you here to "Easy Street," where you begin experiencing entire days without once thinking about wanting to use. While here, e occasional thoughts of wanting to use will become so infrequent, brief and mild that they become laughable.

When it happens, it may begin to feel like our one challenge and day at a time recovery philosophy has outlived its usefulness. But Joel cautions us not to abandon it.

He warns that like never-users, ex-users experience horrible days too. A growing sense of complacency could also leave us toying with temptation in social situations. We will each some day experience tremendous stress at home or work, and we each have loved ones who will eventually die.

The next few minutes are all within your immediate control and each is entirely do-able. The decisions, if any, made during those minutes are yours to command.

Find contentment in today's freedom and healing. It took years to walk this deeply into dependency's forest. It isn't realistic to think that we can walk out overnight. Patience. You'll soon be doing easy time.

Pack a Positive Attitude

Can we make ourselves miserable on purpose? No doubt about it. Throughout our lives we've experienced worry, fear, anger and irritability, only to find out later that our emotions were totally unnecessary, that our concerns didn't occur.

The single greatest source of self-inflicted anxiety in my life flowed from failure to understand my addiction. How could I seriously and intelligently confront something that I didn't understand? Although I often dreamed about freedom, it was easier to reach for that next fix instead. I grew to expect failure.

Combining intelligence with attitude can

National Cancer Institute

destroy baseless fears. Why not reassure your impulsive mind that there is absolutely nothing to fear, that coming home is good not bad.

Picture a board on the ground that's 10 inches wide and 50 feet long. Picture yourself easily and repeatedly walking its entire length, over and over.

Now, picture the same board suspended between two skyscrapers, fifty stories off the ground. What are the odds of you walking its length without falling? Not good.[145]

Recovery is grounded. Why allow false fears to destroy your will? Attitude can either escalate and fuel fears or serve as a calming influence that relaxes and reassures.

Why not choose freedom over bondage, happy over depressed, success over failure? Why not invite your subconscious to pick honesty, healing and safety over lies, toxins and disease?

Why allow resolve, commitment and success to be controlled by dependency induced doubt, anxiety and fear? Why heap layer upon layer of anxiety icing on recovery's cake?

Do you remember when you first learned to swim and found yourself in water over your head? Did you panic? I did. Would I have panicked if I'd been a skilled swimmer?
The more knowledgeable and skilled we become, the easier and calmer recovery. Yes, there may be a few waves along the way. But why fear their arrival? Why not relax and do the backstroke until your swimming skills are needed?

Imagine a positive attitude becoming your subconscious teacher, in sharing the truth about coming home. Imagine confident honesty enlisting it to fight on the side that's right.

Get it to take its finger off of the button controlling your body's fight or flight panic response. Help your subconscious mind understand that what needs to be feared is your dependency. Gradually destroying your body, continued use was threatening survival.

Why adopt an attitude that resists bringing wanting to an end? What harm is there in allowing this temporary journey of re-adjustment to become our most amazing period of self-discovery ever?

Why pretend that the board is too high, the swim too hard, or that there are monsters or demons where none exist?

Reflect on how repeatedly telling yourself that recovery "is too hard," "endless" or "nearly impossible" might tend to eat away at freedom's dreams and desires. Reflect upon how a positive can-do attitude would reassure your subconscious and help diminish self-inflicted stress, worry, anxiety, panic, anger and depression.

Allow your dreams to feel the influence of celebrating each moment of freedom, each challenge overcome?

---

145 Coue, E, Self Mastery through Conscious Autosuggestion, Malken Publishing Co., Inc., 1922.

Picture a plugged-in lamp but without a light bulb. The power switch is turned off. Picture intentionally sticking your finger into the bulb socket and leaving it there. Now picture all of your subconscious nicotine feeding cues being wired directly into the lamp's on-off switch.

If we expect to soon encounter another use cue and anxiety episode but don't know when, what will leaving our finger in the socket all day do to our nerves? Will it keep us on edge?

Will a constant sense of anticipation anxiety have us lashing-out at anyone entering the room? Will we feel like crying? Will worry and concern keep us from concentrating on other things? Will it wear us down and drain our spirit?

Conversely, what if we know that when a shock occurs that it will always be tolerable, that no crave episode will ever harm us, cut us, or make us bleed, break our bones, make us ill or kill us?

What if we know that the crave episode will not last longer than three minutes? What if we know that there's a valued prize at the end, extinguishing another use cue and return of another aspect of life? What if we know that the only path to fully reclaiming life is to extinguish all use cues?

Honesty, confidence, understanding and attitude can make the time and distance between challenges more relaxed. Alternatively, we can allow our thinking to become so infected by fear, doubt and negativism that it becomes the instrument of defeat.

Instead of intense focus upon any anxiety felt when the light switch is briefly turned on, why not focus on learning to relax during the massive amount of time that the switch is off?

If we keep feeding ourselves the thought that recovery is too hard, should we be surprised when our emotions make us feel that it is? Why feed the mind failure? Why fear the swim and needlessly worry when some of us are not even in the water yet? Why fuel the impulsive mind in breeding powerful negative anxieties?

Photo by National Cancer Institute

Fight back with reason, logic and dreams. Look forward with confidence while knowing that nicotine will no longer define who you are. You, not a chemical, will now control your remaining time here on earth.

Embrace recovery as a wonderful journey back to the rich, deep, and tranquil inner calm that resided inside our mind before nicotine first arrived.

Permit yourself to grow stronger, not weaker. Let honesty answer addiction's chatter. Picture your brain and tissues healing, extra money in your pocket, extra time to spend it, and more bounce in each step.

While true that only action, not thought, can rob us of victory, why allow a negative attitude to invite failure? Marvel in the glory of taking back your mind.

The Value of Documenting Your Journey

While "one day at a time" is an excellent victory yardstick, imagine the value of being able to look back and see what each day was like.

Consider jotting down a few calendar notes or diary entries about what early recovery was like and the challenges overcome. Although not necessary to success, doing so could prove valuable later.

Why would anyone want to vividly recall the first few days of recovery, days which could reflect a blend of frustrations, anxieties, crave episodes, anger, bargaining and sadness? The same reason we need to remember, in as much detail as possible, daily life as an actively feeding nicotine addict.

We've all heard that "those who forget the past are destined to repeat it." It's hard to imagine a situation where it rings truer than with drug recovery and relapse.

Humans tend to repress and inhibit negative emotional memories, and emotional experiences in general.[146]   Instead, we remember and replay the good, while forgetting the bad.

Photo by National Cancer Institute

Imagine if it were otherwise. A vivid picture of all the pain, anxiety and hurt of all our yesterdays would be a heavy burden to bear.

While your mind may quickly suppress memories of the challenges overcome, ink on paper or words typed into a computer are durable. The best way to protect against complacency isn't by forgetting what bondage or recovery was like, but by accurately recalling them.

It's wise to make a record of both the reasons you want to break free and what the first couple of weeks were like. Consider sending yourself an e-mail before bed. And here's an example of why.

---

146 Davis PJ, et al, <u>Repression and the inaccessibility of affective memories</u>, Journal of Personality and Social Psychology, January 1987, Volume 52(1), Pages 155-162; also see Depue BE, et al, <u>Prefrontal regions orchestrate suppression of emotional memories via a two-phase process</u>, Science July 13, 2007, Volume 317(5835), Pages 215-219.

Imagine hitting what feels like a recovery plateau, where you no longer sense improvement. Imagine feeling stuck and wondering if it's going to remain this way for good, as if a rose bud had stopped opening.

Now imagine being able to look back and read your own progress notes. Like having a medical chart during a hospital stay, your record can provide accurate perspective of how far you've come.

It can help calm concerns that recovery has stalled. Although at times nearly impossible to see, I assure you, recovery's rose bud continues to slowly unfold.

Consider a present gift of future memory. Consider it free relapse insurance. A few memory-jogging notes when starting out could become invaluable during challenge, lulls or once complacency arrives.

Refueling

While challenge, time and negative memory suppression tend to erode dreams and desires, opportunities abound to reinvigorate the wind beneath our wings.

Ex-users - Ex-users can be an excellent source of support. Most already reside here on Easy Street. But a word of caution about ex-users. As just discussed, their memories of the challenges of early recovery have likely been suppressed.

While most will have forgotten the bad, some have continued to cling tight to a few old nicotine use rationalizations. Doing so has likely kept tantalizing "aaah" wanting relief memories associated with those remaining rationalizations teasingly alive.

Photo by National Cancer Institute

Others will look back upon their years of use as having been "vile, disgusting, expensive, stupid, crazy" or insane.[147] For them, breaking free is now seen as having been common sense, no big deal, a non-event or easy.

Ask the next ex-user you meet how long it has been since their last significant challenge. Try to get them to put a date on it. Ask how long the challenge lasted and what it felt like. How intense was it?

---

147 Spitzer, J, "I don't know if I have another quit in me", http://www.ffn.yuku.com/topic/11406, March 3, 2002.

Then ask about the challenge prior to that. Again, try to get them to be accurate in dating and describing it. A few follow-up questions and I think you'll discover that the event was really a non-event, that it left very little impression.

Ask what they like most about being free. How has it changed their life? Did their success influence others still using? What do they think about while watching others use?

What do they most miss? Try to identify any lingering romantic fixations. Reflect upon the honesty of each. Reflect on how this ex-user succeeded, even though they refused to let go of this rationalization. Imagine if they had. Think about how it places them at greater risk for relapse.

Current-users - If questioned, friends or loved ones still using may not be as open and honest as Katie about their dependency, or about their dream of someday being free. But, words are not necessary. Their dependency will speak for them.

Carefully watching users can be motivational. Often you'll identify them by smell even before they light up.

Watch that first deep puff. Watch their reaction to it, their eyes as 8-10 seconds later nicotine strikes their brain. While doing so, keep in mind that they are not replenishing to tease you. They are doing so because they must.

While stopped in traffic, look for windows rolled down when rain, heat or cold suggest they should be up. Upon spotting the smoker, look closely. What motivated this nicotine feeding? Do they even realize that they're smoking or are they replenishing while on auto-pilot?

Like Pavlov's dogs, did they condition their subconscious to expect replenishment when driving?

Did traffic anxieties turn their urine more acidic, thus accelerating depletion of remaining reserves of the alkaloid nicotine? It's the same acid-alkaloid interaction seen during anger or when consuming alcohol.

Do they extend their arm out the vehicle's window in order to keep tobacco toxins from burning their eyes? And once replenishment is complete, what do they do with their non-biodegradable cigarette butt, with its 12,000 plastic-like cellulose acetate fibers?[148]

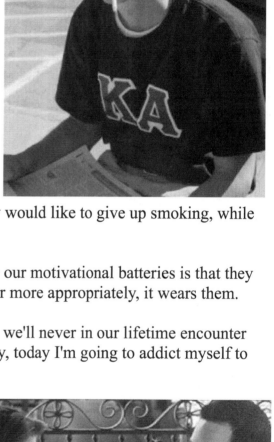

Society is increasingly treating those still in bondage as social outcasts. Notice the smokers standing around outside of buildings in the cold, heat, night, wind or rain. Carefully watch their gestures and posture.

It's almost as if they want all who see them to believe that the only reason they are outside is to enjoy the wonderful health benefits of the great outdoors. But the need to return every thirty minutes or so betrays them.

Watch at the store counter when they re-supply. Are they buying a one-day supply or more? Are you witnessing a daily event in their life? Reflect on their choices.

If already in recovery yourself, what are the odds that this person is envious of you? According to a 2007 Gallop Poll of U.S. smokers, 74% of those polled said they would like to give up smoking, while 67% consider themselves addicted.[149]

The beauty of using unsuspecting current-users to recharge our motivational batteries is that they won't disappoint us. They wear their chemical addiction, or more appropriately, it wears them.

None awoke this morning and decided to put it on. In fact, we'll never in our lifetime encounter any now dependent user who awoke one day and said, "Hey, today I'm going to addict myself to nicotine!"

On a personal note, I hope that none of us ever forget that not long ago that was us.

Never-users - When first starting out, unless a secret closet smoker share your decision. Doing so will invite family, friends and co-workers to offer initial encouragement and support.

Their simple words of praise can inspire and make us look forward to more of the same. But be careful not to develop support expectations, to lean upon them or to transform their praise

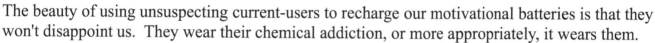

Photo by National Cancer Institute

---

148 Polito JR, <u>Cigarette Butts</u>, WhyQuit.com, July 4, 2002.
149 Saad, L, <u>U.S. Smoking Rate Still Coming Down</u>, Gallup, July 24, 2008, http://gallop.com

or comments into a crutch.

When teenagers, my daughters constantly nagged about my smoking. They both seemed genuinely excited the first few days of my final failed attempt. While their encouragement was extremely uplifting, it ended abruptly. I suddenly felt abandoned. Where was my support?

I'd leaned upon them far too heavily. I'd made them my crutch. I'd made their desire that I stop my primary motivation. It was a mistake. A mistake that left me feeling deprived of support, resentful and wanting to use. Why had they abandoned me? After relapsing I confronted them.

"Dad, we didn't want to bring it up any more because we could see you were succeeding." "We didn't want to remind you and make you keep thinking about smoking."

Is it fair to expect a person who has never been chemically addicted to anything in their life to appreciate the recovery process? Clearly not.

Invite never-users to be part of your support team but be sure to educate them. Let them know that helping you stay focused for the next 90 days would be fantastic. But don't count on them being there. See their support as dessert, never the main meal.

Industry marketing - Store tobacco marketing becomes sadly laughable to the trained eye. Extremely effective, it's a multi-purpose facade through which the dependency savvy brain easily sees.

Effective industry marketing accomplishes three objectives. It encourages youth experimentation, provides use justification, and is bait for relapse.

Look closely. When is your mind first assaulted by use invitations? Are there roadside signs, signs on top of gas pumps, tied to lamp-posts, window signs, exterior building wall signs, signs hanging above candy racks or on the door as you both enter and leave?

Whether noticed or not, almost every aspect of marketing is designed to encourage starting, continued use and discourage stopping. Each time we returned to purchase more, our mind was fed justifications as to why we'd returned.

And when trying to stop, it proclaims why we shouldn't. It wraps around us while trying to purchase gas, food and medicine. Its aim is simple: to force our subconscious to notice it, to stir desire, inflame wanting and contribute to relapse.

Flavor, pleasure, to be true, cool, our gateway to friendship, adventure, rebellion or unbelievable prices, it suggests that we stand at that counter for every reason except the truth, because we must, because our brain is chemically dependent upon nicotine.

Think like a tobacco company. Look closely. What subliminal message is each ad or display attempting to pound into your mind?
Where is the "responsible" merchant's message stating that smoking nicotine may be more addictive and harder to beat than heroin or cocaine? Where's the message warning students that they may only need to use nicotine a couple of times before becoming hooked for life?

Feel the industry's economic muscle as it purchased your subconscious focus at the checkout counter.

What tobacco company won the bidding war at your neighborhood sales location? Look at row after row of the same packs or cartons. The winner's products are the ones on top and most visible. See the winner's sign?

And what's the real purpose of the giant yellow "We Card" or other similar sign above the checkout counter? Don't you find it strange that there isn't one for alcohol?

It's teen bait. Once secret industry documents suggest that the carding sign's primary purpose is to torment neighborhood youth with the ongoing tease that tobacco use is a sign of adulthood, a rite of passage, that it's what "real" grown-ups do.[150]

Look at the hundreds of brightly colored packs, boxes, cartons, tins, cans, bags, pouches and tubes. Collectively this power wall oozes the impression that users can't wait to awaken each day so that they can run down to the store and try a new flavor.

You're looking at the biggest tobacco fib of all. The entire colorful facade is orchestrated to scream the lie that use is a free-choice activity, that everyone's doing it.

In your mind, strip away the rainbow of color, the fancy packaging and the almost 700 documented tobacco flavor additives.[151] Instead, see a vast array of different doses of nicotine, each engineered to penetrate tissues at varying rates of speed.

Turn store marketing on its head. Instead of being used by it, use it as motivation for staying free and keeping your money.

150 Polito, JR, Convenience Stores - Nicotine Addiction Central, WhyQuit.com, March 18, 2006.
151 Polito, JR, Cigarette Additives, Carcinogens and Chemicals, WhyQuit.com, February 7, 2005.

Social controls - How did you react to anti-smoking news stories or to stories about new tobacco health concerns? Did you instantly change the channel, turn the page or otherwise tune out? I did.

News stories that once fostered anxieties can now be used as a source of motivation in helping keep us clean and free.

In case you haven't noticed, there's a movement sweeping the globe as workers and non-smokers demand smoke-free air.

We're seeing stories of smoking being banned on all hospital property, in parks, playgrounds, outdoor sporting events, on beaches, in hotel rooms, and even in company or government owned vehicles.

We're also seeing proposed legislation attempt to ban smoking in all vehicles transporting a child. And smoking is now beginning to factor into family court child custody, visitation and child abuse decision-making.

Science is awakening to the realization that there may not be any living cell in the entire human body that isn't touched and affected by tobacco toxins.

Where allowed by law, employers are beginning to discriminate in refusing to hire anyone testing positive for nicotine. Some employers are threatening to fire all current employees who test positive for nicotine after being afforded a reasonable period of time to break-free.

Fuel and living costs are now rising faster than income in most nations. Millions of hooked parents are increasingly confronted with the choice of buying food for their child or nicotine for their addiction.

It's a situation made worse by cash strapped governments that have become increasingly dependent on tobacco taxes, and the dependability of nicotine's grip upon the taxpayer's brain.

Personally, it's offensive that most politicians either accept tobacco industry campaign contributions or see those still enslaved as a highly dependable source of tax revenue. They just don't seem to get it, or maybe they do.

Whether we accept or deplore the way society treats those still in bondage, news of the latest assault upon them can be used as motivation to prevent assault upon us.

You! - Clearly, your most dependable source of support is "you"! Your three most valuable motivational assets will be:

1. Memories of life as an actively feeding nicotine addict;
2. Your reasons for wanting to be free; and
3. Memories of early recovery.

Again, the early part of this journey can be emotional. It's wise to anticipate and prepare for significant negative memory suppression. You will also suppress old use memories.

Find quality ways to preserve those memories. Make them available both as a recovery progress report and later as an aid in fending off complacency. Doing so will be like owning the best and quickest battery re-charger the world has ever known.

Whether your nicotine use was heavy or light, long or short, out in full view for the world to see or the best-kept secret on earth, your intelligence and conscious thinking mind is your #1 motivational tool.

Closet users - Pretend for a second that you are a closet nicotine addict. If a secret user, your family and friends either never knew you were hooked, or were told that you successfully broke free long, long ago.

Aside from all the lies we told ourselves to rationalize that next mandatory feeding, the closet user lives and breathes the need to constantly deceive the world too.
If a recovering closet-user, in addition to celebrating self-honesty, there's tremendous relief in at last being honest with those we love.

Having lived in almost constant fear of being exposed, whether or not we come totally clean and share our secret, the emotional rewards of no longer living a lie can themselves be extremely supportive. If a closet ex-user, where can you turn for support when your world thinks that you didn't use?

Internet refueling - If you don't own a computer or are not online, consider dropping by your local library as most now offer free Internet access.

Even if you have never touched a computer in your entire life, there is hopefully a library staff member who delights in teaching library patrons how to explore the Internet and print their discoveries.

Once online, a keyboard and mouse will allow you to explore a vast array of empowering recovery tools. Visit WhyQuit.com. Simply type whyquit.com in the address window at the top and then

Motivation, Education and Support for Cold Turkey Nicotine Cessation

WhyQuit.Com

Welcome Video | About Us | Contact Us | Link to Us | News | What's New?

Follow WhyQuit on: FaceBook Twitter YouTube
Share WhyQuit's link via: FaceBook Twitter Google+ Email

Motivation

Why Quit Smoking?

We Died Young
- Bryan Lee Curtis - age 34
- Noni Glykos - age 33
- Quentin Delgado - age 23
- Famous victims - under 60
- Our family member died young
- Your story

Why We Died Young
- Nicotine Addiction 101
- "Nicodemon's" Lies?
- Why I use tobacco
- Nicotine - the sine qua non of smoking
- Carcinogens, chemicals and additives
- Smoking, smoking and more smoking
- World cigarette pack warning pictures

Our Living Nightmare
- Deborah's stage IV battle - age 38
- Kim's missing lung - age 44
- Brandon's 2 missing legs - age 23

How Tobacco Destroys the Body
- Brain damage
- Circulatory disease
- Smoking's Impact on the Lungs
- Pregnancy and breastfeeding
- A Heart-Loving-Heart
- 32-year-old smoker's arteries
- The secondhand smoke battle

More Truth About Tobacco
- Movies and clips
- The smoker's self mutilation
- Why are we dying so young?
- Is the risk of death exaggerated?
- If You Could Spend a Day with Me
- The smoker's body
- Cigarette butts and mother earth

Why Quit Smokeless Tobacco?
- Sean Marsee message - age 19
- Gruen's missing jaw - age 17

Alternatives
- Turkey's Triumphs
- The Smoker's Memorial

Education

Joel's Library

Stop Smoking Library Categories
- Why do people smoke?
- The real cost
- How to quit smoking
- Relapse prevention
- What about weight gain?

Highlight Stop Smoking Articles & Videos
- My cigarette, my friend
- Why do smokers smoke? (video)
- Are you a nicotine junky?
- The smoker's vow
- Quit smoking tip sheet
- Quitting by gradual withdrawal
- Is cold turkey the only way to quit?
- Minimizing common side effects

Joel's free quit smoking materials
- Who is Joel?
- Never Take Another Puff - (Joel Spitzer's free PDF e-book)
- Joel's video stop smoking lessons
- Daily stop smoking video lesson guide
- Joel's Jukebox (audio lessons)
- Ask Joel - Joel's question & answer site
- Language translations of Joel's work

More Education
On Quitting
- Freedom from Nicotine - The Journey Home - (John Polito's free PDF e-book)
- Nicotine Cessation Tips - 8 pg pdf file
- WhyQuit's free quit smoking books
- How long does withdrawal last?
- NRT - do quitting aids work? Chantix
- Stop smoking benefits timetable
- Your guide to "Glory Week"
- Take WhyQuit's quitting quiz
- Quit for Just One Hour at a Time
- Weight gain
- Crave and stress management

Relapse Prevention
- Tearing Down the Wall
- Caring for Your Quit
- Free relapse insurance

Youth Smoking Prevention
- Yesterday, Today, Tomorrow

Support

Freedom - Our Yuku Support Group
A support classroom to stop smoking, quit oral tobacco and break free from NRT

Freedom is an open nicotine dependency recovery forum where 100% of the group's posts and materials are available to all, regardless of membership. A single-minded program, those applying for posting privileges must have quit all forms of nicotine delivery cold turkey within the past 30 days, without use of any products, pills, e-cigarettes or procedures, and remained 100% nicotine-free for at least 72 hours. A nicotine-free forum, any nicotine relapse - even one puff, dip or chew - permanently revokes posting privileges.

Is Freedom Right for You?
- Mission Statement
- Relapse Policy
- Courtesies & Rules
- How to Join

Critical Recovery Insights
- The Law of Addiction
- The "one puff" files
- Tell a newbie how many seconds a day you still want a cigarette
- Index of highlight posts

Key Freedom Destinations
- Freedom's Home Page
- The first 72 hours
- Understanding nicotine dependency
- Navigating the 4 layers of recovery
- Relapse prevention
- Member messages & journals
- Free quit smoking meters

Turkeyville - Facebook Support Group
A cold turkey quit smoking Facebook support group where the focus is on helping new quitters get a solid start
- Group Rules & Mission
- Color Milestones

Other support groups & online forums
- Other stop smoking support groups
- Lung cancer & COPD support groups

Physician, dental & wellness resources
- WhyQuit's patient resources

press "enter" or "return."

Welcome to WhyQuit! As the screen-shot on the next page shows, WhyQuit's home page is broken down into three categories. The left column contains links to motivational articles, the center contains links to educational materials, and the right column is the gateway to free online support.

The site is totally free, declines donations and is staffed entirely by volunteers. WhyQuit's motivation column includes stories of the ordeals endured by young tobacco victims and their families.

Clearly, WhyQuit intentionally shares horrific stories about the youngest of the young. It does so in an attempt to get visitors to appreciate that predicting whom tobacco will harm and at what age is like playing Russian roulette with a gun.

The center education column is home to all of Joel's materials and my articles. Here you'll find every lesson shared in Joel's book, more than 100 short articles on nearly every recovery topic imaginable.

You'll also find links to his free electronic e-book "Never Take Another Puff" and to Joel's nearly 200 video counseling lessons (many formatted as audio files for listening as well).

The right column provides support links and transports visitors to "Freedom," the Internet's most serious and focused peer support group, and to Turkeyville, WhyQuit's new Facebook group. Both groups are exclusively for cold turkey quitters.

At both, education always comes first. It must. We discovered very early that a forum's ability to support and sustain recovery in a purely pep-rally type environment is dismal at best.

While the initial excitement of interacting with other ex-users is often tremendous, it eventually begins to wane. As it does, the forum's value and effectiveness in supporting success diminishes. If no education to fall back upon, group relapse rates become horrible.

Visitors to WhyQuit's support groups don't need to join in order to read each the forum's materials. In fact, most don't. But we still treat them like part of the family.

Freedom and Turkeyville function as virtual classrooms with enormous windows. Maintaining positive control over admissions ensures a classroom type learning experience, prevents chaos, and makes sure that each forum's seasoned volunteer educators are not overwhelmed.

Every message posted at Freedom and Turkeyville must relate to recovery. General socialization is not permitted, including celebration of birthdays, anniversaries or holidays.

Clearly, neither forum is for those seeking to socialize or make new friends. With millions of tobacco related deaths annually, the groups take their missions seriously. Their goal is simple: to aid visitors and members in remaining nicotine-free today.

As for Freedom being 100 percent nicotine-free, we figure there must be at least one place on planet earth where nicotine has no voice. Those applying for membership must certify that they stopped cold turkey without use of any product or procedure and that they've remained 100% nicotine-free for 72 hours.

ffn.yuku.com

Although it may sound harsh, applicants must agree to abide by Freedom's relapse policy. That policy states that should any member relapse that they will permanently lose message board posting privileges. It encourages members to take recovery seriously.

One final point deserves mention. The rules for both groups prohibit mention of any commercially sold book, product, diet or procedure. The forum was built around the concept that every recovery lesson is made freely available to all without cost or obligation.

As such, the forum will not permit any suggestion that any reader need spend any money or make any purchase in order to succeed, including purchasing the paperback or Kindle version of FFN-TJH. If sharing links to FFN-TJH at any online site please share the link to WhyQuit's free version.

Unlike Freedom, there's no 72-hour nicotine-free waiting period at Turkeyville before you can join, and no relapse policy. The group's primary focus is in helping those just starting out in navigating early recovery.

Recovery meters - WhyQuit and Freedom offer visitors links to free stop smoking meters. These are free small computer programs or apps that are either downloaded to and installed on your computer, laptop or mobile device, and designed for use while online.

Once we type in our tobacco use history (how often we smoked, the purchase price and the day we stopped), most will calculate the number of days, months and years we've remained free, the amount of money we've saved, and if a smoker, the total number of cigarettes not smoked and the amount of life expectancy so far reclaimed.

Most meters allow you to copy their calculations to your computer's clipboard for transporting and pasting into e-mails, documents created with your word processing program or for sharing on Internet message boards.

Like a car's odometer, they're a fun way of tracking, marking and measuring our journey home. Links to free meters can be found at both WhyQuit and Freedom.

Support limits - The above recovery support suggestions will hopefully stir your thinking. The only limit to identifying additional ways of keeping our recovery dreams fueled and vibrant is the limits of our imagination.

Our objective is simple. It's to stay sufficiently motivated long enough to allow the time needed to successfully navigate recovery's remaining challenges, if any.

But whether today is good or bad, whether we feel motivated or not, our freedom and healing will continue so long as we stick to one guiding principle ... no nicotine today!

Destroy All Remaining Nicotine

As nicotine addicts, many of us engaged in mind games while pretending to arrest our addiction. One such game was to keep nicotine on hand after stopping, for the purported purpose of proving that we were in full control, stronger than our addiction ... or just in case we need it.

This practice makes as much sense as someone on suicide watch carrying a loaded gun, while fighting the urge to use it. Some carry their nicotine delivery devices with them while others knowingly keep a stash within quick and easy reach.

We'll never be stronger than nicotine but then we don't need to be. Our weapon is our intelligence. Feeling a need to tempt and toy with impulsiveness in order to prove conscious strength reflects abandonment of intelligence.

Why treat quick access to nicotine as though a life jacket? It's a jacket all right but not one that saves, one that enslaves.

The smart move is to destroy all remaining nicotine. Whether in the pocket of a coat hanging in a closet, in your other purse, hidden in the yard, on the balcony, in the garage, in a vehicle, under a seat, or at work, destroy it. And don't forget to empty the ashtrays too.

It's time to get serious. Check for cigarettes that may have fallen under furniture, beneath a cushion or under the car seat.

And throw out all old nicotine replacement products and e-cigarettes, smokeless tobacco and cigars too. Keeping nicotine handy is contrary to learning to live life without it.

Getting rid of all nicotine buys you precious seconds during challenge. With cue triggered crave episodes peaking within three minutes, a few more seconds of delay may be all that's needed to sense anxieties peak and begin to diminish.

"Don't ever forget how cigarettes once controlled your behaviors and beliefs," reminds Joel. "When you stopped smoking you admitted cigarettes controlled you. You were literally afraid that one puff could put you back. That was not an irrational fear. One puff today will lead to the same tragic results as it would have the day you quit."

"Cigarettes were stronger than you before, and, if given the chance, will be stronger than you again, warns Joel. "If you want to show you are now in control, do it by admitting you can function without having cigarettes as a worthless and dangerous crutch."[152]

You'll do just fine, even if your employment requires you to be near or handle nicotine products, or if you live with someone who insists upon leaving their cigarettes, e-cigs, cigars, dip, chew or NRT lying around. It simply means that you'll extinguish use cues associated with those situations more quickly than most.

Photo by National Cancer Institute

But mind games involving conscious temptation are fully within our ability to control. Be smart. Crush, throw-out or flush all remaining nicotine. It's an excellent means of proclaiming that the time for games is over, that you're serious about coming home!

_____

    ɔitzer, J, "I'm going to have to carry cigarettes with me at all times for me to quit smoking," 1988, Joel's Library,
    ʳw.WhyQuit.com.

Chapter 6

Common Hazards & Pitfalls

Early Alcohol Use Risky

A 1990 study found that nearly half who relapsed to smoking (47%) consumed alcohol before doing so. It also found that another 5% had been under the influence of "recreational" drugs.[153]

Early alcohol use is clearly the most avoidable relapse risk of all. Using an inhibition diminishing substance while in the midst of early physical withdrawal is inviting relapse.

Why ex-users may feel alcohol effects sooner - There are a number of nicotine/alcohol interactions. Most obvious is the combined effects (or synergy) of both alcohol and nicotine stimulating the user's brain dopamine pathways and satisfying wanting for more.[154]

Additionally, as explained in Chapter 4 ("Use relieves stress and anxiety"), as with stress, alcohol use causes urine acidification, which in turn causes the user's kidneys to accelerate elimination of the alkaloid nicotine from their bloodstream. A third interaction may leave the use feeling intoxicated sooner.

Nicotine stimulates the body's central nervous system while alcohol depresses it. Alcohol stimulates GABA production (gamma-aminobutyric acid), which produces a sedating effect[155] while impairing muscle (motor) control.[156]

Nicotine stimulates fight or flight pathways, causing release of adrenaline and noradrenaline.[157]

---

153 Brandon, TH, et al, <u>Postcessation cigarette use: the process of relapse</u>, Addictive Behaviors, 1990, Volume 15(2), Pages 105-114.

154 Tizabi Y, et al, <u>Combined effects of systemic alcohol and nicotine on dopamine release in the nucleus accumbens shell</u>, Alcohol and Alcoholism, Sept-Oct. 2007, Volume 42(5), Page 413-416.

155 Koob GF, <u>A role for GABA mechanisms in the motivational effects of alcohol</u>, Biochemical Pharmacology, October 2004, Volume 68(8), Pages 1515-1525.

156 Hanchar HJ, et al, <u>Alcohol-induced motor impairment caused by increased extrasynaptic GABA(A) receptor activity</u>, Nature Neuroscience, March 2005, Volume 8(3), Pages 339-345.

157 Kenneth J. Kellar, KJ, <u>Addicted to Nicotine, Neuropharmacology and Biology of Neuronal Nicotinic Receptors</u>, National Institute on Drug Abuse website, www.DrugAbuse.gov, article updated May 19, 2006.

This is why alcohol induced feelings of becoming sedated or even sleepy can be diminished by stimulating the body with nicotine.[158] Here's what to expect.

When drinking, the user soon begins noticing alcohol's gradual sedation and anesthesia type effects. The more they drink, the more sedated their nervous system becomes. The more they drink, the more acidic their urine becomes and the quicker their kidneys eliminate nicotine from their our bloodstream.

Not only are they starting to feel tipsy, their nicotine reserves are declining faster than normal.

But just one powerful hit of nicotine and, in addition to an alcohol exaggerated "aaah" wanting relief sensation, nicotine kicks in their automatic in-born "fight or flight" neuro-chemical response. The mind has been fooled into believing that danger is present and begins to stimulate an alcohol-sedated body.

Adrenaline, noradrenaline and cortisol are released into the bloodstream. Their heart pounds faster and their rate of breathing increases. Digestion is suspended so that extra blood can be diverted to their muscles. Their pupils dilate, focus improves, hearing perks and stored fats and sugars are pumped into their bloodstream to provide an instant source of energy.

An alcohol-depressed nervous system has just experienced some degree of stimulation. No saber tooth tiger to fight or flee, their new found sense of alertness instead emboldens them to ask for another round. "Bartender, I'm ready for another drink!"

The cycle can be repeated again and again, with an increasingly sedated body gradually becoming less responsive to nicotine-induced stimulation.

What significance does this have to a recovering addict? It may mean that without nicotine periodically slapping you awake, that you may feel alcohol's effects sooner or after fewer drinks.

The solution can be as simple as learning to drink a bit more slowly, spacing drinks a bit further apart or simply drinking less.

Co-dependency concerns - Amazingly, roughly eighty percent of alcoholics smoke nicotine.[159] Has alcohol become central to your life? Are you chemically dependent upon it? If not an alcoholic, have you conditioned your mind to use and expect alcohol too often or to expect too much?

Even social drinkers need to take extreme care when attempting to extinguish alcohol related nicotine use cues. So, what can we do if alcohol use and its inhibition diminishing effects seem to be key factors in preventing us from breaking nicotine's grip upon our mind and life?

If unable to drink in a controlled manner or if drinking is adversely affecting our life, work,

---

158 McKee SA, Effect of transdermal nicotine replacement on alcohol responses and alcohol self-administration, Psychopharmacology (Berlin), February 2008, Volume 196(2), Pages 189-200.
159 DiFranza JR, Alcoholism and smoking, Journal of Studies on Alcohol, March 1990, Volume 51(2), Pages 130-135.

relationships or health, you may be dealing with problem drinking or even alcoholism.

Photo SAMHSA

As Joel sees it, "If a person says that they know that their drinking will cause them to take a cigarette and relapse back to smoking, and if they then take a drink and relapse, they are in effect problem drinkers, for they have now put their health on the line in order to drink."[160]

Is alcohol use your recovery roadblock? If so, while many mental health professionals remain reluctant to suggest simultaneous dual alcohol-tobacco withdrawal,[161] multiple studies suggest that smoking cessation may actually enhance the likelihood of long-term alcohol sobriety.[162]

A 2011 study reviewed 1,185 subjects who 9 years earlier had entered substance use treatment, 716 of whom had also smoked at the time, among which 14% had successfully stopped smoking within a year of substance use treatment.

It found that those who had stopped smoking within a year of entering substance use treatment had 240% greater odds of both remaining abstinent from drugs, drugs plus alcohol, or alcohol alone within the past year, than those who had continued smoking.[163]

The basic insights and skills needed to arrest any chemical dependency are amazingly similar. Recovering alcoholics schooled by quality treatment programs are already skilled in their use.

Research shows that while those with alcohol problems make fewer smoking cessation attempts, they are "as able to stop on a given attempt as smokers with no problems."[164]

WomensHealth.gov

Unfortunately, alcohol recovery programs have a tendency to actually destroy nicotine cessation attempts. "Many, if not most, alcohol recovery programs will inadvertently or very purposely push a new ex-smoker entering the program to smoke," writes Joel.

"Over the years I have in fact had actively drinking alcoholics in smoking clinics - people who made it abundantly clear that they knew they had drinking

160 Spitzer, J, Can people quit smoking and still drink alcohol? Joel's Library, WhyQuit.com, October 2005.
161 Jacques D, et al, Quit smoking? Quit drinking? Why not quit both? Analysis of perceptions among Belgian postgraduates in psychiatry, Psychiatra Danubia, November 2010, 22 Supplement 1:S120-3.
162 Gulliver SB, et al, Smoking cessation and alcohol abstinence: what do the data tell us? Alcohol Research & Health, 2006 Volume 29(3), Pages 208-212.
163 Tsoh JY, et al, Stopping smoking during first year of substance use treatment predicted 9-year alcohol and drug treatment outcomes. Drug and Alcohol Dependence, April 1, 2011, Volume 114(2-3), Pages 110-1188.
164 Hughes JR, et al, Do smokers with alcohol problems have more difficulty quitting? Drug and Alcohol Dependence, April 28, 2006, Volume 82(2), Pages 91-102.

problems and smoking problems but wanted to treat the smoking first."

"I really do try to get them into alcohol treatment concurrently but cannot force them to do it. On more than one occasion I have seen the person successfully stop smoking, stay off for months and sometimes longer, and finally get into AA, only to be assigned a smoking sponsor who tells the person that he or she can't get off smoking and drinking at once, and who actually encourages the person to smoke again."

"Note the sequence here," says Joel. "The ex-smoker has been off nicotine for an extended time period but the smoking sponsor says that the person can't stop both at once. It is unfortunate that most alcohol and drug treatment programs just don't recognize smoking as another drug addiction."

Joel uses heroin to show the insanity of such advice. "You will not often see an AA sponsor say that you can't give up drinking and heroin at once, so if you have been off heroin for six months and now want to stop drinking, you should probably take heroin for a while until you get alcohol out of your system."[165]

Many of the lessons in FFN-TJH can be applied to arresting alcohol dependency. In fact, a number of them, such as a "one day at a time" recovery philosophy have deep roots in alcohol recovery programs.

Confronting alcohol related crave triggers - As discussed in detail in Chapter 11, if a drinker, you have likely conditioned your brain to expect nicotine while consuming alcohol. In fact, you may have created multiple alcohol related use cues. Encountering one of those use cues may cause a brief crave episode that can take up to 3 minutes before peaking in intensity. In that alcohol diminishes inhibitions, it the exception to the rule that we should try to quickly meet, greet and extinguish all learned nicotine use associations.

Regarding alcohol, it's prudent to allow ourselves a few days to get our recovery legs under us and move beyond peak withdrawal before drinking. Even then, due to diminished inhibitions, the smart move is to consider breaking drinking down into more manageable challenges that present fewer potential crave triggering cues.

Use associations between alcohol and nicotine can involve multiple cues. We may have use cues associated with entering a drinking location, engaging in a drinking related activity, sitting down, seeing alcohol containers, hearing ice cubes hit a glass or the sound of a bottle or can opening, picking up a drink, tasting that first swallow, or beginning to sense the onset of alcohol's inhibition diminishing effects.

We may have developed nicotine-alcohol use associations where the use cue is encountering a drinking acquaintance, friend or another nicotine user, being around lots of other users, seeing ashtrays, cigarette packs and lighters within easy reach, seeing a cigarette machine or visible packs or cartons for sale behind the bar, or even sight of a jug filled with free matches.

Use cues could be associated with engaging in conversation while drinking, or having conversation

165 Spitzer, J, Can people quit smoking and still drink alcohol? Joel's Library, WhyQuit.com, October 2005.

shift gears into debate or argument as alcohol's inhibition diminishing effects begin to be felt.

Impaired judgment and diminished inhibitions may have established nicotine use cues associated with hearing music, feeling the beat, singing karaoke, dancing, playing games, flirting, fear, rejection, acceptance, partying, joy, sadness or beginning to feel drunk and turning to nicotine to stimulate the body's nervous system.

So how do we tackle alcohol-nicotine use associations? Consider the benefit of learning to use alcohol and extinguish your primary alcohol-nicotine use associations in the safest environment available (usually your home), away from other potential use associations.

Once able to drink alcohol without using nicotine it's time to extinguish other nicotine-alcohol use associations. Consider not using any alcohol during your first encounter with other potential alcohol-nicotine use situations, or limiting alcohol use so as to allow yourself greater conscious and rational control.

Consider drinking a bit slower than normal, spacing drinks further apart or drinking water or juice between alcoholic drinks. Combine your intelligence with baby steps. Have an escape plan and a backup plan and be prepared to deploy both.

Since half of all fatal vehicle collisions involve alcohol use, if you do drink, make sure that driving a vehicle is not part of the plan.

Avoiding Blood Sugar Swing Symptoms

Hypoglycemia is a big word for what occurs when our "blood sugar (or blood glucose) concentrations fall below a level necessary to properly support the body's need for energy and stability throughout its cells."[166]

Causes of low blood sugar in non-diabetics include skipping or delaying meals, eating too little, increased activity or exercise and excessive alcohol.[167]

Warning signs include an inability to concentrate, anxiety, hunger, confusion, weakness, drowsiness, sweating, trembling, warmness, nausea, dizziness, difficulty speaking and blurred vision.[168]

Keep your blood sugar stable

Each hit of nicotine served as a spoon pumping stored glucose into our bloodstream via our body's fight or flight pathways. It allowed us to skip breakfast and possibly lunch without experiencing low blood sugar or hypoglycemic type symptoms.

166 hypoglycemia. (n.d.). Dorland's Medical Dictionary for Health Consumers. (2007). Retrieved from http://medical-dictionary.thefreedictionary.com/hypoglycemia on August 22, 2008.

167 National Institutes of Health, Hypoglycemia, National Institute of Diabetes and Digestive and Kidney Diseases, NIH Publication No. 03-3926, March 2003.

168 Hepburn DA, et al, Symptoms of acute insulin-induced hypoglycemia in humans with and without IDDM. Factor-analysis approach, Diabetes Care, November 1991, Volume 14(11), Pages 949-957.

One of recovery's greatest challenges is learning to again properly feed and fuel our body. It's not a matter of consuming more calories but learning to spread them out more evenly over our entire day, by eating smaller portions of healthy foods more frequently.

As an aid in blood sugar stabilization, unless diabetic or otherwise prohibited by your health or diet, we recommend devoting the money you would have spent in purchasing nicotine toward purchase and use of some form of natural fruit juice for the first 72 hours.

Juice will not only help stabilize blood sugar levels, it will aid in accelerating removal of nicotine from our blood. But don't over do it or go beyond three days as juice tends to be rather fattening. Make sure it's 100% natural juice, no sugar added and avoid fruit soda drinks and aides.

Cranberry juice is excellent. A 2008 study examined the effects of drinking 480 milliliters or 16 ounces of unsweetened, normal-calorie cranberry juice (280 calories) upon blood sugar. Analysis found that while low-calorie cranberry juice (38 calories) and water produced no significant changes in blood sugar levels, that normal-calorie cranberry juice resulted in significantly higher blood glucose concentrations within 30 minutes, which were no longer significant after 3 hours.[169]

As for fruit juices accelerating nicotine removal, the heart pumps about 20% of our blood through our kidneys. Our kidneys filter approximately 50 gallons or 189 liters of blood daily. This results in removal of about two quarts of waste products and extra water, which pass to the bladder as urine.[170]

The word "renal" means "of or relating to the kidneys." "Renal clearance" is defined as the volume of blood from which a chemical such as nicotine is completely removed by the kidney in a given amount of time (usually a minute).[171]

A controlling factor in determining renal clearance rate is the pH level of urine produced by our kidneys.[172] The more acidic our urine, the quicker nicotine is removed from the bloodstream.

A 2006 study found that drinking one liter of full-strength grapefruit juice (34 ounces or about 2 pints) will increase the rate by which the kidneys remove nicotine from blood plasma by 88%, as compared to when drinking 1 liter of water (231 milliliters of nicotine-free blood produced per

---

169 Wilson T, et al, Human glycemic response and phenolic content of unsweetened cranberry juice, Journal of Medicinal Food, March 2008, Volume 11(1), Pages 46-54.

170 Wilson T, et al, Human glycemic response and phenolic content of unsweetened cranberry juice, Journal of Medicinal Food, March 2008, Volume 11(1), Pages 46-54.

171 renal clearance. (n.d.). The American Heritage Dictionary of the English Language, Fourth Edition. Retrieved August 20, 2008, from Dictionary.com website.

172 Tucker GT, Measurement of the renal clearance of drugs, British Journal of Clinical Pharmacology, December 1981, Volume 12(6), Pages 761-770.

minute using grapefruit juice vs. 123 milliliters of blood when drinking water).[173]

The study found that even if the grapefruit juice was half-strength that nicotine's renal clearance rate increased by 78% (219 milliliters per minute).

The pH scale ranges from 0 to 14 with 7 being neutral. The further below 7 a substance is, the greater its acidity. The higher a substance is above 7, the greater its alkalinity. According to the FDA,[174] the below fluids have the following pH ranges:

- Cranberry juice   2.3 - 2.5
- Grapefruit juice   2.9 - 3.3
- Pineapple juice   3.3 - 3.6
- Orange juice   3.3 - 4.2
- Apple juice   3.4 - 4.0
- Prune juice   3.9 - 4.0
- Vegetable juice   3.9 - 4.3
- Tomato juice   4.1 - 4.6
- Milk   6.4 - 6.8

Depending upon urinary flow rate, renal clearance of nicotine may be as high as 600 milliliters per minute in acidic urine having a pH of 4.4, to as low as just 17 milliliters per minute in alkaline urine having a pH of 7.0.[175]

Aside from juices, adding extra fruit and vegetables to your diet will aid in helping stabilize blood sugars, and may aid in helping diminish weight gain.

A 2012 study found that the odds of successful smoking cessation for 14 months among the one-quarter of study participants consuming the greatest amount of fruits and vegetables daily was three times greater than among the one-quarter consuming the least.[176]

What we don't know is if most within the greater fruit and vegetable group were simply more health conscious to begin with, and thus more motivated.

But don't overdo it. Remember, our primary objective is to stabilize blood sugar during the most challenging portion of recovery, so as to avoid needless symptoms.

173 Hukkanen J, et al, Effect of grapefruit juice on cytochrome P450 2A6 and nicotine renal clearance, Clinical Pharmacology and Therapeutics, November 2006, Volume 80(5), Pages 522-530.

174 U.S. Food & Drug Administration, Approximate pH of Foods and Food products, Center for Food Safety & Applied Nutrition, April 2007.

175 Benowitz NL, et al, Nicotine chemistry, metabolism, kinetics and biomarkers, Handbook of Experimental Pharmacology 2009; Volume 192), Pages 29-60.

176 Haibach JP, et al, A Longitudinal Evaluation of Fruit and Vegetable Consumption and Cigarette Smoking. Nicotine & Tobacco Research, May 21, 2012.

Your Blood Caffeine Level Will Double

Caffeine is a mild central nervous system stimulant found in coffee beans, tea leaves and cocoa beans. The question during early recovery is, can you handle a doubling of your normal daily caffeine intake without experiencing "caffeine jitters" or other symptoms of over-stimulation?

Nicotine somehow doubles the rate by which the body depletes caffeine. What's that mean? It means that if we were drinking two cups of coffee while using nicotine, once nicotine use ends, that the stimulant effect of those two cups might now feel like four.

According to a 1997 study, "continuous caffeine consumption with smoking cessation has been associated with more than doubled caffeine plasma levels. Such concentrations may be sufficient to produce caffeine toxicity symptoms in smoking abstinence conditions."[177]

The study found "a significant linear increase in caffeine sputum levels across 3 weeks post cessation," and that "three weeks after cessation, concentrations reached 203% of baseline for the caffeine user."

An earlier study found that the clearance rate of caffeine from blood plasma averaged 114 milliliters per minute in nicotine smokers and 64 milliliters per minute in non-smokers.[178]

Symptoms of caffeine intoxication have been seen with as little as 100 milligrams of caffeine daily, and may include restlessness, nervousness (anxiety), excitement, insomnia, a flushed face, increased urination and gastrointestinal complaints.

Intoxication symptoms seen when more than 1 gram of caffeine is consumed per day include muscle twitching, rambling flow to thoughts and speech, irregular or rapid heartbeat, irritability and psycho-motor agitation.[179]

Most of us can handle a doubling of our daily caffeine intake without getting the jitters. But how can we tell whether the anxieties we feel are related to nicotine cessation or to too much caffeine? It isn't easy.

Experiment with an up to 50% reduction in daily caffeine intake if at all concerned. Be careful not

---

177 Swanson JA, et al, The impact of caffeine use on tobacco cessation and withdrawal, Addictive Behavior, Jan-Feb 1997, Volume 22(1), Pages 55-68.

178 Joeres R, Influence of smoking on caffeine elimination in healthy volunteers and in patients with alcoholic liver cirrhosis, Hepatology, May-June 1988, Volume 8(3), Pages 575-579.

179 American Psychiatric Association, Caffeine Intoxication, Diagnostic and Statistical Manual of Mental Disorders, Fourth Edition, Text Version, Page 232.

to reduce normal caffeine intake by more than 50% unless you want to add the symptoms of caffeine withdrawal to those of nicotine withdrawal.

Caffeine withdrawal symptoms can include headache, fatigue, decreased energy, decreased alertness, drowsiness, decreased contentedness, depressed mood, difficulty concentrating, irritability, and a foggy mind. Symptoms typically begin 12 to 24 hours after caffeine use ends, reach peak intensity at 20 to 51 hours, and normally last 2 to 9 days.[180]

The following is a sampling of the number of milligrams (mg) of caffeine "typical" in various substances:[181]

- 85mg   coffee - 8 ounces drip brewed
- 80mg   "energy drinks"
- 75mg   coffee - 8 ounces percolated
- 40mg   espresso - 1 ounce servings
- 40mg   tea - 8 ounces brewed
- 28mg   tea - 8 ounces instant
- 26mg   baker's chocolate - 1 ounce
- 25mg   iced tea - 8 ounces
- 24mg   some soft drinks - 8 ounces
- 20mg   dark chocolate - semi sweet - 1 ounce
- 6mg   cola beverage - 8 ounces
- 5mg   chocolate mild beverage
- 4mg   chocolate flavored syrup
- 3mg   coffee - decaffeinated

The stimulant effects of a 24mg soft drink before bed or a 20mg chocolate bar could now feel like two sodas or two chocolate bars. Consider a modest reduction of up to one-half if experiencing difficulty falling to sleep.

Look at it this way, if we were a big caffeine user, it's cheaper now. We get twice the stimulation for half the price.

Crutches

A crutch is any form of reliance that is leaned upon so heavily in supporting or motivating recovery, that if suddenly removed would significantly elevate risk of relapse.

Why lean heavily upon any person, place, thing or activity? Why risk sudden removal? Why allow our freedom, healing and possibly our life to rest upon the presence of a source of support whose reliability is beyond

180 Juliano LM, et al, <u>A critical review of caffeine withdrawal: empirical validation of symptoms and signs, incidence, severity, and associated features</u>, Psychopharmacology, October 2004, Volume 176(1), Pages 1-29.

181 National Institute of Health, <u>Caffeine</u>, National Toxicology Program, webpage updated 04/23/08, http://cerhr.niehs.nih.gov/common/caffeine.html

our ability to control?

Recovery buddies - People can serve as crutches. Creating and leaning heavily upon the expectation that some other person will behave in a supportive manner is dangerous.

While great when our expectations are fulfilled, what happens when they're not? Why tie our fate to the actions or inactions of others, to their sympathies, time demands, comments, emotions, lack of dependency recovery understanding or indifference?

While there's nothing wrong with enjoying their support when it's there, picture your recovery standing entirely on its own.

Picture your core motivations and resolve actually strengthening during moments when those who we thought would be supportive are not. Take pride in the fact that you are standing and saying "no" to wanting without use of any crutches.

Waiting for another nicotine dependent person to join us in recovery is a delay tactic. We're waiting for a crutch.

While wonderful when able to share coming home with a spouse, significant other, family member, friend or co-worker, serious drug recovery programs never partner two new ex-users together.

Such programs understand that risk of relapse during early recovery remains high. Partnering newbies with newbies increases likelihood that should one relapse that the other will follow suit. Instead, effective programs partner new ex-users with stable long-term ex-users.

Successful recovery isn't about learning from someone who may know less about successful cessation than we do. It isn't about coming together to commiserate or share addiction war stories.

Success is not dependent on being able to lean on a person who ended nicotine use with us, but understanding what's required to stand on our own. It's about abiding by the Law of Addiction (Chapter 2).

While obedience to the Law provides 100 percent odds of success, how many smokers have ever heard of it? Statistically, only 1 in 8.7 who attempt recovery succeed in remaining nicotine-free for six months.[182]

That doesn't mean that two new ex-users navigating recovery together can't both succeed. We see it all the time. In fact, it is impossible for either to relapse so long as neither allows nicotine back into their body.

Romeo and Juliet is the tragic tale of a love so great that it would rather be dead than apart.

Each year millions surrender life itself rather than stop smoking. But this isn't Romeo and Juliet

---

182 Polito, JR, Does the Over-the-counter Nicotine Patch Really Double Your Chances of Quitting? WhyQuit.com, April 8, 2002.

being played out on some grand scale. It isn't love reaching for a deadly chemical but physical dependence upon one.

What are the odds that nicotine addiction won't be the cause of ending a marriage or other long-term relationship in which both are smokers and both refuse to stop unless the other stops too?

Statistically, roughly half of adult smokers smoke themselves to death. The death toll is staggering. Smoking is blamed for 20% of all deaths in developed nations.[183] Here in the U.S., the average female claimed by smoking loses 14.5 years of life expectancy, while the average males loses 13.2.[184]

Waiting on our partner to be our "recovery buddy" often proves deadly. One partner needs to be brave, go first, and blaze a trail home that the other can eventually follow.

There were a number of times during my thirty-year struggle where I wanted others to pick me up and carry me home. I waited, and waited and waited for dear friends to stop with me. Finally, I got my wish.

My best friend and I became "recovery buddies" in 1984. I recall two things about that experience. It was the only time during our friendship that we'd ever yelled at each other. I also recall that within an hour of learning that he had relapsed, that I relapsed too.

But the story had a healthy ending. Jim attended a 2002 recovery seminar I presented at the high school from which my daughters graduated.

Standing on the auditorium stage, I shared this crutch and "buddy system" lesson and our mutual failure 18 years earlier. I recall hoping that as a seasoned ex-user that I could now lend a hand in showing Jim the way home. He succeeded. And he's still free today.

As Joel's "Buddy Systems" article proclaims, "Take heart ... your primary focus needs to be on your own [success] now." "Soon you will be the seasoned veteran." "Many programs use the phrase, 'To keep it, you have to give it away,'" writes Joel. "No where is this more true than when dealing with addictions."[185]

---

183 Wald NJ and Hackshaw AK, <u>Cigarette smoking: an epidemiological overview</u>, British Medical Bulletin, January 1996, Volume 52(1), Pages 3-11.

184 Centers for Disease Control, <u>Annual Smoking-Attributable Mortality, Years of Potential Life Lost, and Economic Costs - United States, 1995-1999</u>, Morbidity and Mortality Weekly Report, April 12, 2002, Volume 51, Number 14, Pages 300-303, at Page 301.

185 Spitzer, J, <u>Buddy Systems</u>, April 29, 2000, http://www.ffn.yuku.com/topic/12760

Alcohol or other drugs - Joel's crutches article tells the story of one of his clinic participants turning to alcohol. "Boy did I ever drink my brains out, today," she enthusiastically proclaimed, "But I did not smoke!"

"She was so proud of her accomplishment," recalls Joel. "Two whole days without smoking a single cigarette, to her being bombed out of her mind was a safe alternative to the deadly effects of cigarettes."

"Just 24 hours earlier I had made a special point of mentioning the dangers of replacing one addiction with another," writes Joel. "In [stopping] smoking one should not start using any other crutches which might be dangerous or addictive."

Using alcohol, illegal drugs or addictive prescription medications as nicotine cessation crutches also elevates the risk of relapse due to diminished inhibitions while using them.

It can foster psychological associations that can present problems when unable to obtain or use them. And let's not forget the risk of establishing a chemical dependency upon them, and trading one dependency for another.

As Joel notes, "In many of these cases the end result will be a more significant problem than just the original problem, smoking. The new addiction can cause the person's life to end in shambles, and when it comes time to deal with the new dependence he or she will often relapse to cigarettes."[186]

Some Internet sites teach users to "do whatever it takes" to stop. Advice such as this is disturbing. "I guess that can be translated to taking any food, any drug, legal or illegal, or participate in any activity, no matter how ludicrous or dangerous that activity might be," writes Joel.

"Does the comment smoke crack cocaine, or shoot up heroin, or drink as much alcohol as it takes, or administer lethal dosages of arsenic or cyanide make any sense to anyone as practical advice to stop smoking," asks Joel? "If not, the comment 'do whatever it takes' loses any real concept of credibility."

"As far as stopping smoking goes, the advice should not be 'do whatever it takes to stop smoking,' but rather, 'do what it takes to stop,' " suggests Joel. "What it takes to stop is simply sticking to your commitment to Never Take Another Puff!"[187] And to be a bit more inclusive, to never take another puff, dip, chew, vape, patch or lick.

Exercise programs - At first blush, some crutches appear harmless. For instance, consider an exercise program that was started on your first day of recovery. But imagine your mind so tying the program to successful recovery that you became totally convinced that it was the primary reason you were succeeding.

What would happen if your exercise facility suddenly closed or if bad weather, transportation

---

186 Spitzer, J, Replacing Crutches, WhyQuit.com, Joel's Library, 1987.
187 Spitzer, J, "Do whatever it takes to quit smoking" March 19, 2003, http://www.ffn.yuku.com/topic/12855

problems, illness or injury made exercise impossible?

Exercise is always beneficial and I am in no way trying to discourage activity or exercise. However, while beneficial, exercise is not a nicotine dependency recovery requirement. View your program in terms of the direct benefits it provides, not as a primary source of recovery motivation. In your mind, see your recovery remaining strong with or without it, and your ability and willingness to exercise as a benefit rather than a requirement.

Internet support - The Internet can also become a crutch. While online support groups such as Freedom[188] or Turkeyville[189] can be extremely supportive, take care not to lean too heavily upon them.

What if your computer crashes and you can't afford a new one? What if your Internet service provider has problems and its servers crash for a week? Worse yet, what if the company hosting your online support site goes bankrupt or abruptly discontinues service? Picture your recovery and resolve remaining strong even without a computer.

Hope for the best yet prepare for the worst. Consider printing your favorite articles. If keeping an online recovery journal, diary or log, be sure to print or save a copy every now and then.

Remove as much risk as possible from all sources of support. Create dependability and longevity by preserving what you deem valuable.

Extra food - Food can become an "aaah" wanting satisfaction crutch, as can other oral hand-to-mouth substitutes for cigarettes, e-cigarettes, cigars, pipes, oral tobacco or replacement nicotine products. In fact, any new emotion producing activity or significant lifestyle change can be leaned upon as a crutch.

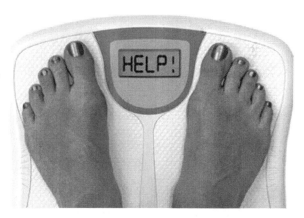

"If you are going to develop a crutch," writes Joel, "make sure it is one which you can maintain for the rest of your life without any interruption, one that carries no risks and can be done anywhere, anytime."

"About the only crutch that comes close to meeting these criteria is breathing. The day you have to stop breathing, smoking will be of little concern. But until that day, to stay free from cigarettes all you need to do is - Never Take Another Puff!"

Consider building your recovery so as to enable it to stand entirely on its own. If you now realize that you have developed a crutch, picture continuing on and succeeding even if it's suddenly removed. You'll be fine. The next few minutes are all we can control and each is entirely do-able.

188   Freedom from Nicotine - http://www.ffn.yuku.com
189   WhyQuit's Facebook Group - https://www.facebook.com/groups/whyquit/

Cessation Products

Open lies and hidden truths - Over the years I've written much on this topic. Two key points need making. First, any smoking cessation product manufacturer whose marketing suggests that few smokers succeed in stopping on their own has already lied to us.

Truth is, each year more smokers succeed by going cold turkey than by all other methods combined.[190] Truth is, while approved cessation products clobber placebo inside clinical trials, that they get clobbered just as badly by cold turkey in real-world use.[191]

Second, what logic is there in paying money to extend nicotine withdrawal for weeks or months when it takes less than 72 hours to rid the body of all nicotine? What sense does it make to buy and use a prescription product that poses risk of death, when our objective is longer life?

Cold turkey is fast, free, effective and smart - We nicotine addicts have been lied to by so many for so long that it's growing harder and harder to believe anyone.

Clearly, the most damaging and deadly lie of all is being told by those seeking to increase their product or procedure's market share by falsely suggesting that few nicotine addicts succeed in going cold turkey, that you need to be a super-hero to do so.

Billions in marketing have been spent during the past three decades in getting us to fear our natural recovery instincts. I submit that it has already cost millions their lives. Both direct and indirect cold turkey bashing not only foster diminished expectations upon being hearing the falsehood that your current attempt is twice as likely to fail, but a cessation confidence crisis for all still using.

Never in history have a greater array of approved smoking cessation products promised to double success rates. Skyrocketing cigarette taxes and prices, the smoke-free air movement sweeping the globe, and a steady stream of new studies on the negative effects of smoking, never in history have the coercive pressures upon smokers to stop been greater.

The latest magic cure varenicline (Chantix and Champix) has been widely used since 2006. Since then, millions of brave and highly motivated users have given it a try. Also, according to the CDC, more than 2.5 million U.S. smokers smoked themselves to death between 2004 and 2010.

Yet, during the six years between 2004 and 2010, decline in the U.S. adult smoking rate was just

---

190 Polito, JR, Are those who quit smoking paying with their lives because of NRT's failure? British Medical Journal, February 7, 2012, Page 344, e866; also see Cancer Council Australia, Most Australians still quit smoking unassisted, Oct. 8, 2010 (survey found that 69% of Australians quit smoking cold turkey); also see Chapman S, MacKenzie R (2010) The Global Research Neglect of Unassisted Smoking Cessation: Causes and Consequences. PLoS Med 7(2): e1000216. doi:10.1371/journal.pmed.1000216 ("Research shows that two-thirds to three-quarters of ex-smokers stop unaided").

191 Doran CM, et al, Smoking status of Australian general practice patients and their attempts to quit, Addictive Behaviors, May 2006, Volume 31(5), Pages 758-766 (88% of successful family practice patients stopped smoking cold turkey with cold turkey doubling success rates for NRT and Zyban); also see Polito, JR, Replacement Nicotine's Killing Fields, WhyQuit.com, February 11, 2012, http://whyquit.com/pr/021112.html

one percentage point, from 20 percent to 19 percent.[192, 193, 194]

Today, up to three quarters of all smokers continue to stop entirely on their own without use of any product, procedure, website or book.[195] And that's despite billions spent trying to get them to purchase replacement nicotine (NRT), rather risky Chantix or Champix pills,[196] stop smoking scapolomine shots invented by a quack now doing hard time for fraud, magic herbs or to motivate smokers to undergo hypnosis, acupuncture or laser therapy.

A 2006 Australian study followed smoking patients of 1,000 family practice physicians. It found that 88% of all successful ex-smokers succeeded by going cold turkey, and that those going cold turkey were twice as likely to succeed as those using the nicotine patch, nicotine gum, nicotine inhaler or Zyban (bupropion).[197]

We nicotine addicts make extremely easy prey. While normal to dream of painless cures, we must not close our eyes to actual results in an arena where the most ridiculous or even fraudulent cessation scheme imaginable should statistically generate success testimonials from 10-11% of users at six months and 5% at one year.[198]

These figures reflect the generally accepted odds of successful smoking cessation by those stopping entirely "on-their-own." It's why so many of us are eventually claimed by our addiction. It's the reason for this book, to share basic recovery insights needed to turn darkness to light.

Pretend that together we concoct a new magic cessation product that we name Billy Bob's Lima Bean Butter. Unless our product somehow undercuts natural cessation (as seen with NRT), 10-11 percent who use it should succeed and still be smoke-free at 6 months.

The beauty/horror of cessation fraud is that nearly all who succeed will deeply believe that our butter was responsible for their success. In fact, we won't be able to convince them otherwise. It would be a waste of breath to try.

It gets worse. We can dramatically inflate our 10-11 percent success rate by creating a study in which our butter gets used in conjunction with other high quality recovery interventions, that have themselves proven to double or even triple success rates.

For example, we could combine our butter's use with coping skills development, behavioral therapy, or individual or group counseling, all of which have their own proven effectiveness.

---

192 Spitzer, J, "Do whatever it takes to quit smoking" March 19, 2003, http://www.ffn.yuku.com/topic/12855

193 CDC, Cigarette Smoking Among Adults - United States, 2007, November 28, 2008, MMWR Vol57, No. 45.

194 CDC, Vital Signs: Current Cigarette Smoking Among Adults Aged ≥18 Years --- United States, 2005--2010

195 Chapman S, MacKenzie R., The global research neglect of unassisted smoking cessation: causes and consequences, PLoS Med. 2010 Feb 9;7(2):e1000216.

196 Polito, JR, "Will Chantix really help me quit smoking?" WhyQuit.com, August 25, 2006.

197 Doran CM, et al, Smoking status of Australian general practice patients and their attempts to quit, Addictive Behaviors, May 2006, Volume 31(5), Pages 758-766; also see Polito, JR, Cold Turkey Twice as Effective as NRT or Zyban, WhyQuit.com, May 19, 2006.

198 Polito, JR, Does the Over-the-counter Nicotine Patch Really Double Your Chances of Quitting? WhyQuit.com, April 8, 2002.

Combining high quality counseling or support with use of Billy Bob's Lima Bean Butter would guarantee newsworthy results. Unfortunately, this success rate inflation tactic has been used in nearly all NRT, bupropion (Zyban) and varenicline (Chantix or Champix) clinical studies to date.

Imagine regular AA meetings where alcoholics come together to educate and support mutual successful ongoing recovery. Imagine the group's support dynamics achieving a rather impressive recovery rate of 35 percent at six months.

Now imagine someone trying to package and sell the program over-the-counter to alcoholics for $200 as a stand-alone, in-home, personal recovery tool, while suggesting that users would experience similar odds.

How long would it take for allegations of consumer fraud to begin flying once it was noticed that 93% buying and trying the program were relapsing to alcohol within six months (over-the-counter NRT's six-month rate is 7%)?

Pfizer's five original varenicline studies broke records for the number of counseling sessions, with up to twenty-five. To this day, Pfizer marketing continues to award full credit to varenicline.[199]

While approved smoking cessation products clobber placebo users inside clinical trials rich in support and counseling, real-world performance has been a disaster.

California,[200] Massachusetts,[201] Minnesota,[202] Quebec,[203] London,[204] Western Maryland,[205]

---

199 Chantix Lisa commercial - You Tube http://youtu.be/Suwx2d0H7XM "In studies, 44% of Chantix users were quit during weeks 9 to 12 of treatment compared to 18% on sugar pill;" also see www.Chantix.com where the site's hompage stated on August 5, 2012, "Proven to Work 44%" "In studies, 44% of CHANTIX users were quit during weeks 9 to 12 of treatment (compared to 18% on sugar pill)." Contrast Polito, JR, Is a 14% Chantix success rate worth risking death? June 14, 2011 WhyQuit.com Press Release at http://whyquit.com/pr/061411.html reviewing the 2011 Hughes Chantix study. Also see the five original Pfizer Chantix studies which include Gonzales D et al, Varenicline, an a4b2 Nicotinic Acetylcholine Receptor Partial Agonist, vs Sustained-Release Bupropion and Placebo for Smoking Cessation: A Randomized Controlled Trial. JAMA. 2006, Volume 296(1) Pages 47-55, during which participants received up to 14 counseling/support sessions lasting up to 10 minutes each by week 12 of varenicline use, with up to an additional 11 counseling/support sessions between weeks 13 and 52 of follow-up.
200 Pierce JP, et al, Impact of Over-the-Counter Sales on Effectiveness of Pharmaceutical Aids for Smoking Cessation, Journal of the American Medical Association, September 11, 2002, Volume 288, Pages 1260-1264.
201 Alpert, HR, Connolly GN, Biener, L, A prospective cohort study challenging the effectiveness of population-based medical intervention for smoking cessation, Tobacco Control, Online First, January 10, 2012.
202 Boyle RG, et al, Does insurance coverage for drug therapy affect smoking cessation? Health Affairs (Millwood), Nov-Dec 2002 Volume 21(6), Pages 162-168.
203 Gomez-Zamudio, M, et al, Role of pharmacological aids and social supports in smoking cessation associated with Quebec's 2000 Quit and Win campaign, Preventive Medicine, May 2004, Volume 38(5), Pages 662-667.
204 SmokeFree London, Tobacco In London, Facts and Issues, [see Figure 14], November 26, 2003.
205 Alberg AJ, et al, Nicotine replacement therapy use among a cohort of smokers, Journal of Addictive Diseases, 2005, Volume 24(1), Pages 101-113.

Nottingham,[206] Australia,[207] the United States,[208] and England,[209] it should bother all of us that after nearly three decades of widespread use that real-world cessation surveys continue to show that those buying and using approved products fail to perform better than those stopping entirely on-their-own.

Such cessation method surveys are inexpensive, quick and easy to generate. And successful ex-users have absolutely no reason to lie about how they finally achieved success.

But NRT stakeholders quickly dismiss such surveys as "unscientific." They argue that we can't trust smokers and ex-smokers to correctly remember the method they used, and whether or not it brought them success.

Frankly, what cannot be trusted and should be dismissed as unscientific is all smoking cessation clinical trial findings whose validity is grounded in use of placebo controls.

Placebo isn't a recovery method and it isn't cold turkey - Let me ask you, if I hand you a piece of nicotine gum or a nicotine lozenge, how long will it take you to tell me whether or not it really contains nicotine or is instead a nicotine-free placebo look-a-like?

Not all of us can do it. However, 3 to 4 times as many of us will be correct as guess wrong, and that's within one week of attempting to stop smoking.[210]

Pretend for a moment that while still hooked and using, that we hear about a new nicotine gum study at a nearby medical school that is offering participants three months of free nicotine gum. There's only one catch. Half signing up for the study will be randomly assigned to receive nicotine-free placebo gum instead.

Would we stick around and allow ourselves to be toyed with for the next 3 months if convinced that we had been given placebo gum instead of the real thing?   Neither did they.

In study after study, 80 to 90 percent of study participants report a history of prior stop smoking

206 Ferguson J, et al, The English smoking treatment services: one-year outcomes, Addiction, April 2005, Volume 100 Suppl 2, Pages 59-69 [see Table 6 where consistent with Doran 2006, 25.5% of those stopping without medication were still not smoking at 1 year versus 15.5% of NRT and 14.4% of bupropion users].
207 Doran CM, et al, Smoking status of Australian general practice patients and their attempts to quit, Addictive Behaviors, May 2006
208 Hartman AM. What does US national population survey data reveal about effectiveness of nicotine replacement therapy on smoking cessation? Paper presented at World Conference on Tobacco or Health, 12-15 July 2006, Washington, DC. Full Text available http://whyquit.com/NRT/studies/Hartman_NCI_NRT.pdf (see PDF pages 33 to 38); also see Pierce JP, et al, Quitlines and nicotine replacement for smoking cessation: do we need to change policy? Annual Review of Public Health, April 2012, Volume 33, Pages 341-356 (see Table 1 indicating that among light smokers of less than 15 cigarettes per day that 26% who stopped unassisted succeeded at 3 months versus only 19% who used NRT or prescription medication, and also that among heavy smokers of greater than 15 cigarettes that 15% of unassisted succeeded versus 9% who used NRT or prescription products).
209 UK NHS, Statistics on NHS Stop Smoking Services in England, April to December 2007 [see Table 6], April 16, 2008.
210 Dar R, et al, Assigned versus perceived placebo effects in nicotine replacement therapy for smoking reduction in Swiss smokers, Journal of Consulting and Clinical Psychology, April 2005, Volume 73(2), Pages 350-353 (3.3 times as many correctly determined assignment); also see Rose JE, Precessation treatment with nicotine patch significantly increases abstinence rates relative to conventional treatment, Nicotine & Tobacco Research, June 30, 2009, where 4 times as many placebo patch users correctly determined their placebo assignment as guessed wrong, and did so within one week of quitting.

attempts. Those attempts taught them to recognize the onset of their withdrawal syndrome. The more prior attempts they had made, the more expert they became at recognizing withdrawal's onset.

If true, what validity would there be in our gum study finding that twice as many nicotine gum users succeeded in stopping smoking as those chewing placebo gum?

Imagine the lack of intellectual integrity required to label victory by default, victories rooted in frustrated expectations, as having been "science-based." It's why use of placebo controls in smoking cessation studies has served as a license to steal.

As I wrote in a letter to the Canadian Medical Association Journal published in November 2008, "pharmacologic treatment of chemical dependency may be the only known research area in which blinding is impossible."[211]

You cannot fool cessation savvy nicotine addicts as to whether or not brain dopamine pathway wanting is being satisfied or not.

A June 2004 study was entitled "The blind spot in the nicotine replacement therapy literature: Assessment of the double-blind in clinical trials."[212] It teaches that anyone asserting that NRT studies were blind is not being honest, as far more study participants correctly determine their assignment as guess wrong.

This might surprise you, but those wanting to stop smoking cold turkey have never been invited to compete in clinical trials against self-selecting smokers seeking months of free replacement nicotine, bupropion or varenicline.[213]

Unlike those going cold turkey, those seeking free "medicine" joined the study in hopes of diminishing, not meeting, greeting and defeating their withdrawal syndrome.

Why are there no head-to-head clinical studies pitting medicine against cold turkey? Because if honest competition had occurred there would be no need for this explanation.

Nearly all cessation researchers have accepted funding and/or personal payments from the pharmaceutical industry. It is not reasonable to expect financially conflicted researchers to bite the hand that feeds them, as they would never receive any pharma money or research projects again.

The industry cannot permit intellectually honest studies as they would cost it billions in profits.

---

211 Polito JR, Smoking cessation trials, Canadian Medical Association Journal, November 2008, Volume 179, Pages 1037-1038; also see original online e-letter selected for publication, Polito JR, Meta-analysis rooted in expectations not science, E-Letter, Canadian Medical Association Journal, July 17, 2008; and a follow-up e-letter rebutting pharmacology meta-analysis editors' suggestion that blinding issues in drug addiction studies are no different than concerns seen in other studies, Polito JR, Why cessation blinding concerns differ from other clinical trials, E-Letter, Canadian Medical Association Journal, November 9, 2008.

212 Mooney M, et al, The blind spot in the nicotine replacement therapy literature: Assessment of the double-blind in clinical trials, Addictive Behaviors, June 2004, Volume 29(4), Pages 673-684.

213 Polito, JR, Flawed research equates placebo to cold turkey, WhyQuit.com, March 12, 2007.

Smoking cessation clinical trial research is increasingly void of scientific integrity. Most calling themselves researchers are now little more than glorified salesmen.

We have now seen more than 200 placebo-controlled smoking cessation NRT, bupropion and varenicline studies, when nearly all agree that placebo affords study participants the worst possible odds of success.

Today, the National Institute of Health's clinical trials registry identifies more than 200 new smoking studies that are using placebo controls.[214]

Why? It's simple. It's all about money.

How many study participants assigned to placebo are facing their final cessation opportunity before experiencing a smoking induced heart attack, stroke, or being diagnosed with terminal cancer or emphysema?

Instead of subjecting them to the worst cessation method known (placebo), why not instead use the best proven treatment as the study's control, and then see how the new method being evaluated compares to the best?

Principle 32 of the World Medical Association's (WMA) Declaration of Helsinki commands that the "benefits, risks, burdens and effectiveness of a new intervention must be tested against those of the best current proven intervention" and that placebos should not be used unless "compelling and scientifically sound methodological reasons" are demonstrated.[215]

How many desperate study participants who were down to their final opportunity have smoking cessation researchers needlessly killed? Do they care or was money more important?

One reasons researchers use placebo instead of the "best current proven intervention" is that placebo promises the greatest margin of victory possible and the biggest news headlines.

Also, in pitting cessation products against each other, unless a tie, one must win and one must lose. Think about GlaxoSmithKline, maker of Nicorette gum, the Commit nicotine lozenge, the Nicoderm CQ patch and Zyban. Would you want any of your products losing to another?

Pharmaceutical companies avoid risk of defeat in head-to-head product competition by use of a control that isn't a real cessation method. This way, no company economic interest gets harmed. Unfortunately, the lives of clinical trail participants are being sacrificed by a near ethic-less headline seeking smoking cessation research industry that's driven by income and study funding.

---

214 National Institute of Health, www.ClinicalTrials.gov, visited December 2008, search: placebo + smoking
215 World Medical Association, <u>Declaration of Helsinki, Ethical Principles for Medical Research Involving Human Subjects,</u> Adopted by the 18th WMA General Assembly, Helsinki, Finland, June 1964, and last amended by the 59th WMA General Assembly, Seoul, October 2008.

What Big Pharma doesn't want us to know - Clinical smoking cessation studies reflect the worst junk-science ever perpetrated upon humans.

Regretfully, real scientists turned their heads as financial stakeholders redefined "cessation" from meaning ending nicotine use to replacing it. They remained silent as the pharmaceutical industry re-labeled a natural poison "medicine" and termed its use "therapy."

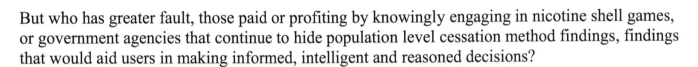

And why total silence when seeing apples compared to oranges? What sense does it make to compare the accomplishment of someone who has stopped using nicotine to stimulate brain dopamine pathways, to someone who continues stimulation by use of NRT, e-cigarettes, smokeless tobacco, Zyban, Chantix or Champix?

But who has greater fault, those paid or profiting by knowingly engaging in nicotine shell games, or government agencies that continue to hide population level cessation method findings, findings that would aid users in making informed, intelligent and reasoned decisions?

Until recently, I struggled trying to understand why government health officials actually discourage natural cessation. For years, I toyed with the possibility that health bureaucrats had grown lazy, don't read cessation studies, are generally stupid or simply don't care.

It wasn't until July 2012 that I learned about the CDC Foundation. Established by Congress in 1995, it's a non-profit organization in which corporations such as GlaxoSmithKline and Pfizer partner with the CDC, by making financial donations towards projects that the industry wants the CDC to study.

Online documents at www.cdcfoundation.org suggest that the amounts actually paid by cessation product makers are secret. What isn't secret is the partnership between the CDC and the industry.

What percentage of over-the-counter (OTC) NRT users are still not smoking at six months or one year? Would this be important to know? I challenge you to locate an answer to this important question on any government, commercial or health website advocating NRT use.

A March 2003 study, conducted by paid NRT industry consultants, combined and averaged all seven OTC NRT patch and gum studies.[216] OTC studies are important because their design is as close as possible to the way these products are used in the real world. Study participants simply walk into the pharmacy, purchase or are given the product, and then use it without any formal counseling, education or support.

Researchers found that only 7% of OTC study participants were still not smoking at six-months. That's right, a product with a 93% failure rate. It's actually worse. The same industry consultants also published a November 2003 study which found that as many as 7% of successful gum nicotine users were still hooked on the gum at six months.[217] Obviously these were two different studies.

---

216 Hughes, JR, Shiffman, S, et al., <u>A meta-analysis of the efficacy of over-the-counter nicotine replacement</u>, Tobacco Control, March 2003, Volume 12, Pages 21-27.
217 Shiffman S, et al, <u>Persistent use of nicotine replacement therapy: an analysis of actual purchase patterns in a population</u>

Even so, the math leaves you wondering if anyone actually breaks free from nicotine by chewing it.

Conclusion: "NRT appears no longer effective in increasing long-term successful cessation in California smokers."

Journal of the American Medical Associaton, Volume 288, Number 10, Pages 1260-1264, Sept. 11, 2002

What are the odds of success during a second or subsequent NRT attempt? Do the user's odds improve or get worse the second time around? Again, I challenge you to locate an answer to this rather important yet elementary question on any government or health organization website advocating use of replacement nicotine by nicotine addicts.

The pharmaceutical industry, government health agencies and health non-profits have known since as early as 1993 that if you have already tried and failed while using the nicotine patch, that your odds during a second patch attempt drop to near zero.[218]

Unlike cold turkey, where each failed attempt actually increases the odds of eventually self-discovering the Law of Addiction, the odds of success for the repeat NRT user dramatically decline with each failure. Why would anyone hide this data?

Nicotine addicts are also not told that by 2003 at least 36.6% of all continuing nicotine gum users were chronic long-term users of greater than 6 months.[219] Unlike the gum, which traps nicotine, the nicotine lozenge fully dissolves, delivering up to 25% more nicotine. We have no reason to believe that the percentage of current NRT users now hooked on the cure isn't climbing.

Let me share the first paragraph of an email I received. "I'm a 24 year old male who smoked cigarettes for about 6 years until stopping 2 years ago. Unfortunately, I did so by switching to Nicorette. In a horror story that I'm sure you've heard dozens of times, I'm now horribly addicted to the gum."

If able to get our brain's dopamine pathways adjusted to functioning without nicotine while at the same time continuing to use it, we should be extremely proud, because we are in fact super-heroes. But if among the 93 out of 100 first time OTC NRT users who quickly relapse, or among the nearly 100% who fail during a second or subsequent attempt, your brain dopamine pathways are functioning as designed.

They made a circuitry-activating event (nicotine's arrival) extremely difficult, in the short term, to

---

based sample, Tobacco Control, September 2003, Volume 12(3), Pages 310-316.
218 Tonnesen P, et al, Recycling with nicotine patches in smoking cessation, Addiction, April 1993, Volume 88(4), Page 533-539; also see Gourlay S. G., et al, Double blind trial of repeated treatment with transdermal nicotine for relapsed smokers, British Medical Journal, 1995 Volume 311, Pages 363-366.
219 Shiffman S, et al, Persistent use of nicotine replacement therapy: an analysis of actual purchase patterns in a population based sample, Tobacco Control, September 2003, Volume 12(3), Pages 310-316; also see Bartosiewicz, P, A Quitter's Dilemma: Hooked on the Cure, New York Times, May 2, 2004.

forget or ignore. Hence, we need to navigate withdrawal once use ends.

Replacement nicotine use defies the very purpose of withdrawal and recovery, the time needed to move beyond nicotine's influence. NRT users are not breaking free because of weeks or months spent toying with replacement nicotine, but in spite of having done so. Their success is testimony to their drive and determination.

Core dreams and desires for freedom are not altered by standing in front of any weaning product or even Billy Bob's Lima Bean Butter. It is "us" doing the work.

So long as we keep our day #1 dreams vibrant and alive long enough to become entirely comfortable within nicotine-free skin, we'll eventually be free to award full credit to any product or procedure we desire.

But should FFN-TJH serve as a tool in aiding your recovery, do understand that it was "you" who put its lessons to work, you who did all the lifting, and the glory is 100 percent yours!

Varenicline - Chantix & Champix - A few words of caution about varenicline (Chantix and Champix). Never in the history of cessation products have we seen such a wide array of serious side effects, including death.

We cannot accurately predict who will and will not sustain harm. What can be asserted with confidence is that varenicline is not the magic cure or nearly as effective in real-world use as marketing suggests.

So far, only 3 studies have pitted varenicline against NRT, Aubin 2008, Tsukahara 2010 and Dhelaria 2012. In each, varenicline failed to show statistical significance over NRT when assessing the percentage of users within each group who were not smoking at 24 weeks.[220]

The Aubin study notes that two varenicline users experienced severe depression, with suicidal ideation causing one to be hospitalized 11 days after ending use.

It found that among 376 Chantix users and 370 patch users that the likelihood of a Chantix users experiencing vomiting was 5.5 times greater, that decreased sense of taste was 5.3 times greater, abdominal pain x5, disturbances in attention x4.5, nausea x4, flatulence x4, constipation x3, headaches x2, dizziness x2, diarrhea x2, with 2.3 times as many Chantix users complaining of

---

220 Aubin HJ, et al, Varenicline versus transdermal nicotine patch for smoking cessation: results from a randomized open-label trial, Thorax, August 2008, Volume 63(8), Pages 717-724; Tsukahara H, et al, A randomized controlled open comparative trial of varenicline vs nicotine patch in adult smokers: efficacy, safety and withdrawal symptoms (the VN-SEESAW study), Circulation Journal, April 2010, Volume 74(4), Pages 771-778; and Dhelaria RK, Effectiveness of varenicline for smoking cessation at 2 urban academic health centers, European Journal of Internal Medicine, July 2012, Volume 23(5), Pages 461-464.

fatigue.

Does it make any sense to assume significantly increased risks, including risk of death, without significantly offsetting greater odds of success?

England's Stop Smoking Services may offer the highest caliber government sponsored cessation services of any nation. Services include free individual or group counseling and support. A 2008 study analyzing program performance found that at four weeks after starting varenicline use (Champix in the UK) that 63% of varenicline users were still not smoking as compared to 48% using nicotine replacement products (NRT) such as the nicotine patch, gum or lozenge, and 51% who stopped smoking without use of any product.[221]

While at first blush it might appear that varenicline has the lead, keep in mind that these are four-week results and that both varenicline and NRT users still face another 4-8 weeks of "treatment" before trying to adjust to living and functioning with natural brain dopamine stimulation.

The only long-term English evidence is from an April 2005 study that examined one-year success rates.[222] That study did not include varenicline as it wasn't yet on the market. It found that while 25.5% of those who attempted to stop without using any pharma product were still smoke-free at one year, that only 15.2% of NRT users and 14.4% of bupropion (Zyban) users were still not smoking.

Bringing together all we so far know suggests that when examining one-year rates, that varenicline will likely perform similar to NRT but well behind cold turkey.

Don't expect any researcher to ever include a copy of FFN-TJH or Joel's book as part of any fair, open-label study pitting cold turkey against varenicline or NRT. Doing so would produce a cold turkey victory that would destroy the industry's golden goose. Also, any researcher bold enough to conduct such a study would never receive pharma industry study funding again.

Joel's poll suggestion - Joel has also written extensively on pharma industry cessation products. He was warning about nicotine gum's ability to foster relapse or become a crutch, as early as 1984.[223]

He encourages those contemplating using industry products to take their own poll of all successful long-term ex-users who have remained nicotine-free for at least a year.[224] He encourages us to believe our own survey findings.

Joel reminds us that smoking declined from 42% to 23% over the past 40 years, but that the drop-off stalled in the 1990s. He finds it curious because that's when pharma industry NRT started experiencing widespread use.

---

221 UK NHS, Statistics on NHS Stop Smoking Services in England, April to December 2007 [see Table 6], April 16, 2008.
222 Ferguson J, et al, The English smoking treatment services: one-year outcomes, Addiction, April 2005, Volume 100 Suppl 2, Pages 59-69 [see Table 6].
223 Spitzer, J, Pharmacological Crutches, Joel's Library, 1984.
224 Spitzer, J, Quitting Methods - Who to Believe? Joel's Library, 2003.

"Nicotine gum was first approved for use in America in 1984, by prescription only. In 1991 and 1992, four patches were approved for prescription use. In 1996 all controls broke loose as the gum and two of the four patches went over-the-counter and Zyban (bupropion) was just coming into the fray."[225]

"Lets hope not too many miracle products for smoking cessation get introduced in the future as it may result in skyrocketing smoking rates," suggests Joel.

Why delay and extend withdrawal and neuronal re-sensitization for weeks or months? Keep in mind that a 7mg. nicotine patch delivers the nicotine equivalent of smoking seven cigarettes a day. In the end, all drug addicts who successfully recover must give-up their drug. In fact, all who successfully arrest their dependency eventually go cold turkey.

It is then and there that the rule for staying free becomes the same for all ... no nicotine just one day at a time.

Negative Support

"You're such a basket case, you should just give up!"

*"If this is what you are like not smoking,
for Gods sake, go back!"*

*"I'm trying but my smoking friends laugh,
tell me I'll fail and offer me smokes."*

No person's comment, look, laugh, stare or offer can destroy our freedom. Only we can do that. According to Joel, most of the time the person making comments or offers such as these has not considered their implications.[226]

It's comparable to telling someone on chemotherapy and in a really bad mood due to hair loss, nausea, and other horrible side effects, that they should get off that stuff because they are so irritable that they are ruining your day, suggests Joel.

"Of course, if analyzed by any real thinking person, the comment won't be made, because most people recognize that chemotherapy is a possible last ditch effort to save the other person's life."

"The decision to stop the treatment is a decision to die. So we put up with the bad times to help support the patients effort to save his or her life."

What's often overlooked, reminds Joel, is that stopping smoking too is an effort to save their life. "While others may not immediately appreciate that fact, the person stopping has to know it for him or herself. Others may never really appreciate the concept, but the person stopping has to."

---

225 Spitzer, J, <u>40 Years of Progress?</u> Joel's Library, 2004.
226 Spitzer, J, Negative Support from Others, February 15, 2001, http://ffn.yuku.com/topic/23019

As Joel notes, such comments are "usually from a spouse, a child of the smoker, a friend, a co-worker or just an acquaintance. It is much more uncommon that the person expressing it is a parent or even a grandparent. I think that says something."

"Parents are often used to their kids outbursts and moods, they have experienced them since they were infants. The natural parental instinct is not to hurt them when they are in distress and lash out, but to try to protect them. I think it often carries into adulthood, a pretty positive statement about parenthood."

But Joel has seen where people have encouraged friends or loved ones to relapse and then months or years later the smoker died from a smoking related disease.

"Sometimes the family member then feels great guilt and remorse for putting the person back to smoking," he says.

"But you know what? He or she didn't do it. The smoker did it him or herself. Because in reality, no matter what any person said, the smoker had to stop for him or herself and stay off for him or herself."

"How many times did a family member ask you to stop smoking and you never listened? Well if you don't stop for them, you don't relapse for them either. You stop for yourself and you stay off for yourself."

"I can't stop. My husband still smokes
and leaves his cigarettes lying around."

"I'm a bartender. How can I stop surrounded
by smoke and smokers at every turn?"

I recall attempts where I hoped smoking friends would be supportive in not smoking around me, and not leave their packs lying around to tempt me. While most tried, it usually wasn't long before they forgot.

I recall thinking them insensitive and uncaring. I recall grinding disappointment and intense brain chatter, that more than once seized upon frustrated support expectations as this addict's excuse for relapse.

Instead of expecting them to change their world for me, the smart move would have been for me to want to extinguish my brain's subconscious feeding cues related to being around them and their addiction.

The smart move would have been to take back my world, or as much of it as I wanted.

As I sit here typing in this room, around me are a number of packs of cigarettes: Camel, Salem, Marlboro Lights and Virginia Slims. I use them during presentations and have had cigarettes within arms reach for years.

Don't misconstrue this. It is not a smart move for someone struggling in early recovery to keep cigarettes on hand. But if a family member or best friend smokes or uses tobacco, or our place of employment sells tobacco or allows smoking around us, we have no choice but to work toward extinguishing tobacco product, smoke and smoker cues almost immediately. And we can do it!

Millions of comfortable ex-users handle and sell tobacco products as part of their job. You may find this difficult to believe, but I've never craved or wanted to smoke any of the cigarettes that surround me, even when holding packs or handling individual cigarettes during presentations.

Worldwide, millions of ex-smokers successfully navigated recovery while working in smoke filled nightclubs, restaurants, bowling alleys, casinos, convenience stores and other businesses historically linked to smoking.

And millions broke free while their spouse, partner or best friend smoked like a chimney.

Instead of fighting or hiding from the world, take it back. Why allow our circumstances to wear us down? Small steps, just one moment at a time, embrace challenge. Extinguish use cues and claim your prize once you do, another slice of a nicotine-free life.

Recovery is about taking back life. Why fear it? Instead, savor and relish reclaiming it.

Maybe I'll have a crave tomorrow. But it's been so many years (since 2001) that I'm not sure I'd recognize it.

Why fear our circumstances when we can embrace them? They cannot destroy our glory. Only we can do that.

Breathing Secondhand Smoke

Photo by National Cancer Institute

"I have to breathe smoke anyway so why not just go back to smoking."

"Contrary to popular opinion or misconceptions, the risks of secondhand smoke exposure are nothing compared to actually smoking yourself," writes Joel.
"As far as causing a relapse to needing nicotine, it can't do that. The trace amount of nicotine that can be absorbed from second hand smoke exposure is usually under 1% of what a smoker gets from smoking."

The primary metabolite that nicotine breaks down into is called cotinine. The benefit of researchers looking at cotinine levels in saliva, blood and urine, instead of nicotine, is that nicotine has a relatively short elimination half-life of about 2 hours. Cotinine's 17-hour half-life makes it a more stable indicator that nicotine was present.

The average of three studies reporting cotinine levels in the saliva of smokers was 260 ng/ml in women and 337 ng/ml in men.[227] Ng/ml stands for nanograms per milliliter. A nanogram is one billionth of a gram and a milliliter is one thousandth of a liter.

A 2006 study used spectrometry (a scope that measures wave lengths or frequency) to analyze cotinine levels of non-smokers after spending 3 hours in a smoke filled bar. Although they experienced an 8-fold increase in cotinine levels, their total average increase was still only 0.66 ng/ml or a little more than half of a nanogram.[228]

Let me quote from a 1979 Surgeon General report:

"Several researchers have attempted to measure the amount of nicotine absorbed by

---

227 Wells AJ, et al, <u>Misclassification rates for current smokers misclassified as nonsmokers</u>. American Journal of Public Health, October 1998, Volume 88(10), Pages 1503-1509.
228 Fowles J, et al, <u>Secondhand tobacco smoke exposure in New Zealand bars: results prior to implementation of the bar smoking ban</u>, The New Zealand Medical Journal, April 21, 2006, Volume 119, Page U1931.

nonsmokers in involuntary smoking situations. Cano, et al. studied urinary excretion of nicotine by persons on a submarine. Despite very low levels measured in the air (15 to 32ug/ma), nonsmokers showed a small rise in nicotine excretion; however, the amount excreted was still less than 1 percent of the amount excreted by smokers."

"Harke measured nicotine and its main metabolite, cotinine, in the urine of smokers and nonsmokers exposed to a smoke filled environment and reported that nonsmokers excreted less than 1 percent of the amount of nicotine and cotinine excreted by smokers. He concluded that at this low level of absorption nicotine is unlikely to be a hazard to the nonsmoker."[229]

It's the same analysis yet even less concern when considering the trace amounts of nicotine found in nightshade vegetables (tomatoes, potatoes, eggplant and peppers).

A 1999 nightshade vegetable nicotine study found that, "on the basis of the observed concentrations and the respective food consumption data for different countries, a distributive analysis of the results suggests that the mean daily dietary nicotine intake for the population of the countries for which consumption data were available is approximately 1.4 micro-grams per day."[230]

Contrast this study's 1.4 micro-gram figure (.0000014) for total daily dietary nicotine intake from nightshade veggies, to the 1 milligram of nicotine (.001) that enters the smoker's bloodstream after smoking a single cigarette. That one cigarette alone introduces 714 times more nicotine than a diet that includes nightshade veggies.

A critical fact that bears repeating is that just one puff of mainstream nicotine is sufficient to stimulate up to 50 percent of the brain receptors that sustain nicotine addiction.[231] Once we ring that bell it cannot be un-rung.

Breathing secondhand smoke introduces vastly more nicotine than nightshade veggies yet vastly less than taking a puff from a lit cigarette. One puff is sufficient to foster relapse, while secondhand smoke cannot.[232]

According to Joel, "as far as secondhand smoke and nicotine goes, you would have to be in a smoke filled room, non-stop for 100 hours, yes I am saying over 4 days to get the equivalent dose of nicotine delivered to a smoker from one cigarette."

"Other chemicals in secondhand smoke can reach some pretty toxic levels much quicker than that, in minutes not days. The side effects felt from being exposed to secondhand smoke are from carbon monoxide, hydrogen cyanide and some other noxious chemicals that can reach levels that

---

229 U.S. Surgeon General, Smoking and Health: A Report of the Surgeon General, 1979, Chapter 11, Page 24.

230 Siegmund B, et al, Determination of the nicotine content of various edible nightshades (Solanaceae) and their products and estimation of the associated dietary nicotine intake, Journal of Agriculture and Food Chemistry, August 1999, Volume 47(8), Pages 3113-3120.

231 Brody AL et al, Cigarette smoking saturates brain alpha 4 beta 2 nicotinic acetylcholine receptors, Archives of General Psychiatry, August 2006, Volume 63(8), Pages 907-915.

232 Spitzer, J, Withdrawal again? Quoting from Second Hand Smoke, November 21, 2001, http://www.ffn.yuku.com/reply/255814#reply-255814

are well above OSHA standards for safety," explains Joel.

But as many newbies discover, being forced to breathe secondhand smoke during recovery can be demoralizing. Breathing it can become a source of junkie thinking during times of challenge. "I have to breathe it anyway so why not just go back to smoking."

What this addict is really saying is, "I'm so concerned about the lesser harms of secondhand smoke and the damage it inflicts that "I'm going to suck main-stream smoke into my lungs and bloodstream, smoke that I know will cause far greater harm."

What they're saying is, "I'm so concerned about a risk that is many times less than I used to face, that I'm going to relapse back to the greater risk and take a 50% chance that I'll smoke myself to death 13 to 14 years early.[233]

Such thinking makes you wonder why it never, ever occurs to non-smokers to take up smoking for the same reason. Such logic only makes sense to a drug addict.

What such junkie thinking is saying is that, "I'm going to again become part of the problem and at times expose others to the smoke, smells and chemicals that my once again badly damaged senses will by then no longer find offensive."
Why allow such smoke screen junkie thinking to obscure the path home? Just one challenge at a time "endeavor to persevere," strive to see through it!

Extremely Vivid Use Dreams

Stay prepared for highly disturbing dreams of smoking, vaping or using oral nicotine products. They may be so vivid and so life-like that you'll awaken totally convinced that you've relapsed to using.

Such dreams are normal and expected. Physical healing makes early dreams the most vivid of all.

Picture a horizontal body of a new ex-user as they sleep during the early days of recovery. Mouth and throat tissues suddenly begin healing and re-sensitizing after years of being deeply marinated in nicotine, flavorings or toxin rich

"Sleep" 1897 Eugene Carriere - National Gallery of Art

---

233 Wald NJ and Hackshaw AK, <u>Cigarette smoking: an epidemiological overview</u>, British Medical Bulletin, January 1996, Volume 52(1), Pages 3-11.

tobacco tars. If a recovering smoker, picture the sweeper brooms lining lung bronchial tubes (your cilia) quickly regenerating and beginning to sweep mucus and tars up to the back of your throat. Add to that, rapidly healing and substantially more sensitive senses of smell and taste.

Now, throw a dream into the mind of this horizontal healing body and presto, the odors, juices, smells and tastes experienced come to life. They are remnants of use and real. What better proof could we possibly feel and sense of the amazing healing happening within? And it isn't unusual to experience more than one use dream.

The dreams that seem to cause the most concern are those that occur later in recovery, weeks or even months after full acceptance that this time is for keeps. Although nearly always described as a "nightmare," they are sometimes mistaken by the ex-user as a sign that they want to start using again.

It's here that we point out the obvious conflict. If a nightmare and not real, then why would any rational person want to invite their nightmare to become a real and destructive part of daily life? As Joel notes, seeing smoking as a nightmare is a healthy sign.

When we need to begin worrying is when we start liking such dreams. Should that occur, it's likely a sign that complacency has arrived, that your recovery is in need of remembering and accurately recalling what it was like to devote a portion of every waking hour of every day to feeding a mandatory chemical need.

And as for having smoking dreams long after ending use, such dreams are normal, yet not nearly as vivid as during the first week or so. We can no more erase from our mind our thousands of old nicotine use memories than we can our name. They reflect who we once were. What's amazing is that they happen so infrequently.

Bad Days

Ex-users should expect to experience bad days. Why? Because everyone has them, including never-users. But when a bad day occurs early in recovery it can become ammunition inside the challenged addict's mind as it searches for any excuse to use.

Blaming a bad day on recovery would never have crossed our mind if it had occurred the week before ending nicotine use. But now, nicotine's absence becomes a magnet for blame.

Would it ever occur to a never-user to reach for nicotine if having a bad day? It's a thought process peculiar to us nicotine

Photo by National Cancer Institute

addicts.

As Joel teaches, if the bad day happens during the first week after ending nicotine use then feel free to blame recovery as "it is probably the reason." "But as time marches on you need to be a little more discriminating."

Acknowledge bad days but allow your healing to live. "Sure there are some tough times," writes Joel, "but they pass and at the end of the day, you can still be free." Staying free means that, "in the greater scheme of things, it was a good day."

If you want to hear about a horrible day, talk to someone who relapsed after having remained clean for a considerable length of time. "They are having bad weeks, months and years," writes Joel. If a smoker, unless they again break free, they will likely face a day when their doctor tells them they now have a serious smoking related disease.

And imagine all the bad days they'll force loved ones to endure if among the 50% of U.S. adult smokers losing an average of roughly 5,000 days of life.[234]

Regardless of how we feel, every hour these minds and bodies are allowed to heal is good. Acknowledge the bad while savoring the good.

And the good only gets better. Ahead are entire days where you'll never once think about wanting to use. Just here and now, let the healing continue.

Weight Gain and Control

Escalating weight gain can gradually erode recovery motivation to the point of making the smoker's 50% odds of losing 13-14 years of life look more appealing than another pound. And let's be frank, many of us need to be concerned about weight gain.

But before going further, it's critical to note that a female smoker who is 64 inches tall (163cms) would need to gain 93 pounds (42kg) before experiencing the elevated risk of chronic heart disease generated by smoking.[235]

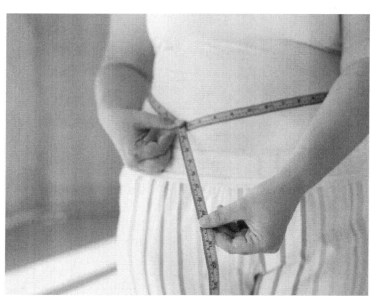

Photo by National Cancer Institute

234 Centers for Disease Control, <u>Annual Smoking-Attributable Mortality, Years of Potential Life Lost, and Economic Costs - United States, 1995-1999</u>, Morbidity and Mortality Weekly Report, April 12, 2002, Volume 51, Number 14, Pages 300-303, at Page 301.

235 Diverse Populations Collaboration, <u>Smoking, body weight, and CHD mortality in diverse populations</u>, Preventive Medicine June 2004, Volume 38(6), Pages 834-840.

As Joel teaches, recovery's battle line is extremely easy to see. As a nicotine addict, "you can't administer any nicotine. There is no gray area here. Eating is more complicated. You will have to eat for the rest of your life."[236]

For many, initial weight gain associated with nicotine cessation can be frightening. It isn't unusual to see up to 5 pounds of water retention weight gain during the first week.[237] It's normally associated with physiological changes and the pounds are easily and quickly shed.[238]

Nicotine increases release of anti-diuretic hormone (ADH or vasopressin). ADH prevents us from dehydrating by increasing water retention. According to Joel, during withdrawal some people experience a rebound type effect, where the normal effect of the drug is actually exacerbated when the drug is stopped.

"That temporary increase is likely what is causing the water retention (bloating) effect that many people notice when they first stop smoking, writes Joel. "The effect can go a few days and at times, even into the second week."

Still, most experience weight gain lasting beyond the second week. But why?

It's normal to notice food starting to taste better as early as day three. And normal to reach for food as a substitute hand to mouth psychological replacement crutch. And normal to attempt to replace missing nicotine generated dopamine "aaah" sensations with "aaah"s from extra food. And normal to need time to discover how to void the onset of hunger by fueling your body early and often, now that nicotine is no longer providing instant energy via your body's fight or flight response.

It is also entirely normal to experience a minor metabolism change associated with our body no longer needing to expend energy in attempting to expel scores of tobacco toxins, and no longer feeling nicotine's stimulant effects in making our body's organs work harder (primarily our heart).

Metabolism is all the chemical processes that occur within a living cell that are necessary to keep it alive. Some substances are broken down to create food energy while other substances necessary for life are synthesized or created.[239]

These processes themselves consume energy. "Basal Metabolic Rate" or BMR is the rate at which the body expends energy while at complete rest. It is expressed as "the calories released per kilogram of body weight [1 kilogram equals 1,000 grams or 2.2 pounds] or per square meter of body surface per hour."[240]

236 Spitzer, J, Patience in weight control issues, http://www.ffn.yuku.com/topic/11636 April 24, 2003.

237 Weight Control Information Network, NIDDK, National Institute of Health, August 2006.

238 National Institutes of Health, You Can Control Your Weight as You Quit Smoking, NIDDK, Federal Citizen Information Center of the U.S. General Services Administration, web page visited August 26, 2008 - http://www.pueblo.gsa.gov/cic_text/health/w8quit-smoke/#1

239 metabolism. (n.d.). The American Heritage Dictionary of the English Language, Fourth Edition. Retrieved from Dictionary.com on August 6, 2008.

240 basal metabolic rate. (n.d.). The American Heritage Dictionary of the English Language, Fourth Edition. Retrieved from Dictionary.com on August 6, 2008.

Were we ever really at complete rest while addicted to a stimulant? Does addiction's impact upon BMR account for nicotine cessation weight gain? Most studies examine short-term weight gain with little or no attempt to determine if the gain is due to diminished BMR, extra food or less exercise.

One long-term study followed weight change and body mass index (BMI) for 36 months. It found that the "contribution of smoking cessation to the BMI increase was practically negligible with "no considerable long-term weight gain."[241]

Most shorter studies report weight change results similar to those shared by the U.S. Surgeon General in his 1990 report on "The Health Benefits of Smoking Cessation."[242]

That report examined 15 studies involving 20,000 people and although "four-fifths of smokers gained weight during recovery, the average weight gain was only 5 pounds (2.3 kg)." "The average weight gain among subjects who continued to smoke was 1 pound.

Thus, smoking cessation produced a four pound greater weight gain than that associated with continued smoking." The Surgeon General also found that less than 4% gained more than 20 pounds.

A 1991 study found slightly greater weight increases than reported by the Surgeon General (2.8 kg or 6.2 lbs in men and 3.8 kg or 8.3 lbs in women). But it also found that while smokers weighed less than never-smokers before commencing recovery, "they weighed nearly the same" at one-year follow-up.[243]

Also noteworthy is a 2009 study which found average cessation weight gain of 3 kg for women and 5 kg for men. What's really interesting is its long-term finding of "no significant differences in weight gain over the 11-year period existed between never smokers and former smokers who had stopped at least five years ago."[244]

Theories as to potential causes are many[245] including genetics,[246] hand to mouth oral gratification replacement, improved senses of smell and taste (most notably sweets and salts), diminished exercise (isolation), changes in diet, and binge eating.

It isn't easy pinpointing the cause for consuming or burning even one extra calorie, especially when

241 John U, et al, <u>No considerable long-term weight gain after smoking cessation: evidence from a prospective study</u>, European Journal of Cancer Prevention, June 2005, Volume 14(3), Pages 289-295.
242 U.S. Surgeon General, <u>The Health Benefits of Smoking Cessation, a report of the Surgeon General</u>, 1990.
243 Williamson DF, et al, <u>Smoking cessation and severity of weight gain in a national cohort</u>, New England Journal of Medicine, March 14, 1991, Volume 324(11), Pages 739-745.
244 Reas DL, et al, <u>Do quitters have anything to lose? Changes in body mass index for daily, never, and former smokers over an 11-year period (1990--2001)</u>, Scandinavian Journal of Public Health, September 2009, Volume 37(7), Pages 774-7777. Epub 2009 Aug 7.
245 Wack JT, et al, <u>Smoking and its effects on body weight and the systems of caloric regulation</u>, The American Journal of Clinical Nutrition, February 1982, Volume 35(2), Pages 366-380.
246 Pietilainen KH, et al, <u>Physical inactivity and obesity: a vicious circle</u>, Obesity (Silver Spring), February 2008, Volume 16(2), Pages 409-414; also see, Waller K, et al, <u>Associations between long-term physical activity, waist circumference and weight gain: a 30-year longitudinal twin study</u>, International Journal of Obesity, February 2008, Volume 32(2), Pages 353-361.

our metabolism slows as we age.

Also keep in mind that study weight findings reflect averages. As seen above, up to 4% clearly go hog wild with food during recovery. Also not reflected by averages is the fact that body weight remains unchanged for many, while actually declining for some.

While natural for the rationalizing "junkie mind" in its quest for relapse justifications to want to blame cessation weight gain entirely on metabolic changes or genetics, factors totally beyond our ability to control (not increased eating or lack of activity), the math simply doesn't add up.

As a general rule, it takes 3,500 extra calories to add one pound of body weight, and burning 3,500 to shed one pound. A study of 6,569 middle-aged men who stopped smoking found that at one year they had consumed an average of 103 fewer calories per day, which the study attributed to metabolic change.[247]

Let's use that finding as our metabolic baseline. Let's assume that the average nicotine addict burns an extra 103 calories a day due to an increase in

Photo by National Cancer Institute

metabolism. If there is zero change in diet or activity after ending nicotine use, it would take 34 days without nicotine before a decrease in metabolism could be blamed for one pound of weight gain (34 x 103 = 3,502).

While true that minor metabolism changes mean fewer calories burned each day, if a former smoker, that change can be easily offset by taking advantage of the enhanced blood flow, greater oxygen levels and improved lung function you'll experience.

According to the Surgeon General, about half of smokers believe that smoking nicotine aids in controlling weight. The obvious question becomes, do "weight-concerned smokers endorse exaggerated beliefs in the ability of smoking to suppress body weight?"

Research suggests they do.[248] It also suggests that education may help correct exaggerated weight control beliefs, making recovery more inviting.

---

247 Hall KD, <u>What is the required energy deficit per unit weight loss?</u> International Journal of Obesity, March 2008, Volume 32(3), Pages 573-576.
248 White MA, et al, <u>Smoke and mirrors: magnified beliefs that cigarette smoking suppresses weight</u>, Addictive Behaviors, October 2007, Volume 32(10), Pages 2200-2210.

How to gain lots of extra weight - Recovery heralds an end to both nicotine's arrival and to the "aaah" wanting relief sensations replenishment generated. Some find themselves camping out inside the refrigerator or potato chip bags where they "aaah" themselves sick with food.

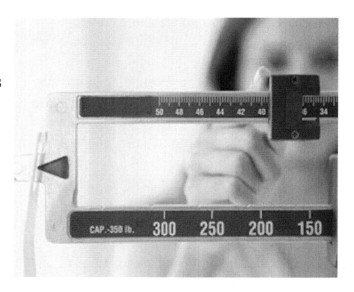

Others intentionally invite weight gain in order to justify relapse. It's a costly ploy. Having outgrown their entire wardrobe and now wearing bed sheets, visible extra pounds is a relapse excuse that's easy to see and sell to ourselves and loved ones.

Why do up the 4 percent who go hog wild continue such destructive behavior to the point of outgrowing their entire wardrobe? Few had any understanding of the dopamine pathway relationship between food and nicotine.

While normal healthy eating stimulates dopamine, during the first few days of recovery stimulation from normal eating obviously won't be sufficient to satisfy all wanting being felt.

Most of us used nicotine to satisfy subtle urges and wanting every waking hour of every single day. Over-eating cannot replace the stimulation effects of missing nicotine, at least not without leaving us as big as a house.

Still, some try. Instead of allowing the brain time to restore natural dopamine pathway receptor counts and sensitivities,[249] it's as if the up to 4 percent gaining more than 20 pounds attempt to make their brain's dependency wiring operate on taste's "aaah" influence instead of nicotine's.[250]

A 2012 study used brain-imaging studies to contrast eating food to smoking. It found that "food and smoking cues activate comparable brain networks" and "there is significant overlap in brain regions responding to conditioned cues."[251]

While compromised dopamine pathways have assigned the same use priority to nicotine as they have to eating food, there's one massive distinction. The brain does not die without nicotine, it thrives!

The sad part about attempting "aaah" relief replacement using large quantities of additional food is that, once the once the addict adopts and acts upon their demoralizing weight increase as their justification for relapse, the extra pounds are likely to remain.

---

249 Picciotto MR, et al, It is not "either/or": activation and desensitization of nicotinic acetylcholine receptors both contribute to behaviors related to nicotine addiction and mood, Progress in Neurobiology, April 2008, Volume 84(4), Pages 329-342.

250 de Araujo IE, et al, Food reward in the absence of taste receptor signaling, Neuron, March 27, 2008, Volume 57(6), Pages 930-941.

251 Tang DW, et al, Food and drug cues activate similar brain regions: A meta-analysis of functional MRI studies, Physiology and Behavior, June 6, 2012, Volume 106(3), Pages 317-324.

That 20+ pound bag of rocks they are carrying makes daily exercise more difficult, and thus less likely.

Now, instead of the former smoker's bloodstream being filled with oxygen reserves sufficient to allow prolonged vigorous physical activity, the significantly heavier relapsed smoker feels the effects of an oxygen-starved bloodstream that is once again occupied by large quantities of toxic carbon monoxide.

Instead of extra pounds being counterbalanced by greater self-esteem and self-worth at having broken free, the relapsed addict is heavier, less healthy and likely more depressed.

Worst of all, the smoker is again engaged in slow suicide via the gradual self-destruction of their body's ability to receive and transport oxygen.

Binge eating - Binge eating reflects a loss of control, that is, being unable to stop eating or control what or how much is consumed.[252] The primary psychological binge-eating cue is waiting too long before eating and sensing the onset of hunger.[253]

Although it may feel like the only way to satisfy a hunger craving is to eat as much food as quickly as possible, repeatedly doing so could result in binge eating becoming hunger's conditioned response.

As mentioned, there is substantial overlap between eating and dependency pathways. Former smokers who relapse to smoking often report an increase in the amount smoked, over the amount

smoked prior to their attempt. Akin to binge eating, it's as if their brain goes into starvation mode upon relapse and begins hoarding nicotine, resulting in a higher level of tolerance and need.

Binge eating is an attempt to satisfy hunger with a shovel. As nicotine addicts, we didn't need to eat regularly, as we used nicotine as a spoon. It pumped stored fats and sugars into our bloodstream via our body's fight or flight response. It allowed us to eat one or two larger meals each day and then use nicotine to release stored calories.

So, what happens when nicotine is no longer there? Can the addition of hunger cravings atop early nicotine withdrawal result in binge eating? Research suggests that it may be more of a concern for those having a high BMI.[254]

The root problem was that the active nicotine addict became conditioned to instantly satisfy the onset of hunger by using nicotine to release stored energy. Non-users who get hungry can't do that.

They have to eat food and then wait for digestion to turn off the body's hunger switch. Once we

---

252 Colles SL, et al, Loss of control is central to psychological disturbance associated with binge eating disorder, Obesity, March 2008, Volume 16(3), Pages 608-614.
253 Vanderlinden J, Which factors do provoke binge-eating? An exploratory study in female students, Eating Behaviors, Spring 2001, Volume 2(1), Pages 79-83.
254 Saules KK, et al, Effects of disordered eating and obesity on weight, craving, and food intake during ad libitum smoking and abstinence, Eating Behaviors, November 2004, Volume 5(4), Pages 353-63.

become non-users, when hunger strikes, whether we eat with a toothpick or shovel, we will need to wait for digestion to satisfy hunger.

It is critical that we quickly re-learn how to properly fuel our body. Yes, it takes a bit of practice to now that instant feedings from liver to bloodstream are history. And we should fully expect to confront hunger if we insist upon skipping meals.

While eating, it's beneficial to learn to chew our food longer and more slowly. Doing so allows a mouth enzyme (salivary amylase) to begin breaking down carbohydrates. This will speed digestion and aid in satisfying hunger sooner.

Research suggests that we eat slower when we turn off and tune out distractions. Maintain your focus on the act of eating and chewing and you'll actually eat less.

But what if you forget to eat and hunger arrives? If you should find yourself reaching for extra food, reach for healthy, low calorie foods such as fresh vegetables and fruits. It's best to have them washed, pre-cut and in the refrigerator in a bowl of cold water, available and ready to eat within seconds of feeling hungry.

Fear's unburned calories - Imagine being so consumed by fear of failure that you withdraw from life. How many calories are burned while hiding in a closet, lying in bed watching television or setting at a computer and clicking a mouse?

Photo by National Cancer Institute

Yes, some of us take the term "quitting" literally and withdraw from life entirely.

Body weight will climb if the amount of daily energy expended substantially declines, while the number of calories consumed remains the same or increases. Also consider that 12 of 15 studies since 2006 have found that exercise reduces smoking cessation cravings.[255]

Demoralizing weight gain is fertile ground for destroying freedom's dreams. The only activity we

---

255 Roberts V, et al, <u>The acute effects of exercise on cigarette cravings, withdrawal symptoms, affect, and smoking behaviour: systematic review update and meta-analysis</u>, Psychopharmacology (Berlin), July 2012, Volume 222(1), Pages 1-15. Epub 2012 May 15.

need end during recovery is nicotine use. Don't allow fear to transform recovery into a prison.

Reaching for a zero calorie "aaah" - The cornerstone of our dependency was nicotine's ability to release dopamine and briefly end wanting. And yes, an extra mouthful of food also provides a short-lived burst of dopamine. But reflect on how many times and how long each day that you devoted to nicotine use.

What if, day after day, you started reaching for and eating extra food, as often and long as you reached for and used nicotine? Yes, reaching for and adopting extra food as a nicotine replacement crutch could turn into a "huge" mistake.

Some researchers classify increased eating as a symptom of nicotine withdrawal.[256] If true, it's clearly one within our ability to minimize.

Consider reaching for a non-fat "aaah" sensation. Take a slow deep breath. Do you feel the "aaah" while exhaling? Drink a glass of cool and refreshing water when thirsty. Do you feel the "aaah" that arrives when satisfying thirst?

Give your favorite person a big, big hug. Are you feeling it now? Take your normal walk, even if just around the yard but this time go a little further or a little quicker than normal. Do you feel accomplishment's "aaah"?

Dopamine "aaah" wanting relief sensations are the mind's way of motivating behavior. Lifetimes of living our priorities teacher's lessons, we each have a hefty collection of durable "aaah" wanting relief memories.

Reach for the healthy zero calorie "aaah" if seeking relief from wanting without weight gain.

Picking mealtime - Nicotine no longer our spoon, increasing the frequency of meals while decreasing the amount eaten may be all that's needed to avoid adding hunger atop withdrawal.

Instead of eating large meals, consider eating little and often as a means to enhance appetite control. One study found that eating more frequently resulted in 27% fewer calories being consumed.[257]

Photo by National Cancer Institute

256 Benowitz NL, <u>Neurobiology of nicotine addiction: implications for smoking cessation treatment</u>, The American Journal of Medicine, April 2008, Volume 121(4 Suppl 1), Pages S3-10.

Consider fueling your body with small, healthy food portions at least five times daily during the first two weeks. Doing so should diminish blood-sugar swings and hunger pains, thus reducing risk of binge eating.

Ending Mealtime - Many of us conditioned our mind to believe that eating was complete and mealtime was over by putting a cigarette between our lips or oral tobacco into our mouth. Now, without a new cue, there may be no clear signal to our brain that our meal is complete. It could result in reaching for additional food with zero leftovers.

Healthy meal completion cues may be as simple as pushing away or getting up from the table, standing and stretching, clearing the table, reaching for a toothpick, taking a slow deep breath, doing the dishes, giving a hug or kiss, stepping outside, brushing our teeth, a stick of sugarless gum or a walk.

Diminishing body weight - A "diet" is a temporary program for losing weight, which by definition ends. The key to sustained weight control isn't dieting. It's in committing to minor changes in our daily calorie intake or activity level that become part of the fabric of our life.

If the removal of one pound of body weight requires the expenditure of 3,500 calories, attempting to burn all 3,500 during a single session of activity or exercise may leave us tired and sore. It might discourage us from being active again tomorrow. Instead, consider a small yet deliberate increase in today's level of physical activity over yesterday's, or if today's level seemed sufficient, maintaining that level tomorrow.

It can be exercise or a bit more of any physical activity that we love and enjoy. Consider gardening, walking your favorite path, visiting or caring for a neighbor, extra house or yard work, a lap around the block, a bike ride or any other activity that expends energy.

Photo by National Cancer Institute

Although a minor daily activity adjustment may seem insignificant, burning just 58 extra calories per day will cause our body weight to decline by half a pound per month (1,740 fewer monthly calories). What if we add a minor change in eating patterns to a minor activity adjustment?

If we consume 58 fewer calories per day we would experience a total monthly decline of roughly 3,500 calories and the loss of one pound per month. Learning to sustain these minor lifestyle adjustments could mean 12 fewer pounds within a year!

How do we lose 12 pounds? Baby steps ... another moment of activity, a few less calories, just one ounce at a time!

Small adjustments can be made anytime. As mentioned, we can eat more often while consuming

257 Speechly DP, et al, <u>Greater appetite control associated with an increased frequency of eating in lean males</u>, Appetite, December 1999, Volume 33(3), Pages 285-297.

the same or less, focus upon, savor and chew each bite longer, take just one less bite, get comfortable leaving something on our plate, use a tad less butter, choose baked over fried, portion control or cooking less food, one cookie versus two, eliminating evening snacks, or trading empty carbohydrates for longer lasting ones.[258]

Get excited about climbing from the deep ditch in which our addiction forced us to live. Savor the richness and flavor of life beyond. Be brave and explore the world that obedience to our dependency's wanting kept hidden from view.

If already impaired or disabled by smoking, your physician should be able to assist in developing an increased activity or exercise plan appropriate to your abilities, even if done while on oxygen, in a wheelchair or in bed.

Photo by National Cancer Institute

Should you find yourself gaining extra pounds during recovery, don't beat yourself up. Your breathing and circulation will improve with each passing day. Whether realized or not, your endurance potential is slowly on the rise.

In a way, we are turning back the clock to a time when we had greater ability to engage in prolonged vigorous physical activity. As smokers, most of us lacked the ability to build cardiovascular endurance. Not any more!

Aging gracefully does not require "dieting." Our slowing metabolism simply requires a minor calorie or activity adjustment now and then, which over time results in the desired body weight.

But what if your dopamine pathways refuse such simplicity when it comes to food? Frankly, I'd rather be slightly bigger and alive, than a tad smaller but dead. Today and tomorrow are worth vastly more than a few extra pounds.

Menstrual Cycle Considerations

A complex interaction of hormones cause many women of childbearing years to experience physical, psychological, and emotional symptoms related to their menstrual cycle.

An estimated 80% experience premenstrual symptoms, which may include: irritability, tension, anxiety, depression, restlessness, headaches, fatigue and cramping. The severity of symptoms can range from mild to disabling.

So how does a woman experiencing significant menstrual symptoms successfully navigate nicotine dependency recovery?

The menstrual cycle can be broken down into two primary segments, the follicular and luteal

258 The Glycemic Index, glycemicindex.com, University of Sidney, 2002, website accessed August 9, 2008.

phases. The follicular or pre-ovulation phase is when significant hormonal changes occur. It announces the first day of a woman's cycle, includes the period of menstrual bleeding and normally lasts in the neighborhood of two weeks.

The luteal phase commences at ovulation, normally lasts two weeks and ends the day before her next period.

A 2008 study tried to determine if the menstrual phase during which a woman attempts to stop smoking affects the risk of smoking relapse.[259]

A total of 202 women were assigned to either commence recovery during the luteal phase or the follicular phase. After 30 days, 34% of women who started during the luteal phase were still not smoking, versus only 14% who started during the follicular phase.

While normal to focus on the 34%, what I find encouraging is the 14%. As they demonstrate, success is achievable even if commencing recovery during the follicular phase, during significant premenstrual symptoms.

Hormone related stress and tension might actually accelerate nicotine elimination by turning urine more acidic, thus causing the kidneys to draw the alkaloid nicotine from the bloodstream quicker (see Chapter 4 "Use relieves stress and anxiety").

The question now being asked is, is addiction to smoking nicotine a cause of premenstrual syndrome (PMS)? A ten year study published in 2008 followed 1,057 women who developed PMS and 1,968 reporting no diagnosis of PMS, with only minimal menstrual symptoms.[260]

After adjustment for oral contraceptives and other factors, the authors found that "current smokers were 2.1 times as likely as never-smokers to develop PMS over the next 2-4 years." The study concludes, "Smoking, especially in adolescence and young adulthood, may increase risk of moderate to severe PMS."

When is it best to face challenge? Early on or delay it? As Joel often states, commencing recovery during a period of significant anxiety increases the odds that anxiety will never again serve as an excuse for relapse.

Can hormonal related symptoms be so profound that it is best to navigate the most challenging portion of recovery -- the first 72 hours -- during the luteal phase? If concerned, discuss it with your physician.

Keep in mind that the smoking woman's unconscious mind has likely been conditioned to reach for a cigarette during specific menstrual cycle hormonal or symptom related events. The more nicotine use cues encountered and extinguished during the luteal phase, the fewer that will remain to trigger crave episodes during the follicular phase.

---

259 Allen SS et al, Menstrual phase effects on smoking relapse, Addiction, May 2008, Volume 103(5), Pages 809-821.
260 Bertone-Johnson ER, et al, Cigarette Smoking and the Development of Premenstrual Syndrome, American Journal of Epidemiology, August 13, 2008.

The beauty of recovery is that next month's cycle will not be affected by the heightened stresses associated with rapidly declining reserves of the alkaloid nicotine. Also, next month's cycle may very well stand on its own, unaffected by either early withdrawal or cue related crave triggers.

Joel encourages doubters to stroll through the hundreds of thousands of indexed and archived member posts at Freedom, the free message board support group, where each day he supports members in navigating recovery.[261]

"Go back one month and see how many of the woman at our site seem to have panicking posts complaining of intense smoking thoughts month after month after month on any kind of regular pattern."

"The fact is, there are no such posts on the board because after the first few months, not smoking becomes a habit even during times of menstruation."[262]

Joel closes by reminding women concerned about menstrual symptoms, that to keep their recovery on course and getting easier and easier over time, it's still simply a matter of staying totally committed, even during tough times, to their original commitment to Never Take Another Puff!

Pregnancy

The awe and excitement of a new life growing inside, the fear and horror that your chemical dependency may harm or destroy it, news of pregnancy can be an emotional kaleidoscope.

Upon confirmation, often within minutes, the mother-to-be makes the biggest mistake of her entire pregnancy. She decides to "stop for the baby." How could something that sounds so right, be so wrong?

Only about half of women claim to be successful in ending nicotine use after learning they are pregnant.[263] Sadly, the real figure is probably closer to one-third.

Researchers conducting third trimester blood tests on women claiming to have stopped smoking report that 25% are untruthful.[264] Why do so few succeed?

Stopping for others, including the unborn, is a formula and recipe for relapse.[265] It can mean an entire pregnancy spent either feeling deprived of nicotine or gradually growing numb to the fears of harm that use would inflict, and eventually surrendering.

---

261 Freedom from Nicotine - http://www.ffn.yuku.com
262 Spitzer, J, PMS and Quitting September 14, 2004, http://www.ffn.yuku.com/topic/12132
263 Tong VT, Smoking patterns and use of cessation interventions during pregnancy, American Journal of Preventive Medicine, October 2008, Volume 35(4), Pages 327-333; also see, Pauly JR, et al, Maternal tobacco smoking, nicotine replacement and neurobehavioural development, Acta Paediatrica, June 12, 2008.
264 George L, et al, Self-reported nicotine exposure and plasma levels of cotinine in early and late pregnancy, Acta Obstetricia Gynecologica Scandinavica, 2006, Volume 85(11), Pages 1331-1337.
265 Spitzer, J, Quitting for Others, WhyQuit.com, Joel's Library, 1984.

What logic is there in making this "the baby's" recovery instead of its mother's? Stop for the baby? Is it the baby who needs help or its mom-to-be?

No longer in harm's way, the precious seconds during and after childbirth are often soured by fixation upon relapse. Instead of savoring life's richest moment, she's plotting the act she knows may bring an early end to both motherhood and life. Each contraction is followed by thoughts that she has sacrificed long enough, that danger of harming the baby is about to pass.

Stopping "for the baby" makes pregnancy cessation vastly harder than need be. Doing it "for the baby" may as well be an open declaration that this baby will have an actively feeding drug addict for a mom. Here are a few quotes from e-mails I've received:

- "I am 33 years old. I started smoking at age 13 and of course never thought I would still be a smoker 20 years later, and a pack to a pack and a half each day. I stopped for nine months while I was pregnant and could not wait the entire pregnancy for just one cigarette. The minute I was home from the hospital I started again."
- "I stopped smoking each time I found out I was pregnant, but right after they were born I was back to a pack a day."
- "I'm 38 years old with three children and have smoked since I was 17, stopping when pregnant only to re-light within hours of giving birth."
- "I started smoking at 13 (well I couldn't draw back like all the other girls) but by the time I was 14, I was smoking at every opportunity. The only time I stopped smoking is whilst I was pregnant and breastfeeding. Then, as soon as my babies weaned, I started again!"
- "When I was pregnant with my first child I gave up smoking as soon as I found out, the same for the second pregnancy. My mistake is I started back up. I'm stopping smoking today even though I'm about to wean my daughter."
- "My daughter is 5 months pregnant and still smokes occasionally. Actually I don't know how much she smokes. For someone who is trying to be so protective of her unborn child she isn't. She is an intelligent person but putting her baby at risk."
- "I am concerned about my neighbor's smoking. She is pregnant again but still smokes. She was smoking while pregnant with her 1st son who is 4 years-old now and deaf."

Approximately half of women who stop smoking during pregnancy relapse within six months of giving birth.[266] Adding it all up, it means that, unbelievably, only about 1 in 5 women who smoked at conception will experience the joys of smoke-free motherhood.

The reasons given in trying to justify relapse following childbirth vary greatly:

- "I am an attractive, 39 year old professional yuppie turned new mom who has been hiding it and in the closet for many years. I stopped successfully when I found out I was 2 weeks pregnant and then started during a brief bout of postpartum depression when my baby was 6 weeks old and I had stopped nursing. I was back to smoking a half a pack to a pack a day."

---

266 Colman GJ, et al, Trends in smoking before, during, and after pregnancy in ten states, American Journal of Preventive Medicine, January 2003, Volume 24(1), Pages 29-35; Kaneko A, et al, Smoking trends before, during, and after pregnancy among women and their spouses, Pediatrics International, June 2008, Volume 50(3), Pages 367-375.

- "I am addicted to nicotine gum. I stopped smoking and started chewing the gum. Then I got pregnant with my daughter and stopped chewing the gum. My mother died right after my daughter was born, so I started smoking again. Three months later, I stopped using cigarettes and started with the gum again. I finally ended gum use in January of 2003. I was totally nicotine-free for about 18 months when my sister-in-law gave me a cigarette. I figured I could handle just one" "I bought a pack the next day. Now, I'm stuck on the gum again...no pun intended."

National Cancer Institute

Driven by significant and very real risks, these women were able to temporarily suspend nicotine use. Then, postpartum depression and a mother's death were used as reasons for relapse. Although not mentioned, it's highly unlikely that relapse and active drug addition improved either situation.

Pregnancy is a golden opportunity. It's a period during which a mind, body and life can be clean, healed and reclaimed in order to prepare for the blessings of nicotine-free motherhood.

Instead, roughly 4 of 5 pregnant smokers spend their pregnancy somewhere between the grips of penetrating guilt over the harms use continues to inflict, and a growing sense of self-deprivation, which they'll satisfy shortly after giving birth.

Let's be clear, it's normal and natural to want to stop for the baby. The risks of harm are tremendous. It isn't a matter of whether or not nicotine will damage the fetus but how bad and noticeable the damage will be.

The risks are so huge that the fears flowing from them consume reason, logic and common sense.

Before learning they were pregnant, most women had their own dream of someday stopping smoking, at a time, place and manner chosen by them. But now gripped by worry of harm to the developing life inside, it's a dream quickly forgotten.

Instead of seeing here and now as the perfect time to live that dream, it's abandoned it in favor of self-sacrifice for the innocent preciousness inside.

Their dream forgotten, some are able to temporarily suspend use for the benefit of the fetus while others do not. Those that don't are forced to invent new nicotine use rationalizations in order to suppress the harms being inflicted. Here are more quotes from e-mails.

- "My daughter just found out that she is pregnant and she smokes. She was going to just stop but then a midwife told her that if she did, her fetus would go into shock and that she should just taper off."

- "I did attempt to stop when I found out I was pregnant the first time, but after thinking about all the people I knew who smoked while pregnant and had normal kids, I kept right on smoking." "I kept my mouth shut, as I had lied to the doctor and the hospital about smoking."

There's also the rationalization that "stopping for the baby is just too hard." She's absolutely correct. The challenge truly is far greater when attempting cessation for others.

Think about the day to day agony and anxiety endured by these women. Imagine the disapproving stares and verbal abuse by those who notice them smoking. Society's disdain only increases her focus upon "stopping for the baby."

Photo by National Cancer Institute

- "I am 8 weeks pregnant and have been struggling with stopping for some time. Even before my pregnancy I was trying to stop. The scariest part for me is the anxiety it creates. Is it dangerous to go through withdrawal cold turkey?"
- "I am 26 years old. I'm 9 weeks pregnant. I've smoked a pack a day for 11 years. I've tried to stop 3 times now in 4 weeks and blown it every time. I am down to about 3-5 cigarettes a day. I am worried about my baby and I have smoked through the whole thing. I am trying to stop again. It has been about 12 hours without a smoke."
- "I am a 22 year-old female who is currently 32 weeks along in my pregnancy. I feel that the reason why I haven't stopped is just that! I am deathly afraid of the feeling of withdrawal."

We can only live in fear for so long before growing numb to it. If this isn't "your" recovery but instead a temporary pause for the baby, how long before that deprived feeling overwhelms diminishing fears? And how much anxiety and guilt would relapse bring?

If the expectant mother has gone two weeks without nicotine, her brain has already substantially completed restoring neurotransmitter sensitivities and counts. Although she will continue to feel the tease of thousands of old nicotine replenishment memories, they belonged to an actively feeding drug addict whose blood-serum nicotine reserves were always on the decline. After two weeks it's nearly all psychological, as there is nothing missing and nothing in need of replacement.

For her, relapse will not match expectations. There will not be an underlying "aaah" wanting relief sensation as nothing was missing. But lapse will immediately re-fire dependency's engines, as nicotine drenched receptors cause her dopamine pathways to re-assign using again, the same priority as eating food.

And the circumstances of lapse will be documented in high definition memory, breathing life into thousands of old use memories that will, in the short term, make lapse nearly impossible to forget.

Her "aaah" missing following lapse, her focus will instead turn to the sensations felt when scores of cigarette toxins strike healing tissues, and carbon monoxide invades an oxygen rich mind.

The toxic assault will likely compel her dizzy and disrupted mind to turn its focus to her now failed objective, "stopping for the baby." She'll wonder whether the burning sensations generated by carbon monoxide, hydrogen cyanide, arsenic, sulfur, ammonia, and formaldehyde are also burning her unborn baby.

But it's too late. Once nicotine is inside, relapse is all but assured, with more assaults and guilt to follow.

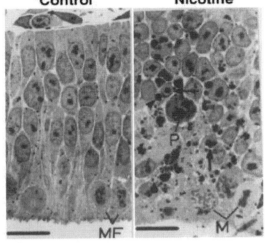

A. Rat Embryo Cultures - Neural Tube Stage

- "Unfortunately, I have given in and I had my first cigarette in 10 months yesterday. I had another today and now I'm feeling absolutely horrible about it. I am breastfeeding and I would like to continue breastfeeding without harming my child."
- "I am 41 years-old and smoked a pack a day since I was 15 years old, with the exception of 9 months when I pregnant (started right up again the day after she was born). I hated myself for failing. I hated the way I smelled. I hated "sneaking" a smoke to get through the day. I hated the disgusted looks of people walking by me as I huddled outside my office building sucking on that disgusting thing, rain or shine, cold or hot. I hated myself for hurting my daughter - thinking for sure, unless I could find the strength and courage to stop that my daughter would lose her mother."

As mentioned, it isn't a matter of whether or not nicotine will damage the fetus but how noticeable the damage will be. Not convinced? Let me share some of the work and findings of those who have devoted their lives to the study of nicotine toxicology and pharmacology.

But before doing so, realize that the primary reason these harms occur is because the woman convinced herself that she had to "give-up" her drug for the "sake of the baby."

Instead, reflect upon the truth that the only way the baby's time with its mother will not be constantly interrupted by the need to replenish missing nicotine is if she embraces recovery for the "sake of the mother." Allow your own dreams and desires to transport you home to the freedom, calmness and beauty that's "you!"

Dr. Heinz Ginzel is a medical doctor and retired University of Arkansas pharmacology and toxicology professor who has devoted decades to the study of nicotine. Dr. Ginzel's medical journal articles use language that tends to speak over-the-heads of most expectant women.

They share concerns over "fetotoxicity and neuroteratogenicity that can cause cognitive, affective and behavioral disorders in children born to mothers exposed to nicotine during pregnancy."[267] But he has also written taking direct aim at pregnant women. Listen carefully to his message:

---

267 Ginzel KH, et al, Critical review: nicotine for the fetus, the infant and the adolescent? Journal of Health Psychology, March 2007, Volume 12(2), Pages 215-224.

"To set the stage, one has to recognize that nicotine interacts with the very basic functions of the peripheral and central nervous system, i.e., the nerves supplying organs and tissues of the body and the vital command stations in the brain. When these systems are formed during fetal life, the nicotine the mother is exposed to from smoking, secondhand smoke or NRT will impair their normal development."

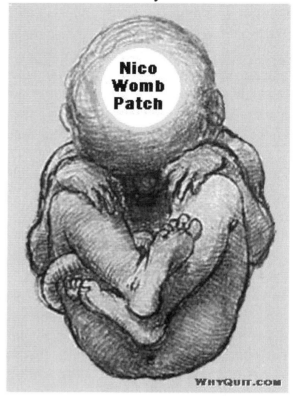

"Such impairment can manifest itself in a variety of symptoms depending on the site, time and intensity of nicotine action. Here are a few examples: The notorious "Sudden Infant Death Syndrome" or SIDS has been traced to prenatal and/or postnatal nicotine exposure. Nicotine exposure is responsible for cognitive and learning deficits in children as well as affective and behavioral problems such as 'Attention Deficit Hyperactivity Disorder' (ADHD), with displays of unruliness and aggression."

"Neonatal nicotine exposure impairs so-called auditory learning, a very specific lifelong handicap. Prenatal nicotine also primes the developing brain for depression and for nicotine addiction in adolescence. Wrongly believing or being told that NRT is risk-free, pregnant smokers who would have stopped during pregnancy may begin using NRT throughout pregnancy."

"As a consequence, intelligence expressed by I.Q. standards may decline in their offspring, but as larger segments of the population are affected, this decline may not be readily discernible."[268]

Warnings such as Dr. Ginzel's make the expectant woman's failure to place her own drug addiction recovery above "stopping for the baby" almost understandable.

Duke Medical University Professor Theodore Slotkin is probably the world's leading nicotine toxicology researcher. He is deeply concerned that nicotine, including replacement nicotine, may cause as much or more harm to the developing fetus than crack cocaine.[269]

According to Professor Slotkin, "NRT, especially by transdermal patch, delivers more nicotine to the fetus than smoking does." "Studies have found that the brains of fetal mice wound up with 2.5 times higher nicotine concentrations than found in the mother's blood when on a slow continuous

268 Ginzel, KH, Why do you smoke? WhyQuit.com, February 6, 2007.
269 Slotkin TA, Fetal nicotine or cocaine exposure: which one is worse? The Journal of Pharmacology and Experimental Therapeutics, June 1998, Volume 285(3), Pages 931-945.

nicotine feed, as would be the case with the nicotine patch."[270]

The patch's continuous delivery of nicotine is believed to somehow overwhelm and saturate the ability of the placenta to perform limited nicotine filtering.

In 2008 Professor Slotkin wrote that, "nicotine by itself is able to reproduce the net outcome from tobacco smoke exposure; that is not to say that the other components are not injurious, but rather, the replacement of tobacco with NRT is likely to produce less improvement than might otherwise be thought, and as shown above, may actually worsen some of the critical outcomes."[271]

Ponder the collective regret of the millions of mothers whose intense focus on protecting the baby actually resulted in harming them.

- "I learned first hand the results of smoking during pregnancy. I had taken lightly my responsibility to him and I will always regret it."
- "My son was born at a comparatively low birth rate, and notably, his umbilical cord, instead of a healthy red color, was a sickly, puss-like shade of yellow. It was not thick and healthy, but tapered and became thinner toward where it was attached to him."
- "So, now my second son is two and a half with developmental delays, and my four year old has Attention Hyperactivity Disorder, with extreme emphasis on the hyperactivity part. I know in my heart that I probably caused these problems but I keep finding other excuses."
- "I smoked very little during my first pregnancy. My child has allergies and catches bronchitis very easily. With my second child I stopped smoking during pregnancy. My husband began smoking again and so did I. When I began breastfeeding after the birth it became another concern for me. I tell myself that it's not hurting the baby, but in my mind it bothers me."

And what will the child say?

- "I hate, hate, hate cigarette smoking, second hand smoke and smokeless tobacco! My mother smoked while she was pregnant (both times) and smoked until I was 17 years old. I was born with a head tumor which continues to give me trouble after two surgeries and more than 35 years of life."
- "My mother smoked, even when pregnant with me. So I guess, being born that way, I've always been addicted to nicotine." "At age 22, my mother died of a sudden and massive stroke caused by hypertension, elevated by smoking. That's exactly what was put on the coroner's report. Even then, I kept smoking."

Imagine never being able to fully bond with your baby because nicotine keeps coming between

270 Slotkin, TA, e-mail from Professor Slotkin to John R. Polito, January 8, 2006.

271 Slotkin, TA, Slotkin, If nicotine iGinzel KH, et al, Critical review: nicotine for the fetus, the infant and the adolescent? Journal of Health Psychology, March 2007, Volume 12(2), Pages 215-224.s a developmental neurotoxicant in animal studies, dare we recommend nicotine replacement therapy in pregnant women and adolescents? Neurotoxicology and Teratology, Jan-Feb 2008, Volume 30(1), Pages 1-19.

you. Alternatively, envision the rich calmness of nicotine-free motherhood.

Why not reach back and seize upon your own pre-pregnancy dream of freedom and make recovery your loving gift of "you" to "you"?

Why not exchange all fears of fetal harm for the celebration of using pregnancy as a golden opportunity to come home to "you"? Picture your new baby basking in liberty's blessings.

Photo by CDC

- "I am very happy to say that I have been nicotine-free for six months now! My kids have not missed any days of school this year. I have started to workout three times a week. I feel better. Most people tell me I look a lot better. My house and car are cleaner. I am so glad I stopped."
- "Now, although I still know I am an addict, I concentrate on keeping my recovery alive by celebrating my freedom. One thought I find very heartening is that I am doing "easy time." Compared with the first days, it is so easy for me not to smoke today. Most of the costs have gone, but I still get the benefits. Smoking is expensive in the UK, and so far I have saved £14,000 (that's U.S. $27,500)! I save so much I can easily justify a weekend away on my annual stopping anniversary. Best of all, I have a 10 week-old son who has a smoke-free mom."
- "I had stopped with my previous pregnancies (three older daughters), but I picked it right back up again with ferocity. After each failure I increased my nicotine intake more and more. At 2 to 2 1/2 packs a day, I saw not much hope for an end. But this pregnancy scared me. Now, I was much older and this baby was counting on me to not just stop during my pregnancy, like with the sisters, but for the rest of my life. I visited WhyQuit and read, and read, and read. I finally learned WHY every time I had picked them back up again in my postpartum periods. I was still in post acute withdrawal. Riddled with anxiety, I did not approach stopping with a recovery mind-set but with a 'suspended sentence' on smoking. For our fifteenth anniversary, I gave my husband another daughter ... and a nicotine-free wife."

Regarding postpartum depression, ready yourself for the possibility. Studies analyzing how often it occurs vary significantly depending on where the women studied lived, the study's definition of depression, and whether or not the results included women who were experiencing depression before giving birth.

Among studies reporting new cases of depression arising after childbirth, 6.9% of 280 new moms in Israel reported postpartum depression at 6 weeks (Glasser 1998), 12.5% among 1,584 Swedish women at 8 weeks, which declined to 8.3% by 12 weeks (Wickberg 1997), 5.8% among 465 Wisconsin women between months 1 and 4 (Chaudron 2001), and 3.7% of 403 Minnesota woman during the first year following childbirth (Bryan 1999).

If depressed following childbirth be sure and let your doctor know. Postpartum depression is not some character flaw or weakness but as real as the nose on our face.

It's believed to be associated with a large increase in progesterone-derived neuro-steroids during pregnancy, and its sharp decline following childbirth, which may have significant effects on GABA receptors.[272]

Emerging research suggests that these receptors could be a path to effective treatment.[273] Clearly, what no physician on earth will suggest as a treatment course is relapse to the highly addictive, fetal teratogen nicotine.

As for replacement nicotine, even its most vocal advocates are forced to admit that, "there is no evidence that NRT is actually effective for smoking cessation in pregnancy."[274]

Keep your eye on the placebos and nicotine should some future "placebo" controlled pregnancy study proclaim NRT "effective." Remember, placebo is not a real-world recovery method.[275] There's no such thing. But it certainly has proven effective in allowing the pharmaceutical industry to make mountains of money.[276]

Also, with any new study, look closely to see if the pregnancy pharma product cessation study examined cotinine levels (the primary chemical nicotine breaks down into), to see if women were truly able to get off nicotine.

If nicotine and cotinine levels were ignored, it immediately tells us that those conducting the study were vastly more interested in selling their product than preventing fetal harm.

Pregnant women would be wise to accept that knowledge and understanding are extremely effective recovery tools. The highest known pregnancy cessation rates continue to be associated with "counseling and behavioral interventions."[277]

It's what we're doing now, reviewing the knowledge, insights and skills needed to embrace and celebrate nicotine-free motherhood. Let this be your loving gift of "you" to "you." Watch the magic unfold as your nicotine-free body heals, mends and repairs while at the same time making a new life.

Why deprive your baby of knowing you? Why sense it feel extreme contentment while in the arms of smokers, especially those who smoke your brand?

---

272 Maguire J, et al, GABA(A)R plasticity during pregnancy: relevance to postpartum depression, Neuron, July 31, 2008, Volume 59(2), Pages 207-713.

273 Nemeroff CB, Understanding the pathophysiology of postpartum depression: implications for the development of novel treatments, Neuron, July 31, 2008, Volume 59(2), Pages 185-186.

274 Coleman T, Recommendations for the use of pharmacological smoking cessation strategies in pregnant women, CNS Drugs, 2007, Volume 21(12), Pages 983-993.

275 Brewster, JM, Pharmacotherapy for Smoking Cessation, electronic letter, Canadian Medical Association Journal, July 29, 2008, http://cmaj.ca/cgi/eletters/179/2/135#19879

276 Polito, JR, Meta-analysis rooted in expectations not science, electronic letter, Canadian Medical Association Journal, July 29, 2008, http://cmaj.ca/cgi/eletters/179/2/135#19781

277 Crawford JT, et al, Smoking cessation in pregnancy: why, how, and what next..., Clinical Obstetrics and Gynecology, June 2008, Volume 51(2), Pages 419-435.

Instead, picture your new baby bonding to its mother's natural skin fragrance instead of the more than four thousand chemicals that cigarette smoke would have deposited upon your hair, skin and clothing.

I encourage you to continue reading, learning and growing. Allow yourself to become vastly more dependency recovery savvy than your addiction is strong.

Baby steps, yes you can! There's only one rule ... no nicotine just one hour, challenge and day at a time!

Photo by National Cancer Institute

Chapter 7

The Roadmap Home

This chapter provides a brief overview of recovery. It's a start to finish look at four distinct yet overlapping phases, followed by a list of health benefits navigating them brings. It lays a foundation for the four chapters that follow:

1. Physical Recovery
2. Emotional Recovery
3. Subconscious Recovery
4. Conscious Recovery

Brief Dependency Review

Nicotine addiction is the result of the introduction of a chemical into the body, which by happenstance is able to unlock and activate the same brain cells and pathways as the neurotransmitter acetylcholine. For us, nicotine's repeated activation of those receptors caused stimulation and permanent compromise of our brain's dopamine pathways, our mind's priorities teacher.

Those pathways were designed to generate urges, wanting and desire, so as to make events that stimulate them, species survival activities, extremely difficult to forget or ignore. But prior to nicotine dependency onset, there was no "wanting" to use again.

Initially, arriving nicotine would cause a burst of unearned dopamine, providing a wanting satisfaction sensation for wanting that didn't yet exist. But for those of us susceptible to dependency onset, continued use would end free stealing.

Soon, our tonic dopamine level started to decline in response to falling nicotine levels. This resulted in "wanting." That wanting would soon be amplified by the anxiety generating tease of an ever growing number of wanting satisfaction memories.

Each of those high definition memories documented exactly how wanting was satisfied, by arrival of a new supply of nicotine. Arrival of more nicotine would generate a sudden phasic burst of dopamine, restoring our tonic dopamine level and temporarily satisfying wanting.

Continued use caused our brain to attempt to de-sensitize itself to nicotine's presence by increasing the number of acetylcholine receptors in multiple brain regions. Continued use also conditioned our subconscious mind to expect a new supply of nicotine when specific times, locations, people, activities or emotions were encountered.

Now, any attempt to stop using nicotine could result in the same wanting related anxieties felt when deprived of food or water.

Declining by one-half every two hours, years of struggling to keep sufficient nicotine in our bloodstream, so as to hold wanting at bay, left us falsely convinced that nicotine was core to our existence, as fundamental as eating. Educated recovery is about understanding both the lie and dependency's effects upon us.

It is my hope that education and understanding will make any remaining fears of life without nicotine so insignificant that it becomes impossible not to notice the beauty that recovery gradually unfolds before you. It's my hope that understanding aids you in appreciating the full glory of again standing on your own, as you fully engage life as "you."

But that's only a hope. Once home, whether our journey is best characterized as having been a cakewalk, a love fest, a non-event, frantic or nightmarish, the only thing that matters is that each challenge and each day remains totally do-able.

Understanding where we now stand is the window to where we've been. An awakening is at hand. Allow your mind to see the lies, the depths to which they took you, and where you now stand.

While such awareness itself can be a tad frightening, why spoil healing with fear? Why fear arrival of a calm and comfortable day where not once do thoughts of using enter our mind? Why fear such days becoming so frequent that they become our new sense of normal?

Ending Nicotine Use

That first courageous step is huge, the biggest baby step of all. Mustering the courage to at last say "no" to that next nicotine fix is the only path to the wonderfulness beyond, a return to a calm, quiet and beautiful mind that dependency and wanting have far too long keep hidden from view.

Contrary to marketing of those pushing an ever growing array of nicotine delivery devices, the only path ending wanting for

Photo by National Cancer Institute

more is to end nicotine's arrival. And the speed of natural recovery can be seen within just one hour of remaining 100% nicotine-free, as the concentration of nicotine within your blood plummets by 25%.

"Half-life" is defined as "the time required for half the quantity of a drug or other substance deposited in a living organism to be metabolized or eliminated by normal biological processes."[278] Most older cessation literature firmly fixes nicotine's elimination half-life at about two hours.[279]

But nicotine's half-life can vary substantially based upon genetic, racial, hormonal, diet, activity and age factors.[280] For now, let's ignore genetic differences, as we have no idea which genes we do or don't have.

As for racial variations, a 1998 study found an average nicotine half-life of 129 minutes in Caucasians and 134 minutes in African Americans.[281] A 2002 study compared Chinese-American, Latino and Caucasian smokers. It found that Latinos had the shortest half-life (122 minutes), Chinese-Americans the longest (152 minutes), with Caucasians in the middle (134 minutes).[282]

Nicotine's half-life is shorter in women (118 minutes) than men (132 minutes), and even faster in women taking oral contraceptives (96 minutes). This is thought to be associated with estrogen.[283]

Its half-life is shorter during pregnancy (97 minutes) than after giving birth (111 minutes).[284] Sadly, new born babies whose mothers smoked endure a nicotine withdrawal period five times longer than what their mother's would have been. Instead of the newborn having a 2-hour elimination half-life, it balloons to 11.2 hours.[285] If considering breast-feeding, nicotine's breast milk half-life averages 97 minutes.[286]

Interestingly, a 1993 nicotine patch study found that when nicotine was administered directly into the bloodstream (intravenously) it had a 2 hour elimination half-life but when administered through the skin via the nicotine patch (transdermally), once the patch was removed nicotine's elimination

278 half-life. (n.d.). The American Heritage Dictionary of the English Language, Fourth Edition. Retrieved from Dictionary.com on August 22, 2008.

279 Benowitz NL, et al, Interindividual variability in the metabolism and cardiovascular effects of nicotine in man, The Journal of Pharmacology and Experimental Therapeutics, May 1982, Volume 221(2), Pages 368-372; also see Feyerabend C, et al, Nicotine pharmacokinetics and its application to intake from smoking, British Journal of Clinical Pharmacology, February 1985, Volume 19(2), Pages 239-247.

280 Benowitz NL, Clinical pharmacology of nicotine: implications for understanding, preventing, and treating tobacco addiction, Clinical Pharmacology & Therapeutics, April 2008, Volume 83(4), Pages 531-541.

281 Perez-Stable EJ, et al, Nicotine metabolism and intake in black and white smokers, Journal of the American Medical Association, July 8, 1998, Volume 280(2), Pages 152-156.

282 Benowitz NL, et al, Slower metabolism and reduced intake of nicotine from cigarette smoking in Chinese-Americans, Journal of the National Cancer Institute, January 16, 2002, Volume 94(2), Pages 108-115.

283 Benowitz NL, et al, Female sex and oral contraceptive use accelerate nicotine metabolism, Clinical Pharmacology & Therapeutics, May 2006, Volume 79(5), Pages 480-488.

284 Dempsey D, et al, Accelerated metabolism of nicotine and cotinine in pregnant smokers, Journal of Pharmacology Exp Therapeautics, May 2002, Volume 301(2), Pages 594-598.

285 Dempsey D, et al, Nicotine metabolism and elimination kinetics in newborns, Clinical Pharmacology Therapeutics, May 2000, Volume 67(5), Pages 458-465.

286 Luck W, Nicotine and cotinine concentrations in serum and milk of nursing smokers, British Journal of Clinical Pharmacology, July 1984, Volume 18(1), Pages 9-15.

half-life was 2.8 hours.[287]   This finding was confirmed by a second patch study which found it to be a minimum of 3.3 hours.[288]

Most nicotine is broken down into six primary metabolites by the liver (mostly cotinine: 70-80%). The kidneys remove (eliminate or excrete) nicotine and its metabolites from the bloodstream.[289]

Thus, any activity which increases blood flow though the liver (exercise or eating) accelerates nicotine depletion. Liver blood flow increases by 30% after meals, with a 40% increase in the rate that nicotine is cleared from arriving blood.[290]

As we learned in Chapter 4, acidic urine accelerates nicotine elimination, while alkaline urine actually allows its re-absorption back into the body .

As suggested by the above half-life data, most of us had sufficient nicotine reserves to comfortably make it through 8 hours of sleep each night (4 half lives leaving us with a minimum of 6.25% of our normal daily supply).

In fact, the amount of nicotine remaining after sleep is actually a tad higher than simple division suggests. It makes sense, as the amount of blood flow and nicotine passing through and being metabolized by the liver decreases while sleeping.

As you can see, our remaining reserves will become so small within 24 hours of ending all nicotine use that they become difficult to detect (.02 or just 2/100ths of our normal daily level). It's here that surgery (nicotine extraction) is nearly complete and deep dependency healing begins in earnest. Within 3 days, with absolute certainty, you will inhabit a nicotine-free body and mind.

As for detection, we often get the question, how long after I stop using nicotine will my insurance company or employer be able to detect nicotine in my system? As seen above, unless examining hair, which permanently records nicotine use, trying to measure rapidly falling nicotine levels in blood, urine and saliva is all but useless as a marker of use.

That's why insurance companies and employers normally test for cotinine, one of nicotine's longer-lasting metabolites, which has a generally recognized half-life of about 17 hours.[291]

In regard to recovery what's important is that remaining levels become so small within 24 hours of ending use that re-sensitization and the brain's adjustment to functioning without nicotine have no choice but to commence.

287 Gupta SK, et al, Bioavailability and absorption kinetics of nicotine following application of a transdermal system, British Journal of Clinical Pharmacology, September 1993, Volume 36(3), Pages 221-227.

288 Keller-Stanislawski B, et al, Pharmacokinetics of nicotine and cotinine after application of two different nicotine patches under steady state conditions, Arzneimittel-Forschung, September 1992, Volume 42(9), Pages 1160-1162.

289 Benowitz NL, et al, Nicotine chemistry, metabolism, kinetics and biomarkers, Handbook of Experimental Pharmacology 2009; Volume 192), Pages 29-60.

290 Hukkanen J, et al, Metabolism and disposition kinetics of nicotine, Pharmacological Reviews, March 2005, Volume 57(1), Pages 79-115.

291 Swan GE, et al, Saliva cotinine and recent smoking--evidence for a nonlinear relationship, Public Health Reports, Nov-Dec 1993, Volume 108(6), Pages 779-783.

Within 24 hours the mind and body will begin to experience overlapping recovery on four levels: physical, emotional, subconscious and conscious. Keep all nicotine on the outside and within 72 hours of ending use, regardless of your body's nicotine half-life or elimination rate, you'll stand atop withdrawal's mountain.

The most challenging portion of recovery will be behind you. While your climb was quick, the slope of the journey down the other side, although initially brisk, is continuous yet ever so gradual. Easier time with fewer bumps, the balance of the journey becomes an exercise in patience.

Yet, violate the "Law of Addiction" - just one hit of nicotine - and forget about any gradual down slope or doing easy time. It's called relapse. You'll either resume life as an actively feeding addict or need to again endure nicotine detox and another climb to the top.

The price of each climb is further depletion of core dreams and desires. Although able to rest and rejuvenate once at or over the top, amazingly few have the stamina of purpose needed to make back-to-back climbs.

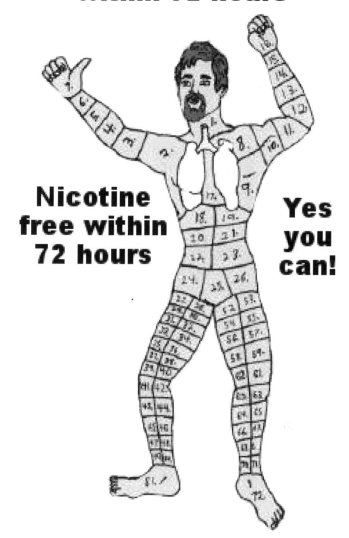

Expect to be teased during both your climb and descent by those selling chemicals that stimulate brain dopamine pathways (tobacco products, cigarettes, e-cigarettes, replacement nicotine, bupropion and varenicline). Expect them to try to discourage you.

Listen for the false and deceptive implication that few succeed in stopping on their own.   Truth is, it's how the vast majority will succeed this year, and they know it.

Clearly, they want your money. And sadly, nearly all are willing to lie to get it.

Expect their tease to falsely suggest that their product makes the climb easy, or as suggested by recent Nicorette commercials, that it make it "suck less." Don't listen. If the product stimulates dopamine pathways, physical withdrawal's climb isn't fully underway until product use ends.

Continued stimulation does not aid recovery but delays it. That's why advertising the product's cessation results on the day product use ends, while still under the chemical's influence, is not about science but salesmanship.

As Joel says, we'd only have ourselves to blame for intentionally extending what should have been a few days of withdrawal into weeks or months. Not only do users face the side-effect risks posed by each product, they face having to someday adjust to living without the dopamine pathway stimulation each provides.

Let's turn our attention to what happens once we muster the courage to say "no." Let's start with the body's physical response to ending all use.

Physical Readjustment

The brain needs time to re-adjust its equilibrium or homeostasis to again functioning without nicotine. Nicotine caused both activation and deactivation of nicotinic-type acetylcholine receptors.[292] A significant increase in the number of receptors (up-regulation) may have occurred in as many as eleven different brain regions.[293]

The brain needs for us to develop the patience necessary to allow the time needed to restore natural sensitivities and remove its defenses against nicotine. If allowed, it will work around-the-clock restoring neurotransmitter sensitivities and returning receptor counts to normal.

Photo by National Cancer Institute

As explained, the pace of healing is amazingly fast. Within three days the mind and body become nicotine-free and we move beyond peak withdrawal.

While the vast majority of physical re-adjustments are generally recognized as being complete within the first two weeks, recent studies have found that some symptoms, primarily related to neuron sensitivity restoration and emotions, may persist for 3-4 weeks.

Aside from the brain, the body needs time for its physiology to adjust to again functioning without nicotine and all other chemicals introduced by our method of delivery. As it does, the withdrawal symptoms experienced may be none, few, some or many.

Although Chapter 9 provides a detailed list (and discussion) of possible withdrawal symptoms, I

---

292 Picciotto MR, et al, It is not "either/or": activation and desensitization of nicotinic acetylcholine receptors both contribute to behaviors related to nicotine addiction and mood, Progress in Neurobiology, April 2008, Volume 84(4), Pages 329-342; also see, Even N, et al, Regional differential effects of chronic nicotine on brain alpha 4-containing and alpha 6-containing receptors, Neuroreport, October 8, 2008, Volume 19(15), Pages 1545-1550.

293 Parker SL, Up-regulation of brain nicotinic acetylcholine receptors in the rat during long-term self-administration of nicotine: disproportionate increase of the alpha6 subunit, Molecular Pharmacology, March 2004, Volume 65(3), Pages 611-622.

encourage you to skip it. That's right. Don't read it. If needed, it'll be there. Such lists have a tendency to transform a sensation that may have been barely noticeable into a full-blown concern. FFN-TJH's primary goal is to destroy fears, not foster them.

Both live and online at Freedom and Turkeyville, we've worked with thousands navigating recovery. Aside from expected anxieties and emotions, many report no noticeable physical symptoms at all.

Also, don't confuse the time needed for the mind to adapt to functioning without nicotine's influence, with the time needed for deep tissue healing and purging of tobacco tars. As suggested by the recovery timetable at the end of this chapter, it takes significant time to fully expel toxins and carcinogens and heal from their assaults.

Emotional Readjustment

Although chemical in nature, a long and intense relationship is ending. For most, it was the most dependable relationship we'd ever known.

Even if our fix was bummed or borrowed and the flavor of the brand was horrible, even if the cigarette was damp, slightly torn, broken and in need of repair, or a stale cigarette butt from an ashtray, the nicotine was always there.

Never once did nicotine let us down in providing temporary relief from urges and wanting. Once inside our bloodstream, within seconds we experienced replenishment: nicotine's stimulation of our nervous system accompanied by satisfaction of our mind's latest cycle of need.

Photo by National Cancer Institute

But now that's all behind us. It's over, finished, done. And as with ending any long-term relationship we must navigate the sense of loss emotions flowing from it.

Denial, anger, bargaining and depression are normal emotional phases associated with any significant loss. Navigating each brings us closer to the final phase marking completion of emotional recovery, acceptance.

Subconscious Readjustment

Nicotine's two-hour half-life compelled us to select replenishment times, situations and patterns. While you may not have recognized the patterns, your subconscious mind did.

When did you replenish? Upon waking each morning, entering the bathroom, before or after a meal, in the yard or garage, while traveling, surrounding work, around friends, while drinking, on the telephone, before bed, when happy, sad, stressed or mad?

Whether or not aware of our use patterns, our subconscious recorded the times, places, circumstances and emotions during which nicotine replenishment occurred. Those situations became conditioned use cues, alerting our subconscious that it was time for more.

Encountering a use cue would trigger a gentle urge reminding us that it was time to feed. Normally we simply obeyed. But if not, anxiety alarms may have sounded triggering a full-blown crave episode.

Subconscious recovery is about meeting, greeting and extinguishing each conditioned use cue. The subconscious mind does not plot, plan or conspire. It simply reacts to input.

Photo by National Cancer Institute

If we say "no" during what's normally a less than 3 minute crave episode (which time distortion may cause to feel far longer), in most instances a single encounter will sever and break the nicotine use association, extinguishing the cue that caused it.

Each time we extinguish a cue we are rewarded with the return of another aspect of a nicotine-free life. That's right, crave episodes are good not bad. It's how we take back life, just one time, place, person, activity or emotion at a time.

In Chapter 11 we'll explore a host of crave coping techniques. For now, understand that: (1) there is no force or circumstance on planet earth that can compel us to introduce nicotine into our bloodstream; (2) we will always be able to handle up to three minutes of wanting anxiety; and (3) the reward at the end of each episode, extinguishing and silencing another use cue, is always worth vastly more than the price of enduring it.

Conscious Readjustment

By far, normally the easiest yet longest layer of recovery is reclaiming normal everyday thinking.

Unlike a less than three-minute subconscious crave episode, the conscious mind can fixate upon a thought of wanting to use for as long as we are able to maintain concentration and focus. How long can you keep your mind focused upon your favorite food? Look at a clock and give it a try. Can you taste it? Does it make your mouth water? Are you feeling an urge?

Now think about your favorite nicotine use rationalization. What was your primary use justification?

Conscious recovery is the period of time needed for new nicotine-free memories to gather, overwrite or suppress all the durable dopamine pathway memories documenting how wanting was briefly satisfied by using more. It's the time needed to move beyond their conscious tease.

Conscious recovery is very much within our ability to accelerate. It is not necessary to destroy drug use memories in order to alter their impact upon us. It's done by seeing our pile of old wanting satisfaction memories for the truth they reflect; that each memory was created by an actively feeding addict in varying degrees of need of more.

It's also accomplished by a willingness to let go of our use rationalizations. This is done by grabbing hold of each use justification, exposing it to honest light, and recasting it using truth.

Photo by National Cancer Institute

Chapter 12 (Conscious Recovery) is about using logic, reason and science to accelerate this final phase of recovery. As seen in Chapter 4 (Rationalizations), some use rationalizations can be laughed away. Others require a bit more distance from active dependency before honesty and clarity of thought allow us to appreciate the truth and let go. And there may be one or more rationalizations may be harder to release and move beyond.

Contrary to nicotine industry marketing, there was only one reason we didn't stop using long, long ago. Our new addiction quickly conditioned us to expect anxiety, irritability, anger and depression to begin building if we waited too long between feedings.

We didn't continue using because we liked it. We did so because we didn't like what happened when we didn't use it.[294]

Arriving Home

What was it like to go entire days without once thinking about wanting to smoke, dip, chew, suck or vape nicotine? What was it like being "you"?

Don't feel alone if you can no longer recall. That's what drug addiction is all about, quickly burying nearly all remaining memory of the beauty of life without using.

Trust in your common sense and dreams. It's my hope that you're curious about what it's like to go days, weeks and then months without once wanting to introduce nicotine back into your bloodstream. Don't be afraid as there's nothing to fear, except the delay fear causes in taking that first courageous step.

---

294 Spitzer, J, "I smoke because I like smoking," 1983, www.WhyQuit.com

We leave absolutely nothing of value behind. In fact, every neuro-chemical that nicotine controlled already belonged to us. As recovering addicts, we can do everything we did while enslaved, and do it as well as or better once free.

Why fight and rebel against freedom and healing when within just two weeks it will be savored, embraced, protected, hugged and loved? Why see challenges, freedom's stepping stones, as frightening when they provides indisputable evidence of just how infected our life had become?

Photo by National Cancer Institute

My prior attempts failed because I fought recovery, and did so in ignorance and darkness. Yes, every now and then I'd get lucky and land a punch, but freedom was short lived. But this time was different.

This time Joel and his insights effectively turned on the lights. Now my opponent couldn't be clearer. My eyes and mind were opened to exactly what it takes to both fail and succeed.

Joel burned an extremely bright line into my mind, one I'll do my very best to keep clean and clear every remaining day of my life. He taught me that I get to stay and live here on the free side of that line so long as it's never crossed, so long as all the world's nicotine remains on the other, so long as complacency isn't allowed to obscure it.

Let's review a few health benefits of life on the free side of dependency's bars.

Recovery Timetable

Most but not all benefits listed below are related to smoking. Why? Because, at least here in the U.S., there are ten times as many smokers as oral tobacco users.[295] By far, smoking reflects the greatest health risks of any form of nicotine delivery, and until recently the vast majority of research has focused on it.

But just because science cannot yet tell us when most oral tobacco, NRT or e-cig recovery benefits occur, doesn't mean they are not happening.

---

295 Centers for Disease Control, Tobacco Use Among Adults - United States 2005, MMWR, Weekly, October 27, 2006, Volume 55(42), Pages 1145-1148.

When ending all tobacco and nicotine use, within ...[296]

- 20 minutes - Our blood pressure, heart rate and the temperature of our hands and feet return to normal.
- 8 hours - Remaining nicotine in our bloodstream will have fallen to 6% of normal peak daily levels, a 94% reduction.
- 12 hours - The ex-smoker's blood oxygen level will have increased to normal while carbon monoxide levels have dropped to normal too.
- 24 hours - Anxieties peak and within two weeks should return to near pre-cessation levels.
- 48 hours - Damaged nerve endings have started to re-grow and our sense of smell and taste are beginning to return to normal. Cessation anger and irritability peaks.
- 72 hours - Our body is 100% nicotine-free and over 90% of all nicotine metabolites (the chemicals it breaks down into) have been ionized or excreted via urine. Symptoms of withdrawal have peaked in intensity, including restlessness. The number of cue induced crave episodes will peak for the "average" ex-user. Lung bronchial tubes leading to air sacs (alveoli) are beginning to relax in recovering smokers. Breathing is becoming easier and the lungs functional abilities are starting to increase.
- 5 to 8 days - The "average" ex-smoker will encounter an "average" of three cue induced crave episodes per day. Although we may not be "average" and although serious cessation time distortion can make minutes feel like hours, it is unlikely that any single episode will last longer than 3 minutes. Keep a clock handy and time them.
- 10 days - The "average ex-user is down to encountering less than two crave episodes per day, each less than 3 minutes.
- 10 days to 2 weeks - Recovery has likely progressed to the point where our addiction is no longer doing the talking. We are beginning to catch glimpses of where freedom and healing are transporting us.
- 2 weeks - Blood circulation in our gums and teeth is now similar to that of a non-user.
- 2 to 4 weeks - Cessation related anger, anxiety, difficulty concentrating, impatience, insomnia, restlessness and depression have ended. If still experiencing any of these symptoms get seen and evaluated by your physician.
- 3-4 weeks - Brain acetylcholine receptor counts up-regulated in response to nicotine's presence have now down-regulated, and receptor binding has returned to levels seen in the brains of non-smokers.[297]
- 2 weeks to 3 months - If an ex-smoker, heart attack risk has started to drop and lung function continues to improve.
- 3 weeks to 3 months - If an ex-smoker, circulation has substantially improved. Walking has become easier. Any chronic cough has likely disappeared. If not, contact your physician.
- 1 to 9 months - Any smoking related sinus congestion, fatigue or shortness of breath have

---

296 Primary sources for this recovery benefits timetable are: (1) U.S. Department of Health and Human Services, The Health Consequences of Smoking: A Report of the Surgeon General, 2004; (2) Hughes, JR, Effects of abstinence from tobacco: valid symptoms and time course, Nicotine and Tobacco Research, March 2007, Volume 9(3), Pages 315-327; (3) O'Connell KA, et al, Coping in real time: using Ecological Momentary Assessment techniques to assess coping with the urge to smoke, Research in Nursing and Health, December 1998, Volume 21(6), Pages 487-497.

297 Mamede M, et al, Temporal change in human nicotinic acetylcholine receptor after smoking cessation: 5IA SPECT study, Journal of Nuclear Medicine, November 2007, Volume 48(11), Pages 1829-1835.

decreased. Cilia have re-grown in our lungs, thereby increasing their ability to handle mucus, keep our lungs clean and reduce infections. The body's overall energy level has increased.

- 1 year - If an ex-smoker, excess risk of coronary heart disease has dropped to less than half that of a smoker.
- 5 to 15 years - If an ex-smoker, risk of stroke has declined to that of a non-smoker.
- 10 years - If an "average" ex-smoker (one pack per day), our risk of death from lung cancer has declined by almost half. Risk of cancer of the mouth, throat and esophagus has also decreased.
- 15 years - Our risk of coronary heart disease is now that of a person who has never smoked.

Chapter 8

The First 72 Hours

Have you accepted the fact that you are a true drug addict in every sense (Chapter 1)? Do you understand the Law of Addiction, the only rule that we addicts need master and follow in order to stay free (Chapter 2)?

Have you discarded destructive use rationalizations such as the false tease of "just one, just once" and the lie that nicotine relieves stress (Chapter 4)?

Are you aware of common hazards and pitfalls such as early alcohol use, blood sugar swings, how your blood caffeine level will double, and how extra food can become a replacement crutch (Chapter 6). If so, you're ready!

Are you a bit apprehensive? It's totally understandable. Still, slow deep breaths as you try your best to relax and embrace your healing and journey home.

Remember, when going smart turkey (educated cold turkey) without use of any product or procedure, nearly everything felt during the first three days is evidence of what may be the most profound healing your body has ever known. It's good not bad.

If coming home smart yet cold, rest assured, you will not experience any cessation product side effect or adverse event. Instead you'll witness and experience the response of your body and mind as they navigate a temporary period of deep and profound repair, cleansing and mending.

If a smoker, this will likely be your body's most intense healing period ever. Picture more than 50 trillion cells,[298] each receiving far more oxygen and far fewer toxins than normal.

Psychologically, that very first step in getting started is the biggest hurdle of all. It's here, during these early magic moments, that we re-discover how to breathe, move about, eat and go to sleep without introducing nicotine back into our bloodstream.

The minutes will pass whether we force ourselves to sit on pins and needles or permit ourselves to relax and remain as calm and comfortable as the moment

---

298 National Institutes of Health, Human Cells 101, NICHD, http://www.nichd.nih.gov - page last updated 9/18/06.

allows.

A clock or watch will soon announce the passing of an hour. When it does, celebrate! You've taken that first giant step home. Congratulations, that's huge!

A new supply of the super-toxin and natural insecticide nicotine did not arrive (Chapter 1, Nicotine). If a smoker, additional brain gray matter was not damaged or destroyed.[299] Unhealthy and damaged cells throughout the body felt the flicker of hope that nicotine's ability to prevent natural cell death (apoptosis) would no longer force them to live on, that at last they'd be permitted to die.[300] And a new round of nicotine-induced angiogenesis did not riddle though and harden plaque build-up within arteries, or accelerate tumor growth rates by providing them with a blood supply.[301]

Most importantly, we arrested our dependency for an entire hour. We traded sides of the bars. Our dependency was now our prisoner, and we were the jailer.

Forget about forever, tomorrow or even two hours from now. All we control are the next few minutes, minutes during which nicotine need not and shall not enter our bloodstream.

You already know the only principle that need be followed in order to enjoy 100 percent odds of success, the Law of Addiction (Chapter 2). The following cold turkey tips are a summary of key recovery insights. Following each tip is the chapter number where you'll find an in-depth review.

Summary of Basic Recovery Tips

1. **Law of Addiction** - Administration of a drug to an addict will cause re-establishment of chemical dependence upon the addictive substance. Fully accept chemical dependency. Nicotine addiction is as real and permanent as alcoholism. The brain dopamine pathway wanting felt for nicotine is no different than the wanting felt by other drug addicts for their drug.

The same brain dopamine pathways that make thoughts of ending food use nearly unthinkable have been taken hostage by nicotine. It's their job to make activities that activate this circuitry nearly impossible in the short term to forget or ignore.

It's why withdrawal and recovery are necessary. It's the time needed to get clean and move beyond this brain circuitry's influence. It's why there is no such thing as just one, or just once. Remember, without food we die, without nicotine we thrive. (Chapter 2)

299 Brody, AL et al, Differences between smokers and nonsmokers in regional gray matter volumes and densities, Biological Psychiatry, January 1, 2004, Volume 55(1), Pages 77-84; also see Kuhn S, et al, Brain grey matter deficits in smokers: focus on the cerebellum, Brain Structure and Function, April 2012, Volume 217(2), Pages 517-522. Epub September 10, 2011.
300 Cucina A, et al, Nicotine Inhibits Apoptosis and Stimulates Proliferation in Aortic Smooth Muscle Cells Through a Functional Nicotinic Acetylcholine Receptor, The Journal of Surgical Research, November 26, 2007; also see Zhang T, et al, Nicotine prevents the apoptosis induced by menadione in human lung cancer cells, Biochemical and Biophysical Research Communications, April 14, 2006, Volume 342(3), Pages 928-934.
301 Cooke JP, Angiogenesis and the role of the endothelial nicotinic acetylcholine receptor, Life Sciences, May 30, 2007, Volume 80(24-25), Pages 2347-2351; also see, Heeschen C, et al, Nicotine stimulates angiogenesis and promotes tumor growth and atherosclerosis, Nature Medicine, July 2001, Volume 7(7), Pages 833-839.

2. **Measure Victory One Day at a Time** - Forget about stopping "forever." It's the biggest psychological bite imaginable. Instead, adopt a do-able "one day at a time" recovery philosophy, or one challenge or hour at a time when needed. (Chapter 5)

3. **Record Your Motivations** - Panic can occur in the heat of battle, with the primitive impulsive mind taking control. Rational thinking is suddenly abandoned as the body's fight or flight response assumes control. Instantly, you've totally forgotten all the reasons that motivated us to begin this journey home. Then all of the sudden you recall that you made a list of your reasons, and that you have it with you. You pull it out, read it and before finishing, the challenge peaks in intensity and begins to subside. Victory is once again yours! (Chapter 5) (Appendix: Form)

4. **Do Not Skip Meals** - Each puff of nicotine was our spoon pumping stored fats and sugars into our bloodstream. Why add hunger craves atop nicotine craves? Why invite your inexperience in dealing with hunger to add lots of needless extra pounds? Eat little, healthy and often. (Chapter 6)

5. **Three Days of Natural Juices** - If your health and diet permit, consider drinking extra acidic fruit juice the first three days. Cranberry is excellent. It will both help stabilize blood sugars and accelerate nicotine's elimination. (Chapter 6)

6. **Stopping for Others** - We cannot stop for others. It must be our gift to us. Doing it for others creates a natural sense of self-deprivation that's a recipe for relapse. (Chapter 5)

7. **Attitude** - Although not mandatory in staying free, a positive attitude will diminish the anxieties felt, and accelerate both letting go and arriving home. Remember, your subconscious is listening. (Chapter 5)

8. **Get Rid of All Nicotine** - Keeping a stash handy is begging for relapse. Totally destroy, beyond salvage, all nicotine products. (Chapter 5)

9. **Caffeine/Nicotine Interaction** - Nicotine doubles the rate by which the body depletes caffeine. Consider a caffeine reduction of up to one-half if troubled by anxieties or poor sleeping. (Chapter 6)

10. **Aggressively Extinguish Nicotine Use Cues** - Most use cues are extinguished by a single encounter during which the subconscious fails to receive the expected result - nicotine. Subconsciously triggered craves peak in intensity within three minutes. But normal cessation time distortion can combine with panic to make the minutes feel like hours. Keep a clock handy to maintain honest perspective. Don't hide from your healing and reclaiming life, attack it. (Chapter

11)

HALT
HUNGRY ANGRY LONELY TIRED

11. **Crave Coping Techniques** - One coping method is to practice slow deep breathing while clearing your mind of all needless chatter, by focusing upon your favorite person, place or thing. Another is to say your ABCs while associating each letter with your favorite food, person or place. For example, the letter "A" is for grandma's hot apple pie. "B" is for warm buttered biscuits. It's unlikely that you'll ever make it to the challenging letter Q before the episode peaks in intensity and victory is once again yours.

Also, try embracing a crave episode's energy by mentally reaching out inside your mind and wrapping imaginary arms around it. A crave cannot cut us, burn us, shock us or make us bleed. Be brave just once. In your mind, wrap your arms around the crave's anxiety energy. Feel the sensation as its anxiety energy slowly fizzles and dies while within your embrace. Yes, another use cue bites the dust, and your healing continues! (Chapter 11)

12. **Alcohol Use -** Alcohol use is associated with roughly half of all relapses. Be extremely careful with early alcohol use. Get your recovery legs under you first.

Once ready, consider drinking at home first without nicotine around, going out with friends but refraining from drinking during the first outing, or spacing drinks further apart or drinking water or juice between drinks. Have an escape plan and a backup, and be fully prepared to deploy both. (Chapter 6)

13. **Avoid Crutches** - A crutch is any form of reliance that is leaned upon so heavily in supporting recovery that if quickly removed would elevate risk of relapse. (Chapter 6)

14. **Extra Fruit & Veggies** - To help avoid weight gain, pre-cut, prepare and have handy vegetables and fruits instead of candies, chips and pastries. Celery and carrots can be used safely as short-term substitutes. A 2012 study suggests that increased fruit and vegetable consumption may substantially increase 30-day cessation rates. (Chapter 6)

15. **No Legitimate Excuse for Relapse -** Recognize that nicotine use will not solve any crisis. Fully accept that there is absolutely no legitimate excuse for relapse, including an auto accident, financial crisis, the end of a relationship, job loss, a terrorist attack, a hurricane, the birth of a baby, falling stocks, or the eventual inevitable death of those we love most. (Chapter 14)

16. **Reward Yourself** - Consider using some of the money you save to be nice to you. You've earned it. (Chapter 5)

17. **Just One Rule** - There is only one recovery rule which if followed provides a 100 percent guarantee of success: no nicotine today! (Chapter 2)

Recovery Sensations - Good, Not Bad

The early days of an educated attempt will be a cakewalk for some, a challenge for others, and easier than expected for most.

Although it sounds strange, within reason, everything felt as you climb to the point where withdrawal's symptoms peak is beneficial and good, not bad.

What more honest signs of healing could we have? Does it make sense to fear healing? Why resist taking back the driver's seat of your mind? Why fight the drive home? Why fear returning to a place where entire days pass without ever once wanting to use?

Don't fight recovery. Embrace it. Hug it hard!

Photo by National Cancer Institute

The balance of FFN-TJH details each layer of recovery: physical recovery (Chapter 9), emotional recovery (Chapter 10), subconscious recovery (Chapter 11), and conscious recovery (Chapter 12), before closing with homecoming (Chapter 13) and complacency & relapse (Chapter 14).

Again, there was always only one rule. It's that lapse equals relapse, that one equals all, that just one hit of nicotine will activate up to half of brain dopamine pathway receptors, forcing this circuitry to again make you believe that not using more is akin to starvation.

Chapter 9

Physical Recovery

Physical recovery is the layer of healing associated with the chemical and physical changes that occur within the body and mind once use of nicotine ends.

What's important from our standpoint isn't the science associated with the neuro-chemical chain reactions that begin within the body once use ends, but the symptoms those changes "may" generate. And the key word is "may."

While physiological cessation changes within the brain are real, the majority of nicotine cessation symptoms are self-induced. Most symptoms can be diminished, corrected or eliminated. Need proof?
Have you ever been so tired that you slept for ten to twelve hours? Nicotine reserves at less than 3%, why didn't withdrawal awaken you?

Have you ever been so sick that you went a day or more without using? How?

And how did the single-session traveling hypnotist give us a day or two of total cessation calm and bliss before reality hit home?

While every attempt is different, why does a physician's warning that smoking's damage is now so profound that "it is time to either stop or die" so often result in a symptom-less recovery?

I'm increasingly convinced that nearly all recovery symptoms are the result of self-induced fears and anxieties, correctable blood sugar issues, caffeine overdose, or the need for a medication adjustment or treatment of a hidden condition that appears after ending use of one or more of the thousands of chemicals present in tobacco.

The primary anxiety culprit is a prefrontal cortex (the large thinking lobe just above our eyes) filled with thousands of old dopamine pathway generated use memories. The greater our need at the moment before use, the more profound wanting's satisfaction, and the greater that memory's influence upon us.

Not understanding that our mind's priorities teacher had been hijacked, we invented scores of explanations as to why that next nicotine fix was so important.

The common thread between extended sleep, illness, hypnotism and standing on the verge of death is a higher priority.

Whether the higher priority is biological, a subconscious suggestion or a death threat, in each case both the lure of old use memories and the appeal of our use explanations was, at least briefly, totally overcome.

No Need to Read About Symptoms Now

If your own personal resolve and understanding is at this moment sufficient to suppress nearly all symptoms, why fill your prefrontal cortex with symptom suggestions? Why load the recovering junky mind with ammo that can both defend or destroy if, as yet, there is no foe to oppose?

It's okay to skip the balance of chapter for now. It will be here later if needed. But should you proceed with reading it now, as you read each symptom ask yourself this, how can this symptom be minimized, corrected or avoided?

Neuronal Re-sensitization

Exactly how and why the brain diminishes the number of active nicotinic-type acetylcholine receptors (down-regulation) after nicotine use ends is still poorly understood. What we do know is that once use ends, that we temporarily have far too many active receptors.

Early recovery can bring us face-to-face with physical evidence of nicotine's influence upon the brain's hard-wired priorities control center. Again, in terms of withdrawal, it is normal to notice that the brain's desire circuitry is temporarily out of whack.

But once nicotine's arrival ends, the brain is works its "butt off" to diminish the number of active receptors and restore sensitivities. Almost as quickly as you notice your sense of smell and taste being enhanced, brain command and control sensitivity restoration is occurring too.

SPECT stands for Single Photon Emission Computed Tomography. It is a scan during which a radioactive substance is put into the bloodstream and followed via pictures as it works its way through the body.

A camera capable of detecting gamma radiation is then rotated around the body, taking pictures from many angles. A computer is then used to put the images together and create a picture of activity within a specific slice of the body or brain.

A 2007 study used SPECT scans to follow dynamic changes in acetylcholine receptor down-regulation binding during smoking cessation. It compared those finding to receptor activity inside the brains of non-smokers.[302] It found that within four hours of ending nicotine use that acetylcholine receptor binding potential had already declined by 33.5 percent.

The good news is that binding potential has already rebounded by 25.7% within ten days of ending nicotine use, and then "decreased to levels seen in non-smokers by around 21 days of smoking cessation."

We don't need to put radiation into our bloodstream or do a SPECT scan of our brain to know that the de-sensitized period felt and sensed during recovery is temporary, normal and expected.

---

302 Mamede M, et al, Temporal change in human nicotinic acetylcholine receptor after smoking cessation: 5IA SPECT study, Journal of Nuclear Medicine, November 2007, Volume 48(11), Pages 1829-1835.

It's enough to know that what we are sensing and feeling is happening inside a brain that's working hard to readjust to functioning without nicotine. Why fear your brain's healing? Savor it.

Symptoms

> **WARNING**: **The following symptoms relate to cold turkey nicotine cessation only. They are not intended for those using Chantix, Champix, Zyban, Wellbutrin, nicotine replacement products (NRT) or any other cessation product. Regardless of cessation method, immediately consult your health care provider or pharmacist if experiencing any symptom causing concern, including changes in thinking, mood or behavior.**

> **WARNING**: **The list of symptoms below is NOT MEDICAL ADVICE but simply an outline of documented cold turkey recovery symptoms.**

> **IMMEDIATELY** contact our physician should you experience any condition or symptom that causes you CONCERN or ALARM, including continuing depression.

Within reason and common sense, if going cold turkey it is fairly safe to blame withdrawal for most effects felt during the first three days, but not always. Pay close attention to what your body is telling you and if at all concerned contact your doctor.

While reviewing the symptoms below, keep in mind that I am not a physician. I am a nicotine cessation educator. The below information is intended to support not replace the relationship that exists between you and your doctor.

> **Do not rely upon any information in this book to replace individual advice from your physician or other qualified health care provider.**

Every recovery is different. The variety and intensity of effects experienced during recovery varies from person to person, and even between each person's own cessation experiences.
Over the years we've seen thousands of new ex-users surprised to find that they experience few symptoms, if any, while others were confronted with multiple symptoms.

By understanding some of the symptoms, how frequently they occur and how long they last, it may be possible, in some instances, to minimize their impact by action or thought.

As we just learned, brain dopamine pathway sensitivities can take up to 3 weeks before fully restored. Although physical withdrawal symptoms normally peak within the first 3 days, a 2007 study reviewed all symptom studies and found that recovery symptoms has passed with 2 weeks for most but not all. The study found that if symptoms remain "slightly elevated" beyond 2 weeks that they should fully resolve within 3-4 weeks.[303]

---

303 Hughes, JR, Effects of abstinence from tobacco: valid symptoms and time course, Nicotine and Tobacco Research, March 2007, Volume 9(3), Pages 315-327.

Even so, within 2 weeks the ongoing process of restoring and fine-tuning natural sensitivities reaches a point where most begin experiencing confidence building glimpses of the full flavor of life beyond.

A serious concern with symptoms lists such as this is that "smokers with higher levels of perceived risk may find it more difficult to stop and remain abstinent due to higher levels of anticipated or experienced withdrawal symptoms."[304]

As mentioned, they provide a "junkie-mind" looking for relapse justifications a rich source of fuel for accentuating or highlighting something that may otherwise have remained minor, secondary, suppressed or ignored. But how can we not notice symptoms?

If we have a toothache at the same time as a headache, the one that will receive the most attention and focus is the one generating the greatest pain or discomfort. As soon as the discomfort from our primary concern falls below that of our secondary concern, our focus immediately shifts to what was our secondary concern.

We do the same type of primary/secondary refocusing with the effects of withdrawal and layers of recovery. Sometimes we don't even notice a particular symptom until a prior one subsides.

Although the intensity of each remaining effect is likely far less significant than the one preceding it, the mind of the uneducated recovering drug addict is impatient. And some are actually on the lookout for that perfect excuse to relapse and get their drug back.

Upon decline of initial symptoms (if any), recovery remains continuous yet at times may be so gradual that - like trying to watch a rose bud open - it almost becomes impossible to notice change.

Reading symptom lists such as this may tend to cause the mind to look for and expect symptoms to occur. In fact, mental expectations are capable of generating physical symptoms. This phenomenon - known as psychological or functional overlay - is very real.

Few starting home will experience the majority of the symptoms listed below. So why even share this list? You may very well experience one or more symptoms. Knowing how often they occur and how long they normally last offers potential to diminish anxieties, thus increasing your chances of success.

This list is shared to alert you to symptoms commonly seen and to hopefully motivate you to communicate with your doctor regarding any symptom, whether listed or not, that's causing you ongoing concern.

But don't allow this symptoms lists such as this one to sell you on the belief that beginning your journey home will be horrible or intense. Instead, relax, dump irrational fears, maintain a positive attitude, and keep your reasons for wanting to break free in the forefront of your mind. Also, abandoning unrealistic victory standards such as "stopping forever." Instead, adopt a totally do-

---

304 Weinberger AH, et al, Relationship of perceived risks of smoking cessation to symptoms of withdrawal, craving, and depression during short-term smoking abstinence, Addictive Behaviors, July 2008, Volume 33(7), Pages 960-963.

able standard such as celebrating after each hour, challenge or day of freedom and healing.

Avoid needless symptoms by eating smaller and healthier portions of food more frequently, by not skipping meals, by sipping on some form of natural fruit juice for the first three days, and if a big caffeine user, by considering a modest reduction of up to one-half of normal daily caffeine intake. Get plenty of rest while following these simple rules, and this adventure home could turn out to be the most deeply satisfying personal experience of your entire life!

As mentioned, some withdrawal symptoms have roots in the absence of nicotine, and the time needed for the mind to physically adapt to functioning without it. The brain isn't just down-regulating the number of receptors associated with dopamine pathway stimulation. It is resuming full control of all neuro-chemicals that were influenced by nicotine.

While it may take science decades to untangle, measure and quantify all cessation sensitivity interplays, researchers are already cataloging subjective symptom reports from tens of thousands who have attempted cessation. As with the SPECT scan, they're also using brain-imaging studies and other non-invasive exams to discover how the brain is physically altered by nicotine's absence.

Homeostasis is defined as "the ability or tendency of an organism or cell to maintain internal equilibrium by adjusting its physiological processes."[305] It's the body's tendency to return home.

Our enslaved mind had no choice but to adapt and learn to function within a sphere of nicotine normal. Once nicotine's arrival ends, the brain's grand design will cause it to re-adjust, as maintaining homeostasis is a critical part of our ticket home.

Anxiety

Whether dealing with heroin dependency, alcoholism or nicotine addiction, anxiety is a common recovery symptom seen with nearly every drug of addiction.[306] Recovery anxiety can have many sources.
Most obvious, nicotine is no longer stimulating dopamine pathways, resulting in declining levels of background or tonic dopamine, thus elevating wanting. That wanting will from time to time be teased by thousands of old replenishment memories, each sharing the false message that the way to end wanting is to use more nicotine.

One study suggests that much of the

Photo by National Cancer Institute

---

305 <u>Homeostasis</u>. The American Heritage Science Dictionary. Retrieved July 12, 2008, from Dictionary.com website: http://dictionary.reference.com/browse/homeostasis

306 Hall SM, <u>The abstinence phobias: links between substance abuse and anxiety</u>, The International Journal of the Addictions, September 1984, Volume 19(6), Pages 613-631.

underlying current of anxiety felt during the first seven days may in part be the product of a mind preoccupied with risk of relapse.[307]

Remember, it is impossible to fail so long as no nicotine enters the bloodstream. And contrary to the primary message of thousands of use memories, recovery is the only path home. Thinking and dreaming about nicotine use do not cause relapse. Use does.

The primitive limbic mind has been fooled into believing that using nicotine is as important as eating food. It may see ending use as danger, almost as though trying to starve yourself to death. A deep internal belief in this falsehood can generate substantial anxiety.

We can also generate, fuel and feed anxieties on purpose. An addict could easily sabotage his or her own recovery by purposefully focusing on the negative, allowing emotions to fester and build. The plotting junkie mind can then intentionally explode and crash their emotions in hopes of

creating sufficient chaos to justify relapse.

Now for the good news. Any undercurrent of anxiety associated with receptor re-sensitization will peak within 72 hours. By then, nicotine's half-life guarantees that you'll reside inside a nicotine-free body. By then, you may begin noticing that both background anxieties and brain function are starting to improve.

Oh, you may still feel disconnected and foggy for a while (as discussed below) but overall brain function is now on the mend.

While simple to sit here writing about the benefits of dumping needless anxiety generating fears, and about how there's no need to afraid of coming home after years or even decades of chemical captivity, I sincerely appreciate that it's easier said than done.

For some, emptying the mind of nicotine may briefly feel like an emotional train wreck. If so, it's wreckage that's quickly cleared, as the brain works around the clock to restore homeostasis.

If we remain 100% nicotine-free for just 72 hours, unless in the grips of self-induced fears and anxieties, we should begin noticing the underlying current of anxieties begin easing off. By then, billions of brain neurons are basking in nicotine-free, oxygen rich blood serum. Yes, as early as 72 hours and homeostasis sensitivity re-adjustments should begin bearing fruit.

Early healing is rapid. Slow, deep breathing while intentionally working to relax and reassure a frightened mind may help diminish anxieties. It also can't hurt to use physical activity or exercise to stimulate blood circulation.

As reviewed in Chapter 6, keep an eye on caffeine intake as caffeine intoxication can foster anxieties. Keeping an eye on sugar intake can have a calming effect too. Also, eating small portions of healthy foods more frequently should help stabilize blood sugars and prevent you

---

307 Brown RA, et al, Anxiety sensitivity: relationship to negative affect smoking and smoking cessation in smokers with past major depressive disorder, Addictive Behaviors, Nov-Dec 2001, Volume 26(6), Pages 887-899.

having to deal with anxieties associated with the onset of hunger induced wanting, urges and craves.

A 2001 study by Ward entitled "Self-reported abstinence effects in the first month after smoking cessation" may be the most detailed withdrawal symptom study ever. It provides fascinating recovery symptom insights.[308]

The Ward study found that, on average, anxieties peak on day one (within 24 hours), and that, for most, return to pre-cessation levels within two weeks.

Irritability (anxiety's aftermath) peaks at about 48 hours, while restlessness peaks at 72 hours. According to the Ward study, both should return to near pre-cessation levels within two weeks.

Anger

On average, anger peaks at about 48 hours (after 2 days) and within 72 hours is beginning to return to near pre-cessation levels.

Adrenaline stimulation was a non-addictive but now missing element of our nicotine high. The rational mind can use anger to invoke the body's fight or flight response, thus stimulating an adrenaline release.

Anger may also reflect the boiling point of anxiety driven fears, or a normal emotional phase of any significant sense of loss.

Photo by National Cancer Institute

The good news is that it only takes a couple of days of recovery patience to begin sensing improvement. Look for ways to vent frustrations that won't cause needless hurt to family, loved ones, friends, co-workers or pets.

Walk, run, vent into a pillow, find a punching bag, bend a piece of steel, or bite your lip if need be. Share your feelings with your family, friends or other support network. And be sure to let all you spend significant time around know that you've stopped using, as irrational behavior could lead them to believe you're on drugs.

Impatience

Whether impatience is an independent recovery symptom, or simply an expected result associated with anxiety, anger and restlessness, is subject to debate. What isn't debatable is the fact that as nicotine addicts we were each conditioned by our dependency to be extremely impatient when it came to satisfying wanting, urges and craves.

---

308 Ward, MM et al, <u>Self-reported abstinence effects in the first month after smoking cessation</u>, Addictive Behaviors, May-June 2001, Volume 26(3), Pages 311-327.

As active users, we were each in full control in responding to and quickly satisfying those early urges announcing that it was once again time for more. Satisfaction within 10 seconds if slave to inhaled nicotine, we didn't need patience.

Increasingly, neither do users of snuff, chew or dip. Nicotine delivery engineering is mastering the science of using alkaline pH buffering and abrasives to shorten the time needed for nicotine to penetrate oral mouth tissues and enter the bloodstream.[309]

Photo by National Cancer Institute

Nicotine laden smoke would travel into our mouth and throat, past our larynx (housing our vocal cords), down four inches of trachea or windpipe, and then branch into our left and right lungs via our two main bronchial tubes.

Once inside each lung, smoke descended down ten smaller bronchial tubes before striking an estimated 240 million thinly walled air sacs called alveoli.[310] Here nicotine passed through each alveoli membrane and into the bloodstream's pulmonary veins.

Inside the bloodstream, nicotine was pumped over to our heart where between beats it collected in the left atrium. The next beat would pump it through the left ventricle before being ejected upward into the aorta.

There, it branched and traveled up to our brain via either the carotid or vertebral arteries. A small molecule, it easily passed through the brain's protective blood brain barrier.

The amount of nicotine from that first puff would be sufficient to occupy up to 50% of our brain's nicotinic-type acetylcholine receptors. Activating these receptors would trigger a burst of dopamine, which would elevate background or tonic dopamine, while simultaneously generating an "aaah" wanting relief sensation.

When smoked, the entire journey takes less than 10 seconds. If sucked, chewed or dipped, the oral nicotine user's impatience is satisfied in a minute or two, depending on the brand's pH buffers or added abrasives.

Is it any wonder that we nicotine addicts have very little patience when it comes to satisfying recovery related wanting, urges, craves and anxieties?

So, how do we develop the patience to navigate the 3 days needed to move beyond peak physical withdrawal, the up to 3 minutes needed to outlast a cue induced crave episode, or the duration

---

309 Benowitz NL, <u>Systemic absorption and effects of nicotine from smokeless tobacco</u>, Advances in Dental Research, September 1997, Volume 11(3), Pages 336-341.

310 Ochs M et al, <u>The number of alveoli in the human lung</u>, American Journal of Respiratory and Critical Care Medicine, January 1, 2004, Volume 169(1), Pages 120-124.

patience needed to allow new nicotine-free memories time to bury old replenishment memories?

We do so by staying focused on here and now, just one moment and challenge at a time.

Inability to Concentrate or Foggy Mind

According to the Ward study, the feeling that our concentration is not as good or that our mind now lives in a fog is experienced, to one degree or another, by almost two-thirds during recovery. The return of clearness of mind and concentration may seem ever so gradual but within two weeks most begin experiencing concentration levels very close to those of never-smokers.

Photo by National Cancer Institute

As explained in detail in Chapter 6, poor concentration, focus and an inability to think clearly is often associated with low blood sugar. Nicotine force-fed us stored fats and sugars, allowing us to skip meals without feeling hungry.

If we continue attempting to skip meals after ending use, we should expect our blood glucose level to decline and our concentration to suffer. It is not necessary to eat more food but to learn to spread our normal daily calorie intake out more evenly over the entire day.

Women would be well advised to put a very small amount of fuel into their stomach about every three hours and men at least every five.

As reviewed in Chapter 6, unless diabetic or our health care provider recommends otherwise, consider drinking some form of natural fruit juice during the first 72 hours. Cranberry is excellent. Not only will it aid in helping stabilize blood sugar, it is acidic and will slightly accelerate elimination of the alkaloid nicotine.

If concentration concerns persist, consider reducing or avoiding alcohol, as alcohol reduces brain oxygen and impairs concentration. Brisk walks, other physical exercise or slow deep breathing may help enhance focus by increasing oxygen to the brain.

Remember, life-giving oxygen is a vastly healthier brain stimulant than destroying brain gray matter through smoking,[311] or damaging learning and memory via nicotine.[312]

311 Brody, AL et al, Differences between smokers and nonsmokers in regional gray matter volumes and densities, Biological Psychiatry, January 1, 2004, Volume 55(1), Pages 77-84.

312 Pickens LR et al, Sex differences in adult cognitive deficits after adolescent nicotine exposure in rats, Neurotoxicology and Teratology, July-August 2013, Volume 38, Pages 72-78; Ernst M, et al, Smoking history and nicotine effects on cognitive performance, Neuropsychopharmacology, September 2001, Volume 25(3), Pages 313-319.

Sadness & Depression

WARNING - *The following depression discussion is not medical advice. It is a general overview for those going cold turkey, not for those using any cessation medication or product. Regardless of method, seek emergency medical attention if you, your family or your caregiver notice agitation, depressed mood, or changes in behavior that are disturbing or alarming, or if you develop suicidal thoughts or actions.*

The above warning is necessary in part because the meaning of the word "depression" can vary greatly. Like the vague word "crave" ranging from a barely noticeable urge to full-blown panic, the word depression can range from a short period of normal and expected sadness to full-blown clinical long-term (chronic) depression with suicidal thoughts, planning or attempts.

Let's briefly overview depression generally before focus upon sadness or depression associated with ending nicotine use. First, the good news for those experiencing pre-cessation depression.

While evidence that adolescent nicotine use contributes to causing depression continues to build,[313] researchers report no difference in either short-term (less than 3 months) or long-term recovery success rates (greater than 6 months), between smokers with a history of depression and those without.[314]

Photo by National Cancer Institute

According to the U.S. National Institute of Mental Health (NIMH), we all occasionally feel sad or blue but normally such feelings pass within a couple of days. There are many types of depression and no one single cause. It likely results from a combination of factors including psychological, biochemical, environmental and genetic.

The NIMH states that symptoms of depression may include persistent sadness, anxiousness or "empty" feelings, feelings of hopelessness and/or pessimism, feelings of guilt, worthlessness and/or helplessness, irritability, restlessness, loss of interest in activities or hobbies once pleasurable including sex, fatigue and decreased energy, difficulty concentrating, remembering details and making decisions, insomnia, early morning wakefulness, or excessive sleeping, overeating, or appetite loss, thoughts of suicide, suicide attempts, persistent aches or pains, headaches, cramps or

313 Iniguez SD, et al, <u>Nicotine Exposure During Adolescence Induces a Depression-Like State in Adulthood</u>, Neuropsychopharmacology, December 17, 2008 [Epub ahead of print]; also see, Goodman E, et al, <u>Depressive symptoms and cigarette smoking among teens</u>, Pediatrics, October 2000, Volume 106(4), Pages 748-755; and also Boden JM, et al, <u>Cigarette smoking and depression: tests of causal linkages using a longitudinal birth cohort</u>, British Journal of Psychiatry, June 2010, Volume 196(6), Pages 440-446.

314 Hitsman B, et al, <u>History of depression and smoking cessation outcome: a meta-analysis</u>, Journal of Consulting and Clinical Psychology, August 2003, Volume 71(4), Pages 657-663.

digestive problems that do not ease even with treatment.[315]

The American Psychiatric Association's DSM-IV manual (Diagnostic and Statistical Manual of Mental Disorders, Fourth Edition) provides standards for diagnosing depression.

What are the symptoms of major clinical depression? Before reviewing them, do NOT use the following list to attempt to self diagnose yourself, as the DSM-IV standards have other depression definitions too, which include many, many qualifiers. It's why we have highly trained mental health professionals such as psychiatrists.

Generally, under DSM-IV standards, a person must exhibit at least 5 of the following 9 symptoms for at least two weeks in order to be diagnosed as having "major depressive disorder" or MDD: (1) feeling sad, blue, tearful; (2) losing interest or pleasure in things we previously enjoyed; (3) appetite much less or greater than usual, accompanied by weight loss or gain; (4) a lot of trouble sleeping or sleeping too much; (5) becoming so agitated, restless or slowed down that others begin noticing; (6) being tired without energy; (7) feeling worthless or excessive guilt about things we did or didn't do; (8) trouble concentrating, thinking clearly or making decisions; (9) feeling we'd be better off dead or having thoughts about killing ourselves.

Even if a person exhibits 5 of the above 9 symptoms, the symptoms cannot indicate a mixed episode, must cause great distress or difficulty in functioning at home, work, or other important areas and may not be caused by substance use (e.g., alcohol, drugs, medication).

Even if a patient otherwise meets the DSM-IV criteria to be diagnosed with depression, they are excluded and denied the diagnosis if their depression is a normal reaction to the death of a loved one (the "bereavement exclusion") or induced by alcohol or drug use.

So, why exclude drug induced depression but not depression related to ending drug use? Why is it normal to experience depression related to the loss of a loved one, but not when the loss is associated with ending a long and intense chemical relationship?

Normal Sense of Emotional Loss - Sadness and depression are commonly seen in association with withdrawal from most addictive substances. During nicotine withdrawal, both temporary neuro-chemical de-sensitization and a normal psychological emotional loss can give rise to sadness and depressive-type symptoms.

Recovery reflects the end to a long and intensely dependent chemical relationship. As the brain restores sensitivities, physiological, psychological and emotional bonds are broken. Some degree of sense-of-loss sadness is normal and expected.

Should moods fostered by a healing brain or due to normal and expected sadness be classified as clinical depression and mental illness? "Probably not," says a leading U.S. expert.

Dr. Michael First is a physician and psychiatry professor at Columbia University Medical Center,

---

315 U.S. National Institute of Mental Health, Depression, Internet article last reviewed April 3, 2008, accessed July 19, 2008.

and was an editor who helped write the DSM-IV standards.[316] Dr. First did an interview with National Public Radio in April 2007.

During the interview he discussed a study he co-authored that sheds light on the question of whether or not the DSM-IV "bereavement exclusion" should extend to "other types of losses," where it is normal to expect temporary depression to be seen.

"For some people a very messy divorce, a loss of a job, suddenly, those can be just as traumatic as the loss of a loved one," said Dr. First. According to Dr. First, in order to fall under the "bereavement exclusion" for normal, expected and temporary depression, the depression has to "last less than two months and be relatively mild."

"For instance it would not include symptoms such as suicidal ideation or severe slowing down in the way you talk. So it was a mild version of depression that occurred following a loss such as divorce and other things like that."[317]

Dr. First's 2008 study reviewed a national mental health survey and found that "25% of people who were diagnosed with major depressive disorder in the study looked just like the people who we would consider to have normal grief."[318] "So it really raises questions about whether or not these individuals should be considered normal in the same way someone who has normal grief would be considered normal."

He was asked about treatment of those experiencing normal and expected sadness. "When a clinician makes a decision about whether to use psychotherapy or mediation or some combination, the severity of the symptoms play an important role," he notes.

"And certainly if someone is felt to have a normal reaction to the loss of a loved one or a stressful situation, probably the clinician would err on the side of being less aggressive

Photo by National Cancer Institute

with respect to treatment." Although normal sadness might benefit from medication, Dr. First reminded listeners that "medications have side effects" and any potential benefits must be weighed against them.

Although recovery may feel like the death of a friend or loved one, in truth it's an end to chemical captivity. While normal to feel a sense of loss, how do we know that what we're feeling is normal sadness and not full-blown major clinical depression?

316 Columbia University Medical Center, Department of Psychiatry, <u>Michael First MD, Faculty Profile</u>, updated 2005, viewed July 24, 2008.

317 National Public Radio, All Things Considered, <u>The Clinical Definition of Depression May Change</u>, April 3, 2007 www.npr.org; also see Wakefield JC, et al, <u>Extending the bereavement exclusion for major depression to other losses: evidence from the National Comorbidity Survey</u>, Archives of General Psychiatry, April 2007, Volume 64(4), Pages 433-440.

318 Wakefield JC, et al, <u>Extending the bereavement exclusion for major depression to other losses: evidence from the National Comorbidity Survey</u>, Archives of General Psychiatry, April 2007, Volume 64(4), Pages 433-440.

Self-diagnoses can be dangerous. The best advice I can give is that if you sense you are experiencing depression that isn't lifting, or your family is noticing mood changes, get seen and evaluated as soon as possible by your medical provider or at the nearest emergency medical facility.

In regard to depressive type symptoms associated with cold turkey nicotine cessation, it may fall under the "bereavement exclusion" if symptoms are relatively mild and it doesn't last longer than two months.[319]

The more fundamental question is, "why" is sadness or depression a normal step in the emotional grieving process? What's the purpose of depression?

While the anger phase of emotional recovery is fueled by anxiety (Chapter 10), depression is emotional surrender. It reflects a wide spectrum of varying degrees of hopelessness, where anxieties often subside.

Psychiatrist Paul Keedwell suggests that depression is part of what it means to be human, that it's a defense rather than defect. Dr. Keedwell contends that depression forces us to pause and evaluate loss, to change or alter damaging situations or behavior, and that upon reflection and recovery we often experience greater sensitivity, increased productivity and richer lives.[320]

Photo by National Cancer Institute

While successful nicotine dependency recovery demands a degree of reflection, obviously not all depression falls within the "bereavement exclusion," is "relatively minor" in nature, nor improves within 60 days.

In the Ward "abstinence effects" study, 39% of smokers entering the study reported experiencing depression on the day before commencing recovery. By comparison, 19% of never-smokers in the control group were also then experiencing depression.

The percentage experiencing depressive type symptoms during recovery peaked at 53% on day three, and fell to 33% (6 points below their starting baseline) by day seven. Amazingly, only 20% of ex-smokers were reporting depressive-type symptoms by day twenty-eight, just one percentage point above the rate of non-smokers in the control group.[321]

It was once thought that those with depression smoked in order to self-medicate. But as suggested

---

319 National Public Radio, All Things Considered, The Clinical Definition of Depression May Change, April 3, 2007
    www.npr.org; also see Wakefield JC, et al, Extending the bereavement exclusion for major depression to other losses:
    evidence from the National Comorbidity Survey, Archives of General Psychiatry, April 2007, Volume 64(4), Pages 433-440.
320 Keedwell, Paul, How Sadness Survived, the evolutionary basis of depression, 2008, Radcliffe Publishing, ISBN-10 1 84619
    013 4
321 Ward, MM et al, Self-reported abstinence effects in the first month after smoking cessation, Addictive Behaviors, May-June
    2001, Volume 26(3), Pages 311-327.

by Ward's finding, researchers are now asking, "Which came first, nicotine addiction or depression?"[322]

Photo by National Cancer Institute

We know that if nicotine replenishment is delayed, that an escalating sense of depression is part of each low felt between each nicotine fix, which is accompanied by increasing anxiety and frustration. We also know that youth who take up smoking report increased levels of anxiety, stress and depression, and that adults experience "enduring mood improvements" after stopping.[323]

Hopefully, education and self-honesty will aid in more quickly putting any normal sense of loss blues behind you. If depressed while you were using, once through withdrawal, hopefully that will change for the better.

Zyban, Wellbutrin, Chantix and Champix - Keep in mind that the physician's depression treatment resources include not only counseling but scores of non-nicotine and non-addictive medications including Wellbutrin (whose active chemical is bupropion), which is marketed as the stop smoking pill Zyban.

Although long-term results from real-world cessation method surveys indicate that Zyban may be no more effective than attempting recovery without it,[324] it doesn't mean that bupropion does not benefit those experiencing depression.

I also want to briefly mention varenicline which is marketed in the U.S. as Chantix and elsewhere as Champix. Although we have no reported case or medical journal article discussing anyone stopping cold turkey having ever attempted suicide, on April 1, 2008 the U.S. Food and Drug Administration reported that:

> "Chantix has been linked to serious neuropsychiatric problems, including changes in behavior, agitation, depressed mood, suicidal ideation and suicide. The drug may cause an existing psychiatric illness to worsen, or an old psychiatric illness to recur. The symptoms may occur even after the drug is discontinued."[325]

I mention varenicline for two reasons. First, in arguments intended to help salvage varenicline

322 Xu Z, et al, Adolescent nicotine administration alters serotonin receptors and cell signaling mediated through adenylyl cyclase, Brain Research, October 4, 2002, Volume 951(2), Pages 280-292; also Boden JM, et al, Cigarette smoking and depression: tests of causal linkages using a longitudinal birth cohort, British Journal of Psychiatry, June 2010, Volume 196(6), Pages 440-446.

323 Parrott AC, Cigarette-derived nicotine is not a medicine, The World Journal of Biological Psychiatry, April 2003, Volume 4(2), Pages 49-55.

324 Doran CM, et al, Smoking status of Australian general practice patients and their attempts to quit, Addictive Behavior, May 2006, Volume 31(5), Pages 758-766, also see Ferguson J, et al, The English smoking treatment services: one-year outcomes, Addiction, April 2005, Volume 100 Suppl 2, Pages 59-69 [see Table 6]; also Unpublished 2006 U.S. National Cancer Institute Survey of 8,200 quitters, as reported in the Wall Street Journal, Page A1, February 8, 2007.

325 U.S. Food and Drug Administration, FDA Patient Safety News, New Safety Warnings About Chantix, Show #74, April 2008.

from the FDA recall chopping block, Pfizer (the pharmaceutical company marketing varenicline) has come dangerously close to suggesting that depression in those stopping cold turkey can become so great that they too commit suicide. Nonsense!

Varenicline is what's termed a partial agonist. It stimulates dopamine pathways via the same nicotinic-type acetylcholine receptors that nicotine would have occupied, while at the same time blocking nicotine's ability to occupy the receptor and induce stimulation.[326]

But receptor stimulation by varenicline is significantly less than with nicotine (35 to 60%).[327] This reduced level of stimulation may be insufficient to keep some having certain pre-existing underlying disorders (such as depression or other mental health disorders) from experiencing the onset of serious depression and/and behavioral changes.

The problem is that varenicline's elimination half-life is 24 hours.[328] It means that even if the user realizes that the medication is affecting mood or behavior, that even if they stop taking varenicline immediately, that they'll only reduce its influence by half after a full day without it.

So long as varenicline's stimulation blocking effects remain present, could it be that for some small percentage of users, that the only way they see to bring their suffering to an end is to contemplate ending life itself? It's only a theory. We don't yet know.

The National Institute of Health maintains the www.PubMed.gov website, which indexes and allows searching of the summaries (abstracts) of nearly all medical journal articles and studies. My June 14, 2012 search of the term "smoking cessation" returned 22,042 papers, while a search of "suicide" identified 56,345. But when the two terms were combined into a single search ("smoking cessation" + suicide) only 61 papers were returned, and nearly all were associated with cessation medications.

I could not locate a single research paper documenting that anyone going cold turkey had ever attempted suicide. Not one.

Those going cold turkey do not use chemicals that prevent their dopamine pathway receptors from being stimulated naturally. Nor is there any chemical preventing their brain from rapidly re-sensitizing receptors and down-regulating receptor counts to levels seen in non-smokers. As an avenue of last resort, even if they were to begin feeling the effects of untreated major depression, there was no chemical preventing stimulation.

Photo by NIH

What we know with certainty is that smokers attempt to stop smoking in order to save and extend their life, not end it.

326 Pfizer, Chantix Full Prescribing Information, May 2008, www.Chantix.com
327 Coe JW, et al, Varenicline: an alpha4beta2 nicotinic receptor partial agonist for smoking cessation, Journal of Medicinal Chemistry, May 2005, Volume 48(10), Pages 3474-3477.
328 Pfizer, Chantix Full Prescribing Information, May 2008, www.Chantix.com

If feeling overwhelmed by feelings of depression and sadness get help immediately! Go to the nearest emergency medical facility if necessary.

Why allow treatable depression to bring you to the brink of relapse? Why allow it to serve as an excuse for continued use when chronic nicotine use likely contributed to causing it?[329] Instead, put a physician on the team!

Given proper treatment, there is absolutely no evidence to suggest that anyone with a mental health condition - including chronic depression - cannot succeed in gaining freedom from nicotine.

Loneliness or Feeling Cooped Up

Akin to the "sense of loss" felt with depression, loneliness is natural anytime we leave behind a long-term companion, even if a super-toxin. It's time to gift ourselves a new companion, a healing and healthier "us!" Climb from the deep, deep rut we once called home and taste the flavor of nicotine-free life.

Many of us smokers severely limited the activities we were willing to engage in, either because they were too long and interfered with our ability to smoke nicotine, or because our body could not muster the stamina needed to do them.

Carbon monoxide's four-hour half-life robbed our blood of the ability to deliver enough oxygen so as to allow the moderate to heavy smoker to engage in prolonged periods of vigorous physical activity.

Lonely? Get to know the gradually emerging you. Be brave, climb from dependency's ditch and head in directions once avoided. If able, consider pushing your body a bit harder than normal and sampling the healing within.

One of the most satisfying aspects of recovery can be exploring life as an ex-user. Climb out, look around, savor and enjoy.

Insomnia

Nicotine is a nervous system stimulant known to affect subconscious thought. Some evidence suggests it alters EEG monitored brain waves during sleep,[330] and diminishes the percentage of deep REM sleep (our high quality sleep), while increasing REM dream imagery.[331]

Photo by National Cancer Institute

329 Sobrian SK, et al, <u>Prenatal cocaine and/or nicotine exposure produces depression and anxiety in aging rats</u>, Progress in Neuropsychopharmacology & Biological Psychiatry, May 2003, Volume 27(3), Pages 501-518.
330 Zhang L, <u>Power spectral analysis of EEG activity during sleep in cigarette smokers</u>, Chest, February 2008, Volume 133(2), Pages 427-432.
331 Page F et al, <u>The effect of transdermal nicotine patches on sleep and dreams</u>, Physiology and Behavior, July 2006, Volume 30;88(4-5), Pages 425-432; also see Underner M et al, <u>Cigarette smoking and sleep disturbance</u> (article in French), Rev Mal

Our sleep's sense of "nicotine normal" can become disrupted and "sleep fragmentation" is not unusual. Gradually, new or pre-nicotine sleep patterns emerge. Over time we may find that we don't need nearly as much sleep as we did while using, or we may find that our body requires more.

Take a close look at caffeine intake if sleep is disrupted. Nicotine somehow doubles the rate by which the body eliminates caffeine.[332] During recovery, with no nicotine in the bloodstream to accelerate caffeine elimination, if we continue to consume the same amount of caffeine, we should expect to find twice as much circulating in our bloodstream.

If you normally drink a cola before going to bed imagine now feeling the effects of two. If you can handle doubling your normal caffeine intake without disrupting sleep, then this isn't an issue. But if not, or if a heavy user, consider a reduction of up to one-half of your normal caffeine intake to avoid over-stimulation.

Relaxation through mind clearing and slow deliberate breathing can help induce sleep. Mental relaxation can be as simple as slowly clearing our mind of all other thoughts by focusing exclusively on a single object or color.

If sleep continues to be fragmented or is affecting your health, safety or performance, turn to your physician or pharmacist for assistance. There are many sleeping aids available. Don't allow sleep disruption to become another lame excuse to sabotage recovery and destroy your freedom.

Chest Tightness

Although rarely mentioned in symptom studies, it isn't unusual to hear chest tightness complaints during early recovery. Whether arising from tension, stress, depression or somehow related to coughing, lung healing, or lung disease, be extremely careful as chest tightness can also be a sign of more serious health problems, including life threatening heart conditions.

If at all concerned, pick up the phone and contact your doctor. If tightness is related to anxiety or tension, it may benefit from relaxation exercises, a warm shower, slow deliberate breathing or moderate exercise.

Sore Mouth or Throat

Study results are mixed on whether recovery actually causes sore throats. Years of tobacco use clearly damaged and irritated tissues. Powerful toxins numbed them to tobacco's daily assaults. As tissues re-sensitize and heal they may feel temporarily irritated. If so, ice or cool liquids may provide soothing, and cough drops may generate moisture and temporary relief from minor discomfort.

But as a site of other more serious diseases, if mouth or throat pain or discomfort persists, the smart move is to get seen and have it medically evaluated.

Respir. June 2006, Volume 23(3 Suppl), Pages 6S67-6S77.

332 Swanson JA, et al, The impact of caffeine use on tobacco cessation and withdrawal, Addictive Behavior, Jan-Feb 1997, Volume 22(1), Pages 55-68.

Coughing, Mucus or Nasal Drip

According to the Ward study, roughly 60% in recovery reported coughing on day two, 48% by day seven, 33% by day fourteen, and 15% by day twenty-eight.[333] Consider making an appointment to have a thorough check-up if still coughing after having stopped smoking for one month.

A chronic cough can be a warning sign of disease, including lung cancer. A thorough examination that includes a simple chest x-ray can bring piece of mind. Get seen immediately should a cough ever produce blood in sputum.

Cilia are microscopic hair-like projections that line nasal passages, our windpipe (trachea) and bronchial tubes. Cilia inside lung bronchial tubes linking air sacs (alveoli) to our windpipe oscillate in unison at a rate between 5 to 11 cycles per second.[334] They act as a wave-like broom or slow moving carpet that sweeps secreted mucus, containing trapped contaminants, up and out of our lungs.[335]

Tobacco toxins inflict extreme damage and near total destruction of a smoker's cilia. It results in roughly 50% developing a chronic cough (chronic bronchitis), as inflamed bronchial tubes and lungs fight to expel trapped mucus containing pathogens, toxins and particulate.

The good news is that within three days of commencing recovery our cilia begin regenerating and within six months they've fully recovered.[336] They will soon be engaged in cleaning and clearing gunk from the lungs.

Years of tar build-up are loosening. Some will be spit out in phlegm or mucus but most will be swallowed. Mucus and coughing are common, yet according to the Ward study many experience neither.

Clearly, healing lungs benefit from fluids to aid with cleansing and healing. Although the "8 x 8" water drinking rule is under attack for not having any studies to back it (drinking 8 ounces of water 8 times daily),[337] "absence of evidence is not evidence of absence."

Ice can sooth and moisten healing tissues. Cough syrups or decongestants may also bring temporary relief from coughing or irritation. But, again, do not hesitate to get seen should your cough persist.

Although destroyed lung air sacs can never be replaced, those not yet destroyed clean up nicely.

---

333 Ward, MM et al, Self-reported abstinence effects in the first month after smoking cessation, Addictive Behaviors, May-June 2001, Volume 26(3), Pages 311-327.

334 Selwyn DA, et al, A perfusion system for in vitro measurement of human cilia beat frequency, British Journal of Anaesthesia, January 1996, Volume 76(1), Pages 111-115 [4.6 cycles per second]; also see, Clary-Meinesz C, et al, Ciliary beat frequency in human bronchi and bronchioles, Chest, March 1997, Volume 111(3), Pages 692-697 [11 cycles per second].

335 Stannard W, Ciliary function and the role of cilia in clearance, Journal of Aerosol Medicine, Spring 2006, Volume 19(1), Pages 110-1155.

336 Spitzer, J, Smoking's Impact on the Lungs, 2001, WhyQuit.com, Joel's Library.

337 Valtin H, "Drink at least eight glasses of water a day." Really? Is there scientific evidence for "8 x 8"? American Journal of Regulatory, Integrative and Comparative Physiology, November 2002 Nov, Volume 283(5), Pages R993-1004.

And many ex-smokers see a significant increase in lung function within six months.[338]

I couldn't run 200 feet while still smoking and thought I'd never do so again. With early emphysema, it isn't like I'm some big runner now. But I do run-walk a few hundred feet at a time at least weekly and I'm not nearly as winded when the running stops and the walking phase starts.

I thought I'd destroyed these lungs beyond repair. Sometimes it's wonderful being wrong.

Bad Breath or Nasty Tastes

Your healed sense of smell and taste may find the horrible odors and tastes rising-up from healing lungs or oozing from tobacco marinated gums and mouth tissues disgusting.

Guess what? This is what it was like inside your mouth every day while still using. It was just that our senses were so dulled by tobacco toxins that we couldn't notice.

Picture layer after layer of cells slowing dying and being replaced. Depending upon how long, frequently and intensely we used tobacco, it could take significant time for these tastes and odors to fully dissipate.

Time, oxygen rich blood, and fluids will keep mouth, nasal, throat and respiratory tissues on the road to maximum recovery. Brushing a bit more frequently and mouthwash should help control odors released from slowly healing tissues.

Bleeding Gums

Gum bleeding is not unusual during recovery. Aside from the impact of brisk brushing that attempts to whiten tar stained teeth, our gums are feeling the impact of tobacco and nicotine-free living.

Surprisingly, like never-users, the ex-user's gums are more prone to bleeding, not less. Nicotine is a vasoconstrictor that actually constricts and diminishes blood flow. It's thought that this may account for smokers having thicker gum tissues.[339]
According to a 2004 study, the gingival (gum) blood flow rate is "significantly higher at 3 days" into recovery. Within 5 days the liquid sticky plasma proteins normally released by healthy gums have significantly increased, and within 2 weeks are comparable to those of non-smokers.[340]

But if it takes a bit of bleeding to begin gradually reversing the risk of experiencing 240% greater tooth loss than a non-smoker,[341] so be it. Call your dentist if at all concerned about gum bleeding.

---

338 Buist AS, The effect of smoking cessation and modification on lung function, The American Review of Respiratory Disease, July 1976, Volume 114(1), Pages 115-122.

339 Villar CC et al, Smoking influences on the thickness of marginal gingival epithelium, Pesqui Odontol Bras. Jan-March 2003, Volume 17(1), Pages 41-45.

340 Morozumi T et al, Smoking cessation increases gingival blood flow and gingival crevicular fluid, Journal of Clinical Periodontology, April 2004, Volume 31(4), Pages 267-272.

341 Krall EA, Smoking, smoking cessation, and tooth loss, Journal of Dental Research, October 1997, Volume 76(10), Pages 1653-1659.

Headaches

No study has yet identified headaches as a significant recovery concern. While the Ward study notes a slight day-three increase, it also provides evidence that recovery may actually reduce headaches.

It found that 33% of smokers reported having headaches immediately before commencing recovery. Interestingly, those reporting headaches peaked on day three (72 hours) at 44%, dropped to 17% on day seven, and declined to a low of just 11% by day fourteen.[342]

Ward's finding of greater incidence of headaches in active smokers is supported by other studies, which suggest nicotine, a known vasoconstrictor, as a primary culprit.[343]

Vasoconstriction is the narrowing of blood vessels with restriction or slowing of blood flow, caused by contraction of the vessel's muscular wall.[344]

Among smokers, once nicotine's arrival ends, brain blood-oxygen and carbon monoxide levels are restored to normal within twelve hours.

Should a day three headache occur, keep in mind that according to the U.S. National Institutes of Health, "the most common type of headache is a tension headache. Tension headaches may be due to tight muscles in our shoulders, neck, scalp and jaw. They are often related to stress, depression or anxiety."[345]

Relaxation and slow deep breathing, rest, mind clearing with thought focusing exercises, a warm bath or shower, or physical exercise may help relieve tensions and bring relief. Aspirin and a host of other over-the-counter headache medications are available.

Nausea

Nausea is "an uneasy or unsettled feeling in the stomach together with an urge to vomit. Usually it isn't serious and benefits by avoiding solid foods for at least six hours."[346]

The Ward study found that 16% reported nausea on day one, as compared to 2% at pre-cessation baseline. The rate dropped to 11% on day three, 16% on day seven, 9% at two weeks, and 4% on day twenty-eight.

---

342 Ward, MM et al, <u>Self-reported abstinence effects in the first month after smoking cessation</u>, Addictive Behaviors, May-June 2001, Volume 26(3), Pages 311-327.

343 Payne TJ, <u>The impact of cigarette smoking on headache activity in headache patients</u>, Headache, May 1991, Volume 31(5), Pages 329-332.

344 National Institutes of Health and U.S. National Library of Medicine, <u>Vasoconstriction</u>, Medline Plus, Medical Encyclopedia, web page updated January 22, 2007, http://nlm.nih.gov/MEDLINEPLUS/ency/article/002338.htm

345 National Institutes of Health and U.S. National Library of Medicine, <u>Headache</u>, Medline Plus, Medical Encyclopedia, web page updated July 18, 2008, http://www.nlm.nih.gov/medlineplus/headache.html

346 National Institutes of Health and U.S. National Library of Medicine, <u>Nausea and Vomiting</u>, Medline Plus, Medical Encyclopedia, web page updated July 28, 2008, http://www.nlm.nih.gov/medlineplus/nauseaandvomiting.html

Take heart, 37% of Chantix and Champix users report nausea, and in some cases its severe.[347]

Constipation

A 2003 study found that one in six new ex-smokers developed constipation and that for one in eleven the problem became severe ("very or extremely constipated"). It found that constipation levels peaked at about two weeks.[348]

According to a 2006 study, nicotine interacts with digestive tract smooth muscle contractions (peristalsis). The digestive system needs time to adjust to functioning naturally without it. But constipation is correctable and we need not suffer.

"Magnesium salts are the first-line treatment for this problem. If they fail, neostigmine, an anticholinesterase with parasympathomimetic activity, appears remarkably effective in correcting this disorder."[349]

Aside from adjusting to nicotine's absence, what other factors contribute to constipation? According to the U.S. National Institutes of Health (NIH) "the most common causes of constipation are poor diet and lack of exercise." Regarding diet, it's caused by "a diet low in fiber or a diet high in fats, such as cheese, eggs, and meats."[350]

Aside from more fiber, less fats and increased activity, the NIH recommends plenty of water, juice or other liquids free of alcohol and caffeine, which may worsen constipation. "Liquids add fluid to the colon and bulk to stools, making bowel movements softer and easier to pass."

"As food moves through the colon, the colon absorbs water from the food while it forms waste products, or stool," explains the NIH. "Muscle contractions in the colon then push the stool toward the rectum. By the time stool reaches the rectum it is solid, because most of the water has been absorbed."
"Constipation occurs when the colon absorbs too much water or if the colon's muscle contractions are slow or sluggish, causing the stool to move through the colon too slowly. As a result, stools can become hard and dry."

Why extra fiber? "Fiber is the part of fruits, vegetables, and grains that the body cannot digest," says the NIH. "Soluble fiber dissolves easily in water and takes on a soft gel-like texture in the intestines. Insoluble fiber passes through the intestines almost unchanged. The bulk and soft texture of fiber help prevent hard, dry stools that are difficult to pass."

The NIH defines "constipation" as "having a bowel movement fewer than three times per week."

---

347 Aubin HJ, et al, Varenicline versus transdermal nicotine patch for smoking cessation: results from a randomised open-label trial, Thorax, August 2008, Volume 63(8), Pages 717-724.

348 Hajek P, et al, Stopping smoking can cause constipation, Addiction, November 2003, Volume 98(11), Pages 1563-1567.

349 Lagrue G, et al, Stopping smoking and constipation, [Article in French], Presse Medicale, February 2006, Volume 35(2 Pt 1), Pages 246-248.

350 National Institutes of Health, Constipation, NIDDK, NIH Publication No. 07-2754, July 2007, http://digestive.niddk.nih.gov/ddiseases/pubs/constipation/

According to the NIH, "some people think they are constipated if they do not have a bowel movement every day. However, normal stool elimination may be three times a day or three times a week, depending on the person." Consult your physician or pharmacist and obtain relief should constipation concerns arise.

Fatigue Not a Symptom

The majority of studies conclude that physical fatigue is not a normal withdrawal symptom.[351] In fact, exercise induced fatigue has been found to be a symptom of smoking.[352]

The body is shedding the effects of years of dependence upon a stimulant. If anything, the body is working less not more. We actually experience a metabolism reduction. Our heart beats slower, our breathing becomes shallower and our body is no longer feeling the effects of, and working to expel, an endless stream of arriving toxins.

While early recovery may leave us feeling emotionally drained, physically we should soon be feeling much better with more energy than we've felt in years.

It is not normal to feel physically tired or fatigued. If it occurs, get seen and find out why.

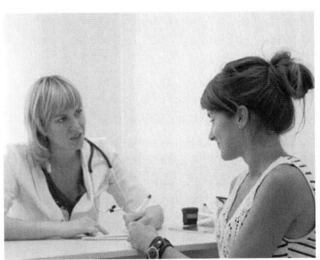

Photo by National Cancer Institute

Possible Medication Adjustments

As noted, tobacco, both oral and smoked, contains thousands of chemicals, some of which may have interacted with medications we were takings. "Often when people stop smoking they may find that medications that were adjusted for them while smoking may be altered in effectiveness," writes Joel.[353]

"People on hypertensives, thyroid, depression, blood sugar drugs, and others may need to get re-evaluated for proper dosages."

"The first few days, it can be difficult telling the difference between 'normal' withdrawal symptoms and medication dosage issues," notes Joel. "But once through the first few days, if a person who is on medications for medical disorders finds him or herself having physical symptoms that just seem out of the ordinary, he or she should speak to the doctor who has him or her on the medications."

"Point out to the doctor that you have recently stopped smoking and started to notice the specific symptoms just after stopping, and that they haven't improved over time."

---

351 Hughes, JR, <u>Effects of abstinence from tobacco: Valid symptoms and time course</u>, Nicotine & Tobacco Research, March 2007, Volume 9(3), Pages 3215-327.

352 Hughes JR, et al, <u>Physical activity, smoking, and exercise-induced fatigue</u>, Journal of Behavioral Medicine, June 1984, Volume 7(2), Pages 217-230.

353 Spitzer, J, Medication Adjustments, July 19, 2001, http://www.ffn.yuku.com/topic/23017

Don't think only in terms of new symptoms. Old symptoms can disappear. During a 2008 question and answer session before roughly 200 inmates in a woman's prison that had recently gone tobacco-free, one woman in the back raised her hand.

"Yes mam, your question." "I don't have a question but a comment," she replied. "I knew this policy change was coming so I stopped a month ago. At the time, I was on eight different medications for my heart, blood pressure, hypertension, cholesterol and breathing. Now I'm down to just two." A big cheer went up.

Key to quality and effective medical treatment is effective communication between patient and physician. Be sure to accurately describe any symptoms, when they were first felt, how frequently they occur, how long they last, what aggravates them and the medications you've been taking.

A complete picture will greatly aid our doctor in determining whether there is a need to increase, decrease, change or discontinue medications.

Possible Underlying Hidden Conditions

Stay alert for the possibility that medical conditions were being masked and hidden by your dependency.

The oral tobacco user introduces more than 2,550 chemicals into their body.[354] A burning cigarette gives off more than 4,000. A mini-pharmacy, these chemicals were capable of hiding a host of medical conditions, including some caused by tobacco use. One that could be noticed during the first 72 hours is difficulty breathing.

Photo by National Cancer Institute

"Why am I having trouble breathing?"
"It's like I need to keep breathing in deep, breath after breath after breath."

Rarely a day passes in overseeing our Internet sites (WhyQuit, Joel's Library, Freedom and our Facebook group) without arrival of an email inviting us to play Internet doctor.

Although well intended, I am a cessation educator who teaches recovery, including symptom possibilities.

I am not a trained and skilled physician, qualified to evaluate, diagnose and treat actual conditions. Even though the symptom being described may sound like normal recovery, how could I possibly know the actual cause? I'd be guessing.

---

354 U.S. Surgeon General, <u>Reducing the Health Consequences of Smoking: 25 Years of Progress: A Report of the Surgeon General: 1989</u>, Page 79.

Difficulty breathing or shortness of breath is not normal.

Still, such concerns are not uncommon. When I hear them, my initial thoughts are outrage and sadness. This could be a smoking induced breathing disorder that until now tobacco industry cigarette engineering had kept hidden from them.

But again, I'd just be guessing. Instead, I tell them it isn't normal, that they need to get seen by a doctor as soon as possible.

How wrong and damaging could guessing be? Shortness of breath can be caused by "lung disease, asthma, emphysema, coronary artery disease, heart attack (myocardial infarction), interstitial lung disease, pneumonia, pulmonary hypertension, rapid ascent to high altitudes with less oxygen in the air, airway obstruction, inhalation of a foreign object, dust-laden environments, allergies (such as to mold, dander, or pollen), congestive heart failure (CHF), heart arrhythmias, de-conditioning (lack of exercise), obesity, compression of the chest wall, panic attacks, hiatal hernia, or gastroesophageal reflux disease (GERD).[355]

Possible hidden conditions aside, what are the odds of someone in the first few days of recovery developing pneumonia or noticing a hiatal hernia? Never-users develop hernias too. They also catch colds, the flu and get sick.

Remain mindful that a coincidental illness or other condition could occur during recovery.

Can cigarette engineering contribute toward hiding symptoms of early asthma or emphysema? Although disputed by the tobacco industry, it's reported that cocoa may cause cigarette smoke to act as a breathing nebulizer.[356]

A chemical within cocoa, theobromine, is known to relax airway muscles and expand bronchial tubes. It's suggested that this might allow more nicotine-laden smoke to penetrate deeper and faster, resulting in a bigger hit or bolus of nicotine assaulting brain dopamine pathways sooner. In theory, this could keep the user loyal to their brand and coming back for more.

According to Philip Morris, maximum concentrations of cocoa can be up to 5%. Theobromine within cocoa accounts for 2.6% of its weight. If a cigarette contains 5% cocoa it also contains up to 1 milligram of theobromine.[357]

The tobacco industry knows that cigarette smoking constricts lung bronchial tubes,[358] that theobromine relaxes bronchial muscles, and that in competition against theophylline, a chemical

355 National Institutes of Health and U.S. National Library of Medicine, Breathing difficulty, Medline Plus, Medical Encyclopedia, web page updated April 12, 2007, http://nlm.nih.gov/medlineplus/ency/article/003075.htm

356 ASH, Tobacco Additives, cigarette engineering and nicotine addiction, July 14, 1999, http://old.ash.org.uk/html/regulation/html/additives.html; as brought to my attention by Schwartz, L, "I'm an ADDICT! Hooray!" March 2, 2002, http://www.ffn.yuku.com/topic/115

357 Philip Morris USA, TMA Presentation on Cocoa to the Department of Health, Carmines, October 18, 1999, Bates #2505520057

358 Hartiala J, et al, Cigarette smoke-induced bronchoconstriction in dogs: vagal and extravagal mechanisms, Journal of Applied Physiology, October 1984, Pages 1261-1270.

used in breathing nebulizers, theobromine compared favorably in improving breathing in young asthma patients.[359]

Philip Morris argues that it is "unlikely" theobromine in cocoa added to cigarettes can produce "a clinically effective dose."[360] Once secret industry documents evidence ongoing industry monitoring of both cigarette cocoa and licorice extract levels for at least three decades. Licorice extract contains glycyrrhizin which some contend is another means by which cigarettes act as bronchodilators.

But Philip Morris says its research shows that licorice extract is "pyrolyzed extensively" (decomposed due to heat), by the up to 900-degree temperatures found in cigarettes.[361]

Although additives have likely changed significantly since 1979, a Brown & Williamson report then documented that cigarette brands containing more than 0.5% cocoa included: Belair, Benson & Hedges, Camel Lights, Doral, Kool Super Lights, Marlboro Lights, Merit, Now, Salem Lights, Tareyton Lights, Vantage, Viceroy Lights and Winston Lights.

Brands then containing more than 0.5% licorice included: Belair, Benson & Hedges, Camel Lights, Marlboro Lights, Merit, Parliament, Pall Mall Lights, Salem Lights, Tareyton Lights, Vantage, Viceroy Lights and Winston Lights.[362]

Other possible once hidden health conditions include thyroid problems masked by iodine in tobacco,[363] chronic depression masked by nicotine,[364] and ulcerative colitis, also somehow suppressed, hidden or controlled by nicotine.[365]

Remember, nicotine is not medicine. It is a natural poison.

Celebrating Two Weeks of Healing!

As seen, nearly all symptoms of physical recovery resolve within two weeks. As for brain dopamine pathway function, yes, there's likely another week or so of ongoing fine tuning of the number of acetylcholine receptors needed to achieve balance and normalcy. But any remaining adjustment is minor in comparison to the healing completed.

While the body's physical readjustment is all but complete, the scars of use remain and deep tissue

359 Simons FE, The bronchodilator effect and pharmacokinetics of theobromine in young patients with asthma, The Journal of Allergy and Clinical Immunology, November 1985, Volume 76(5), Pages 703-077.
360 Philip Morris USA, TMA Presentation on Cocoa to the Department of Health, Carmines, October 18, 1999, Bates #2505520057
361 Carmines EL, Toxicologic evaluation of licorice extract as a cigarette ingredient, Food and Chemical Toxicology, September 2005, Volume 43(9), Pages 1303-1322.
362 Brown & Williamson Tobacco Corporation, Cocoa & Licorice Contents of Competitive Hi-Fi Cigarettes, June 12, 1979, Bates #680224319
363 Vejbjerg P, The impact of smoking on thyroid volume and function in relation to a shift towards iodine sufficiency, European Journal of Epidemiology, 2008, Volume 23(6), Pages 423-429.
364 Covey LS, et al, Major depression following smoking cessation, American Journal of Psychiatry, February 1997, Volume 154(2), Pages 263-265.
365 Lakatos PL, et al, Smoking in inflammatory bowel diseases: good, bad or ugly? World Journal of Gastroenterology, December 14, 2007, Volume 13(46), Pages 6134-6139.

healing, cleansing and repair will be ongoing for years. For example, while our sense of smell and taste have mended, the after-effects of years of marinating tissues in thousands of tobacco chemicals may linger for weeks.

The beauty of two weeks is that our physical addiction is no longer doing the talking. Overall, we've progressed far enough that we begin sampling what it means to be free. And the massive dependency lie we each lived is now far easier to see.

While thousands of old nicotine replenishment memories continue to declare that use satisfies wanting, by two weeks the truth is becoming clearer. By now, increasing periods without wanting begin suggesting that the only path to bringing wanting to a permanent and lasting end is the one now traveled.

We've gifted ourselves a nicotine-free body. The body's readjustment period is nearly complete. By now, the vast majority of subconscious use cues have been extinguished, and our emotional readjustment is well under way. And, the number of wanting-free minutes each day continues to grow.

Photo by National Cancer Institute

Yes, our body has adjusted to functioning without nicotine and we're standing on our own. Whether measurable or not, whether appreciated or not, with each passing day the challenges continue to grow fewer, generally less intense and shorter in duration (see Chapter 13, the comments of 72 ex-users).

Although nicotine assaults have ended and normal function has been restored, the scars of the paths and tracks taken by nicotine have been permanently burned and etched into our brain.

There's only one way to ensure that those paths and tracks are never traveled by nicotine again. There's only one way to guarantee that our mind's priorities circuitry is never again hijacked, so as to place nicotine use on a par with food.

No nicotine today!

Chapter 10

Emotional Recovery

Feelings reflect awareness of our emotions stirring within. The structure and function of these beautiful minds blend and melt subconscious and conscious awareness to create an emotional richness that rivals the stars.

Yet, if the only emotions remaining were those untouched by our addiction, our mind's unfeeling night sky would be empty and dark.

That isn't to say that as nicotine addicts we didn't have emotionally rich, full and meaningful lives. It's that, to varying degrees and frequency, our addiction infected every emotion.

Rising and falling blood-serum nicotine levels not only impacted dopamine but a host of other neuro-chemicals affecting feelings, emotions and mood, including: serotonin, norepinephrine, acetylcholine, gamma-aminobutyric acid and glutamate.[366]

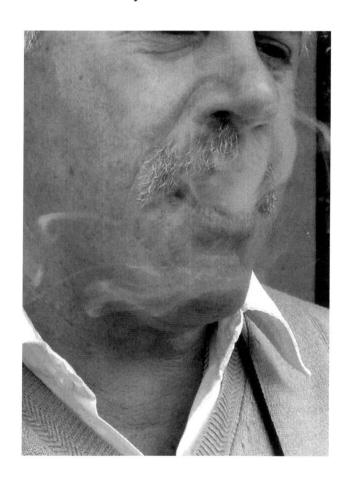

Nicotine dependency is associated with anxiety and mood related disorders.[367] Research shows that the user's mood improves after their first nicotine fix each day. The more badly in need of nicotine, the greater the improvement.

Mood scores are lower in users than non-users throughout the day, with delayed and lower peaks, and decreased subjective feelings compared to non-users.[368]

Emotion can be broken down into three overlapping categories: (1) primary emotions, (2) secondary emotions and (3) background emotions.[369]

366 Quattrocki E, et al, Biological aspects of the link between smoking and depression, Harvard Review of Psychiatry, September 2000, Volume 8(3), Pages 99-110; also see Slotkin TA and Seidler FJ, Nicotine exposure in adolescence alters the response of serotonin systems to nicotine administered subsequently in adulthood, Developmental Neuroscience, 2009, Volume 31(1-2), Pages 58-70.

367 Grover KW, et al, Does current versus former smoking play a role in the relationship between anxiety and mood disorders and nicotine dependence, Addictive Behaviors, May 2012, Volume 37(5), Pages 682-685.

368 Adan A, et al, Effects of nicotine dependence on diurnal variations of subjective activation and mood, Addiction. December 2004, Volume 99(12), Pages 1599-1607.

369 Mosca, A, A Review Essay on Antonio Damasio's The Feeling of What Happens: Body and Emotion in the Making of Consciousness, Psyche, Volume, 6(10), October 2000.

Primary human emotions include surprise, fear, anger, joy, sadness and disgust.[370]

The common thread is that each reflects an almost instant reaction as seen in facial expressions, with no processing or routing inside the frontal lobe of the brain (the prefrontal cortex), the seat of intelligence and thought.

Secondary emotions are all other emotions, and result primarily from frontal lobe and intellectual processing and analysis of the influence of primary emotions.

A truly dynamic being, although appearing as just a list of words, varying emotions are the product of neuron and chemical interactions. Although not easy, while reviewing the following list, reflect on how life as a nicotine addict may have touched upon each.

Human secondary emotions can include feeling:

Accepting, affectionate, amused, anticipating, appreciated, bitter, blissful, bold, bored, bewildered, cautious, caring, cheerful, compassionate, competent, composed, confused, constrained, contempt, contented, cowardly, cruel, curious, courageous, dejected, delighted, depressed, detached, disrespectful, distant, dreadful, disappointed, dismayed, displeased, eager, elated, embarrassed, enjoying, enthusiastic, envious, euphoric, exhausted, exhilarated, expecting, familiar, fond, free, gaiety, generous, grieving, guilty, hateful, homesick, hopeful, hopeless, humiliated, impatient, incomplete, independent, indifferent, infatuated, innocent, insecure, insulted, interested, irritated, isolated, jealous, jolly, jubilated, loathing, interested, longing, lonely, lost, loving, lustful, malicious, melancholy, modest, obligated, optimistic, overwhelmed, painful, mysterious, panicky, passionate, pleasured, pitiful, prohibited, proud, regretful, rejected, relaxed, relieved, reluctant, resentful, resistant, revulsion, satisfied, scornful, sentimental, shameful, sluggish, smug, spiteful, secure, stressed, sympathetic, tender, tense, timid, troubled, uncomfortable, uneasy, weary, woeful and zealous.

Relaxed? How could we expect to ever in our lifetime know total calm or experience full relaxation with nicotine making our heart pound 17.5 beats per minute faster?

Stressed? Try to imagine what stress alone would feel like, if not for urine acidification throwing you into early withdrawal by accelerating elimination of the alkaloid nicotine from your bloodstream.

Uncomfortable or uneasy? Imagine entire days, weeks, months or eventually even years (like millions of us, including me) where you are not once punished with wanting, an urge or use crave.

What would it feel like to untangle and free your emotions from your dependency?

The final category of emotion is background. Background emotions reflect feelings present when at rest or homeostasis.

370 Libkuman TM, et al, <u>Multidimensional normative ratings for the International Affective Picture System</u>, Behavior Research Methods, May 2007, Volume 39(2), Pages 326-334; also see Shaver P, et al, <u>Emotion knowledge: further exploration of a prototype approach</u>, Journal of Personalty and Social Psychology, June 1987, Volume 52(6), Pages 1061-1086.

Our background emotions were ridden hard by an endless roller-coaster ride of neuro-chemical lows and highs, transporting us from badly needing a nicotine fix to the "aaah" wanting relief sensation upon getting one.

Emotional recovery isn't only about navigating the feelings and emotions brought on by recovery. It's about freeing them from our addiction, about brightening each star that fills life's sky.

Before you is an opportunity to heal pride and self-esteem. Imagine the sea of emotions when you first realize that you really love being free, that you never, ever want to go back.

When they occur, every physical symptom reviewed in the last chapter (Chapter 9) will be wrapped in emotions. Likewise, the subconscious mind's healing (Chapter 11) cannot be divorced from the feelings we make it sense. And how bland would our thinking and conscious recovery be (Chapter 12) if not painted with emotion?

Although I've separated recovery's layers for purposes of review, in reality they are so intertwined that the best we can hope for is to grasp the obvious.

Such complexity reflects the beauty of who we are, and why it's so sad to continue paying the nicotine addiction industry to pull our emotional strings, as if its puppets.

But why has it taken so long for us to awaken to the fact that our emotions have become as hostage to our dependency as every other part of our being? And what emotions are normal and should be expected during recovery?

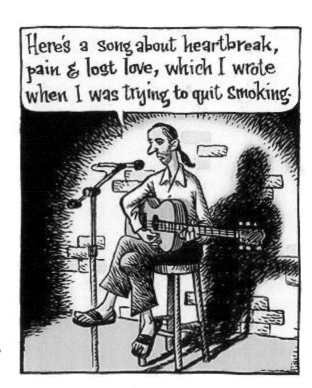

The human mind is designed to adapt, protect and insulate itself from circumstances that seem beyond its control. It does so by employing defense mechanisms that work by distorting or blocking reality and natural instincts.

The brain's well-stocked arsenal of defense mechanisms includes denial, displacement, intellectualization, projection, rationalization, reaction formation, regression, repression, sublimation, suppression, compensation, dissociation, fantasy, identification, undoing, and withdrawal.[371]

Dependency recovery understanding and insights can help fuel and inspire our own personal dreams of freedom, including causing our mind's dependency defenses to crumble before our eyes.

If they were to crumble, what might emotional recovery be like? Let's review the natural grief cycle in hopes that understanding it helps accelerate your healing.

---

371 Defense mechanism, New World Encyclopedia, April 3, 2008, http://newworldencyclopedia.org/entry/Defense_mechanism

Kubler-Ross Grief Cycle

The Kubler-Ross model identifies five discrete stages in the grief cycle when coming to terms with any significant emotional loss.[372]

Albeit chemical, dependency upon nicotine may have been the most intense and dependable relationship in our entire life.

As a smoker, unless wet and it wouldn't light, never once did puffing on a cigarette let me down. Even if a brand we hated, nicotine's "aaah" wanting relief sensation was always a few seconds away.

If we smoked nicotine ten times per day and averaged 8 puffs per cigarette, that's 80 times a day that we puckered our lips up to some nasty smelling butt spewing forth more than four thousand chemicals that included hundreds of toxins, 81 of which are known to cause cancer.

What human on earth did we kiss 80 times each day? Who did we depend upon 80 times a day? How many days during our life did we think or say our name more than 80 times? Any? Imagine being closer to our addiction than our own name.

In 1982, Joel Spitzer applied the Kubler-Ross grief cycle model to the emotional journey navigated during recovery.[373] The five stages of emotional healing include:

(1)   Denial: "I'm not really going to quit. I'll just pretend and see how far I get."

(2)   Anger: "Have I really had my last nicotine fix? "This just isn't fair!"

(3)   Bargaining: "Maybe I can do it just once more. Two days without, I've earned it!"

(4)   Depression: "This is never going to end." What's the use?" "Why bother?"

(5)   Acceptance: "Hey, I'm feeling pretty good!" "I can do this!" "This is great!"

It's important in navigating emotional recovery to not get stuck in any stage before reaching acceptance. Understanding the roots of each will hopefully help empower a smoother and quicker transition.

As we review each stage, keep in mind that the Kubler-Ross's grief cycle of emotional loss is not etched in stone, nor need it occur in the order presented. One or more phases may be absent, while another is revisited.

Obviously, it's hoped that by spending time now reflecting on denial, anger, bargaining and

---

372 Kubler-Ross, Elizabeth, "On Death and Dying," 1969, Routledge, ISBN 0415040159.
373 Spitzer, J, Joel's Library, Understanding the Emotional Loss Experienced When Quitting Smoking, 1982, http://whyquit.com/joel

depression that each can be minimized if not avoided altogether.

In the perfect world, knowledge and understanding would allow us to skip the first four phases entirely and jump right to acceptance.

And that actually happens far more often than you might think. But if it doesn't, don't fret. You'll navigate each just fine.

Denial

Cessation denial is a state of disbelief. The denial phase of emotional recovery is associated with coming to terms with the fact that a long and intense chemical relationship has ended.

It's almost the opposite of active dependency denial, which uses distortion and blocking techniques to provide cover and insulation, so as to enable continued use.

Denial is the unconscious defense mechanism - just below the surface - that allowed us to resolve the emotional conflict and anxiety that would normally be felt by a person living in a permanent state of self-destructive chemical bondage.[374]

While using, we were protected by a thick blanket of rationalizations, minimizations, fault projections, escapes, intellectualizations and delusions. Our denial helped insulate us from the pain and reality of captivity. For most, it also helped us pretend that the problem was somehow being solved.

But here, during recovery, those same anxiety coping defenses begin to distort reality about what's really happening.

As mentioned, I start seminars by asking for an honest show of hands to the following question, "How many of you feel that you will never, ever smoke again?" Rarely will a hand go up. Even though all attending came wanting to stop, then and there, all were in denial, as none believed they would.

Although we want to stop, on a host of levels the mind isn't yet convinced. If convinced, why do so many of us treat recovery as though some secret? And why leave an escape path such as that one hidden cigarette, or a means to quickly obtain more?

---

374 <u>Denial</u>. (n.d.). The American Heritage Dictionary of the English Language, Fourth Edition. Retrieved July 21, 2008, from Dictionary.com

Denial is normal. But if allowed, it can transform disbelief into failure.

"I don't want to stop just yet," decides Ryan. "I am perfectly healthy using, so why stop now," asks Emily? "I'm different, I can control use and keep it to just one or two a day," asserts Ashley.

Regrettably, relapse is at hand for Ryan, Emily and Ashley. While denial acts as protective insulation in allowing us to get our toes wet in beginning this journey -- including allowing you the courage to reach for FFN-TJH - cessation disbelief can easily become a path of betrayal.

The denial phase protects us against the immediate emotional shock of leaving the most intense relationship we've likely ever known, even while embarking upon a journey from which there should be no return.

It's a shock buffer that allows us time to come to terms with where we now find ourselves. It operates unconsciously to diminish anxiety by refusing to perceive that recovery and success will really happen.

A number of times I went three days and then "rewarded" myself with that one puff that always spelled defeat. Clearly, I hadn't made it beyond denial. But if I had, the next phase encountered would likely have been anger.

Anger

Anger is a normal and expected emotional recovery phase. It's also a way to experience the flow of missing adrenaline that was once part of our nicotine high.

Anxieties flowing from anger can also be used to intentionally fuel rage. I take no pride in recalling that I could became so nasty and create so much turmoil among those I loved, that I could convince them that I needed my cigarettes back.

But there are important distinctions between anger felt during the emotional recovery stage and using it as an adrenaline crutch or a sick relapse ploy.

The anger phase of recovery is a period of healing where we begin to awaken to the realization that it may actually be within our ability to pull this off and succeed. It's awareness that, just maybe, our last puff, dip, chew or vape ever is already behind us.

Durable nicotine use memories flowing from captive dopamine pathways elevated that next fix to one of life's top priorities. But emotional recovery has now transported us from fear of stopping to fear of success.

Photo by National Cancer Institute

Is it any wonder that anger would be the mind's reaction? It's now sinking in. Success is occurring in spite of denial. A relationship that was once high-priority is ending. This realization can feel overwhelming.

Now, all the new ex-user requires is some excuse, any excuse, to let it all out, to vent, to turn an ant hill into a mountain. Conflicting motivations, freedom or feed-em, risk of succeeding and fear of the unknown. Just one spark, any spark, and the uneducated ex-user stands primed to lash out.

While this high-energy phase of the emotional stage of goodbye is a normal step in recovery, the educated ex-user both recognizes anger's arrival and understands its roots.   Recognition is critical as it provides a protective seed of reason inside a mind looking for a spark, a fear driven mind poised to abandon rational thought.

If allowed, that spark may activate the body's fight or flight response, releasing a cascade of more than one hundred chemicals and hormones.

The prospect of success is not a logical reason to get mad, enraged or fight. The educated mind knows that emotion can be contrary to our well-being and best interests. Anger ignores all positives while pretending a sense of loss, a loss based largely on false use rationalizations.

So how does a mind trained in recognizing and understanding recovery anger prevent it from harming us and the world around us? Chapter 11 on subconscious recovery provides a number of techniques for navigating a crave episode which may not peak for three minutes.

In that anxiety underlies both crave episodes and anger episodes, they should serve you well. Let me leave you with one exercise that may aid in generating the patience needed to move beyond anger.

Another day of freedom causes a sense of loss to collide with the likelihood of success. A spark is generated. It's time for patience, just one micro-second at a time.

Recognize the anger building within. Understand what's happening and why. Realize that unless being physically assaulted, that only bad can
come from unleashing your body's fighting
chemicals.
Anger is almost never a solution.

It reflects primitive impulsive instincts out of
control. It carries strong potential to harm
innocent victims, leaving emotional scars that
may never fully heal.

If possible, sit down. Slowly close your eyes
while taking a slow deep breath into the bottom
of both lungs. Focus all concentration on your
favorite color or object, or upon the sensations

Photo by National Cancer Institute

associated with inhaling and exhaling your next breath. Feel the cool air entering, and its warmth while slowly exhaling.

Baby steps, just one second at a time. Take another slow deep breath while maintaining total inner focus. Feel the sense of calm and inner peace as it begins to wash over you. As calmness arrives slowly open your eyes. Now, if you wish, respond to the situation with logic, reason and calm.[375]

How long will the anger phase last? As briefly or as long as we allow.

Clearly, knowledge can provide the insights needed to recognize transitions and hopefully react in healthy, non-destructive ways. It's what anger management is all about. Hopefully, understanding and acceptance will help accelerate emotional recovery. But if not, don't be disturbed as each step reflects normal emotional healing.

Fears, cycling emotions, an addict's relapse ploys, or feeling a sense of loss, recovery presents plenty of opportunities to encounter anger. We also need to remain mindful that normal everyday life produces anger too, even in never-users. At times, anger's causes may overlap and get tangled. But even then, we have it within us to fully control anger impulses, without harm to anyone.

Success at hand, where does the mind turn next? What is anger's ultimate solution? A debate is about to begin. How do we keep our cake while eating it too? But this isn't about cake. It's about a highly addictive chemical with tremendous impact upon our physical, subconscious, conscious and emotional well-being.

Bargaining

"Maybe I'm the exception to the Law of Addiction.
Maybe I can use just once!"

Chapter 4 reviewed use rationalizations employed by the still feeding addict in an attempt to justify that next fix. Using many of the same rationalizations, here bargaining's primary hope is more about continuing this journey home while also visiting with nicotine now and then.

Instead of grief simply accepting an end to nicotine use, dependency ignorance toys with breaking free while remaining great friends.

Bargaining can be with our particular nicotine delivery device, another form of delivery, ourselves,

Photo by National Cancer Institute

---

375 While debate abounds about meditation's ability to heal the body, and study quality to date has been horrible, there is limited evidence of some forms of meditation diminishing blood pressure. See, U.S. Agency for Healthcare Research and Quality, Evidence Report/Technology Assessment Number 155, Meditation Practices for Health: State of the Research, AHRQ Publication No. 07-E010, June 2007.

loved ones or even our higher power. Its aim is the impossible feat of letting go, without letting go. If allowed, the emotional conflict of wanting to say "hello" while saying "goodbye" can easily culminate in relapse.

"Just one," or "just once" can evolve into "this is just too hard," "too long," "things are getting worse not better," "this just isn't the right time to stop!"

Although a significant portion of FFN-TJH is about bargaining, if allowed, this book itself can and will provide an abundance of fuel for the bargaining mind.

For example, every user and every recovery are different. Sharing "averages" and "norms" with primary focus upon the most common form of delivery will naturally generate tons of ammunition for those whose dependency or recovery traits are beyond "average" or don't involve smoke.

Key to navigating conflicted feelings is to demand honesty, while keeping our primary recovery motivations vibrant, strong and on our mind's center-stage. The wind beneath our wings, allowing freedom's desire to die invites destructive and intellectually dishonest deals to be made.

Instead of buying into relapse, remember, so long as 100% of the planet's nicotine remains on the outside it's impossible to fail. But what happens inside the grieving and bargaining mind once it realizes that brain dopamine pathway design makes it impossible to arrest our dependency while letting it run free?

Depression

Please refer to the prior chapter, Chapter 9, under Symptoms for a detailed discussion of depression. While a brief period of sadness and depression is normal and expected when ending any long and intense relationship, even a chemical one, don't hesitate to get seen and evaluated if at all concerned about ongoing depression.

If already taking medication for depression, keep in mind that your prescription may need adjustment. And do remain alert as nicotine can mask hidden underlying depression. It's why getting seen is important if your period of sadness

Photo by National Cancer Institute

isn't both brief and mild.

Acceptance

The victory phase of the Kubler-Ross grief recovery cycle is acceptance. It's the "this is do-able" moment of an emotional journey that can mark the transition from a "user trying to stop" to "ex-user."

It may or may not have been pretty getting here. Now and then, you may still encounter infrequent or seasonal un-extinguished subconscious feeding cues.

And it's likely that your pile of old replenishment memories will, for now, continue their gradually waning tease. It's also likely that the pile's lure will continue to be fueled by a lingering romantic fixation or two, that might benefit from focused honesty. But you did it!

In regard to your emotional recovery, if you've been able to let go and fully accept letting go then your emotional journey is complete. Congratulations!

Still only one rule ... none today!

Chapter 11

Subconscious Recovery

The Unconscious Mind

Endlessly hammered by flavor, aroma, pleasure, friendship, adventure, rebellion and affordability marketing, our subconscious mind is the nicotine addiction industry's hidden target.

If it didn't work they wouldn't annually spend billions doing it. The subconscious is listening. Twice the traveling cessation hypnotist sold me a full day of unbelievable hypnotic bliss before I tested it and relapsed.[376]

But looking upon our subconscious mind only in terms of being the playground of others cheapens and makes it look dumb, while ignoring our conscious ability to do the same in retraining it.

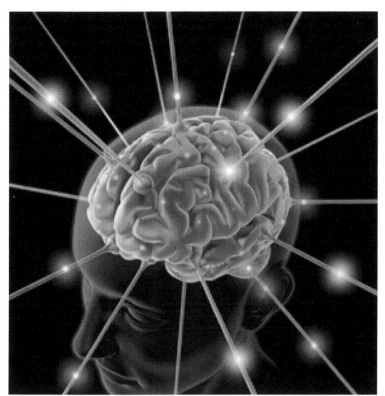

Image by National Institute of Mental Health

If so dumb, why can our subconscious see subliminal messages invisible to the conscious mind, or feel the influence of tobacco marketing that our consciousness has totally ignored? Why can it react to triggering cues written upon it by hypnotic suggestion or self-conditioning, cues meaningless to conscious awareness?

Dumb? When typing on a keyboard, what part of the mind and level of awareness is locating and correctly striking each key? While operating a vehicle, who is really controlling which foot needs to push on which pedal and how hard, or doing the driving as we read billboards, talk on the phone or daydream?

Our conscious mind has unknowingly aided in helping teach our subconscious skills and how to perform activities, including using nicotine.[377] Now it's time to knowingly teach it how to function without it.

---

376 Abbot NC, et al, <u>Hypnotherapy for smoking cessation</u>, Cochrane Database of Systematic Reviews, 2000;(2):CD001008, which examines 9 hypnotherapy studies and concludes: "We have not shown that hypnotherapy has a greater effect on six month quit rates than other interventions or no treatment."

377 Bargh JA, et al, <u>The Unconscious Mind</u>, Perspectives on Psychological Science, January 2008, Volume 3(1), Pages 73-79.

Whether referred to as our subconscious, unconscious or preconscious, science is still in the early stages of discovery in understanding the scope of its involvement in day-to-day life. It's every bit as real as the never seen portion of an iceberg. Think of Disney World and awareness of the magic above ground, while a massive unseen city beneath lives and breathes in bringing the magic to life.

It's normal for us to deeply believe that our consciousness is the one doing things, that it causes our actions after careful deliberation, that our behavior was our idea.

While this is our self-perception, a growing body of evidence suggests that like Disney's puppets, the conscious mind is not the primary source motivating behavior, that in many cases our subconscious has already made up our mind for us.[378]

It's suggested that the subconscious mind has evolved as a highly adaptive "behavioral guidance system" which acts on impulse. It's becoming more widely accepted that the impulse for behavior flows from our subconscious, that our consciousness then seizes upon the idea as its own.

It's suggested that the real role of our consciousness is as impulse gatekeeper, and trying to make sense after the fact of behavior that the gatekeeper allowed to occur.[379]

Sources of subconscious impulses can include evolutionary motivations, past personal preferences, cultural norms, family values, past experiences in similar situations, how others in the same situation are currently behaving, or be the product of conditioning, both reinforcement (operant) and association (classical).

Multiple sources of subconscious behavioral impulses make conflicts inevitable. Drug addiction reflects a conflicts war zone.

Our subconscious has its own behavioral goals, goals hidden from awareness.[380] Reading these words is clear evidence that "you" want to break free. It's likely your subconscious does too.

But after being conditioned by years of nicotine dependency wanting, use and relief, and by false gatekeeper explanations as to why use was again necessary, without honesty and teamwork subconscious recovery can be messy and longer than necessary.

---

378 Galdi S, et al, Automatic mental associations predict future choices of undecided decision-makers, Science, August 22, 2008, Volume 321(5892), Pages 1100-1102.

379 Wegner DM, Precis of the illusion of conscious will, Behavioral Brain Science, October 2004, Volume 27(5), Pages 649-659; as reviewed in Bargh JA, et al, The Unconscious Mind, Perspectives on Psychological Science, January 2008, Volume 3(1), Pages 73-79.

380 Bargh JA, et al, The automated will: Unconscious activation and pursuit of behavioral goals, Journal of Personality and Social Psychology, December 2001. Volume 81, Pages 1004-1027.

Operant Conditioning

Operant conditioning is a process that operates to modify behavior, in our case nicotine use. It does so through positive or negative reinforcement. In our case, we've associated relief from wanting, urges or craves with use of our nicotine delivery device. Operant conditioning conditioned us to associate the relief produced by the reinforcement with a specific behavior.[381]

Drug use behavior conditioning reflects unintended expectations training of the subconscious mind. Hundreds or thousands of annual nicotine use repetitions created strong subconscious associations between using nicotine and the adrenaline charged "aaah" sensation that followed.[382]

Operant conditioning associated with experiencing "aaah" wanting relief was actually only one side of operant control.

We were also controlled by displeasure and fear conditioning associated with the consequences of ignoring nicotine's two-hour half-life.

Once hooked, we discovered that delaying replenishment for too long made us anxious, irritable and depressed our mood, while replenishment brought temporary relief.

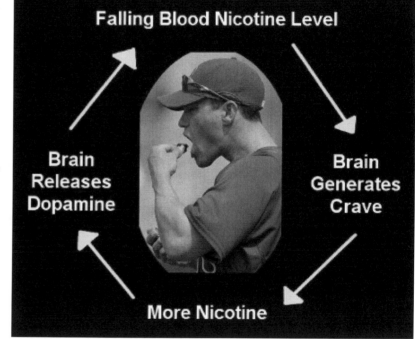

Like being beat with a whip or receiving an electrical shock, the anxiety consequences of having waited too long between feedings operated to condition us to avoid anxieties by engaging in replenishment early and often.

Trapped in a perpetual cycle between wanting and relief, is it any wonder that both our subconscious and conscious grew to deeply believe that nicotine use defined who we were, that replenishment was as important as eating, and that life without it would be empty, meaningless or nearly impossible?

The good news is that within 72 hours of ending use the subconscious has no choice but to begin noticing that peak withdrawal has been achieved and is now gradually beginning to subside, yet life goes on.

---

381 operant conditioning. (n.d.). The American Heritage Stedman's Medical Dictionary. Retrieved August 31, 2008, from Dictionary.com website.
382 Rose JE, et al. Inter-relationships between conditioned and primary reinforcement in the maintenance of cigarette smoking, British Journal of Addiction, May 1991, Volume 86(5), Pages 605-609.

While likely still anxious and alert, the most intense period of recovery is over. So long as all nicotine remains on the outside, fears and anxieties associated with avoiding withdrawal's onset need never again be encountered.

While negative reinforcement operant conditioning is quickly extinguished by diminishing punishment for not using, positive reinforcement operant conditioning associated with the tease of thousands of old "aaah" replenishment memories will take additional time to overcome.

While we cannot erase thousands of old "aaah" memories, conscious honesty and dependency understanding enable us to see those memories for what they truly are, an accurate record of the times when an actively feeding drug addict's replenishment briefly satisfied drug wanting.

Recasting them in truthful light can diminish or even end their remaining tease and influence upon us. But let's not fool ourselves. Each memory remains tied to the same dopamine pathway that created it.

Even if we go years without nicotine, the effects of just one powerful puff, dip, chew or vape somehow breathes new life into old "aaah" memories, and at least one aspect of positive operant conditioning. Whether recognized or not, activated dopamine pathways would immediately re-assign nicotine use the same priority as eating. Whether wanted or not, use would soon have our brain demanding more and us obeying.

The good news is that simply becoming mindful of how subconscious positive and negative operant conditioning played a part in controlling us can aid in helping extinguish it and take back control.[383]

Although not always easy, the solution always remains simple ... no nicotine today!

Classical Conditioning

As it relates to nicotine, classical or Pavlovian conditioning is conditioning in which, through repetition, a person, place, thing, activity, time or emotion (a conditioned stimulus or use cue) becomes so paired with using nicotine, that encountering the use cue alone becomes sufficient to trigger wanting, an urge or crave.[384]

Subconsciously triggered anxieties are the mind's means of commanding that we again bring nicotine into the body.

---

383 Brewer JA, et al, <u>Craving to Quit: Psychological Models and Neurobiological Mechanisms of Mindfulness Training as Treatment for Addictions</u>, Psychology of Addictive Behaviors, May 28, 2012.

384 <u>classical conditioning</u>. (n.d.). Merriam-Webster's Medical Dictionary. Retrieved August 31, 2008, from Dictionary.com website.

Like Pavlov's dogs, which he conditioned to expect food and begin salivating upon the ringing of a bell, we each conditioned our subconscious to expect arrival of a new supply of nicotine in specific situations.

For example, your mind can be trained to want nicotine upon simply seeing a picture of a green triangle. A 2012 classical conditioning study did just that. It conditioned smokers to associate smoking with an object that had previously been entirely neutral.[385]

The conditioning was created by 80 times pairing a picture of a green triangle with a smoking related picture (people holding or smoking cigarettes). Each pairing was shown to smokers for less than half a second (400 milliseconds). Although less than a second, the subconscious mind was watching and learning.

Not only did smokers report increased cravings upon being shown the green triangle alone without the smoking related image, brain responses recorded by EEG (electroencephalograph) supported their claims.

Researchers have successfully used sight, smell and hearing to establish new conditioned use cues in smokers.[386] Encountering the new cue triggers use expectations and an urge to smoke, with an increase in pulse rate.

Researchers find it easier to establish new cues among light smokers, who obviously have fewer existing cues than heavy smokers.

If crave episodes feel real and physical in nature there's good reason. Although nicotine-feeding cues are psychological in origin, they trigger physiological responses within the body.

Not only do the stimulant effects of using nicotine increase pupil size, researchers found that encountering a visual nicotine use cue will increase pupil size, an autonomic response.[387]

Using brain scans, researchers discovered increased blood flow during cue-induced cravings in brain regions associated with "aaah" wanting relief or anxiety (the ventral striatum, amygdala, orbitofrontal cortex, hippocampus, medial thalamus and left insula).[388]

They also found that the amount of brain blood flow (perfusion) was tied to the intensity of the cue induced cigarette cravings in brain regions known to control attention, motivation and

385 Littel M and Franken IH, <u>Electrophysiological correlates of associative learning in smokers: a higher-order conditioning experiment</u>, BMC Neuroscience, January 11, 2012, 13:8.
386 Lazev AB, et al, <u>Classical conditions of environmental cues to cigarette smoking</u>, Experimental and Clinical Psychopharmacology, February 1999, Volume 7(1), Pages 56-63.
387 Chae Y, et al, <u>Subjective and autonomic responses to smoking-related visual cues</u>, The Journal of Physiological Sciences, April 2008, Volume 58(2), Pages 139-145.
388 Franklin TR, <u>Limbic activation to cigarette smoking cues independent of nicotine withdrawal: a perfusion fMRI study</u>, Neuropsychopharmacology, November 2007, Volume 32(11), Pages 2301-2309.

expectancy (the prefrontal cortex and posterior cingulate).[389]

Years of subconscious conditioning had us reaching for a nicotine fix and engaging in replenishment without our conscious mind recognizing that we had encountered a use cue (conditioned stimulus), and often without noticing that replenishment was underway.

Study the next smoker you see. As if on autopilot, it is very likely that the drags you'll watch being inhaled will be taken while their unconscious mind is in full control.

I can't begin to count the number of times I looked down and was surprised to see the ashtray full and the pack empty.

Nicotine's half-life combined with our dependency's level of tolerance to determine the number of times daily we'd need to replenish. Although probably unaware, we each established daily replenishment patterns that conditioned our subconscious when to expect more.

Crave Episode Intensity

As we navigated our day. our sight, smell, sound, taste, touch or an emotion would alert our subconscious that a use cue had been encountered. Although often unnoticed, a gentle urge was generated alerting us that it was again time for replenishment.

If ignored or replenishment was long overdue, the urge's anxiety energy could grow into a full-blown crave episode. A 2007 study suggests that your right insula (just above your ear and an inch or so in) acts as a control center for urge and crave anxiety routing and intensity control, including recognition of each time, place, person met, activity or emotion during which we conditioned our subconscious to expect nicotine.[390]

The intensity of a particular crave episode appears to be influenced by a number of factors. A 2007 study found that the two most significant were how recently we had used and our level of impulsiveness.[391] Obviously, the longer without nicotine, the longer anxieties have to build.

You'd think that once we end all use and become 100 percent nicotine-free that our subconscious

389 Small DM, et al, The posterior cingulate and medial prefrontal cortex mediate the anticipatory allocation of spatial attention, NeuroImage, March 2003, Volume 18(3), Pages 633-641.

390 Naqvi, NH, et al, Damage to Insula Disrupts Addiction to Cigarette Smoking, Science, January 2007, Vol. 315 (5811), Pages 531-534.

391 Zilberman ML, et al, The impact of gender, depression, and personality on craving, The Journal of Addictive Diseases, 2007, Volume 26(1), Pages 79-84.

would notice that we are still alive, well and functioning and abandon demands for more. While getting clean and allowing time for re-sensitization aids in diminishing underlying withdrawal anxieties, urge and crave anxieties tied to subconscious conditioning are independent.

Still, once beyond peak withdrawal, all levels of awareness are confronted with escalating awareness that we've been living a lie, that once all nicotine is out of our system that things slowly start getting better not worse. It's here that fears of failure butt heads with fears of success.

As for impulsiveness, it's the trait that played a key role in many of us experimenting with using nicotine in the first place. Now that same trait sees relapse as a quick-fix solution.

Patience in standing up to impulsivity can, itself, foster confrontation anxieties. Our hopes and dreams of a lasting dependency solution are pitted against thousands of old "aaah" memories promising instant yet temporary relief from wanting.

Truth is, only one choice provides a way out. Truth is, the only path home is to choose the bigger, better yet delayed reward. Truth is, use triggering activity done while under nicotine's influence can be done as well as or better without it.

Ask yourself, what is the only permanent solution to ending replenishment urges and craves?

Why not invite your subconscious to switch teams, to join in your quest to stay clean instead of trying to keep your dependency active by issuing urges and craves for more nicotine. Invite your impulsiveness to act as guardian over the next few moments in remaining 100 percent nicotine-free.

Talk to your subconscious. Encourage it to serve as a vigilant ally in protecting your freedom, healing, pride and growing self-esteem.

Photo by National Cancer Institute

Imagine the creation of healthy, positive impulses that instantly respond to protect us from challenge. Imagine all levels of awareness forming a skilled firefighting team that remains on scene, ready to quickly extinguish any blaze.

Although one study noted that the level of depression among women, but not men, was capable of impacting crave episode intensity,[392] study after study finds little or no difference between

---

392 Zilberman ML, et al, <u>The impact of gender, depression, and personality on craving</u>, The Journal of Addictive Diseases, 2007, Volume 26(1), Pages 79-84.

male and female success rates.[393] Although the thought of a depressed woman having to endure a slightly more intense crave episode is disheartening, keep in mind that all episodes are extremely short lived, and within a week the majority are silenced. But as reviewed in Chapter 9, whether male or female, do not ignore or make light of ongoing depression.

A food craving study found that vividness of imagery associated with food influenced food craving intensity.[394] Go ahead. Give it a try. Picture your favorite food. Now make the mental image as vivid and detailed as possible. Feel the urge?

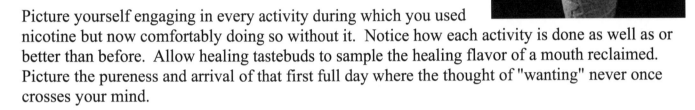

Now picture your particular brand of nicotine delivery device. What color is it? Hold it in your hand. Smell it. Do you sense an urge?

Why not use recovery imagery as a subconscious re-training tool? Why not flash our own subliminal messages?

Picture yourself engaging in every activity during which you used nicotine but now comfortably doing so without it. Notice how each activity is done as well as or better than before. Allow healing tastebuds to sample the healing flavor of a mouth reclaimed. Picture the pureness and arrival of that first full day where the thought of "wanting" never once crosses your mind.

See such days soon becoming more and more common, until becoming your new sense of normal. Listen as the diminishing noise of addiction's daily chatter as it gradually comes to an end. Feel the beauty and emotion of a brain responding to life instead of nicotine.

Controlling expectations - A 2001 conditioning study taught smokers to expect to be able to smoke during specific situations. It encouraged participants to try to identify when a use cue had occurred.[395]

As with the green triangle study, researchers discovered that encountering and noticing the use cue would generate cravings, with increased salivation and skin conduction. It found that the more aware we become of our use cues, the more profound use expectations become.

Far more importantly, it found that once study participants were told that they would no longer be able to smoke once the previously identified use cue appeared, that cravings were thereafter absent and extinguished.

Can conscious expectations control both subconscious expectations and the presence or absence of craving? Absolutely! It means that what we think and believe is critical, that what is

---

393 Etter JF, et al, <u>Gender differences in the psychological determinants of cigarette smoking</u>, Addiction, June 2002, Volume 97(6), Pages 733-743.

394 Tiggemann M, et al, <u>The phenomenology of food cravings: the role of mental imagery</u>, Appetite, December 2005, Volume 45(3), Pages 305-313.

395 Field M, et al, <u>Smoking expectancy mediates the conditioned responses to arbitrary smoking cues</u>, Behavioural Pharmacology, June 2001, Volume 12(3), Pages 183-194.

expected can occur.[396]

My most dreaded use cue was walking into the pub after work and having a couple of beers with the guys, as we debated and solved the world's problems. But I'd lost my longest attempt ever by combining alcohol with a false belief that I could handle "just one."

This time, online peer support taught me about use cues triggering craves and I expected a massive one. I feared it so much that I delayed the after-work gang for three weeks. I kept thinking how I missed my friends, our discussions, and a cold beer, and I wanted it all back.

Finally, heading into my fourth week, I mustered the courage. Upon opening the door, my healed sense of smell was immediately struck by an overpowering stink. Had it always been this bad? Indirect sunlight highlighted a thin indoor cloud that swirled as the door closed behind me. There they were, thirty or so after-work buddies tackling the day's events.

Scanning the room I was shocked to discover that all of them, without exception, were either smoking a cigarette or had a pack and ashtray within reach. Why hadn't I noticed this before? Although less than one-quarter of Americans smoked, I was now discovering that nearly all of my friends were nicotine addicts. How could this be? Was it coincidence?

I was prepared to turn and run if needed but it didn't happen. A crave didn't come. After a couple of minutes I grew brave and ordered a beer. It still didn't happen. What was going on? This was my most feared situation of all and yet no craves, zero, none.

How could I be standing here, beside smokers puffing away and yet no urge? I'm sure I could have stayed and drank another but I'd been in there for nearly a half hour.

I found myself thinking about my still healing lungs every time sunlight pierced the smoke filled room. Increasingly, I felt a slight burning sensation. My lungs didn't deserve this. It was time to leave.

Looking back, it's likely that I'd given so much thought to my biggest fear, while harboring dreams of reclaiming that aspect of life, that desire somehow severed all nicotine use associations.

Again, think about the traveling smoking cessation hypnotist using their conscious mind to relax our conscious mind, so as to allow them to rewrite subconscious expectations.

The problem with single-session hypnosis is not that it does not or cannot work, at least briefly. It's that it only addresses a single layer of recovery, the subconscious, while ignoring the ongoing negative influence of conscious stimulation and use related thoughts.

Think about the repeated subconscious impact of the title of Allen Carr's book "The Easy Way to Stop Smoking." Each time the book is opened the subconscious is hit with the message that stopping is easy.

---

396 Dols M, et al, Smokers can learn to influence their urge to smoke, Addictive Behavior, Jan-Feb 2000, Volume 25(1), Pages 103-108.

Inside, Allen does the same thing that Joel Spitzer does in the first two chapters of his free ebook "Never Take Another Puff." It's the same thing done here in Chapter 3 ("Quitting You"), Chapter 4 (Rationalizations) and Chapter 12 (Conscious Recovery).

We invite the enslaved mind, both conscious and subconscious, to see through the long list of use lies our addiction compelled us to invent, in an attempt to try and justify or explain that next fix.

If willing to engage in open and truthful analysis, once done there may be little or no sense of loss. You might skip emotional recovery altogether. If nothing to lose, there's nothing to fear. If no fear, there may be little or no anxiety.

Could letting go entirely generate an "easy" or even cakewalk recovery? Absolutely! But even if seriously challenged, as I was, recovery is entirely do-able.

We don't need to be trained hypnotists to use our conscious mind to calm, reassure, sooth or create subconscious expectations. Draw near and use truth to reassure your subconscious. It's listening.

Try engaging in slow deep breathing while progressively relaxing your body. Quiet all chatter inside your mind by focusing, to the exclusion of all other thoughts, upon an image of your favorite place.[397] Once totally relaxed, share your dreams and rewrite expectations.

Reassure your subconscious. Let it know that there is absolutely nothing to fear in coming home to entire days where you never once want for nicotine. Teach it that, contrary to the lies, you need not lose a single friend or give-up any activity, that life will be better not worse.

Photo by National Cancer Institute

Encourage your subconscious to join forces in embracing recovery, to ignore the tease, lure and false message of that pile of old replenishment memories, each created by a drug addict in need. Ask it to fear relapse instead of freedom, toxins instead of oxygen, your self destruction and slow suicide instead of healing, health and extra life.

Make it aware that your mind and body are experiencing the most intense period of healing they'll hopefully ever know, and that you could use a little help. Invite your subconscious to defend and bask in freedom's glory, to feel the delight of your ongoing victory and growing sense of pride.

Deep relaxation may be challenging during the first 72 hours. If so, think about how relaxed the

397 Anbar RD, <u>Subconscious guided therapy with hypnosis, American Journal of Clinical Hypnosis,</u> April 2006, Volume 50(4), Pages 323-334.

conscious mind and body become immediately before slumbering off into sleep. Seize upon and use these precious seconds before sleep, when our conscious and subconscious draw near. Calm subconscious fears as you slumber into sleep. Throw out the lies!

Celebrate today's victory and picture tomorrow being your most fruitful day of recovery yet. Slide off into sleep feeling free and proud.

Common Use Cues

When during each day did your subconscious expect nicotine? Was its cue the smell of morning coffee, starting the car, placing a plate into the sink, the sound of a bottle or can opening, or ice cubes filling a glass?

While few of us appreciated the precise cue recognized by our subconscious, we each have a pretty good feel for most situations during which we trained our mind to expect replenishment.

What follows is a brief review of possible use cue situations. Don't be intimidated. Use this review to think about your own use patterns. And then imagine navigating each situation and claiming the prize at the end. Why fear your healing? Welcome it!

Activities - Our morning activity trigger may have been climbing out of bed, making the bed, getting dressed, caring for a pet, associated with breakfast, reading the paper, drinking coffee, stepping outside, brushing our teeth, watering plants, or using the bathroom.

Mandatory daily activities such as eating and sleeping compel us to quickly meet, greet and extinguish any and all associated cues.

Imagine so tying nicotine use to using the bathroom that once use ends that you are briefly left wondering whether you'll ever be able to have a bowel movement again.

If parents, cues may be associated with waking your children, feeding them, making lunch and getting them off to school. Once home, there's homework, after school or weekend activities, summer planning and activities, scraps, tears, illness, concern, tending to their daily needs, fixing dinner, baths, getting their clothes ready, bedtime, reading or singing them to sleep, and the quiet period that follows.

There's housework, daily planning, caring for pets, talking on the phone, laundry, taking a break, paying bills, worry about paying bills, television, using the computer, walking outside, and gardening or yard work.

And then there's the workplace. There, you may have conditioned yourself to see nicotine replenishment as a reward (a "smoke break") for having accomplished some task.

Traveling to work, arriving, either nicotine-use breaks or using while working, deadlines, lunch, stress, the end of the workday and catch-up replenishment while traveling home. Some of us had so tied nicotine use to work that we can't imagine ever being productive workers again.

Delay in confronting and extinguishing work associated conditioning can be costly. Work avoidance can add mountains of needless pressure and anxiety to recovery. Why fear silencing all work related use cues and being rewarded with a use-free workplace?

Be brave. Take that first step. Just a tiny one, and the step that follows will become easier.

Then there are possible cues associated with arriving home, reading mail and email, preparing dinner, the evening news, hobbies or leisurely activities, social time, caring for pets, preparing for bed or romance.

As reviewed in Chapter 6, the only use cues we suggest delay in encountering are associated with using alcohol or other inhibition diminishing chemicals. As there discussed, unless you have co-dependency concerns (also Chapter 6), alcohol use is a non-mandatory activity that can be delayed a few days, at least until beyond peak withdrawal.

As reviewed in Chapter 6, alcohol can be associated with multiple use cues, including the location, people present, the presence of cigarettes or other users, peer pressures, music, singing, relaxation, dancing, celebration or intoxication.

Locations - Think about the locations you frequented that may have become conditioned use cues: entering the house, bathroom, a work area, your smoking room, garage, backyard, the garden, outdoors, a vehicle, bus stop, train or subway station, walkway, workplace, bar, pub or restaurant, or entering or leaving a store.

We encounter some use locations far more often than others. How often did we use in association with our place of worship, a doctor or hospital visit, or in association with a movie, concert or sporting event? If we established associated use cues, when might they next be encountered?

People - We may have established cues associated with specific friends, acquaintances or co-workers. If so, when will you next see them? Then, there are those people whose personalities somehow increased our anxieties. Just seeing them could trigger a crave.

And don't forget those who didn't use nicotine and tended to visit and stay longer than our unfed addiction could tolerate. What will happen the next time they visit and then leave?

Times - Our most fundamental and core use cue is likely related to time, the fact that unless replenished, our body's nicotine reserves decline by roughly half every two hours.

Other specific time use conditioning could be associated with waking, meal or break-time, or related to the hours or minutes appearing on a clock or watch. They may be associated with the time that our workday ends, a television program or the time when we awake or prepare for bed.

Times of the year may serve as conditioning: a vacation, spring and blooming flowers, arrival of summer heat, fall's cool temperatures, falling leaves, that first frost, winter or snowfall.

But don't be surprised if by then your crave generator seems to have lost its punch. Instead of full-blow cravings, remote, infrequent or seasonal cues may by then feel more like a few seconds of stiff breeze.

Eventually, the time and distance between remote un-extinguished use cues will become so great that any breeze is barely noticeable or even laughable. They'll become a long overdue reminder of the amazing journey you once made.

Events - There were some events that served as cues for most of us. Research has found that seeing and smelling a burning cigarette will cause a cue induced craving during early recovery.[398] Would watching another oral tobacco user put tobacco into their mouth trigger a craving in most oral users? Probably.

Weddings, funerals, the birth of a baby and offer of a cigar, holidays, birthdays, New Year's, recovery is about silencing conditioning and taking back life, just one piece at a time.

The smell of morning coffee, seeing a smoking friend, hearing laughter, tasting your favorite drink, touching your nicotine delivery device, wouldn't it be fascinating to have full and accurate awareness of all nicotine use conditioning while navigating recovery?

Although conventional wisdom suggests that we attempt to discover our cues beforehand, frankly, even when we think we've identified the exact cue adopted by our subconscious, we'll often miss the mark. Instead of frustrations associated with being unable to accurately predict subconscious cues, it's probably best to remain calm yet fully prepared to react on a moment's notice.

Emotions - As reviewed in Chapter 10, the range of human emotion provides our subconscious with a vast spectrum to pick from. Laughter, sorrow, a sense of accomplishment or defeat, worry or calmness, each has potential to generate a craving if the mind created a use association.

Extended emotions such as those associated with financial strain, serious illness, injury, or the death of a loved one, were ripe for cue establishment.

Withdrawal cues - Overlaying operant conditioning expectations atop craves associated with classical conditioning, atop physical withdrawal and emotional recovery, brings potential to foster a somewhat intense initial 72 hours.

The good news is that we move beyond peak withdrawal within three days. That time period also offers tremendous potential for extinguishing our most basic daily use cues, cues associated with waking, dressing, walking, talking, eating, working and sleeping.

It's why watching pharmaceutical companies sell expensive products which drag withdrawal out for weeks or months is so disturbing. And how does popping a piece of nicotine gum or a nicotine lozenge into our mouth when a use cue is encountered extinguish conditioning? Add in

---

398 Niaura R, et al, Individual differences in cue reactivity among smokers trying to quit: effects of gender and cue type, Addictive Behavior. Addictive Behaviors, March-April 1998, Volume 23(2), Pages 209-224.

products like Chantix/Champix, which has been linked to suicide and it makes you wonder whose interests are being protected.

We are each unique when it comes to the number and types of use cues we established. Although natural to want to run and hide from conditioning, extinguishing each is a stepping-stone to freedom.

Are Crave Episodes Really Less Than 3 Minutes?

Yes, generally. Although we don't yet know why, within three minutes it is normal for crave episode anxieties, anxiousness and/or panic to peak and begin easing off. Although amazingly little research in this area, it's a basic recovery lesson widely shared across the Internet.

Photo by National Cancer Institute

While possible that more than one un-extinguished subconscious cue may be may encountered within minutes of each other, years of online cessation group discussions suggest that it isn't as common as we might think.

What is often seen are periods of conscious thought fixation being confused with a subconsciously triggered crave episode.

Think about your favorite food. How long can you continue to stay focused and fixated upon it? Can you do so for 10, 20 or even 30 minutes? The only limit upon the duration of fixation is our ability to maintain conscious concentration and focus.

The primary distinction between a subconscious crave episode and conscious fixation is control.

While we have substantial direct control over the duration of fixation, and significant control over how the conscious mind reacts when a subconscious cue is encountered, our subconscious controls the timing and duration of cue-triggered episodes.

The importance of the distinction is the recovery confidence provided in knowing that subconscious challenge will pass within 3 minutes. But if cue triggered crave episodes peak and begin to subside in less than three minutes, why do the minutes sometimes feel like hours?

Time Distortion

A 2003 study found that distortion of time perception is one of the most common nicotine dependency recovery symptoms.[399]

Smokers were asked to estimate the passing of 45 seconds both while still smoking nicotine and during a second session after which they had not smoked any nicotine for 24 hours. Their time estimates were also compared to a control group of non-smokers.

While at a loss to explain why, researchers found that time estimation accuracy was significantly impaired (300%) in smokers who had not smoked or used nicotine for 24 hours, as compared to estimates made while smoking.

The ability of smokers who had not smoked for 24 hours to estimate the passing of 45 seconds was also impaired when compared to estimates made by non-smokers. But timing estimates were found to be similar between non-smokers and smokers while smokers were allowed to continue smoking.

Keep a watch or clock handy - What the study didn't assess was the estimation of time during occurrence of a crave episode.

Whether cessation time distortion is ultimately found to be physiological, psychological or some combination, knowing that it exists suggests the need to look at a clock or watch during an episode, in order to bring honest perspective to time.

When a crave arrives, immediately look at your watch or a clock and note the time. The episode's false message that the only way to make the crave end is to bring more nicotine into your body will soon peak and then pass. Not only will your recovery remain alive and well, you are highly likely to receive a reward, the return of yet another aspect of nicotine-free life.

It's important to note that for the 1.7% of adults diagnosed with panic disorder under diagnostic standards such as the American Psychiatric Association's DSM-IV manual, that DSM-IV criteria indicates that panic attacks may not peak for up to 10 minutes.[400]

Focus your panic attack coping skills training on handling nicotine cessation panic attacks. Already highly skilled, hopefully you'll find this aspect of nicotine dependency recovery the least challenging of all.

We're each fully capable of handling a few brief moments of anxiety. All of us can. Accurately measuring the episode's duration will prevent time distortion from making it appear 300 percent longer than reality.

Don't let time distortion deprive you of your dream of again comfortably engaging life as "you."

399 Klein LC, Smoking Abstinence Impairs Time Estimation Accuracy in Cigarette Smokers, Psychopharmacology Bulletin, May 2003, Volume 37(1), Pages 90-95.

400 American Psychiatric Association, Panic Disorder, Diagnostic and statistical manual of mental disorders, fourth edition, 1994

Crave Episode Frequency

How often do crave episodes occur? The best we can do in answering this question is to share study averages. The obvious problem with averages is that we may not be average.

A 1998 real-time crave coping study followed smokers for two 2 weeks and collected fascinating data.[401]

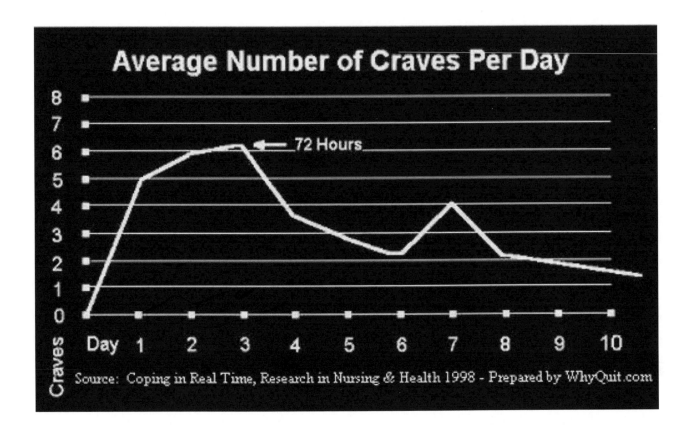

It found that the day on which the most crave episodes were encountered was the third day of recovery, with an average of 6.1 craves. Day four's average dropped to 3.5, with day five generating just 3 craves per day. By day ten the average fell to just 1.4 episodes per day.

If each crave episode is less than 3 minutes, and the average on the most challenging day is 6.1, that's a total of 18.3 minutes of crave anxiety on your most challenging day of recovery.

Can you handle 18.3 minutes of serious challenge in order to reclaim your mind and life? Absolutely! We all can.

But what if you're not average? What if you conditioned your subconscious to have twice as many cues as the average user? That would mean that you could experience a maximum of 37 minutes of total crave episode anxiety on your most challenging day, dropping to just 8 minutes by day ten.

401 O'Connell KA, et al, Coping in real time: using Ecological Momentary Assessment techniques to assess coping with the urge to smoke, Research in Nursing and Health, December 1998, Volume 21(6), Pages 487-497.

Is there any doubt whatsoever that you handle 37 minutes of challenge in order to permanently reclaim the driver's seat of your mind? And you won't be asked to do it all at once. Just up to three minutes at a time, and then take a break.

You should also prepare for the possibility of a small spike on day seven. While the average study participant was down to just over 2 episodes per day by day six, day seven brought an average of 4 cravings, before returning to 2 on day eight. We can only guess as to why.

And there are lots of theories. One is that life is measured in weeks and a full week of freedom provided the first significant reason for celebration. Did your subconscious associate use with celebration? If so, what about the celebration that turns sour, like when everyone but mom forgets our birthday? Could that generate a second episode?

Again, we can only guess. What we do know is that every new ex-user is fully capable of handling 12 minutes of challenge on day seven, followed by 6 minutes on day eight.

Looking at the study's chart, reflect on how the average newbie both moves beyond peak physical withdrawal within 72 hours and navigates the peak number of use cues. Coincidence? Not necessarily.

While we have little control over nicotine's half-life, the recovery day on which we decide to fully engage life and confront the bulk of our normal daily use cues is very much within our control.

Joel always started his clinics on a Tuesday night. Historically, many programs encouraged users to start on the weekend, thinking that it will help avoid work pressures. If so, Monday brings day three, work, and the first full engagement of life.

Extinguishing Use Cues

Real-world evidence (empirical) suggests that most subconscious use cues are extinguished after a single encounter, during which the conscious mind tells the subconscious mind "no."

This does not mean that encountering the same nicotine use reminders day after day won't cause the conscious mind to focus or fixate upon "thoughts" of wanting.

It means that the first encounter, where the subconscious learns that our consciousness will no longer respond to the cue is normally sufficient to break the use association and extinguish the urge, crave or mini-panic-attack which would have followed.

Recovery is about re-learning to engage in every activity we did as users, but without nicotine. As Joel notes, ending all nicotine use almost immediately compels us to confront and extinguish all nicotine-use conditioning related to survival activities such as breathing, eating, sleeping and using the bathroom.[402]

---

402 Spitzer, J., Alcohol and Quitting, June 9, 2001, http://www.ffn.yuku.com/topic/11776

While essential to feed the children and get them off to school, early fears of encountering another crave trigger can motivate postponement of non-essential activities such as housework or proper personal hygiene, at least briefly.

Some try to hide from life. But, not without a price. A dirty house or tall grass may breed their own escalating internal anxieties or cause needless family frictions.

Joel cautions that aside from threatening our livelihood and making us look like a slob, if we attempt to hide and avoid confronting use cues associated with non-survival activities for too long, we may begin to feel intimidated that we will never be able to engage in one or more of these activities ever again.

Then, there are non-mandatory activities such as partying, dating, nurturing relationships, television, the Internet, sports, hobbies and games. The only way to extinguish use cues associated with an activity is to engage in the activity, confront the cue and reclaim that aspect of life.

Again, holding off too long can intimidate us into feeling that we can never do it again. Recovery anxieties generated by delay in reclaiming any aspect of life are totally within our ability to eliminate.

At worst, the activity is just three minutes of challenge away from again being yours. Then again, there may not even be a challenge.

Last night I walked into a convenience store to pay for gas while wearing my "Hug me I stopped smoking" tee shirt. The clerk behind the counter asked if it were true.

While literally surrounded by cigarette packs, cartons, oral tobacco products and cigars he asked, "Did you really quit?" "Yes," I said. "After thirty years and being up to three packs-a-day!"

"I haven't had a cigarette for a week," he said. You could feel his pride. While heading out the door I heard the lady who had been behind me say, "Two packs of Marlboro Lights, please."

Think about his first day on the job after his last nicotine fix. Imagine your livelihood requiring you to repeatedly reach for and handle cigarettes, a conditioned use cue for nearly all.

Yes, his first time may have triggered a cue induced mini anxiety attack. If so, what are the chances he was so busy that it peaked and passed before he had an opportunity to take a break and quiet it by relapse?

While subsequent sales may have caused urges associated with conscious thoughts of wanting, the difference was the absence of an uncontrollable anxiety episode. This time, the intensity and duration of the experience was almost totally within his ability to control.

But be careful here. Some conditioned use cues are so similar to others that we fail to grasp their distinction. For example, the Monday through Saturday newspaper may have only been associated with smoking one cigarette, while Sunday's paper is much thicker and may have required replenishment two or more times to read.

Cue exposure therapy - Cue exposure therapy or CET is intentional exposure to drug-related use cues in order to more quickly extinguish learned associations.[403] A tool of modern drug treatment programs, it can be our tool too. We can either wait for time and life to bring nicotine use cues to us, or seek out and extinguish them as quickly as we desire.

For example, it's likely that nicotine use cues are associated with our daily work schedule or chores. We can fear and delay encountering these work related cues or intentionally target them for extinction. Our problem in using CET is the same problem confronting researchers and drug treatment programs. We can't possibly know all the use cues adopted by the subconscious mind.

Even if we did, some situations, such as changing seasons or holidays, would be beyond our ability to reproduce. CET is, at best, only a partial tool. Although we have the ability to boldly and quickly reclaim most aspects of life, we need to accept that some cues will survive and arrive when presented by time or circumstances.

Still, intentionally confronting as many as possible will foster confidence and help prepare us to eventually extinguish all of them. Also, when encountering what appears to be a use cue, how do we distinguish between true subconscious classical conditioning (an uncontrollable response) and conscious thought fixation (a controllable situation)?

It isn't always easy. Even after nearly all of our subconscious use cues have been extinguished, it's normal and natural for our senses to notice old use situations. The difference is that now we're in full control of our mind's response.

Try to imagine and picture a high quality photograph of your favorite food. Picture the best photo of it that you've ever seen. It oozes and drips with flavor. Can you smell it? Imagine that first bite. Savor the flavor and sense the "aaah" wanting relief sensation that follows.

While I controlled the imagery cues, you controlled the intensity and duration of any desire or urge felt. You were totally free to stop at any time.

Researchers have discovered that young smokers respond to CET better than long-term smokers.[404] Younger users often have established fewer nicotine use associations and their memories house significantly less dependency baggage.

CET and intentionally trying to rapidly meet, greet and extinguish use conditioning is contrary to historic cessation lessons, the remnants of which can still be found at some Internet sites.

For example, the U.S. government's leading cessation booklet is 37 pages and called "Clearing the Air." Page 9 tells readers to stay away from places smoking is allowed, and stay away from

---

403 Lee J, Nicotine craving and cue exposure therapy by using virtual environments, Cyberpsychology & Behavior, December 2004, Volume 7(6), Pages 705-13.

404 Traylor AC, et al, Assessing craving in young adult smokers using virtual reality, The American Journal on Addictions, Sep-Oct 2008, Volume 17(5), Pages 436-440.

people who smoke. The title of page 24 reads, "Stay away from what tempts you."

Readers are then told to "Stay away from things that you connect with smoking," like not sitting in their favorite chair or watching their favorite TV show. They're told to drive a different route to work or not drive at all and take the train or bus for a while.[405]

How can we reclaim driving or our favorite TV program if taught to fear and avoid it? Unfortunately, my government's primary cessation booklet is loaded with serious conflicts.

The title of page 9 reads, "Meet those triggers head on." Sounds great, right! But then the first two sentences on page 9 state, "Knowing your triggers is very important. It can help you stay away from things that tempt you to smoke."

Well, which is it, "meet those triggers head on" or "stay away" from them? Clearly, it's wise to stay away from nonsense booklets such as "Clearing the Air," as they will only cloud it further.

Let me share one more glaring "Clearing the Air" conflict. Page 17 is entitled, "Medicines that help with withdrawal."

The page tells readers, "You may feel dull, tense, and not yourself. These are signs that your body is getting used to life without nicotine. It usually only lasts a few weeks." There are medicines that can help with feelings of withdrawal: ... "nicotine gum, nicotine inhaler, nicotine lozenge, nicotine nasal spray, nicotine patch."

The obvious question becomes, how does the body get "used to life without nicotine" by feeding it "nicotine?" Obviously, it can't.

Back to extinguishing use cues. What if you could extinguish some of your conditioned cues without experiencing any cravings? Research suggests that through conscious thought and its subconscious influence that we have the ability to create new expectations conditioning that overpowers old use conditioning, thus creating a possible avenue by which you can avoid a particular crave episode altogether.[406]

Again, think about how the single-session traveling hypnotist is able to briefly interrupt use urges and craves. It isn't magic. They relax our consciousness and then create new expectations. Again, reflect on the subconscious impact of the title to Allen Carr's book "The Easy Way to Stop Smoking."

Our conditioning patterns mirrored how we lived life. We cannot reclaim life by avoiding it.

A 2002 study found that 97% of inmates forced to stop smoking while in prison had relapsed within 6 months of release.[407] When arrested, each was still an actively feeding nicotine addict.

---

405 National Institutes of Health, <u>Clearing the Air</u>, April 2003, NIH Publication No. 03-1647.
406 Dols M, et al, <u>Smokers can learn to influence their urge to smoke</u>, Addictive Behavior, Jan-Feb 2000, Volume 25(1), Pages 103-108.
407 Tuthill RW et al, "<u>Does involuntary cigarette smoking abstinence among inmates during correctional incarceration result in continued abstinence post release?</u>" (poster). 26th National Conference on Correctional Health Care, Nashville, Tennessee,

Once released, imagine their first time driving a car, walking into a bar, running into an old smoking buddy, or the moments following romance.

They were hit head-on by conditioned nicotine use cues associated with a host of situations that their arrest and imprisonment had prevented from being extinguished.

As the correct portion of "Clearing the Air" states, "meet those triggers head on." They mark the path home. Yes, you may find that there are some aspects of life that you no longer desire, but that will be your choice.

The Bigger the Better

Although the crave episode chart reflects averages of data from a specific study of a unique population, it shows two factors common to every recovery.

It evidences that the number of daily crave episodes quickly peaks. It also shows that the number of episodes then begins to gradually decline.

Let's focus upon what happens once the number of daily crave episodes experienced, if any, begins to decline. I say "if any" because knowledge and understanding have potential to make recovery a cakewalk.

Unless hiding in a closet in order to avoid temptation, locked up in prison or laid up in the hospital, we have no choice but to meet, greet and extinguish the bulk of our subconscious feeding cues within the first week.

The number and frequency of early challenges helps keep us alert, prepared and ready to deploy our crave coping defenses on a moment's notice.

As shown by the crave episode chart, by day 10 the average study participant was experiencing just 1.4 crave episodes per day. That translates to less than five minutes of significant challenge. But what about the days that follow?

What would be the natural and expected consequences of beginning to go entire days without challenge? What will happen to your battle plans, defenses, to your preparedness and anticipation once you experience a day or two without encountering a cue driven crave episode?

For purposes of discussion only, let's pretend that during recovery days 14, 15 and 16, although you remained occupied in dealing with conscious thinking about wanting to use, that you did not once encounter any un-extinguished subconscious feeding cue or experience any full-blown crave episode.

Although unlikely you would have noticed, wouldn't it be normal to begin to relax a bit and slowly lower your defenses and guard?

October 21, 2002.

And then it happens. On day 17 you encounter a still active use cue.

Surprised, it catches you totally off-guard and unprepared. You scramble to muster your defenses but it's as if you can't find them. It's as if they too are being swallowed by a fast moving tsunami of rising anxieties.

You feel as if you've been sucker-punched hard by the most intense crave ever. It feels endless. Your conscious thinking mind begins suggesting that things are getting worse, not better. The thought of throwing in the towel and giving-up suddenly begins sloshing about inside a horrified mind.

It's then, when things seem worst, that you need to briefly pause and reflect upon what you're really seeing. Things are not getting worse, but better.

Think about how long it had been since your last significant challenge and how relaxed you allowed yourself to become. It's likely that this episode is no more intense than prior ones. It's just that you had taken off your life jacket and you couldn't quickly locate and put it on. You panicked.

If such an event should ever happen to you, I encourage you to stop, reflect and then celebrate! You've reclaimed so many once conditioned aspects of a nicotine dependent life that serious challenges are beginning to grow rare.

Oh, you may still encounter remote or even seasonal triggers. But with the passing of time they'll grow further apart, shorter in duration and generally less intense. Remember to keep a clock handy so as to defend against time distortion.

None of us will ever be stronger than nicotine but then we don't need to be as it's simply a chemical with an IQ of zero. Trust your dreams to your vastly superior intelligence, your greatest weapon of all.

No matter how far we travel or how comfortable we become, there's still just one guiding principle allowing us to remain here on the free side of the bars, while keeping our dependency under arrest on the other ... no nicotine today.

Rewards

Consider reversing your mind-set. Recovery isn't about punishment but rewards.

Our chemically enslaved survival instincts teacher was compromised by an external

Photo by National Cancer Institute

chemical and fooled. Its job was to make dopamine pathway activating events nearly impossible in the short term (the time needed for recovery) to forget or ignore.

Except for responding to the wrong input, it functioned as designed. It did its job and did it well. But now it's time for a mind schooled in nicotine dependency and recovery to save the day. Extinguishing each conditioned use cue rewards us with the return of another aspect of a nicotine-free life. Why fear being able to finish work, a meal, exit a store or drive without experiencing an urge or crave commanding replenishment?

When a crave arrives, think about the prize at the end. Reflect on wanting for more nicotine being permanently evicted from the yard, bathroom, porch, car, work and play, and no longer associated with our relationships, activities or emotions.

Crave episodes reflect evidence of where we've many times been, and what we were forced to do once there. But not anymore! The moments can again be ours.

Moments of subconscious healing are good not bad. Soon, you will have reclaimed so many aspects of life that, like putting together a puzzle, it will reflect a life reclaimed.

Crave Coping Techniques

How do we successfully navigate a less than three minute crave episode? We've already reviewed a few ways, including reaching for your list of reasons for commencing recovery.

Let's take a look at additional coping techniques.

Embracing crave episodes - Upon sensing danger, our survival instincts tell us to either prepare to stand and fight or get ready to run. What approach will you use? Upon encountering a crave episode will you duck and run, or turn and fight?

While the objective is clear - to not use nicotine - our natural instincts on how best to achieve that objective may not be the easiest path to travel.

Can we hide from cravings or will they find us? Can we runaway or will they catch us? It's the same with going toe to toe in battle, isn't it? Can we beat-up craves and make them surrender or cry uncle? Can we scare them away?

Encountering and extinguishing use cues is how we mend, heal, repair and reclaim a nicotine dependent subconscious mind. It's how we destroy use expectations and take back life.

While nicotine is a natural poison, what about craves? Can a crave that lasts a couple of minutes destroy tissues, clog arteries and cause a heart attack or stroke, promote cancer, or contribute to early dementia?

Will a crave cut us, make us bleed or send us to the emergency room? Can it physically harm us? If not, then why fear it, why run, why hide?

How much of the anxiety associated with recovery is self-induced? Nearly all.

So, why agonize over the anticipated arrival of that next crave? Once it does arrive, why immediately begin feeding our mind additional anxieties that only fuel the fire?

Photo by National Cancer Institute

Let's not kid ourselves. The anxiety associated with a craving for nicotine is as real as the eyes reading these words. And fear of anxiety hides solutions.

While fully capable of mentally embracing a crave episode's anxiety energy, few have ever done so. Instead, what we feel is a tremendously inflated experience fueled by anticipation, driven by fear, and possibly tense due to a history of prior relapse.

Try this, just once. Instead of inviting your body's fight or flight response to inflame the situation, when the next crave arrives, stop, be brave, drop your guard, take slow deep deliberate breaths and in your mind imagine reaching out and wrapping your arms around the crave's anxiety energy.

It won't harm or hurt you. It's normal to be afraid but be brave for just one moment.

Continue wrapping yourself around the episode while fully embracing it. Continue taking slow deep breaths as you clear your mind of all chatter, worries, fears and thoughts so that you can sense and appreciate the episode's level of raw anxiety.

Touch it, sense it, hug it hard. Doing so will not make it any more intense than it otherwise would have been. You're witnessing a moment of beauty, the most profound subconscious healing you've ever allowed your conscious mind to touch.

Yes, there is anxiety. But possibly for the first time ever, it's not being fed and fueled by you.

Now, feel as the crave episode's energy peak and then begin to gradually subside. You've won! You've reclaimed another aspect of life. And you did so by way of courage not dread, by a hug, not hiding.

You've seen that the greatest challenge presented by natural recovery cannot hurt you. Only we can do that. Embrace recovery don't fear it. There's a special person waiting down the road. Your birthright, it's a long lost friend you'll come to know, savor, enjoy and love.

Distraction coping - Far less courageous, distraction is any mental exercise or physical activity that occupies the conscious mind long enough to allow challenge to pass.

Alphabet or counting association schemes demand some degree of focus and concentration. They provide an instant means of occupying the mind. An alphabet association scheme can be as simple as going through the alphabet while trying to associate each letter with a person, place, animal or food.

Photo by National Cancer Institute

Take food for example. The letter "A" is for grandma's hot apple pie. "B" is for a nice crispy piece of bacon. "C" is for a rich and moist chocolate cake. I challenge you to try and get to the challenging letter "Q" before three minutes pass and challenge subsides.

Physical distraction possibilities include turning to your favorite non-nicotine activity, a brief period of physical exercise or something as simple as brushing your teeth.

Activities such as screaming into a pillow, squeezing a tree or biting your lip are available should you ever feel a need to vent. The pillow won't scream back, I doubt you'll hurt the tree and your lip will heal.

Relaxation coping - Embracing crave episodes is one means of increasing relaxation by preventing the addition of self-induced anxieties. Meditation is another tool for navigating a cue induced crave episode.

Most forms of meditation use breathing and focus as a means to foster inner peace and tranquility. Research confirms their ability to calm anxieties.[408]

Try this. Comfortably sit in a chair or on the floor. Straighten yet relax your spine. Near the level of your naval, lay one hand in the palm of the other with thumbs slightly touching. Gently close your eyes.

Photo by National Cancer Institute

Now allow your breathing to slow and deepen. Calm and settle your mind by focusing exclusively upon the feelings and sensations of breathing.

---

408 Agency for Healthcare Research and Quality, <u>Meditation Practices for Health: State of the Research</u>, Evidence Report/Technology Assessment Number 155, AHRQ Publication No. 07-E010, June 2007.

Focus entirely upon that next breath. Feel the cool air entering your nostrils, and its warmth as you slowly exhale.

When a thought arises don't chase it but instead breathe it away. Continue focusing upon each breath. As challenge subsides, allow yourself to become increasingly aware of your surroundings as you slowly open your eyes.

Instead of focusing upon breathing, other forms of meditation, such as panic attack coping or mindfulness based stress reduction, encourage exclusive focus upon your favorite color, person or that "special place."

We also should mention laughter. Research shows that laughter activates various muscle groups for a few seconds each, which immediately after the laugh leads to general muscle relaxation, which can last up to 45 minutes.[409]

Laughter also induces sporadic deep breathing.[410] There's also evidence suggesting that among those with a sense of humor, that laughter and smiling may result in diminished anxiety and stress.[411]

Remember, this is conditioning that you created. It's now commanding relapse, the introduction of nicotine back into your body. Why not give laughter's calming effects a try. What's there to lose?

Analytical coping - Here, moments of challenge are spent focusing upon and analyzing the situation. Embracing a crave episode fits nicely here too.

So does pulling out and reviewing your list of reasons for commencing recovery. Also consider reviewing them when not feeling challenged, so as to help keep your motivational batteries fully charged.

What cue triggered the episode? While we can't know for certain, what's your best guess? What activity, emotion, person, place or time will you likely be awarded once this episode passes?

Look at a clock and time the episode. How long did it take before its anxieties peaked? Is that shorter or longer than your last challenge? How long had it been since your last significant challenge?

409 Paskind J, Effects of laughter on muscle tone, Archives of Neurology & Psychiatry, 1932, Volume 28, Pages 623-628; as cited in Bennett MP, et al, Humor and Laughter May Influence Health: III. Laughter and Health Outcomes, Evidence-Based Complementary and Alternative Medicine, March 2008, Volume 5(1), Pages 37-40.
410 Fry W, The respiratory components of mirthful laughter, Journal of Biological Psychology, 1977, Volume 19, Pages 39-50; as cited in Bennett MP, et al, Humor and Laughter May Influence Health: III. Laughter and Health Outcomes, Evidence-Based Complementary and Alternative Medicine, March 2008, Volume 5(1), Pages 37-40.
411 Yovetich NA, et al, Benefits of humor in reduction of threat-induced anxiety, Psychological Reports, February 1990, Volume 66(1), Pages 51-58.

Consider keeping a crave episode log. They make interesting reading. Like medical records, they allow us to quickly look back and see how far we've come. A log can prove valuable while waiting for the final recovery layer to pass, conscious recovery. It's here that the pace of noticeable change will naturally begin to slow.

Oral coping - Oral coping is a form of crutch substitution. It is capable of itself fostering use conditioning which results in continuing crutch use long after all challenge has ended. Using food as an oral crutch can obviously add extra pounds.

All oral coping strategies should be avoided, especially any that imitates use or the handling of any object that imitates your nicotine delivery device.

Imitating any addiction related behavior helps maintain that behavior, delays suppression of old use memories, invites use fixation, prolongs recovery and thus elevates risk of relapse.

If you find yourself reaching for something more substantial than a toothpick or toothbrush, make sure it isn't fattening, that will always be available within seconds, and something you'd be able to do anywhere and anytime for years to come. As Joel suggest, about the only thing that meets that definition is slow deep breathing, which passes air through the mouth.

Consider eating healthy if having difficulty avoiding reaching for extra food. Can you eat an entire apple in 3 minutes? If so, that's 80 calories and 4 grams of fiber.

Pre-cut veggies   *Photo by National Cancer Institute*

Five asparagus spears are 20 calories, one medium sized stalk of broccoli is 50, a seven inch carrot is 40 calories, one-sixth of a medium head of cauliflower or two medium stalks of celery total 25 calories, a medium cucumber is 45 calories, a medium orange 80, one medium peach is 40 calories, seven radishes total 20, eight medium strawberries are 70, and one medium tomato is 35 calories.

Seasonal, Holiday and Infrequent Cues

Expect to arrive home with a few seasonal, holiday and infrequent use cues not yet encountered and extinguished. Infrequent cues can be associated with a vacation, a wedding, death, funeral, meeting an old friend or illness. Many infrequent cues have their own histories.

For example, when a cold or flu struck while still using it likely diminished use, thus possibly adding early withdrawal to the illness. When your cold or flu symptoms started to improve you likely quickly increased nicotine use in an effort to catch up and avoid withdrawal. Thus, you may have trained your subconscious to expect a sudden increase in use following an illness.

The good news is that any remaining subconscious use associations after arriving on Easy Street were likely weak to begin with, as death and illness have hopefully been rare.

Also, like any relationship, the mind's crave anxiety generator depends heavily upon vibrant and reinforced new use memories for its punch. No new use memories are serving as memory bank infusion reminders for thousands of old use memories. Thus, your crave generator may become so weak over time that future episodes become laughable reminders of your journey home, and an aid to fending off complacency.

During your second nicotine-free lap around the sun, with few exceptions, nearly all nicotine use cues will have been extinguished. Oh, you'll still have conscious use thoughts now and then (Chapter 12). But if you have let go of your junkie use thinking, they too will grow rare, harmless and laughable.

Now that you know more about subconscious recovery than most physicians (as few medical schools devote any class time to studying cessation), what if it were possible to minimize or eliminate crave episodes altogether? What if use cue extinction could occur without crisis?

The next chapter, Chapter 12, reviews the primary source of crave episode anxieties, our thousands of old nicotine replenishment memories documenting use having satisfied wanting, and the scores of explanations we invented to explain why we would soon use again.

KEEP YOUR BRAIN HEALTHY

There's still just one rule. It's that one equals all, that lapse equals relapse, that just one puff and nicotine will activate the same brain dopamine circuitry that makes going without eating seem nearly impossible. Why pretend or expect a different result? Still only one rule ... none today!

Chapter 12

Conscious Recovery

Think of it as journey thinking. The final yet longest layer of recovery is rooted in the time needed to move beyond use related memories, beliefs and thoughts. This chapter's objective is to accelerate conscious recovery.

First, we'll focus on the truth about that pile of old wanting satisfaction memories, the anxiety inviting bars that helped form our prison cell.

Simply put, why invite torment by the lie each memory delivers, that use is the solution to wanting? Also, why be teased by a biological need to feed which no longer exists within 2-3 weeks of ending use?

Next, we'll examine a few additional false use beliefs that our lack of dependency understanding may have forced us to invent.

Simply put, why allow use lies invented by a mind that knew almost nothing about chemical dependency to combine with thousands of old wanting satisfaction memories and fuel irrational fears, anxiety or even panic?

Imagine what would happen if willing to totally let go of all use justifications.

Why not give truth a chance? While freedom begins the moment we say "no" to more, truth offers potential to accelerate transforming "no" into calm.

The Final Truth

Although I have no idea where you are in recovery, or if you've even started yet, let's assume for a moment that you're almost home.

You adopted a protective "one day at a time" recovery outlook that has kept you rooted and grounded in here and now. You learned to remain patient during a less than 3 minutes crave episode clamoring for compliance. You stuck with it for the full 72 hours needed to empty your body of nicotine. At last you were clean!

Your healing and glory continued for the two to three weeks needed to re-sensitize and down-regulate receptor counts, allowing your brain to fully adjust to functioning without nicotine.

You confronted and extinguished all but remote, infrequent or seasonal subconscious use cues, and are now less than two weeks away from that first full day of total and complete mental quiet and calm, where you never once think about wanting to use.

Still, now, you find moments each day where your mind continues to be occupied with thoughts of using. The waning tease of years old "aaah" wanting satisfaction memories continue to call, each proclaiming that the way to end wanting is to use.

It normally happens something like this. Your eyes, nose or hearing sense some aspect of use, or a fleeting thought turns your attention to the subject of using.

Before you know it, old use memories begin suggesting that use can end wanting. An internal debate commences, as an old use justification enters your mind and bumps heads with the reality that you've already stopped.

Before considering the use rationalization that surfaced, let's reflect on a few truths about the pile of old use memories that awakened it. Why? Because while we cannot erase them, honest light can diminish or even eliminate their pester and tease.

Recall the 1990 Brandon study reviewed in Chapter 2. It followed and examined lapse and relapse in smokers who'd successfully completed a two-week cessation program.[412] It also documented the primary emotion felt immediately after relapse.

Assume that many of them were close to where I've asked you to pretend you are now, a couple of weeks away from that first full day without wanting.

You've already succeeded in fully navigating physical withdrawal. There is no chemical missing and no chemical in need of replenishment. Your brain has fully re-sensitized and down-regulated. The biological need for nicotine in order to maintain the addict's sense of "nicotine normal" no longer exists. Your brain's sense of normal (homeostasis) has been restored. Background dopamine levels (tonic levels) are elevated, and their decline no longer induces wanting for nicotine.

So, with nothing missing, what would be the primary emotion you'd expect to experience if you lapsed and used nicotine? According to the Brandon study, the vast majority had a negative reaction.

Among them, 13% felt depressed and hopeless, 33% experienced anxiety and tension, 16% were angry and irritated, and 12% felt boredom or fatigue. Only 3.6% reported what most of us would have expected following normal replenishment, which was "feeling relaxed."

There's no denying that sagging blood nicotine levels reduced background or tonic dopamine, which generated wanting. Each nicotine fix stimulated the release of a burst of dopamine (a phasic release) which elevated tonic levels and

Photo by National Cancer Institute

412 Brandon, TH et al, Postcessation cigarette use: the process of relapse, Addictive Behaviors, 1990; 15(2), pages 105-114.

satisfied wanting.

Each use also created a new high definition dopamine pathway memory of how wanting was satisfied. Collectively, thousands of old such use memories daily pounded home the message that use satisfies wanting. Together, they helped form our prison cell, a thick wall preventing us from seeing truth.

More easily seen during this final layer of recovery, their collective influence invites and fosters use anxieties. While still using, those anxieties motivated us to invent use compliance rationalizations.

Now during recovery, if allowed, debating and struggling with our use rationalizations can foster anxiety.

Yes, although temporary, each fix brought the addict a true sense of relief. And yes, wanting satisfaction memories were valid when made. However, one critical factor has changed. The brain has now fully adjusted to functioning without nicotine. There is nothing missing.

If we visit online recovery forums and dig back through messages describing relapses that occurred beyond week 2-3 weeks, those describing the sensations they experienced have a common ring.

They read like this, "I had a mouth full of smoke, I was dizzy and I coughed, but I didn't get the sense of satisfaction I expected. It just didn't come!"

Lizzy, a member of WhyQuit's Freedom support site wrote:

> "The first cigarette after four years tasted like Luther's Boot. It was horrible. I smoked the whole thing wondering why I was smoking it (answer: tequila and complacency). I woke up the next morning feeling worse than any hangover could possibly feel, because I wasn't hungover."
>
> "I'd inhaled poison the night before. My head was killing me, I felt nauseous and my lung felt as though I'd sucked up broken glass. There was no 'aaah' feeling. It was more like 'aauugghh!!!' What had I done to myself?"[413]

Falling Blood Nicotine Level

Brain Releases Dopamine

Brain Generates Crave

Inhale New Nicotine

Thousands of enticing old use memories stored in the prefrontal cortex tell the relapsing person to expect a sense of relief and satisfaction, that use will satisfy wanting.

---

413 LizzyB, The Final Truth, Response #11, Freedom from Nicotine, June 26, 2006.

But in that their brain had already fully adjusted to functioning without nicotine, their wanting itself was memory based, and the expected "aaah" wasn't there. Unlike when those old "aaah" sensations were recorded, there was nothing missing and nothing in need of replenishment.

Memories suggested a physical need that no longer existed. We blamed the absence of nicotine for each memory's tease, thus, in our minds, transforming the culprit into a cure. So, with great expectations they took that first hit of nicotine and it failed to measure up.

What happens next? Sadly, the uneducated user is likely clueless as to why lapse didn't match expectations. They'll find the absence of an "aaah" wanting relief sensation hard to believe.

They know that the satisfaction message being shouted by thousands of old replenishment memories was true when made. Although relapse has already occurred and full blown wanting and begging will soon return, they'll likely keep digging inside the pack, pouch, tin, packet, tube or box, trying to get use to match expectations.

Eventually they'll succeed. Active dependency is soon restored, often with an increase in level of use (a tolerance increase possibly due to nicotine binge gorging following relapse).

Now, they can look in the mirror and say to themselves, "See, I was right." "Smoking did bring me a relaxed "aaah" feeling and sense of relief!"

Still, the basic wanting satisfaction message suggested by each old use memory was a lie even when made. Use cannot and does not end wanting. To the contrary, it's the only way to ensure its survival. The only way to end wanting is to navigate this temporary period of re-adjustment called recovery.

Photo by National Institute on Drug Abuse

Realize that all memories of that "perfect" fix were created inside the mind of an actively feeding drug addict riding an endless cycle of nicotine/dopamine highs and lows. While thousands of old replenishment memories document use giving us a brief pause in wanting, they belong to who we once were.

While who we once were demanded explanation, our dignity needed to survive.

Dignity's Denial

As teenagers, what most of us thought would be a brief rebellious experiment was quickly transformed into a powerful permanent chemical addiction, as occasional nicotine use became regular, and optional use mandatory.

Studies confirm that for some of us it only took coughing and hacking our way through a couple of cigarettes before slavery's shackles began to tighten.[414]

Five, ten, fifteen nicotine fixes a day - when would enough be enough? "Tomorrow, tomorrow" became the lifetime cry of millions. Welcome to the realities of chemical servitude, a world built upon lies.

Science calls our lies denial. Denial is an unconscious defense mechanism, just below the surface, for resolving the emotional conflict and anxieties that naturally arise from living in a permanent state of self-destructive bondage.

The three primary areas of denial relied upon by nicotine addicts are dependency denial, cost denial and recovery denial. In each, truth is sacrificed for piece of mind or to justify relapse.

Nearly every nicotine addict we'll see today is insulated from the pain of captivity by a thick blanket of denial rationalizations, minimizations, fault projections, escapes, intellectualizations and delusions.

Together, they create the illusion that a problem either doesn't exist or is somehow being solved.

The average addict musters the confidence to challenge their addiction once every two to three years. Not knowing the Law of Addiction and fighting in total darkness, each year, only about 1 in 20 attempts will succeed in breaking free for an entire year.

With respect to smoking, by far the most destructive and deadliest form of nicotine delivery, eventually roughly half successfully commit slow suicide via smoke's toxins.

There are more than five million senseless self-destructions annually. They stand as irrefutable evidence of denial's depth in insulating us from the extreme price paid with each puff, a bit more of life itself.

Once we've accepted that the basic message delivered by thousands of old replenishment memories is false, this final layer of recovery offers opportunity to laugh at use explanations once deeply believed.

---

414 DiFranza JR, <u>Hooked from the first cigarette</u>, Scientific American, May 2008, Volume 298(5), Pages 82-87.

First, let's be clear. One need not do anything to succeed except to fully end use.   It's how the vast majority of "real-world" ex-users did it.

They simply waited and allowed sufficient time to pass until both the tease of their pile of old wanting satisfaction memories and their use justifications faded into calm.

Can we accelerate the process by seeing the truth about both? Absolutely!

Photo by National Cancer Institute

Imagine having a brain wanting disorder, a mental illness as real and permanent as alcoholism and not knowing it. Imagine residing inside a chemically dependent mind yet not realizing that it had de-sensitized itself by growing millions of extra receptors in multiple brain regions. Imagine no awareness that nicotine controls the flow of more than 100 chemicals inside our body.

But we didn't need such details to know we were hooked. We'd already experienced increased anxieties after having waited too long between feedings. Deep down, we knew we'd lost the ability to simply turn and walk away.

And even though we'd tried to tune it out, we also couldn't help but hear the dull roar of the endless stream of new medical studies. They reminded us how each and every puff destroys more of our body's ability to receive and transport life-giving oxygen.

They warned of the deadly consequences of continuing to inhale the 81 cancer causing chemicals so far identified in cigarette smoke, or the 28 found in smokeless tobacco juices. We knew we were slowly building cancer time bombs throughout our body. What we didn't know was how to stop building and start diffusing.

So how did our conscious mind cope with the sobering reality that our brain was slave to its own self-destruction? How did we look in the mirror each morning and maintain any sense of dignity, self-worth or self-respect while constantly being reminded that we were prisoners to dependency, decay, disease and death?

As smokers, how did we cope with each day bringing ourselves a bit closer to completing the act of committing chemical suicide? It was easy. We learned to lie.

We called upon our intelligence and conscious mind to help build a thick protective wall of denial that would insulate us from our dependency's hard, cold realities. Our basic wall building tools were conscious rationalizations, minimizations and blame transference.

We could then hide when those on the outside felt the need to remind us of who we really were, and what we were doing. It was also a place to hide when craves and urges reminded us that nicotine use was no longer optional, a home to explanations for our involuntary obedience to them.

Although nicotine's two-hour half-life was the basic clock governing mandatory feeding times, we became creative in inventing alternative justifications and explanations.

While most of us admitted to being hooked, we minimized the situation by pretending that all we really had was some "nasty little habit."

In our pre-dependency days (if there were any, as some of us were born hooked), there was no dopamine pathway wanting motivating use. But once feedings became mandatory, it didn't matter how we felt about them. Choice was no longer an issue.

Even if we didn't fully appreciate our new state of permanent chemical captivity, we rationalized the situation based upon what we found ourselves doing.

Tearing Down the Wall

In Chapter 4 we reviewed common use rationalizations. We learned that Nicodemon does not exist. Nor are there any other internal monsters. Repeated use fathered dopamine pathway chemical dependency. Dependency combined use patterns, conditioning, sensations and rationalizations to father a full-blown addiction.

Nicotine is not a friend and using isn't about love, flavor, pleasure, boredom, concentration, making coffee taste better or stress reduction.

Such rationalizations insulated us from a harsh world that was often in our face and just wouldn't let up. They were bricks in a wall made thicker by each empty pack, tin, pouch, tube, box or cartridge. Our only wall building limitation in adding new bricks was our imagination.

Have you ever noticed just how challenging it is to coax a smoker or oral user out from behind their wall? Give it a try. It's one of life's greatest challenges.

After years and hundreds of additions, like a turtle drawing into its shell, it's a solid and secure place to hide from those seeking to impose their will upon us.

Dependency's protectors, during recovery the wall's bricks, the lies we invented, become the enemy. Unchallenged, they provide super fuel for relapse. Especially here, during recovery's final phase, once no longer clouded or obscured by physical, emotional or subconscious challenge.

Here, a simple sight, sound or smell can awaken our use memory bank's collective influence. Its tease invites remaining use rationalizations to surface. Combining old use memories with a use justification can leave the new ex-user feeling overwhelmed and debating whether it's all worth it.

Rest assured, take heart. The peace and tranquility once addiction's chatter ends is worth thousands of times more than the price of admission.

Again, it's not necessary that any of us set out to intentionally dismantle our wall of denial. Time will eventually wear it down so long as, just one hour, challenge and day at a time, we keep our dependency under arrest.

But in that our wall simply reflects rationalizations that we ourselves created, we have it within us to rethink each, thus diminishing or even destroying their influence upon us.

Still, that's easier said than done. Why? Because each use justifications is rooted in truth avoidance, the exact opposite of what's needed to let go of it.

"Just think about something else"? - Our natural instinct is to try to ignore or suppress "junkie thinking" when it attempts to take root and play inside our mind. "Just try to think about something else."

Research shows that attempts at thought suppression may actually have the reverse effect of causing the thought to-be-suppressed to intrude with greater frequency into our consciousness.[415]

Photo by National Cancer Institute

Trying to think about something else often backfires making things worse. As Joel notes, the core of most internal debates likely involves fixation on the thought of having "just one," "one puff," "one cigarette" or "one fix."

"It's hard to think about something else because one puff seems like such a wonderful concept. They are often reminiscing about one of the best cigarettes, or more accurately, about the sensation around one of the best fixes they ever had. It may be one they smoked 20 years earlier but that is the one they are focused on," notes Joel.

"So what about thinking about something else? Well, it's hard to think of something else that can deliver such pleasure as this magic memory," suggests Joel. "Even if they successfully think of something else and overcome that urge, they walk away from the moment with a sense of longing or sadness with what they have just been deprived of again."

Keep in mind that their "pleasure" and "magic memory" is likely associated with ending one of the most intense moments of wanting their addiction ever mustered.

So, what works instead? "Change the tactic," advises Joel. "Instead of trying (often unsuccessfully) to think of something else, acknowledge the desire. Don't tell yourself you don't want one, you do and you know it."

"But remember there is a catch. To take the one you have to have all the others with it. And with the others, you have to take all the problems that go with 'them.' The smell, the expense, the embarrassment, social ostracization, the total loss of control, and the health implications."

415 Rassin E, et al, <u>Paradoxical and less paradoxical effects of thought suppression: a critical review</u>, Clinical Psychology Review, Nov. 2000, Volume 20(8), Pages 973-995.

Joel encourages us to see "just one" for the falsehood it reflects. By thinking about the entire spectrum of dependency that comes with "just one" we can walk away from the encounter feeling good about breaking free. We won't feel deprived but grateful.

The more vividly and accurately we are able to recall full-blown dependency, the less we'll think about it. "In a sense forcing yourself to remember will help you forget," Joel notes. "Not forget using, but the fantasy, the appeal of a nicotine fix."[416]

As with "just one," "just once," instead of trying to run or hide from use rationalizations that enter your mind, grab each by the horns. And don't let go until you've turned it inside out.

Think about the enslaved mind that created it. How much did any of us then know about nicotine dependency? Examine each use rationalization in honest light. Do you recall where it came from? Is that how you felt the very first time you used nicotine? Does tobacco industry store marketing play to it?

Would relapse somehow make the rationalization permanently go away, or instead guarantee its survival? Can you say with certainty that it's true and honest, or was it invented by a mind that needed justification for answering nicotine's next dinner bell?

Whether we choose to attempt to destroy rationalizations with honesty or wait for new non-use memories to suppress them, the day is approaching when you'll awaken to an expectation of going your entire day without once wanting to use.

Oh, you'll still have thoughts now and then, but with decreasing frequency, shorter duration and declining intensity. They'll become the exception, not the rule.

They say that "truth shall set us free" but there's an even better guarantee. It's impossible to lose our freedom so long as we refuse to allow nicotine back into our body.

The next few minutes are all that matter and each is entirely do-able. Thoughts or no thoughts, there was always only one rule ... no nicotine today, NONE (**NO N**icotine **E**ver)!

More Lies

In Chapter 4 we examined the primary, common, and most threatening use rationalizations. That's why they were placed in the front of FFN-TJH. If just getting started, they posed the greatest threat.
Let's look at a few more. But why? Because use justifications invaded nearly every aspect of our thinking. Unless willing to let go, we not only risk becoming a reluctant ex-user, down the road they become complacency's seeds for relapse.

Letting go requires awareness that something is being retained. While we each invented our own unique list of use excuses, between Chapter 4 and here we'll hopefully touch on most. It's my hope that the following additional examples provoke awareness of additional areas of use thinking in

---

416 Spitzer, J, "Just think about smoking else," August 31, 2002, http://www.ffn.yuku.com/topic/12581

need of honest reflection.

As mentioned earlier, conscious rationalizations usually fall into one of three categories: dependency, cost or recovery.

Dependency Rationalizations

Dependency rationalizations seek to deny or minimize being hooked, or suggest reasons for continuing use. Let's look at a few examples.

- **"I don't even know if I'm hooked. I've never tried stopping"** - Some have never made a serious recovery attempt. But why? What better way of never having to admit chemical dependency or experience defeat than by avoiding evidence that a problem exists?

- **"I only use once daily!"** - Some rationalize that their use level is too little to be addicted, lie about how much they use, or if addicted, believe that they are somehow better than other users because they used less frequently. The need for such minimization is evidence itself of dependency denial. Being a little bit addicted is like being a little bit dead.

- **"I don't use!"** - Even worse are the closet smokers like my grandma Polito who constantly tried to convince us that the thick cloud of smoke rolling out of the bathroom behind her simply wasn't there. How much more visible could denial be?

- **"I only smoke because it gives me something to do with my hands"** - Whittling wood, knitting and juggling are also things to do with our hands and they don't come with a 50 percent chance of life ending 13-14 years early.

  Such weak dependency denial rationalizations ignore that doodling with a pen, playing with coins, squeezing a ball or using strength grippers may be habit forming but are non-addictive. While we might get ink on ourselves, become rich or develop massive forearms, our chance of serious injury, disease or death is near zero.

- **"It's my right to blow smoke!"** - Truth is, we were chemically obligated to blow smoke. And as far as smoking rights, they continue to evaporate. Social controls to protect the rights of non-smokers continue sweeping the globe.

  If smoking nicotine truly is as addictive as heroin, should we be surprised as society continues its march toward banning smoking within view of children? It's already happening in parks, on beaches, on hospital grounds, and on entire college campuses. It's increasingly an issue in determining child custody and visitation obligations in divorce actions.

  And where permitted by law, employers are beginning to refuse to hire those testing positive for nicotine or cotinine.

- **"These new flavors are fantastic!"** - Pina colada, pumpkin pie, watermelon, pralines n' cream, marshmallow, raspberry cheesecake, peach schnapps, maple, sugar cookie, key lime, chocolate mint, bubble gum, pineapple, electronic cigarette e-liquid nicotine is today available in every flavor imaginable.

The nicotine addiction industry is providing those hooked on replacement nicotine or e-cigarettes plenty of reasons to explain continued use.

But how many chew expensive cinnamon or fruit flavored nicotine gum 5, 10 or 15 times daily because of great tasting fruit, mint or cinnamon? How many suck or vape cappuccino flavored nicotine because of a deep love for the taste of coffee?

And where does the e-cigarette user turn when their last atomizer breaks? A straw maybe? Slow deep breaths? I don't think so.

- **"I'll cut down or smoke just one now and then"** - Such rationalizations pretend that chemical dependency is some nasty little habit capable of manipulation, modification and control. We are drug addicts. Although accompanied by alertness, the dopamine pathway wanting we feel for nicotine is no different from the dopamine pathway wanting felt by the crack, heroin or meth addict.

Using less than our level of tolerance demands will likely leave us in a perpetual state of withdrawal. While we may use less often, we can compensate by smoking, chewing or sucking harder, or if a smoker by sucking deeper and holding it longer.

Cost Rationalizations

Cost rationalizations either deny or minimize use harms or costs. Here are a few of the more common ones.

- **"I vape e-cigs and it's vastly safer."** - While likely and hopefully true, we have little current appreciation for what "safer" really means. Long overdue research into health risks associated cleaner forms of delivery is finally receiving attention. It's being motivated by an increasing percentage of users transferring their dependency to oral tobacco, replacement nicotine or electronic cigarettes.

But results will arrive slowly. A glaring defect in most current harm reduction risk analysis is that risk calculations are being created by studying oral tobacco or snus users, most of whom had little or no prior smoking history. For example, it may be decades before we have a firm grasp on the health risks of inhaling vaporized nicotine into lung already damages by years or decades of smoking.

A 2008 study found that the odds of a smokeless tobacco user experiencing a fatal ischemic stroke were 72% greater than for non-users.[417] How many more years before e-cig users know their stroke risks?

Does it make sense to suggest to a smoker with 20 pack-years of damage to their body that

417 Hergens MP, et al, <u>Smokeless tobacco and the risk of stroke</u>, Epidemiology, November 2008, Volume 19(6), Pages 794-799.

if they transfer to smokeless tobacco that they'll suddenly have the same risks as a smokeless user who never smoked?

- **"I smoke lights and they're not as bad"** - Lights and ultra-lights are fully capable of delivering the same amount of tar and nicotine as most regular brands, depending on how they're smoked.

  They do not reduce most health risks including risk of heart disease or cancer. In fact, those who smoke them often compensate by covering the holes with their lips or by taking longer or deeper drags, thus introducing more tar not less.

- **"I'm only hurting me!"** - Reflect upon the emotional pain and financial loss your needless dying and death would inflict upon loved ones. How should they explain your death? Was it an accident? Were you murdered? Was it stupidity? Was it suicide? Did you intentionally kill yourself?

- **"Cessation causes weight gain and that's just as dangerous"** - This intellectual denial pre-assumes a large weight gain and then makes an erroneous judgment regarding relative risks. Recovery does not increase body weight, eating does.

  Metabolic changes may account for a pound or two. But you'd have to gain an additional 75 pounds in order to equal the health risks associated with smoking one pack-a-day (Whelan, A Smoking Gun, 1984).

- **"It's too painful to stop!"** - Compared to what? Imagine a diagnosis of lung cancer and having your left lung ripped out, followed by chemotherapy. Imagine years spent trying to recover from a serious stroke or massive heart attack, or fighting for every breath through emphysema-riddled lungs as the twelve steps to the bathroom totally exhaust you, as you drag your oxygen along too.

- **"There's still plenty of time left to stop"** - Keep in mind that one-quarter of all adult smokers are being claimed in middle-age, each an average of 22.5 years early. Also keep in mind that such figures are just averages, that many die sooner. We've been sharing stories of young victims at WhyQuit since 1999. The common thread among most claimed in their 30s or 40s is that they started using while still children or in their early teens.

- **"A cure for cancer is coming soon"** - Between Europe and North America, tobacco will claim more than one million victims this year. How many of them thought that a cure was on the way? Sadly, it was false hope.

  Which type of lung cancer are you hoping they'll cure: squamous cell, oat cell, adenocarcinoma, or one of the less common forms?

  Even if the right cure arrives, what will be left of your lungs by the time it gets here? If gambling on "how" tobacco will kill you, don't forget to consider heart attack, stroke and emphysema.

- **"Lots of smokers live until ripe old age"** - Look around. Old vibrant smokers are rare. If you do find old smokers almost all are in poor health or in advanced stages of smoking related diseases, with many on oxygen. Smokers tend to think only in terms of dying from lung cancer when tobacco kills in many ways.

  For example, circulatory disease caused by smoking kills more smokers each year than lung cancer. Some point to actor George Burns who smoked cigars and lived to age 100. But how long would George have lived and how healthy would he have been if he hadn't smoked cigars? What's wrong with living a long and healthy life?

- **"It's too late now to heal these lungs"** - Nonsense! Tissues not damaged beyond repair will heal and may provide a substantial increase in overall lung function.[418] Even with emphysema, although destroyed air sacs will never again function, recovery will halt the needless destruction of additional tissues.

- **"We have to die of something"** - This rationalization all but admits our own intentional slow-suicide. But I challenge you to locate even one terminal lung cancer patient who wasn't horrified upon learning that they'd actually succeeded.

  Some apply the cup half-full rationalization to smoking's 50% adult kill rate,[419] suggesting that what it really means is that there's a 50% chance that "smoking won't kill me." Try to name any other activity in which we'd willingly participate if there were a 50% chance of death.

Recovery Rationalizations

Here are a few recovery rationalizations, each designed to postpone or delay cessation.

- **"I'll stop after the next pack, next carton, next month, my next birthday or New Years' day"** - I hate to think about how many times I lied to myself with such nonsense. And which pack, carton, month or birthday offers the best chance for success?

  Why did I limit myself to always purchasing only a one-day's supply? Because tomorrow was always the day I'd stop and I couldn't see throwing extra packs away.

- **"I'll stop next week"** - For some of us it was always next week, next month or next year. Others go so far as to actually set a date. Doing so always made today's use more tolerable, as we pretended that our problem would soon be solved.

- **"I'm waiting on a painless cure"** - Don't hold your breath. The day science can make our mother's death painless -- so as to avoid any emotional loss -- is the day it will be capable of

418 Buist AS, The effect of smoking cessation and modification on lung function, The American Review of Respiratory Disease, July 1976, Volume 114(1), Pages 115-122.

419 Wald NJ and Hackshaw AK, Cigarette smoking: an epidemiological overview, British Medical Bulletin, January 1996, Volume 52(1), Pages 3-11.

erasing the emotional loss associated with ending the most dependable chemical relationship we've likely ever known.

- **"The 3rd generation vaccine is coming!"** - NRT, Zyban, Chantix or Champix, and failure of two generations of vaccines, nicotine addicts have been teased for decades with promises that new magic cures were on the way.

Most recently, the promise was that four to five vaccine shots over six months would cause the body's immune system to create large antibodies, that would quickly bond with nicotine molecules, making them too large to cross through the blood-brain protective filtering barrier and stimulate dopamine pathways.

It was wishful thinking. It didn't work. Vaccine users found ways to relapse even with all those expensive injections and antibodies everywhere.[420]

Wall Street Journal headlines declared in June 2012 that "Vaccine Shows Promise for Nicotine Addiction."[421] Instead of injecting antibodies, the new vaccine tricks the liver into constantly producing them, at least in mice.

And as the WSJ article notes, therein lies the problem, "making the leap from [mice] to people will be a challenge. Other recent attempts failed to prove effective in people after initially encouraging animal studies."

- **"My family can't handle recovery"** - Blame transference seeks to place the cause for defeat upon others. It's easy to intentionally exaggerate withdrawal via anger or other antics, to the point of making life a living hell for friends, loved ones or co-workers.

Transference can blame relapse on a lack of support, a relationship, stressful times, financial hardship, other smokers, alcohol or even our job.

- **"I won't be able to stop unless someone stops with me"** - Many pretend that they cannot succeed because their husband, wife or friend won't stop too. This procrastination brick allows use to continue until someone else takes action. What if they never stop?

Sadly, millions ride this waiting rationalization all the way to an early grave. It's nice when friends or loved ones make this journey with us. But if not happening, someone needs to be brave and go first. Then, it's simply a matter of being patient and teaching by example, allowing them to observe freedom's full glory.

- **"Mom just died. Now just isn't the time"** - Smoking won't bring back mom or dad, nor cure any other ill in life. As Joel teaches, success during a period of high stress insures that future high stress situations won't serve as justification for relapse.

---

420 Cornuz J, et al, <u>A vaccine against nicotine for smoking cessation: a randomized controlled trial</u>, Plos One. 2008 Jun 25;3(6):e2547.

421 Winslow, Ron, <u>Vaccine Shows Promise for Nicotine Addiction</u>, Wall Street Journal, June 27, 2012

- **"I'd stop but withdrawal never ends!"** - Hogwash! Why not disprove this one by living the truth? Give it a go!

- **"If I stop, I'll just start back again. I always do"** - Truth is, we do not have to relapse. Relapse occurs because we fail to respect the Law of Addiction. We violate the Law because we allow ourselves to forget why we stopped or invent some lame excuse such as those above.

  In fact, this recovery is absolutely guaranteed to be our last ever, so long as nicotine never again finds its way into our bloodstream, so long as we continue to live on the right side of the "Law."

Conscious Fixation

As mentioned, we do our thinking inside our prefrontal cortex, the large lobe behind our forehead. Conscious fixation is the ability of the rational thinking mind to become completely engrossed, absorbed and preoccupied with a single subject, issue or train of thought.

As you'll recall, while subconscious conditioning somehow limits the duration of a cue triggered crave episode to three-minutes or less, conscious fixation can last as long as our ability to concentrate, remain focused and stay absorbed.

How will you react when thoughts of "wanting" to use begin bantering about inside your mind? Will you fixate upon them or instead seize the moment as an opportunity for conscious healing?

Wanting's arrival presents a chance to reflect upon both wanting's source or foundation, and the thinking or debate that follows.

Don't worry. Neither fixation nor analyzing it can harm us. In fact, as Joel often reminds us, it's impossible to relapse by thinking. Only action can destroy our healing and glory.

Photo by National Cancer Institute

Clearly, we cannot erase thousands of old wanting satisfaction memories, or the use justifications we invented to explain creating another. What we can do is use honesty and insights to destroy their influence upon us.

Instead of an addict's use memories becoming fuel for fixation and relapse, truth and understanding can transform them into laughable reminders of the prison we once called home.

While still using, how many times did we reach for and rely upon each of our use excuses? During recovery, how many times will each use excuse pop into our mind? The arrival of each is a golden opportunity for a mind no longer under nicotine's influence to analyze a drug addict's use justifications in honest light.

It's a chance to use insight and understanding to recast hundreds or even thousands of similar dependency memories all at once. Such repainting or recasting of use thinking can accelerate recovery.

Still, there may be one or more elements of junkie thinking that seem difficult to let go. There may be one or more attractions to nicotine use that truth and insight fail to impact. If so, accept them, for now, and move on. But in doing so, try to fit any such remaining attractions into the bigger dependency picture.

If willing to be brutally honest about the prison cell we once called home, little will remain to embrace. Like eyes on a potato, any lingering romantic use rationalizations will be surrounded by tasty and edible truths.

The concern is that once home and residing here on Easy Street that, like fertilizer, complacency can cause those remaining eyes to begin to sprout, grow and eventually destroy the tastiness surrounding them.

Staying focused on dependency's bigger picture -- that one equals all -- can help keep their influence in perspective.

We sometimes encounter long-term ex-users whose remaining use rationalizations are beginning to combine with complacency to elevate risk of relapse. Some will disclose that they still think about using and have recently found themselves doing so more frequently. A few questions may aid in helping them regain perspective.

Photo by National Cancer Institute

- When was the last time you experienced an urge to use?
- What thoughts went through your mind?
- How long did it last? How intense was it?
- How long before that urge did you experience your previous urge?
- If you don't mind sharing, what did you like most about using?
- What did you dislike most?
- Do you understand that for ex-users that there's no such thing as just one?

Those in the first few days of recovery would laugh at what the long-term ex-user considered an "urge." Normally it's a brief passing thought that lasts seconds and is quickly abandoned.

Digging deeper may allow identification of the particular rationalization that was likely never directly confronted during recovery. Unchallenged, like a cancer, its significance now grows.

So called "experts" claim that nicotine dependency is a chronic relapsing condition. But it doesn't have to be. Still, you'll sometimes meet current smokers who'll tell you that they once stopped for 5, 10 or even 20 years and then smoked one, and soon found themselves smoking more than ever.

Many can recall the use rationalization they fixated upon in the seconds before relapse. Amazingly, some still believe in it even though it cost them their freedom.

Imagine for a moment that once here on Easy Street that you've brought one or two remaining romantic use notions with you. If so, consider wrapping them in this often quoted recovery mantra:

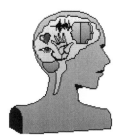 

"I'd rather be an ex-user who sometimes thinks about using
than a user always thinking about stopping."

The Joy of Smoking?

Out on the town, you watch as your good friend Bill lights-up and sucks down a deliciously deep puff, and then lays the pack on the table between you.

Cindy, your talkative co-worker, blows smoke your way while gloriously waving her cigarette like a conductor's baton.

Arthur and Denise, two smoking strangers, gravitate toward one another and engage in light-hearted conversation while guarding a store's entrance.

While stopped at a light, Ellen inhales a deep and relaxing puff in the car beside you.

"Oh but to again share in the joys of smoking," you think to yourself, "to puff, to taste, to blow, then relax."

The joys of smoking? Joy?

Yesterday, Bill stepped in a pile of dog dung but failed to notice until he turned and was puzzled by the strange brown tracks across his sky blue carpet that lead to his right shoe. Bill's sniffer has been almost useless for more than 20 years.

A pack and a half a day smoker, he's experienced two cases of pneumonia over the past 3 winters, with the last one putting him in bed for 6 days. Struggling for each breath, Bill still managed to smoke a couple each day. His doctor has pleaded with him for years to stop. But, having already tired and failed using every new product his doctor recommended, he feels like a total and complete failure.

Cindy's two teenage sons harass her almost daily about her smoking. They can't walk anywhere as a family without her cigarette smoke finding the boys. When it does, they make her want to crawl into a hole, as they both start coughing and gagging as if dying. When smoking, they never walk together. It's either ahead or behind for mom.

Her parents are non-smokers. She dreads the seven hour drive to their home next week but can no longer make excuses for visiting only once in 3 years. Cindy knows that they'll pass three rest areas along the interstate, but it will be difficult to fib about having to go to the bathroom at all three. Two will have to do.

The date for the trip arrives. She skips making breakfast to ensure that the boys will demand that they stop to eat along the way. Cindy shakes her head after coming back in from loading up the car. Not only does she have a cigarette in her hand, the ashtray on the table is smoking one too.

Before leaving town, she stops to fill up with gas. She feels far more secure after stuffing two new packs into her purse, while sneaking two quick puffs on the way back to the car.

Arthur, a 54-year-old pack-a-day smoker, has small cell lung cancer in the right lobe. His fast growing tumor is now almost three months old and a little bigger than an orange. As he sits rolling coins to purchase the 20 milligrams of mandatory daily nicotine needed to stay within his comfort zone, he does not yet know he has cancer.

Although he has twice coughed up a small bit of bloody mucus, he quickly dismissed it both times. Frankly, he just doesn't want to know. There is a bit of chest pain but that's nothing new, as chest tightness has occurred on and off for the past couple of years.

Additional thick bloody mucus will soon scare Arthur into a doctor visit and a chest x-ray. The delay will cost him a lung. During the 4 months that follow, he'll battle hard to save his life. In the end Arthur will lose. His fate is the same as 92% diagnosed with stage III small cell lung cancer, death within five years.

A workaholic, Ellen has done very well financially. Her life seems to have everything except companionship. A three pack-a-day smoker, she constantly smells like a walking tobacco factory and often turns heads and noses when entering a room. A serious chain-smoker, she tells those around her that she enjoys her cigarettes.

Deep down, she knows that she is a drug addict and believes that she just can't quit. Her car windows, house blinds and forehead continually share a common guest, a thin oily film of tobacco tar. Ellen has a date next Friday, a two pack-a-day smoker named Ed. They'll find comfort in sharing their addictions.

Denise started smoking at age 13 while her lungs were still developing. Constantly clearing her throat, month by month her breathing capacity continues to slowly deteriorate. Smoking lines and wrinkles above and below her lips have aged a once attractive face far quicker than its 32 years.

Considered "cool" when she became hooked, the government recently banned smoking in all public buildings. The headline in the local paper she's holding is about the city proposing a ban on smoking in the park across the street.

About to lose her smoking park bench and feeling like a hopelessly addicted social outcast, a single tear works its way down her cheek.

Why? Because 15 pounds overweight to begin with, a year ago Denise successfully broke free for almost 2 months by exchanging cigarettes for a new crutch called food. She threw in the towel after outgrowing her entire wardrobe. Three months following relapse and still depressed over her defeat, all the new weight remains with her.

Already on high-blood pressure medication, Denise is about to become a regular user of anti-depressants too.

The joy of smoking? Joy?

Fortunately for Denise, a caring friend will tell her about a free online forum called WhyQuit.com. There, Denise will discover the core principles underlying her almost two decades of chemical dependency upon nicotine.

She'll develop the patience, outlook and understanding needed to navigate this temporary period of re-adjustment called recovery. She'll also develop the mental skills and healthy body needed to successfully tackle her unwanted pounds. How? Just one ounce at a time.

All that matters are the next few minutes and each is entirely do-able. There will always be only one rule that comes with a 100% guarantee of success for all who follow it ... no nicotine today!

Chapter 13

Homecoming

How do we know when we're home? If you've ever moved, you know there's a big difference between moving into a house and having it feel like home.

The correct answer is, you are home when you feel it! Some feel at home in a couple of weeks while others need months.

A Silent Celebration

Amazingly, within 2 to 4 months the adjustment process transports most in recovery to a point where they experience that very first day where they never once "think" to themselves, "gee, I'd sure like a smoke," "dip," "chew," "lozenge," "vape" or "piece of nicotine gum."

Photo by Centers for Disease Control

After the first such day, such days become more and more common. Soon, they become our new norm in life, with the distance between the occasional "thought" growing further and further apart.

If it happens sooner or takes longer, don't fret! If sooner, enjoy it, If longer, patience, it's coming!

Long-Term Quiet and Calm

Imagine entire days, weeks, months, or eventually even years without your mind ever once feeling an urge to use nicotine.

Imagine living in a constant state of total comfort without any nicotine use related anxieties whatsoever - none, zero, nil, complete and total tranquility.

It's where hundreds of millions of comfortable ex-users reside today. Were any of them truly stronger than nicotine? Were any of them stronger than us? Or, is that just another lame use excuse?

After arresting my thirty-year dependency, my recovery evolved

Photo by National Institute on Drug Abuse

to the point of substantial comfort by about eight weeks, a few weeks earlier than most but later than some. It was then that I experienced my last major subconscious crave episode.

And about then when I started to notice that the once steady stream of thoughts of wanting were ever so slowly becoming fewer, shorter and generally less intense. During the first few weeks I worked hard to maintain a strong positive attitude while refusing to allow negative thoughts to infect my thinking and dreams.

While feeding myself large doses of positive thought, I also confronted and analyzed those remaining thoughts that kept inviting relapse. Soon, it was no longer a matter of trying to believe what I was telling myself. I did believe in the new nicotine-free me!

Although at times intense, I did my best to remain focused on the long overdue healing occurring within. I saw each and every day as a full and complete victory in and of itself. Today I was free. Today was about healing!

And there were lots of little gifts along the way. New smells, tastes, energy, extra pocket change, the whiteness emerging in my smile, pride, empty pockets, a bit bigger step, odorless fingers, hope, endurance, an ash-less world, new found time, long overdue self-respect, gradually lengthening periods of comfort, freedom and even a few extra pounds, it was simply me coming home to meet me.

Eventually the minor urges and periods of thought fixation became further and further apart. After two years of freedom I found myself going months without an urge. And the last time I experienced anything that can be fairly called an "urge" was in December 2001, two years and seven months after starting my journey.

Gradually Diminishing Thoughts and Urges

Most ex-users report that recovery was less challenging than expected. Many report cakewalks.

But it certainly wasn't for me. There were a couple of moments where I felt totally overwhelmed. Thank goodness such moments were few and brief.

The beauty of recovery is that with each passing day after peak withdrawal that the frequency, duration and intensity of challenge is "generally" on the decline.

But like trying to watch a rose bud open, seeing the decline while living it can at times seem nearly impossible. Before we know it, the storms turn to breezes, with a possible gust now and then.

Photo by Centers for Disease Control

It's entirely normal during the first couple of years to experience occasional thoughts of wanting, or even encounter a remote, seasonal or infrequent use cue. It's also possible to retain a romantic attachment to using, a link capable of fostering desire until ready to let go.

One of the most popular discussions at WhyQuit's peer support group Freedom is entitled, "Tell a newbie how many seconds a day you still want a cigarette." Below are messages posted to the discussion. Each opens by indicating how long the person had been nicotine-free. They then tell us how long each day they still want a cigarette.

Keep in mind as you read them that, for the most part, these are educated ex-users. It's likely that part of their reason for posting to this particular discussion was excitement over how much easier an educated recovery can be.

- 4 days: "My experience so far has been tough but tolerable. I'm 35 and have been smoking a pack/day since 17. Up until 4 days ago, I felt completely powerless in the face of nicotine, like I was especially weak to its powers - but reading has helped me to realize that nicotine has done the same exact thing to all of us." Gus
- 5 days: "I think there are probably 150 seconds in my current days that I want a cigarette, and I have to remind myself, I am a non-smoker and the reasons why and that smoking a cigarette is stupid and will do nothing but harm me. My dad died in December of lung cancer." Darla
- 6 days: "I probably only get one real crave a day now. The first two days I had really bad cravings at all the usual times that I would light up. Third and fourth days seemed like I only had 2-4 bad craves. Day 5 through now it seems like its just one. And even that one crave isn't that big of a deal. However, I do get those 'pangs.' Not pangs of "need" though. It's more like I'm just missing something and a second of sadness comes over me...then I just realize that 'Oh yeah, I would have been smoking a cigarette now!'" Casey
- 7 days: "I think about smoking maybe once or twice a day for 1 or 2 minutes. I'm so turned off by smoking that some days I don't think about smoking at all and I am only one week in." Gina
- 8 days: ""Even though it's been just over a week I can honestly say I don't really CRAVE a cigarette anymore. I'm not saying I don't think about them, I've been an addict for 24 years. But I don't crave them. I don't want them. Time spent remembering them, probably a couple of minutes a day, but when you consider that I use to spend over 3 hours a day abusing myself with them and much of the rest of the time wishing I wasn't abusing myself, that's small potatoes! As one of my favorite quotes says: 'I'd rather be an ex-smoker who occasionally thinks about a cigarette than a smoker who is obsessed by them!'" Pheonix
- 10 days: "Ten days now and I still think about it a few times an hour for a few seconds. But I'm mostly thinking about how I don't smoke anymore! Very simple! Maybe once a day, I get blind-sided with a very strong and powerful thought of "I have to have a cigarette, NOW!" My responding thought is "But, I don't smoke anymore" and it's GONE! HAHAHA! The "gotta smoke" thoughts are getting rather wimpy. There seems to be absolutely NOTHING behind them! It's a beautiful thing :-)" Glynda
- 13 days: "Still haven't wanted one and it is day 13, yes on a Friday, lol, I have thoughts like 'gee I would have just lit up,' 'again,' 'another instance.' What is more amazing is the thoughts that come 'I HAVEN"T THOUGHT OF A CIGARETTE!' Not craves, thoughts." Tagsgirl

- 13 days: "For the past two days I have actually gone hours without thinking about a smoke. Hours! That has not happened in a long time. I look forward to the time when I can go for days without hardly a thought of those nasty little things." Tubes

- 14 days: "I think about cigarettes about 3 times a day, they last about 3 minutes each, which is the actual time it took to smoke one cigarette. I don't want one, it is just a thought that does not last long, and it goes away. I feel awesome and now have a much better life with my children and husband." Barbara.

- 15 days: ""I've been nico-free for 2 weeks, 1 day and now only have 4 or 5 urges each day. This is a definite improvement over the constant craves of the first 3 days! I know I have to be patient ... and also try to enjoy each victory over every urge that I defeat!" Judy

- 16 days: "Surprisingly, only a couple of times a day, for not more than 30 seconds each time. Averaging about a minute-and-a-half on the usual day. Also, these are just habit-driven thoughts; thinking about smoking on the way to the car, but I'm perfectly fine once I get there, or thinking about having a cigarette before bed, but knowing that I sleep so much better without it. These are just thoughts; by facing them, they have no power over me!" MichelleNC

- 17 days: "I think about a cigarette several times a day, but only one or two of those is an actual "want" and not just a thought. That's a change from actually crying for want of a cigarette on day two, to shrugging off a couple of little wants in the course of a day in just over two weeks' time ...awesome." Stef

- 18 days: "I don't think about smoking very much, maybe 10-20 seconds a day. But I do think about not smoking a lot !!!!!!" Rob

- 18 days: "Probably about 4 minutes thinking about it, maybe 30 seconds with a bit of an empty feeling, craving something that might be nicotine." Maisie

- 19 days: "I smoked for 40 years, at least a pack a day. Am I having craves? Yes. Are they easier or harder than I thought they would be? Easier. Do they become less and less in duration as time goes by? Yes they do! I have craves about 4 to 5 times a day lasting seconds." Jill

- 21 days: "I crave a cigarette maybe once a day. It lasts about 45 seconds. I feel sooooo much better since I quit!!! The craves I can handle..." Ah0304

- 22 days: "I never want one. Oh, I may occasionally think I should be having one. But I can't say I want it. Even those thoughts have become rarer and rarer. I have been totally amazed at how quickly I went from needing one every couple of hours (if I was doing good) and having no desire for one. I am thrilled to be smoke free." Leigh

- 23 days: "Some days I don't crave at all, and the most is just once and it last for a few seconds." Suez

- 24 days: "I am into my 24th day and honestly I don't even think about cigarettes unless I see someone smoking or smell it and then I think how nasty and disgusting it is! After smoking for 37 years that is pretty amazing ... of course there is an occasional trigger but not on a daily basis!" Bev

- 25 days: "After just three weeks I am down to once or twice a day. I have even gone entire days without thinking about it! After 19 years of smoking up to two packs a day, that's pretty amazing to me." Joe

- 26 days: "I do think about smoking every now and then, but I definitely don't think as much about smoking as I did when I still smoked 30 cigarettes a day." Klinka

- 26 days: "I would say I probably think about a cigarette 3 to 5 times a day (which is down from like a million!! haha) and I actually 'want' a cigarette 1 time a day. This is fantastic to me! I was so scared that I would fight for the rest of my life like I was in the first week, but have come to realize this simply is not true." Amy79

- 29 days: "This has gone textbook as described on this site. Today I have one crave a day but everyday it gets a little more vague." Phillip
- 30 days: "After one month I still think of cigarettes. The thoughts are in 2 forms. The first is not a crave but just thinking about a situation or activity that relates to smoking. It doesn't bother me at all. This happens about 3 to 4 times a day. The second is the crave. It only lasts about 10 to 20 seconds. The craves are not as bad as they were a few weeks ago." John
- 31 days: "It's still early in the recovery process so I'm not going to say I don't think about them...because I do, but in all honesty it's not really that much. The thoughts come quickly from time to time, but they leave just as quickly." Abu Daud1
- 32 days: "I don't have cravings. Ever. I sort of feel like having a cigarette maybe 2-3 times a day for a total of about 60-90 seconds (at most). That's about 1 1/2 minutes a day." Matt
- 32 days: "I work with smokers and dippers all day. Every time I saw someone smoking I would think Hmmm ... time for a smoke and actually go for my pocket to get one out and then remember- I can't! This went on for the first two weeks and I was wondering if this was how it was going to be for me forever. I had smoked a pack plus a day for 30 years it was so much a part of my life that I figured I would always feel the urge to smoke when I saw someone else smoke. After the 2nd week I was feeling much more confident and determined and when I thought about smoking it was that I was sooo ... glad that I didn't anymore. Now after four weeks plus I think about smoking maybe 20 seconds a day and it's never an urge to smoke, it's a sense of something missing but not missed. The law of addiction is the first thing I think of when I think about smoking and I know that as long as I remember that I will Never Take Another Puff." Ginz
- 34 days: 1-3 minutes per day on average I still want a cigarette. It's not a craving that happens during the first 3 days, not an itch that goes for 1-3 weeks after you quit. It's just a small thought." Levaser
- 37 days: "The thought of smoking is not even a daily occurrence anymore. When I do think of it, it is not an urge but just a thought. It does get better. At one time I didn't think it would but it did." Saree
- 38 days: "I can honestly say that I never want a cigarette. Sometimes I will get a random thought about having one, but it is quickly gone once I remind myself that I don't smoke any more." Jason
- 45 days: "It has been at least two weeks since I actually WANTED a cigarette. What I have now are vagrant thoughts about smoking that pass in a matter of a few seconds--and I have actually had one day where I realized the next morning that I hadn't thought about smoking at all. That's after 45+ years as a smoker of at least 2 packs a day." Cliff
- 46 days: "I am a newbie at just 1 month, 2 weeks, 2 days. I still think about smoking quite often. I would say at least a half an hour a day. I was worried about this but now that I have written it down I realize that it really isn't to bad, considering I used to think about smoking about every half hour or so. But I do realize that I think much more about not smoking than I do about smoking." Steve
- 47 days: "I maybe spend 2 minutes out of an entire day thinking about cigarettes. I no longer obsess about them, and I find the act of smoking, well, filthy. I haven't yet had those wondrous days where there are no thoughts at all, but I've come pretty close." Diana

- 51 days: "How often a day do I think about cigarettes? Not very often. If I do think about cigarettes it is only for a few seconds a day but today I spent zero seconds thinking about cigarettes." Herman
- 58 days: "I think about smoking most days but spend NO time wanting to smoke now. There is nothing I want back about nicotine and cigarettes." Doc
- 60 days: "...thought a few times of having a smoke but it's a passing thought now, it has little strength." Dave T
- 67 days: "Thoughts have completely dropped off to random, fleeting, a spit second if I choose to notice them. Occasionally, there is a new trigger but relatively easy to deal with now that I'm no longer struggling." Ilona
- 69 days: "On a usual day, I don't want a cigarette at all. Sometimes I have a craving or two, and they last for about 3 seconds each. Then they're gone. It's brilliant!" RedSunFlower
- 71 days: "I'm 58, smoked since 16, a pack a day, have been nicotine-free for 71 glorious days and I don't want them, don't need them, don't miss them and rarely think of them. I don't even remember smoking." Sarah
- 72 days: "I only think about cigarettes on the weekend at a nightclub when a smoker stands next to me and I have to move because it smells so bad." Rochelle
- 74 days: "Maybe 3-5 seconds every couple of days. Seriously, it does get so much easier." Beth
- 77 days: "I am amazed at how quickly I went from needing a cigarette every hour or less to going days without wanting one at all. I was a very heavy smoker (3 to 4 packs a day) and I expected years of wanting to smoke. I had my first day without any urges at least 2 weeks ago. I can't remember the last time I wanted a cigarette. At least a few days ago. For the last 3 or 4 weeks the rare urges have been so easy to deal with that I think they pass without me remembering I had one. I know I can get through 3 minutes without nicotine, so why dwell on it?" Jim H
- 86 days: "Once every two weeks for about 3-5 minutes." Diane
- 105 days: "Three and a half months in I want a smoke 0 seconds. There are still occasional triggers I run across, but I would say that is about once a week and 10 days now, and getting longer in between. I have achieved comfort. P.S: My wife still smokes, so it is possible to be around it and not want it." Roy
- 108 days: "Rarely, very rarely, do I even think about smoking. I am not quite four months quit and I had smoked for 40 years. To me that is absolutely incredible! Quitting is so much easier, and so much more rewarding, than I ever dreamed it could be. And I know I'll never go back to a life of feeding the addiction." Stella
- 4 months: "...maybe six or seven seconds of "thoughts" a week. I'm one very happy camper." Pat
- 5 months: "I sometimes get hooked into a romantic thought about smoking, a memory, but it is merely a thought and not a desire or a need or a want." Moira
- 5 months: "I smoked for 38 years, in the end at 3 1/2 packs a day. Stopped cold turkey on Jan. 11, 2012, my first attempt. I now have smoking thoughts just a few times per week, and they're not 'dwelling' thoughts - they just last 1 or 2 seconds or less. I'm very proud of my progress." VoltMan
- 6 months: "I'm thinking that I'd like a cigarette for 6 seconds a week. When I smoked, there were probably at least 2 occasions each day when I wanted to smoke but couldn't, because I was in a no-smoking office or a restaurant or on a train. Each of those occasions lasted say

30 minutes average. That amounts to 25,200 seconds a week when I was suffering significant anxiety and withdrawal symptoms, far worse in intensity than any discomfort I have suffered from not smoking since I stopped." Marty

- 7 months: "Never a want, need or crave ... Passing thought? Maybe a couple times a week." RJW

- 8 months: "Thinking about a cigarette is no longer a daily activity. If I have a thought it is weeks apart and lasts for only 5 seconds or less. I treat the thought like a pesky, dirty fly and swat it from my mind! Freedom is sweet!!!" Jrock413

- 9 months: "Zero. I do still think about them once in awhile, but never want one. My hard won freedom is too precious at this point to throw away over a lousy puff." Roy

- 10 months: "I have not wanted a cigarette even once for many months now. Even a couple of unexpected triggers did not result in my wanting a cigarette, just the realization that a brief craving is a minor annoyance NOT a desire to smoke!" JefferyRW

- 10 months: "I have not wanted to have a cigarette is many months now. I have no craves at all and there is only an occasion (every 3-4 weeks) that I will think for a second, 'Wait, something is missing,' only to smile as I realize I would be having a cigarette if I was still living in my addiction. But I do NOT want to smoke. It is only a reminder of how chained I was. I was a heavy smoker for so long, I thought I couldn't stop! Yes, comfort does come. Much faster than I thought possible. The rewards are so plentiful, I am full of gratitude." Endura

- 10 months: "When I think about cigarettes (which is hardly ever), I am grateful that I don't have to buy them, roll them, smoke them, cough after them, wake up in the morning feeling tight in the chest after smoking too many of them, smell my clothes, hair, skin after smoking them, worry about my health after smoking them, feel shame and guilt after smoking them ... you get the point. Freedom is HUGE! Best thing I've ever done." Lara

- 11 months: "I might have had a thought about having a cigarette a few days ago but I'm not sure. It could be my old age kicking in. They pop into my head and out again so rarely and so quickly they don't even register anymore." Pat
  1 year: "Today is exactly 12 months since I had my last puff. This is the greatest gift I have ever given myself, and let me assure you, I NEVER think of having a smoke, but think often of how free I am. If you think I'm just a strong person, let me tell you how weak I am. I am an alcoholic and a compulsive gambler. I am as weak as can be to my addictions. But today I choose not to puff." Steve

- 1 year: ""It's been a long, long time since I last wanted one - months, I suppose. The cigarettes, urges and craves have simply vanished out of my life. I stay prepared, and with the knowledge gained here I'll always be ready for an urge, but the truth is, I think it's over now. I don't want cigarettes any more, that's all there is to it." Susanne

- 1 year, 2 months: "I haven't wanted a cigarette for a very long time, I do however think about smoking fairly often but only because it is a reminder of how wonderful it is to be free!!" Lucie

- 1 year, 3 months: "zip, zero, nada!" Melrose

- 1 year, 4 months: "I think about having one on what probably amounts to about 6 seconds a week!" Annies1

- 2 years: "I am very happy to report that I don't ever have urges anymore. If I think about nicotine at all, it's about how proud I am" to be free. Whelen

- 2 years: "I never thought I could stop smoking or that I would completely stop thinking about cigarettes - but I have and its wonderful!" Sally

- 2 years: "I never think of smoking really. I think I had a fleeting thought one spring day when I was having a glass of wine and standing on the deck." Jeff
- 2 years: "ZERO!" Melrose
- 2 years: "I can truthfully say that I just do not think of smoking. I never thought I would be able to say that, but it's true!!" Vicki
- 3 years: "Null, nix, none, nothing, zip, zero ... honestly, my nicotine-related thoughts are annoyance at the smell of cigarettes if I can't avoid it." Meg
- 3 years: "A few times in the past year the thought of smoking crossed my mind." Joseph
- 4 years: "How many seconds a year? None!!!" Laura
- 4 years: "I never think about smoking, except the occasional wish for a friend or acquaintance to know the peace that comes with never taking another puff." Kevin
- 5 years: "I came to this website over 5 years ago struggling with addiction like everyone else. Had tried stopping many times in life, but cigarettes always came back to me until I educated myself. Now I can happily say I am still free from my addiction, and I never want a cigarette." JazzLady
- 7 years: "My family smokes. I never desire it even if they're around me smoking." Anne
- 10 years: "Every so often -- maybe once every 3 or 4 months -- I'll pass by someone who's freshly lit up, and there will be a fleeting nostalgia. Never lasts for more than a few seconds, and I'd definitely never describe it as wanting a cigarette. Maybe a bit like a poison dart frog... curious to look at, but I don't have any desire to lick its skin." OBob

It's been more than a decade since I've experienced anything that could be considered a crave. During that time there have beenBut an article by Joel teaching this point ("What should I call myself?") compelled critical thinking. a couple of darting thoughts, none of which lasted long enough to grab.

Maybe someday an urge or crave will occur again. Maybe tomorrow. But if so, I'm certain that I'll wear a smile during the entire brief encounter, as it will be a long overdue reminder of the amazing journey I once made.

"What should I call myself?"

While the exact moment of transition from use to non-use is clear, what we call ourselves once use ends is not. Are we an ex-user or non-user, ex-smoker or non-smoker, an ex-dipper or non-dipper? And when have we earned that title?

Regarding former smokers, the primary choice is between non-smoker and ex-smoker. Clearly, non-smoking applies as soon as use ends. We are in fact non-smokers. But there's a major distinction between being a never-smoker and non-smoker, a distinction the term non-smoker fails to declare.

Never-smokers don't have to worry about relapse. Chemical dependency has not permanently grooved and wired their brain for nicotine.

This critical distinction between non-smoker and ex-smoker applies equally to oral, nasal and transdermal nicotine users. If staying free is important, remembering that we are different can have as a protective effect as a self-reminder of our vulnerability.

While both a non-user and ex-user, I always refer to myself as an ex-smoker or former smoker as doing so reminds me that I remain just one powerful puff of nicotine away from three packs-a-day.

Initially, my mind rebelled against the thought that I wasn't fully "cured." I wanted to be like the average never-smoker. I thought I'd earned the right to hide among them. But an article by Joel teaching this point ("What should I call myself?") compelled critical thinking. Soon resistance and disappointment passed as I found myself wanting to embrace both the term ex-smoker and the world of ex-smoker-hood.

I love my freedom. I love residing on this side of the bars. So why wouldn't I want to remind myself of exactly what it takes to stay here?

If you want to consider yourself a non-smoker or non-user that's fine, you truly are. But be careful not to totally entrench your thinking in non-smoker-hood.

Also don't forget that certain legal documents, such as a life or health insurance policy application, may demand disclosure that we are ex-smokers. Failure to fully disclose our prior use status could later result in coverage concerns.

A related question is when should we see ourselves as being an ex-user or non-user? When do we cross the line from "trying to stop" to having done so? It's one of the most wonderful self-realizations of our entire journey. It's a deeply personal moment that's different for each of us, the crossing of a self-defined threshold.

For me, it occurred when my fears subsided to the point that I knew for certain that this was for keeps, that I wasn't going back. I'd already told the world I'd stopped but the difference now was that I actually believed it.

I'd already surrendered three decades of control to inhaling this chemical. Now, even if I were diagnosed with lung cancer tomorrow, I'd take comfort in one sure-fire fact. I would not die with my true killer still circulating inside.

The time before such conviction arrived was not some preplanned dress rehearsal. Starting out, I didn't foresee some magic moment in the future where success would become certain. In fact, the most frightening moment of all was the decision to stop putting nicotine into my body.

I didn't think I could do it. I thought I would fail. Everything after that first brave step was a journey of confidence that transported me from just one moment and challenge at a time to a deep seeded conviction that I will never ever use nicotine again!

Anyway, if here, welcome home! If not yet home, baby steps and it won't be long. And once here, never forget that we get to stay so long as we remain committed to a single principle ... no nicotine today!

Chapter 14

Complacency & Relapse

Caring for Our Recovery

First, the good news. The risk of relapse declines with the passage of time! While roughly 95% of uneducated smokers who attempt to stop smoking relapse within a year, the relapse rate declines to just 2 to 4% per year from years 2 to 10, and then falls to less than 1% after 10 years.[422]

Keep in mind that those rates were generated by ex-users who generally had little understanding of nicotine dependency and no formal respect for the Law of Addiction. If obedient to Law, our risk of failure remains zero. But just one powerful hit of nicotine and the addict is back.

While ignorance of the Law is no excuse, the vast majority of ex-users do not remain ex-users because of understanding or respect for the Law, or because of "one puff" relapse rates seen in studies. They've never heard of the Law.

They do so because once home they discover that life without using is vastly better than using.

Photo by National Cancer Institute

While the relapse rate for years 2 though 10 may seem small, when added together the risk becomes significant. A 2008 study suggests that as many as 17% who succeed for 1 year may eventually relapse.[423]

These ex-users don't relapse because they dislike being home. They do so because they lose sight of how they got there, who they are, and the captivity they escaped.

---

422 Krall EA, et al, <u>Smoking relapse after 2 years of abstinence: findings from the VA Normative Aging Study</u>, Nicotine and Tobacco Research, February 2002, Volume 4(1), Pages 95-100.

423 Hughes JR, et al, <u>Relapse to smoking after 1 year of abstinence: a meta-analysis</u>, Addictive Behaviors, December 2008, Volume 33(12), Pages 1516-1520.

Among educated ex-users there appear to be three primary factors associated with relapse: (1) a natural suppression of memories of recovery's early challenges, (2) they rewrite, amend or decide to test the Law and (3) they pretend that they have a legitimate excuse to break or ignore it.

Should these factors combine with an offer of a free cigar, alcohol use around those still using[424] or occur in an impulsive-type person,[425] the risk of relapse gets magnified.

Recovery Memory Suppression

It's normal to slowly grow complacent during the months and years after ending nicotine use. Complacency is fueled by failing memories of daily captivity and the factors that compelled us to seek freedom. It's also fueled by an inability to recall the intensity of early withdrawal anxieties, the power of cue triggered crave episodes, or the duration of conscious fixation.

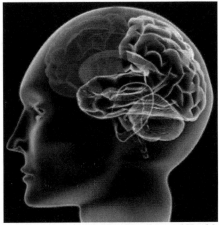

National Institute of Health

Most of us failed to keep a detailed record of why we commenced recovery or what those first two weeks were like. Without a record to remind us, we're forced to rely upon our memory to accurately and vividly preserve the truth, the whole truth and nothing but the truth. But now, the memory in which we placed our trust has failed us.

It isn't that our memory is bad, faulty or doing anything wrong. In fact, it's working as designed to preserve in as much detail as possible life's joyful events, while suppressing and helping us forget life's stressful events, anxieties, trauma and pain.

To do otherwise would make life inside these minds unbearable. In fact, post-traumatic stress disorder (PTSD) is believed to reflect a breakdown in the mind's ability to forget.[426] If women were forced to remember the agony and pain of childbirth, most would likely have only one child. We are each blessed with the ability to forget.

So how does the recovered nicotine addict who failed to record their journey home revive their passion for freedom and recall liberty's price? If we forget the past are we destined to repeat it? Not necessarily.

But just as any loving relationship needs nourishment to flourish, we should not take our recovery for granted or the flame could eventually die, and the fire go out.

---

424 Krall EA, et al, Smoking relapse after 2 years of abstinence: findings from the VA Normative Aging Study, Nicotine and Tobacco Research, February 2002, Volume 4(1), Pages 95-100.

425 Doran N, Impulsivity and smoking relapse, Nicotine and Tobacco Research, August 2004, Volume 6(4), Pages 641-647.

426 Geraerts E, McNally RJ, Forgetting unwanted memories: directed forgetting and thought suppression methods, Acta Psychologica (Amst), March 2008, Volume 127(3), Pages 614-622; also see, Levy BJ, Anderson MC, Individual differences in the suppression of unwanted memories: the executive deficit hypothesis, Acta Psychologica (Amst), March 2008, Volume 127(3), Pages 623-635.

It's my goal to protect my freedom until I draw my last breath. If you feel the same, then we need to nourish our desires. If we do, we win. If not, we risk complacency allowing nicotine back into our bloodstream. We risk dying as slaves.

Whether daily, monthly or just once a year, our recovery benefits from care. But where do we turn if our recovery memories have been suppressed and we've kept no record? Our best resource is probably our brothers and sisters still in bondage. Why not enlist their help in revitalizing our own memories of active dependency?

Talk to them. Let them know what you seek. Encourage them to be as candid and truthful as possible. Although it may look like they're enjoying their addiction, their primary objective is to stay one step ahead of insula driven urges and craves.

Tell them the truth about where you now find yourself. Although not always the case, with most you'll find their responses inspiring. Be kind and sincere. It wasn't long ago that those were our shoes.

Try hard to recall those first two weeks without nicotine. Think about earlier uneducated attempts. What were they like? Can you recall your mind begging to be fed? Feel the anxieties. Were you able to concentrate? How was your sleep?

Photo by National Cancer Institute

Did you feel depressed, angry, irritable, frustrated, restless or anxious? Were there rapidly cycling emotions, irrational thinking or emotional outbursts? Do you remember these things? Do you remember the price you paid? Do you recall the reasons you willingly paid it?

If you have access to a computer, go online and visit any of the scores of smoking cessation support groups. There we'll find thousands of battles being fought, hear a multitude of cries and watch hundreds struggling for survival as they dream of the calmness and quiet you now call home.

The newbies you'll see cannot begin to imagine traveling so far, that recalling the turmoil they now feel will someday soon become their greatest challenge of all.

If permitted, send a message to those in need. The most important thing you can tell them is the truth about why you came. If still in the first few days, they may be facing significant anxieties. Their mind may have them convinced that their emotional storm will never end.

Don't pretend that you can feel their anxiety. Instead give them what they need, the truth. Let them know that you've traveled so far that it's now difficult to relate. Tell them how comfortable and complacent you've grown. Describe last week and how many seconds, if any, that you devoted to thinking about using.

Fear of the unknown is frightening. Teach them what life on Easy Street is like. By aiding them we aid ourselves.

It may be that complacency has you at a point where thoughts of wanting are again taking root. But think back. How long had you gone without wanting?

If it is happening, rekindling pride in the amazing journey you once made may silence such chatter.

If occurring, I'd encourage you to re-read Chapters 4 and 12, as I suspect that you've either developed a romantic fixation with using, or failed to let go of one during recovery.

Amending the Law of Addiction

The second complacency factor working against us is a strong, natural desire to want to believe that we've been fully cured, that we can now handle "just one" or "just once."

But just one puff, dip or chew and "do not pass go, do not collect $200." Go directly to the addict's prison and surrender your freedom.

It isn't that we don't believe the Law. It's probably more a matter of growing to believe that we're the exception to it. We convince ourselves that we're stronger, smarter or wiser than all addicts who came before us.

We amend the law. We put ourselves above it. "Just once, it'll be ok, I can handle it." "I'm stronger than them." "A little reward, it's been a while, I've earned it."

Such thoughts infect the mind and feed upon themselves. Unless interrupted by reason and truth, our period of healing and freedom may be nearing an end. If allowed to fester, all our dreams and hard work risk being flushed like a toilet.

Instead of pretending we can handle" just one," such encounters demand truth. Before reaching the point of throwing it all away we need to be honest about what's about to happen. If this moment should ever arrive, try telling yourself this before bringing nicotine back into your body:

> "My freedom will now end!" "I'm going back." "I can handle all of them, give them all back to me, my entire addiction, all the trips to the store, the buys, the money, and the empties." "I want it all back." "Go ahead, slowly harden my arteries, depress by life and eat my brain."

If a smoker, "fill my world with ash, cover me in that old familiar stench, and let morning again be for coughing." If an oral user, "take my hair, destroy my teeth, and put sores back into my mouth."[427]

"Put me back behind bars, make me an outcast, throw away the key and let me die with my master still circulating in my veins." "I accept my fate" "I'm ready to surrender!"

It's far easier for the junkie mind to create a one puff, dip or chew exception to the "law" than to admit the truth.

Instead of picturing just one or once, picture all of them. Try to imagine fitting them into your mouth all at once. Because day after day, month after month, year after year after year, that's exactly where they'll be going.

"To thine own self be true." You navigated recovery. You paid the price, if any. You deserve the truth! If you find yourself attempting to rewrite the Law, stop, think, remember, reflect, read, revisit, revive and give to others, but most important, be honest with you!

The Perfect Excuse

The final ingredient is an excuse. For many, any excuse will do, even joy. It could be a reunion with an old buddy who uses, one too many drinks with friends, a wedding, graduation, or even a baby's birth and someone handing you a cigar.

Imagine being curious about the new electronic or e-cigarette with its atomization chamber, smart chip, lithium battery, and cartridge filled with apple, cherry, strawberry, chocolate, vanilla, coffee, mint or tobacco flavored nicotine.

Imagine watching an e-cigarette instantly vaporize nicotine when sucked and seeing a little light at the end imitate a real cigarette's heat.

What about a chance encounter with a self service display offering two pieces of Nicorette's new Cinnamon Surge," "Fruit Chill" or "Cappuccino" flavors of nicotine gum for one penny!

What about being tempted to try one of the other new nicotine delivery devices now hitting the streets? It's exactly what those selling them are hoping will happen.

Imagine being offered the new fully dissolvable tobacco/nicotine toothpicks, sticks, film or candy flavored orbs.

But joyful or even stupid nicotine relapse is harder to explain to ourselves and to those we love.

427 Polito JR, Long-term Nicorette gum users losing hair and teeth, WhyQuit.com, December 1, 2008.

The smart addict waits for the great excuse, the one that will be easy to sell to both themselves and others. As sick as it may sound, the easiest to sell is probably the death of a loved one.

Although everyone we love is destined to die and it will happen sooner or later, for the reformed addict it's the perfect excuse for relapse. I mean, who can blame us for ingesting highly addictive drugs upon the death of our mother.

Anyone who does would have to be extremely insensitive or totally heartless! Right? Wrong! There is no legitimate excuse for relapse.

Losing a job, the end of a relationship, a serious illness, disease, a terrorist attack, financial problems, a flood, earthquake, hurricane, an auto accident, are all great excuses too - it's drug time again! The addict is back!

Utterly terrible events will happen in each of our lives. Such is life. Adding full-blown nicotine relapse to any situation won't fix, correct or undo our underlying concern.

Take a moment now and picture yourself fully navigating the worst nightmare your mind can imagine.

Sooner or later it will happen. When it does, staying clean and free may be the most positive factor during this period of darkness.

Remember, we've only traded places with our chemical dependency and the key to the cell is that one hit of nicotine that will force your brain's survival instincts teacher to teach a false lesson, and make that lesson nearly impossible in the short term to forget.

As long as we stay on freedom's side of the bars, we are the jailers and our dependency our prisoner.

There are only two choices. We can complete this temporary period of adjustment and enjoy comfortable probation for life, or introduce nicotine back into our bloodstream, relapse, and intentionally inflict cruel and unusual punishment upon these innocent bodies for the remainder of their time on earth.

If the first choice sounds better - lifetime probation - then we each need only follow one simple rule ... no nicotine today!

Relapse - The Lesson Learned

One of two things happens following relapse. The user will think they have gotten away with using and, as a result, with the passage of time a "false sense of confidence" will have

Lapse Equals Relapse: Why challenge your brain's "wanting" generator?

them using again. Or, they'll quickly find themselves back using nicotine at their old level of daily intake or higher.

Although it sounds strange, as Joel notes, the lucky ones are those who quickly find themselves once again fully hooked.[428]

Why? Because this group stands a far better chance of associating that first puff, dip or chew of nicotine with full and complete relapse. Instead of learning the Law of Addiction from some book such as this, they stand a chance of self-discovering the law through experience and the school of hard-knocks.

It's a lesson that's become increasingly difficult to self-discover since 1984, when the FDA approved the first of a now vast array of nicotine replacement products (NRT), the nicotine gum. Today, the lesson that just one hit of nicotine spells relapse gets muddied and buried by promotion and marketing associated with ineffective nicotine weaning schemes.

Those standing to profit from the sale of NRT have re-labeled a natural poison medicine. They teach that instead of ending nicotine's use that you need to replace it, and describe doing so as "therapy."

It's why teaching and sharing the "Law of Addiction" with those still in bondage is the most important gift we can give.

Pre-NRT generations enjoyed clean mental chalkboards upon which to record prior relapse experiences. Today the chalkboards of millions are so filled with conflicting messages that identifying truth has become nearly impossible.

This generation needs us. They need our insights.

No Legitimate Justification for Relapse

Over the years we've heard nearly every relapse justification imaginable. Some relate extremely horrific and brutal life situations and then put their back against the wall as if daring you to tell them that their nicotine use and relapse wasn't justified.

Guess what? Again, there's absolutely no legitimate justification for relapse. None, zilch!

As Joel puts it, we understand why the person failed. They "violated the Law of Addiction, used nicotine and are paying the mandatory penalty - relapse. We also know that any excuse that the person is attempting to give for having re-awakened an active chemical dependency is total nonsense. There is no acceptable reason for relapse."[429]

Don't expect any serious support group or competent nicotine dependency recovery counselor to allow relapse excuses to stand unchallenged. They can't, as silence is a teacher too. Here, a deadly

---

428 Spitzer, J, <u>The Lucky Ones Get Hooked</u>, WhyQuit.com, Joel's Library 1984.
429 Spitzer, J, <u>We Understand Why You Relapsed</u>, WhyQuit.com, Joel's Library, 2002.

one.

It's "like someone standing on a ledge of a building," writes Joel. "Do you want the people standing on the ground giving the person on the ledge reasons not to jump, or after listening to all the woes in the individual's life saying, 'Gosh, I understand what you are saying.' 'I feel that way too.' 'I guess if I were in your shoes I would jump too.' 'Don't feel guilty, though, we understand.'"

"I don't want this statement to be read like a mockery of those attempting to offer help," says Joel. "I am trying to illustrate an important point. Obviously, if the person on the ledge jumps he or she will die. But understand, that if a person relapses and doesn't quit, he or she is likely to face the same fate, just time delayed."

"Yes, if you saw a person on a ledge you would try to use empathy to coax him or her back. But, empathy would be in the form of explaining that you understand his or her plight but totally disapprove of his or her current tactic for dealing with it. There are better ways to resolve these problems than committing suicide."

"You may understand the feelings the person had. You may have even felt them at some point yourself. But you don't give into the feeling," writes Joel.

We are nicotine addicts: real, live honest to goodness drug addicts. If we were all heroin addicts sticking needles into our arms, when one of us relapsed and started again injecting heroin into their veins, would the rest of us pat them on the back and tell them that "it's ok"?

Would we tell them "don't worry about it," "it's just a little slip, nothing big" "you just keep slipping and we'll just keep hugging you each time you come back." "Hey, we all slip every once in a while, it's just part of life," that "it's no big deal"?

No big deal? Surrendering control of life to an external chemical is a big, big deal. The smoker waiting for the sky to fall while committing slow motion suicide is massive.

Continuing Use Rationalizations

While the relapsed addict may feel that their reason for relapse was sufficient, it will not be sufficient to explain the fact that they continue to find themselves still using.

They now need a new rationalization to explain why their relapse justification has passed, yet they haven't stopped using.

"I'm just too weak to stop."[430]

This excuse dismisses or ignores having been successful up to the point of relapse. Obviously, they were not too weak then. This user would benefit by focusing upon and breathing renewed life into freedom's neglected dreams and desires.

---

430 Spitzer, J, "I'm just too weak to quit smoking!" WhyQuit.com, Joel's Library, 1984.

During their next recovery, they need to master not only putting but keeping those dreams in the driver's seat of their mind, especially during challenge. They'd be wise to review the crave coping techniques shared in Chapter 11 and prepare for battle by arming themselves with additional coping skills.

They need to appreciate that the growing pride they felt before they relapsed can take root anew in just a few hours, as they navigate withdrawal again, just one challenge at a time.

"Well, at least I tried."[431]

As Joel notes, chalking the attempt up to "experience" will mean absolutely nothing unless the user "objectively evaluates what caused his relapses."

"Instead of recognizing his past attempts as failures, he rationalizes a positive feeling of accomplishment about them. This type of rationalization all but assures failures in all future attempts."

He needs to understand that claimed use justifications never cause relapse. Administering another dose of nicotine is what causes relapse, not the circumstances surrounding it.

"I know I will stop again."[432]

This addict justifies continued use today by promising to navigate withdrawal in the future. But what if their now shattered dreams and desires never again become sufficient to motivate them to stop? What if there just isn't time?

What if continuing use causes fats and plaque building and gathering within an artery delivering oxygen to their brain, becomes fully blocked before arrival of the courage to again say "no"?

Once sufficiently re-motivated, why should they expect a different result if they still have little or no understanding as to why the last relapse occurred? If their motivations are sufficient now and they understand why they relapsed, what are they waiting for?

They are likely waiting because they've invented some new silly drug use rationalization as to why now just isn't the time.

"I've tried everything to stop and nothing works."

Joel tells the story of a clinic participant named Barbara. She "told me that she had once attended another clinic and liked it more than ours. I asked her how long she had stopped after that program and she said, 'Oh, I didn't stop at all.'"

"I then asked her how many of the other people succeeded. She replied, 'I don't know if anybody

---

431 Spitzer, J, <u>"Well, at least I attempted to quit. That is better than not trying at all"</u> WhyQuit.com, Joel's Library, 1986. Note: references to the word quit have been replaced with the word stop or stopped.

432 Spitzer, J, <u>"I know I will quit again"</u> February 22, 2001, http://www.ffn.yuku.com/topic/22978

stopped.' I then asked, if nobody stopped then why did she like the program more? She answered, 'When I completed the program, I didn't feel bad about smoking!'"[433]

I often hear, "I've already tried cold turkey plenty of times!" What this person doesn't yet appreciate is that education is a recovery method.

In contrast to uneducated abrupt nicotine cessation, it's like turning on the lights. Products and procedures clearly can fail to produce as advertised. But it's a little hard to blame knowledge and understanding when our actions are contrary to them.

Like the public library, knowledge cannot take credit for being used, or blame for being ignored. Unlike products, FFN-TJH can never claim credit for having endured a single challenge for any reader.

Credit for their ongoing victory will always be 100 percent theirs. Likewise, responsibility for allowing nicotine back into their bloodstream and brain is totally theirs too.

"Maybe I'm different."[434] "Maybe I can't quit."[435]

It isn't that this person is different. In fact, they're the same as us. Relapse after relapse, with at least a dozen serious failed attempts of my own, I eventually came to believe that it was impossible for me to stop.

After one last failed attempt in early 1999, I surrendered to the fact that I was a drug addict, hopeless and would die an addict's death.

What I didn't then realize was that each of those battles was fought in ignorance and darkness. I was swinging blindly at an unseen opponent.

What I didn't realize was that I'd never once brought my greatest weapon to the battlefield, my intelligence.

433 Spitzer, J, "I've tried everything to quit and nothing works" February 16, 2002, http://www.ffn.yuku.com/topic/12121
434 Spitzer, J, "Maybe I'm Different" WhyQuit.com, Joel's Library, 1985.
435 Spitzer, J, I Can't Quit or I Won't Quit, WhyQuit.com, Joel's Library, 1986.

I'd made recovery vastly more challenging than need be. I skipped meals, added hunger anxieties, mind fog, experienced caffeine doubling associated with at least a pot of coffee daily, and leaned heavily upon others for support.

Insanely, more than once I celebrated and rewarded myself with just one cigarette after three days, once the early anxieties began easing off a bit. I knew nothing of the body's abilities to rid itself of nicotine.

And having inter-spaced cold turkey with at least four NRT attempts, I was totally lost. Was nicotine medicine or was it what was keeping me hooked? How could I possibly self-discover the Law of Addiction via one puff and relapse when being taught that nicotine was medicine?

Was I weaker than the hundreds of millions who had successfully stopped? Was I different?

Certainly not with respect to what happens once nicotine enters the brain. As Joel notes, it is impossible to locate any person who relapsed who didn't introduce nicotine back into their bloodstream.

More Excuses Coming

As far as relapse excuses are concerned, life will provide an abundant supply for anyone looking for them. We will have friends or loved ones who will get sick, diseased and die.

Dying is a normal part of life. If the death of someone close to us is an acceptable reason for relapse then the freedom and healing of nearly a billion now comfortable ex-users is at risk.

Expect imperfect humans to do the unthinkable. We change, disagree, sometimes break promises, argue, and start and end relationships. Expect financial distress as food, medicine, fuel and living costs continue to rise. The loss of a job or inability to work may only be an injury, disease or pink slip away.

Floods, droughts, fires, tornadoes, earthquakes and hurricanes will happen. People die, vehicles collide, sports teams lose, terrorists attack and wars will be waged, won and lost. Life promises loads of excuses to relapse. But freedom's promise is absolute. It is impossible to relapse so long as all nicotine remains on the outside.

We each have a 100 percent guarantee of staying free today so long as no nicotine gets inside.

Harm Reduction

What if we do relapse? What then? Hopefully, relapse will instill a deep and profound respect for the power of one hit of nicotine to again take the mind's priorities teacher hostage.

Hopefully, belief in the Law of Addiction will thereafter forever remain beyond question. Hopefully, we'll immediately work toward reviving and strengthening our dreams and soon start home again. But if not, what then?

And what if our relapse was to the dirtiest, most destructive and deadliest form of nicotine delivery ever devised, the cigarette?

We're told it accounts for 20% of all deaths in developed nations.[436] According to the World Health Organization, smoking is expected to claim more than one billion nicotine addicts by the end of the 21st century.

Respected nicotine toxicologist Heinz Ginzel, MD writes, "burning tobacco ... generates more than 150 billion tar particles per cubic inch, constituting the visible portion of cigarette smoke. But this visible portion amounts to little more than 5 to 8 percent of what a lit cigarette discharges and what you inhale during puffing. The remaining 90% of the total output from a burning cigarette is in gaseous form and cannot be seen."[437]

Many health officials wish they could immediately transfer all smokers to less destructive forms of nicotine delivery. And some are now strongly advocating it.

How many fewer deaths would occur? We don't really know. Although most harm reduction advocates are extremely optimistic and expect massive reductions, their suppositions ignore the fact that most smokers have already logged years of tobacco toxin and carcinogen exposure.
How does their continuing use of the super-toxin nicotine factor into the damage already done?

What are the long-term risks associated oral tobacco, electronic cigarettes, and replacement nicotine in long-term ex-smokers? It may take decades before science can untangle relative risks and draw reasonably reliable conclusions.

As for any traditional combustion-type cigarette claiming to be less harmful than another brand of burning cigarette, don't buy it. Inhaling gases and particles from a burning mini toxic waste dump is inherently dangerous and extremely destructive.

A 2008 study examined the effects of smoke from three brands claiming harm reduction upon normal embryonic stem cell development. It found that smoke from these so-called harm-

436 Wald NJ and Hackshaw AK, Cigarette smoking: an epidemiological overview, British Medical Bulletin, January 1996, Volume 52(1), Pages 3-11.
437 Ginzel, KH, Why Do You Smoke? WhyQuit.com, February 6, 2007.

reduction cigarettes inhibited normal cell development as much "or more" than traditional brands.[438]

Some public health advocates are alarmed that harm reduction campaigns may actually backfire, keeping millions who would have successfully arrested their chemical dependency hooked and cycling back and forth between cigarettes and other forms of nicotine delivery.

They are also concerned that harm reduction campaigns tossing about terms such as "safe," "safer," or "safety" may actually entice ex-smokers to relapse.

I hold in my hand sample packets containing two 2mg pieces of "Fresh Fruit" and "Ice Mint" Nicorette gum with tooth whiteners. I was told that these sample packs were being sold at self-service checkout counter displays in Canadian beer stores for one penny.

How many ex-smokers will be tempted to give it a try while drinking alcohol? How many will relapse? How much of this sample gum will end up in the hands of youth?

The second sentence on the back of each Canadian sample pack tells smokers that Nicorette gum isn't just for stopping smoking.

"Nicorette gum can also be used in cases in which you temporarily refrain from smoking, for example in smoke-free areas or in other situations which you wish to avoid smoking."

Imagine pharmaceutical companies dove-tailing their marketing with that of tobacco companies in order to make continued smoking easier or more convenient.

Have you ever wondered why you have never once heard any pharmaceutical industry stop smoking product commercial suggest that, "Smoking causes lung cancer, emphysema and circulatory disease, that you need to buy and use our product because smoking can kill you"?

You haven't and likely never will. But why?

As hard as this may be to believe, the pharmaceutical and tobacco industries have operated under a nicotine marketing partnership agreement since about 1984. The once secret documents evidencing their agreement are many, and suggest that neither side may directly attack the other side's products.[439]

---

438 Lin S, et al, Comparison of toxicity of smoke from traditional and harm-reduction cigarettes using mouse embryonic stem cells as a novel model for preimplantation development, Human Reproduction, November 29, 2008.

439 Shamasunder B, Bero L., Financial ties and conflicts of interest between pharmaceutical and tobacco companies, Journal of the American Medical Association, August 14, 2002, Volume 288(6), Pages 738-744; also see the following once secret tobacco industry documents available at TobaccoDocuments.org: PM USA internal memo dated 7/21/82, Bates #2023799798; PM USA internal memo dated 5/7/84, Bates #2023799799; PM USA internal memo dated 10/25/84, Bates #2023799801;   PM USA letter dated 12/17/84, Bates #2023799804; PM USA internal memo dated 1/22/85, Bates #2023799803; PM USA internal memo dated 9/6/85, Bates #2023799796; 2nd PM USA internal memo dated 9/6/85, Bates #2023799795; PM USA internal memo dated 12/16/85, Bates #2023799789; PM USA internal memo dated 1/8/88, Bates #2500016765; PM USA letter dated 5/8/91, Bates #2083785672; British American Tobacco collection letter dated 8/1/91, Bates #500872678; PM International letter dated 4/23/98, Bates #2064952307.

The primary purpose of their partnership is to ensure the purchase and use of each side's dopamine pathway stimulation products.   They want you to pay them to satisfy your dependency's wanting. FFN-TJH's purpose is to aid you in arresting it.

Back to harm reduction where both sides in the debate appear to be overstating their case.

Some opposed to harm reduction have argued that the risks associated with a smoker transferring to oral tobacco is like getting hit by a small car instead of a large truck, like shooting yourself in the foot instead of the head, or like jumping from a three-story building rather than one ten stories tall.

Lacking accurate relative risk data themselves, the harm reductionist counters by asserting that, "Based on the available literature on mortality from falls, we estimate that smoking presents a mortality risk similar to a fall of about 4 stories, while mortality risk from smokeless tobacco is no worse than that from an almost certainly non-fatal fall from less than 2 stories."[440]

"We estimate"? It's disturbing to see us stoop to educated-guessing when it comes to life or death.

It is also disturbing that no serious harm reduction advocate has yet been willing to provide an accurate accounting of known and suspected harms associated with chronic nicotine use.

They know that the amount of nicotine needed to kill a human is 166 times smaller than the amount of caffeine needed to do so (40-60 milligrams versus 10 grams).[441]

Yet, in order to sell smokers on "safer" delivery many have resorted to falsely portraying nicotine as being as harmless as caffeine.

Harm reduction advocates have also done little to quiet concerns about the impact of marketing upon youth, messages already bombarding them with a wide array of tempting flavors being portrayed as vastly safer than smoking.

They seem unconcerned by an increasing number of adolescent nicotine harm studies showing nicotine's horrific toll on the developing adolescent brain.[442] Let me give just one example among many. Ever wonder why those who started using nicotine as children or early teens tend to have greater difficulty learning through listening?

Research shows that adolescent nicotine disrupts normal development of auditory brain fibers. This damage may interfere with the ability of these fibers to pass sound, resulting in greater noise and diminished sound processing efficiency.[443]

---

440 Phillips CV, et al, Deconstructing anti-harm-reduction metaphors; mortality risk from falls and other traumatic injuries compared to smokeless tobacco use, Harm Reduction Journal, April 18, 2006, Volume 3, Pages 1-5.

441 Polito, JR, Nicotine 166 Times More Deadly than Caffeine? WhyQuit.com, February 16, 2006.

442 Slotkin TA, et al, Adolescent nicotine treatment changes the response of acetylcholine systems to subsequent nicotine administration in adulthood, Brain Research Bulletin, May 15, 2008, Volume 76 (1-2), Pages 152-165; also see, Slotkin TA, If nicotine is a developmental neurotoxicant in animal studies, dare we recommend nicotine replacement therapy in pregnant women and adolescents? Neurotoxicology and Teratology, January 2008, Volume 30, Issue 1, Pages 1-19.

443 Jacobsen, LK, et al, Prenatal and Adolescent Exposure to Tobacco Smoke Modulates the Development of White Matter Microstructure, The Journal of Neuroscience, December 5, 2007, Volume 27(49), Pages 13491-13498.

Harm reduction advocates not only ignore the harms inflicted by nicotine, they ignore nicotine's greatest cost of all, living every hour of your life as an actively feeding drug addict.

They must, otherwise they couldn't sell it. They focus on dying not living.

Some have resorted to accusing cessation educators and counselors unwilling to incorporate harm reduction lessons into their recovery programs as having a "stop or die" mentality.

It is as if they have no appreciation for the fact that bargaining is a normal phase of recovery, and there may be no more inviting bargain for a drug addict than one which invites them to keep their drug.

It's why it pains me to include this harm reduction section here at the tail end of FFN-TJH.

I worry that some new struggling ex-user reading this book, who would have succeeded if this section had not been included, will instead seize upon the words that follow as license to relapse.

But the alternative, the potential for relapse and then smoking yourself to death because relative risk had never been discussed or explained, is totally unacceptable.

Still, as Dr. Ginzel notes, it would be nice if we knew the actual relative risks in contrasting oral tobacco to NRT but we don't.

What is the relative risk when comparing cigarettes to oral tobacco or to electronic cigarettes or replacement nicotine?

We know that cigarettes currently contribute to nearly five million deaths annually, and that cigarettes release more than 4,000 chemicals while oral tobacco releases 2,550 chemicals. We also know that 81 potential cancer-causing chemicals have been identified in cigarette smoke[444] versus 28 in oral tobacco.[445]

The only as yet known harmful agent in both the new electronic or e-cigarettes (which uses an atomizer to create a nicotine mist)[446] and replacement nicotine (NRT) is nicotine, and trace amounts of tobacco-specific nitrosamines (TSNA's), which will hopefully be corrected via quality control.

Still, additional research is badly needed as we have little long-term data for pure nicotine, as nearly every user has years of cigarette or oral tobacco exposure, which makes it nearly impossible to determine direct and proximate cause.

Clearly, smokers face serious risk of many different types of cancers, a host of breathing disorders including emphysema, and serious circulatory disease as carbon monoxide combines with nicotine

444 Smith CJ et al, IARC carcinogens reported in cigarette mainstream smoke and their calculated log P values, Food and Chemical Toxicology, June 2003, Volume 41(6), Pages 807-817.

445 IARC Monographs on the Evaluation of Carcinogenic Risks to Humans, Smokeless Tobacco and Some Tobacco-specific N-Nitrosamines, 2007, Volume 89.

446 Polito JR, Do Kennedy and Waxman know about electronic or e-cigarettes? WhyQuit.com, March 29, 2008.

to destroy vessel walls and facilitate plaque buildup.

Smoking's risks and roughly 50% adult kill rate are well known. What wasn't being studied until recently were the health concerns being expressed by long-term NRT users.

Although we still don't know whether or not NRT user health concerns are in fact directly related to chronic nicotine use, online complaints among those who have used nicotine gum for one year or longer include:

> Addiction with intense gum cravings, anxiety, irritability, dizziness, headaches, nervousness, hiccups, ringing in the ears, chronic depression, headaches, heart burn, elevated blood pressure, a rapid or irregular heart beat, sleep disruption, tiredness, a lack of motivation, a heavy feeling, recessed, bleeding and diseased gums, diminished sense of taste, tooth enamel damage, tooth loss, jaw-joint pain and damage (TMJ), canker sores with white patches on the tongue or mouth, bad breath, dry mouth, sore or irritated throat, difficulty swallowing, swollen glands, bronchitis, stomach problems and pain, gastritis, severe bloating, belching, achy muscles and joints, pins and needles in arms and hands, uncontrollable foul smelling gas that lingers, a lack of energy, loss of sex drive, acid reflux, stomach ulcers, fecal impaction from dehydration, scalp tingling, hair loss, acne, facial reddening, chronic skin rashes and concerns about immune system suppression.[447]

As you can see, while the list of unproven possibilities are many, few concerns come anywhere near smoking's known risks. Clearly, smoking's harms are vastly greater and far more life threatening than nicotine's.

How many millions of additional air sacs would these lungs have today if I'd permanently transferred my dependency to nicotine gum the first time I used it in 1985 or 86?

If my goal had been long-term gum use instead of 8 to 12 weeks during cessation, would I have been more willing to accept gum's slower, less precise and less controllable delivery? If I'd permanently transferred my dependency to cleaner delivery in 1986, would I be able to run for more than a few hundred feet today? Would I have more teeth?

If I had allowed myself to become hooked on the cure, as an estimated 37% of U.S. nicotine gum users were as of 2003,[448] would I have had the motivation to eventually break free from all nicotine, as I did on May 15, 1999 when I stopped smoking?

Would I have created WhyQuit two months later in July? Would I have met Joel Spitzer in January 2000? Would FFN-TJH have been written?

I don't know. Maybe, maybe not. Hopefully you understand a bit better my reluctance to suggest that if you relapse to smoking nicotine, that if a non-pregnant adult, that you consider attempting to adapt to a cleaner form of delivery. But there, I've done it. You should.

---

447 Polito JR, Long-term Nicorette gum users losing hair and teeth, WhyQuit.com, December 1, 2008.

448 Bartosiewicz, P, A Quitter's Dilemma: Hooked on the Cure, New York Times, Published: May 2, 2004; quoting, Shiffman S, Hughes JR, et al, Persistent use of nicotine replacement therapy: an analysis of actual purchase patterns in a population based sample, Tobacco Control 2003 November; 12: 310-316.

But my dream isn't about seeing you develop the patience to allow yourself time to adapt to and remain slave to a cleaner and less destructive form of delivery. It's that you develop the "one day at a time" patience needed to go the distance and allow yourself to sample the amazing sense of quiet and calm that arrives once your addiction's chatter ends.

Closing Thoughts

My hope is greater than just "you" breaking and staying free. If you've read this far and have ended use, you may well be the most knowledgeable ex-user you've yet to meet. It's my hope that you won't be shy about sharing what you've learned with others in need.

One of life's greatest challenges is penetrating the actively feeding addict's thick protective wall of denial. We may only get a few seconds or a single chance before their defenses tune us out entirely. As with Twitter, what could we possibly say that would make a difference if limited to a maximum of 140 characters?

I leave you with this Tweet:

> Once ready to stop, there's only one rule, that we are REAL drug addicts. For us there is no such thing as just one, as one equals all.

As for your ongoing victory, please understand that it's totally your doing. As with any library, knowledge is simply a tool to be used or ignored. You are the one who put it to work. And the glory is 100% yours.

As Joel often reminds us, in that we refuse to accept the blame when someone violates the Law of Addiction, we have no business taking credit when they don't. I wish I could say that I endured even a single challenge for you. But, it simply isn't true.

Once free and comfortable, I pray you never forget the most important lesson of all. As my mentor taught me, the true measure of nicotine's power isn't in how hard it is to stop, but in how easy it is to relapse.
More than 100,000 words yet just one simple principle determining the outcome for all ... no nicotine today! Yes we can!

Breathe deep, hug hard, live long,

Appendix: Recovery Journal/Diary

1. My nicotine use history:

2. My core motivations for wanting to end nicotine use:

3. My recovery attempt history and the real reason each attempt failed:

4. A brief summary of what the first week of this recovery was like:

5. The total minutes daily I spent thinking about wanting to use nicotine at:

30 hours	6 weeks:
72 hours:	2 months:
1 Week:	3 months:
2 Weeks:	6 months:
4 Weeks:	1 year:

6. The benefits I noticed during recovery included:

7. Things I want to remind myself of on my one-year anniversary:

8. The names of two other active users that I've taught the Law of Addiction:

9. The names of two children or teens that I've taught the true power of nicotine:

Printed in Great Britain
by Amazon.co.uk, Ltd.,
Marston Gate.